Lecture Notes in Computer Science   1368

Edited by G. Goos, J. Hartmanis and J. van Leeuwen

Springer
Berlin
Heidelberg
New York
Barcelona
Budapest
Hong Kong
London
Milan
Paris
Santa Clara
Singapore
Tokyo

Yoshifumi Masunaga   Takuya Katayama
Michiharu Tsukamoto (Eds.)

Worldwide Computing and Its Applications – WWCA'98

Second International Conference
Tsukuba, Japan, March 4-5, 1998
Proceedings

 Springer

Series Editors

Gerhard Goos, Karlsruhe University, Germany
Juris Hartmanis, Cornell University, NY, USA
Jan van Leeuwen, Utrecht University, The Netherlands

Volume Editors

Yoshifumi Masunaga
University of Library and Information Science
1-2 Kasuga, Tsukuba, Ibaraki 3050821, Japan
E-mail: masunaga@ulis.ac.jp

Takuya Katayama
Japan Advanced Institute of Science and Technology
1-1 Asahidai, Nomigun, Tatsunokuchimachi, Ishikawa 9231292, Japan
E-mail: katayama@jaist.ac.jp

Michiharu Tsukamoto
Electrotechnical Laboratory
1-1-4 Umezono, Tsukuba, Ibaraki 3050045, Japan
E-mail: Tukamoto@etl.go.jp

Cataloging-in-Publication data applied for

Die Deutsche Bibliothek - CIP-Einheitsaufnahme

Worldwide computing and its applications : second international conference ;
proceedings / WWCA '98, Tsukuba, Japan, March 1998. Yoshifumi Masunaga ;
Takuya Katayama (ed.). - Berlin ; Heidelberg ; New York ; Barcelona ; Budapest
; Hong Kong ; London ; Milan ; Paris ; Santa Clara ; Singapore ; Tokyo :
Springer, 1998
  (Lecture notes in computer science ; Vol. 1368)
  ISBN 3-540-64216-1

CR Subject Classification (1991): C.2.4, D.1.3, F.1.2, C.2, D.4, D.3, H.5

ISSN 0302-9743
ISBN 3-540-64216-1 Springer-Verlag Berlin Heidelberg New York

Typesetting: Camera-ready by author
SPIN 10631853   06/3142 – 5 4 3 2 1 0   Printed on acid-free paper

Preface

WWCA'98 is an international conference and a continuation of WWCA'97 held in Tsukuba, March 10–11, 1997. The purpose of these international conferences is to provide a place for the free exchange of ideas and discussion concerning the technologies and science of the Web and the Cyber Age that we have now entered, and contribute to the development of distributed information processing technologies for the coming 21st century.

As with the previous conference, WWCA'98 is being sponsored by the Electrotechnical Laboratory of the Ministry of International Trade and Industry (MITI) of Japan (Director-General, Koichiro Tamura). The main feature of this conference is that it enables the participants to directly attend presentations given by many of the world's most renowned scientists and technicians. Since this conference is held in cooperation with the Internet Workshop (IWS), there will also be a wide range of sessions and high-level presentations relating to the field of the Internet.

There will be an opening remark and three invited lectures given on the morning of the first day (March 4, 1998), followed by a total of 30 paper presentations given in 10 technical sessions that afternoon and the next day. The 10 sessions will be as follows: Distributed Objects, Distributed Component Ware, Distributed Systems Platforms, Internet Technology, Mobile Computing, Inter-Culture Technology, Collaborative Media, Collaboration Support, Information Discovery and Retrieval, and Novel Network Applications. As with WWCA'97, each session will be an hour and a half long and consist of three presentations, one of which will be given by an invited speaker recommended by the Session Chair. The remaining 20 presentations will be papers which were publicly submitted to and selected by the program committee. Although only 31 papers were submitted due to the tight schedule, the 20 that were selected cover many extremely worthwhile and timely topics which are sure to be of great interest. Each paper was examined by three reviewers, and we would like to express our thanks to these reviewers (program committee members and external referees) for devoting their time to WWCA'98.

Tsukuba Science City is known for its academic organizations, such as its approximately 50 national research institutions (including the Electrotechnical Laboratory), two national universities (University of Library and Information Science and University of Tsukuba), and many private research laboratories. Tsukuba is also close to New Tokyo International Airport at Narita and the Tokyo Metropolitan Area. These conditions make it the most suitable location in Japan for providing information on the results of research and development activities through international conferences. WWCA'98 has been made possible through the efforts of General Chair Professor Hideo Aiso, members of the Organizing and Advisory Committee, the Program Committee, and the Executive

Committee (Co-Chairs Yoichi Hamazaki and Shuichi Tashiro), and the staff of the WWCA'98 secretariat. We hope that WWCA international conferences will continue to be held in Tsukuba Science City.

Tsukuba, March 1998

Yoshifumi Masunaga
Takuya Katayama
Michiharu Tsukamoto

Message from the General Chair

The connection of each and everyone throughout the world via information networks used to be a great dream of ours. And now, the Internet has made this a reality. We can stroll and shop in 3D virtual malls, and wander through museums, all from the comfort of our desktops. Networking is changing our lives and the activities of enterprises, and will soon alter the society in which we live. In such an emerging era, what are the researchers and engineers pursuing?

To answer this question, we should gather not only the academic, but also the industrial world to discuss the future and their vision of the coming 21st century. The WWCA'97 conference was held early last spring to provide an international forum. More than 300 people participated in this event to share their R&D results and opinions with the world. Needless to say, it was a great success. It is our great pleasure to be able to hold the second WWCA, WWCA'98. The preceding meeting, Internet Workshop '98, is held in cooperation with WWCA'98. The volunteers of the workshop will also cooperate in preparing the conference. I strongly believe that our WWCA is extending to related societies.

I would like to express my sincere appreciation to the organizing and executive committees, consisting mainly of researchers from the Electrotechnical laboratory of the Agency of Industrial Science and Technology, and MITI (Ministry of International Trade and Industry), for making this conference possible. Last but not the least, my special gratitude goes out to the Information Processing Society of Japan and the Electrotechnical laboratory for their unsparing cooperation as organizers, and the Association for Computing Machinery, Institute of Electronics, Information and Communication Engineers, and the Information-Technology Promotion Agency of Japan for their invaluable support.

March 1998   Hideo Aiso

WWCA'98 Committees

General Chair
  Hideo Aiso, Keio University

Organizing Committee
Advisery and Organizing Chair
  Michiharu Tsukamoto, Electrotechnical Lab.
Members
  Kazuhiro Fuchi, Keio University
  Satoshi Goto, NEC Corp.
  Yoichi Hamazaki, Electrotechnical Lab.
  Hiromu Hayashi, Fujitsu Labs. Ltd.
  Seiichi Ido, NTT Software Labs.
  Takashi Iida, Communications Research Lab., M.P.T.
  Kazuo Iwano, IBM Japan Ltd., Tokyo Research Lab.
  Masanori Kataoka, Hitachi, Ltd.
  Katsura Kawakami, Matsushita Research Inst. Tokyo Inc.
  Takashi Masuda, The Univ. of Tokyo
  Yoshifumi Masunaga, Univ. of Library and Information Science
  Hitomi Murakami, KDD R&D Labs.
  Takayuki Nakajima, Sharp Corp.
  Tamotsu Nomakuchi, Mitsubishi Electric Corp.
  Kazuhito Ohmaki, Electrotechnical Lab.
  Saburo Ohno, Nihon Sun Microsystems Inc.
  Shuichi Tashiro, Electrotechnical Lab.
  Akio Tojo, Information-technology Promotion Agency
  Mario Tokoro, Sony Corporation
  Koji Torii, Nara Inst. of Science and Technology
  Ikuo Yamada, Mitsubishi Research Inst., Inc.

Program Committee
Co-Chairs
  Yoshifumi Masunaga, Univ. of Library and Information Science
  Takuya Katayama, Japan Advanced Inst. of Science and Technology

Members
  Mikio Aoyama, Niigata Inst. of Technology
  Rudolf Bayer, Technical Univ. of Munich
  Kenneth Birman, Cornell University
  Kilnam Chon, Korea Advanced Inst. of Science and Technology
  Shigeki Goto, Waseda University
  Jonathan Grudin, Univ. of California, Irvine
  Masayuki Ida, Aoyama Gakuin University

Kazuhiko Kato, Univ. of Tsukuba
Yasushi Kiyoki, Keio University
Isao Kojima, Electrotechnical Lab.
Robert Kummerfeld, Univ. of Sydney
Wen-Syan Li, NEC USA, Inc.
Thomas Little, Boston University
Eric Manning, Univ. of Victoria
Jun Murai, Keio University
Ken-ichi Okada, Keio University
Toshio Okamoto, Toshiba Corporation
Robin Stanton, Australian National University
Hideki Sunahara, Nara Inst. of Science and Technology
Tin-Wee Tan, National University of Singapore
Jiro Tanaka, Univ. of Tsukuba
Shuichi Tashiro, Electrotechnical Lab.
Fumio Teraoka, Sony CSL
Hideyuki Tokuda, Keio University
Michiharu Tsukamoto, Electrotechnical Lab.
Keisuke Uehara, Keio University
Ken Urquhart, JavaSoft

Executive Committee
Co-Chairs
Yoichi Hamazaki, Electrotechnical Lab.
Shuichi Tashiro, Electrotechnical Lab.

Members
Yuuichi Ichisugi, Electrotechnical Lab.
Noboru Akima, Information-technology Promotion Agency
Shigeru Chiba, Univ. of Tsukuba
Akihito Nakamura, Electrotechnical Lab.
Masaya Nakayama, The Univ. of Tokyo
Naoki Tomikawa, Mitsubishi Research Inst., Inc.
Osamu Nakamura, Keio University

External Referees

Table of Contents

Session B-1: Distributed Systems Platform
Chair: Hideyuki Tokuda

Session B-2: Internet Technology
Chair: Jun Murai

Session B-3: Mobile Computing
Chair: Fumio Teraoka

Session B-4: Interculture Technology
Chair: Tan Tin-Wee

Session C-1: Collaborative Media
Chair: Yasushi Kiyoki

Session C-2: Collaboration Support
Chair: Ken-ichi Okada

Session C-3: Information Discovery and Retrieval
  Chair: Isao Kojima

Session C-4: Novel Network Application
  Chair: Shigeki Goto

WWC and the Hyper Information Age

Koichiro Tamura

ktamura@etl.go.jp

Electrotechnical Laboratory

Abstract. It is well discussed that the computerization or "informatization" definitely affects and characterizes our present civilization and society. But on the way of the growth of the technology, the coming age should be distinguished from the past 50 years since we see significant paradigmatic change recently. Thus we call the coming age "hyper information age". The aspects of not only the technology but organizations,and even peoples way of looking at the world shall dramatically be changed. We discuss those features we shall see in the coming age, the reason that the development is necessary, and, on the contrary, the danger that the technology may originate.

1 "Hyper" Information Age and Society

Only a few years remain until the start of the 21st century starts. I will not be alone in feeling that the entire world is experiencing drastic change. The rapid development of information technology has become one of the driving forces of this change.

The arrival of the "information society" and of the "advanced information society" has been predicted. But I have a strong feeling that even more drastic movements are evolving than the predicted social changes. The images implied by words such as the "information society" or the "advanced information society", appear to have tacitly presupposed a simple efficiency supremacy doctrine, dependent on centralized computing power typified by mainframes.

The word "information society" was used as early as the 1960s to predict a society in which computers prevail in all social activities. But most computers at that time were of the stand-alone type so that their availability was limited. In the 1970s, time sharing systems started to be widely used in areas such as banking systems and ticket reservation systems. Then, people wanted to distinguish the emerging style of those systems and the society to make use of them. The phrase people used to identify these phenomena was the "advanced information age". In fact, the appearances were different, but the essence of building both types of systems was the same; the simple efficiency supremacy doctrine, dependent on centralized computing power. A popular cliche at that time was that the larger the computer, the more efficient it is. It was said around 1980 that if we could have a computer large enough to handle everything in the world, it would be the final solution.

However, the decline of this efficiency supremacy doctrine is now evident. The ongoing change in information technology today is not at all what pundits originally predicted. The real world is too complicated to be handled by any single machine, however powerful it is. It can be viewed as a similar phenomenon to the disintegration of the former Soviet Union's political system. In fact, society, organization and even people's way of looking at things are becoming increasingly fragmented and the world is plunging into an epoch of major change. Once we understand this, the assertion that we are witnessing the arrival of the "advanced information society" already sounds out of date. I, then, prefer to use the term "hyper information society". In this kind of society, the systems are decentralized and first consideration is given to the value of information itself rather than the conventionally pursued efficiency of information processing.

2   Coping with Energy Crisis by Informatization

Information processing is made up of four functions: information generation (to be input into systems), distribution (to be transferred), processing (to be computed and edited) and accumulation (to be retrieved). The traditionally pursued information-oriented society aimed at increasing the efficiency of these functions. The need for more efficient functions will never diminish. But yet, what is regarded as all the more important in the hyper information society will be the amount of and, after all, the quality of information generated, processed, distributed and accumulated. You can generate as much information as you like, and information does not waste itself by processing. Therefore, it goes without saying that information itself could be the most valuable resource in a country like Japan which lacks natural resources.

It is not only Japan that will see a shortage of the natural resources: The whole world is facing the serious danger of exhausting the earth's resources. The average rate of growth of energy consumption in the long term has been approximately 2 % per year, which means even the whole lithium in the sea water supposed to be fuel for nuclear fusion will be exhausted in only 600 years. Oil, coal, gas, and other resources now available for conventional energy systems are in much shorter supply; maybe less than 100 years. Soft energies such as solar and wind energies are too poor to keep up with the growing consumption. If we, all mankind, cannot *radically* change the paradigm of civilization to consume massive amounts of material and energy, we will hardly be able to survive in the near future. We have to reexamine the direction of our civilization. In this sense, *"informatization"* of the whole structure of civilization is vital. The advent of the hyper Information age is not a simple predicted term, but a necessity for human kind.

3   Some Aspects of Hyper Information Age

Information is useless if it adds nothing new. The number or quantity is important when it comes to, for instance, cars or bread, regardless of their model or kind. But information does not gain value by being simply copied. This makes originality highly valuable. The value of information falls abruptly with decreasing accuracy. Even though there may be plenty of information available, it is of no use unless you can find from it what you want to know or what is useful to you. In addition, information needs to be up-to-date. These are the reasons why quality, rather than quantity, of information is of key importance.

To prepare for such an epoch, there is a yet stronger demand for innovative technology. The Internet boom may give the impression that information technology has come of age, but this is an illusion.

The so-called "information highway" idea was almost realized by the recent Internet. Offices, factories and even ordinary homes are connected to Internet through personal computers, workstations and servers. The whole system is open to anyone who wants to connect to it, while the old proprietary systems were closed within each company or organization, even if their networks are global. But, we are heading to the more advanced stage in that *anything in any environment is going to be connected* to the Internet-like global information network, via wire or wireless.

By anything, I mean literally any thing from home utilities such as refrigerators and washing machines to everyday clothes, to buildings materials, to roads in town. What will or can happen in this situation depends entirely on the imagination of engineers and customers. The most certain prediction is that what nobody imagines now shall happen. The followings are some aspects of the hyper information age which I can imagine.

4 Agents and Information Field

If everything is connected to a network to enable them communicate with each other, some good results shall be attained which cannot be done by stand alone machines. Even now, hive computing is a well known research issue that is a kind of computing method for doing one thing with a cluster of computers connected to a network. Thus, cooperation of a kind of "agent" becomes important. Agents are emerging concept now, for example, user interface agent, network agent, and security agent. I think agents may be viewed as an advanced concept of "objects". Object orientation has been a leading concept through the 1970s to 1980s in research communities of information sciences, and in the 1990s has become one of the hottest practical issues in every computing engineering field. An agent can be viewed as an advanced version of an object in the sense that it is active and adaptive to the environment whereas an object is passive and unchanged, although both are entities for processing information.

An agent should also be regarded, in my view, as a unit for forming a software architecture as an object is, and in this sense, cooperative agents and an architecture consisting them are the new and key concept which should be pursued in the coming age. Thus, any computer including microcomputers embedded in things has agents and those agents are in cooperation through the network. We call this group of information entities an *information field*, since the group constructs a kind of field, where the network is not only for simple communication between agents but for construction of information processing organizations.

Communication among agents shall be in a kind of artificial language which is as close as possible to natural languages. Artificial languages used so far in computers provide expressions only for talking about computation and computational structure, whereas natural languages are means for expressing the real world we live in. We cannot talk about pretty girls or delicious foods in any programming languages in any operating system. That is one of the reasons for making computers still difficult for people to use. Users in the coming age shall not use stand-alone computers but information field, which will make it harder for users if much more advanced user interface is not available. Thus, a new approach to attacking semantics shall become very important.

Semantics relates directly to common sense, which is the basis of high level communication. Embedding common sense in information processing systems will then continue to be important although this problem has long been pursued by the artificial intelligence community. To advance the user interface, much more built-in knowledge about the real world is necessary, while the quality of communication among agents in the information field also demands the common sense. Eventually, teams of cooperative agents in an information field will yield new useful knowledge that human beings have never known.

5 Integration of 3 Infrastructure Networks

Information networks have already become one of the most important infrastructure of our world. Our everyday work and life is going on over the network. We have another two infrastructure networks: Commodity flow network and Energy flow network. In the coming age, we will see the integration of these three networks. By the integration of the Information net and commodity net, self driving car transportation can be done, which means achievement of ultimate energy conservation in the commodity flow. Similarly, the integration of the information net and energy net means not only quick response to demand but also achievement of ultimately efficient energy distribution. An energy version of the Internet may come true some day in which energy is transferred and distributed in the shape of packets responding to each unit of demand. All of these matters are some examples of "informatization" of our civilization and culture. It can be expected to be a means to save our energy crunching society from fatal destruction.

6 Danger in the Hyper Information Age

At the same time, we must think about the dangers that the hyper information age may develop. I think this could reside in the gap between the real world and the information world. The information world or virtual world consists of direct information of the real world and information derived from the raw information. It should be a right reflection of the real world in many aspects. We make use

of information to deal with the real world. We can act much more easily based
on the information from the virtual world than from the real world. That is one
of the reasons why we construct an information world. In the long history, we
have been constructing many kinds of information worlds based on things such
as books and computer data. In the hyper information society, we can get almost
all of the useful information from the information field instead of the real world.
If the gap between the two worlds grows too wide, our activities will be based on
false information and become void, and that shall lead to the ruin of our whole
society. We see urgent research issues around this problem.

7 Concluding remarks to WWC

Needless to say, the development of Worldwide Computing technologies is indispensable in this context. I hope that researchers and all those involved in the
WWC project will continue their efforts to open up this new field.

Global High Performance Research Network: An Asia-Pacific Perspective

Kilnam Chon

KAIST, Taejon, Korea

Abstract. Broadband testbeds have been deployed around the world since 1980s, and their successors, high performance research networks are being deployed in Asia- Pacific, Europe, and North America. These networks are forming the global high performance network through their interconnections. Various applications are being carried out using the network to carry on global research activities. Many meetings are being held to coordinate the interconnections and the applications.

This paper surveys the research networks around the world, and analyze on the interconnections and the funding aspect as well as various global collaborations to realize the global high performance research networks.

1 INTRODUCTION

The Internet and the related networks go through four phases in each generation as originally proposed by Campos and modified by various people. [1,2,3] See Fig. 1 for the diagrammatical description. The four phases are

Phase 1: Experimental Research and Development Network,
Phase 2: Production Research and Development Network,
Phase 3: Privatization, and
Phase 4: Commodity Network (through commercialization).

During the second and third phases, collection of the network partnership is very important.

The first phase of the first generation started with experimental research and development networks in USA and Europe in 1970s. The notable network in this phase is Arpanet in USA. The second phase with production research and development networks was introduced in 1980s around the world such as NSFnet in USA, SDN in Korea, and JUNET in Japan.[4] The third phase is the privatization such as ANSnet in USA, and HANA in Korea. The final phase is the commodity network, which typically comes with commercialization, such as commercial Internet service providers around the world. Some remain as non-profit networks such as academic networks in Asia and Europe.

The second generation started with broadband testbeds in 1980s and 1990s. Notable examples are regional Gigabit testbeds and the original vBNS in USA, National Testbed Network of CANARIE in Canada, JAMES and other projects in Europe, and similar projects in countries of the Asia-Pacific region.[5,6,7,8]

The second generation network is moving toward the second phase now with the various network initiatives;

Asia:	APAN
	national research networks
Europe:	TEN-34
	national research networks
North America:	CA*net2
	vBNS and Internet2
	mission-oriented networks

Various efforts are being put to interconnect these networks around the world. G7 GII/GIBN and CCIRN are some of these efforts.[10,11] The interconnection leads to formation of global high performance research networks. The current discussion focus on the network topology with appropriate exchange points and the relevant funding issues. The discussion have been carried out in various conferences, too.[9,26,27]

As the global high performance research networks are being formed, the international high performance applications based on these networks are also being developed around the world. The development of these high performance applications as well as the next generation networks impact the commodity Internet through the next phases; privatization and commercialization.

2 SURVEY

Figure 2 shows the research networks around the world seen from the STAR TAP. In North America we find most intensive development effort on the high performance research networks. National Testbed Network of CANARIE in Canada, an experimental research and development network, evolved to CA*net 2, a production research and development network recently.[6] Each province has its own GigaPoP, which is linked to one or more GigaPoPs. CA*net 2 is linked to USA at STAR TAP in Chicago, and to Europe with 155 Mbps link now. In USA, Next Generation Internet Initiative is funded by the federal government through DoD, DoE, NIH, NIST, and NSF to develop the technologies necessary to build the second and future generation networks.[12] vBNS is being expanded to 100 sites or more with higher bandwidths. Internet 2 Consortium with more than 100 member universities as well as various industry partners are developing the

second generation Internet for the university community with 20 or more GigaPoPs.[9]

Asia-Pacific Advanced Network(APAN) is being developed for the Asia-
Pacific research community.[3] See Fig. 3 for the member countries and regions
as well as their links. APAN is the high performance research network to serve
the research community as the network environment and as the network research
testbed. It is founded by four countries in 1997; Australia, Japan, Korea, and Singapore. It covers over 10 countries in Asia-Pacific and has the liaison members of
USA and Canada now. APAN connects national testbed networks and research
networks. In Japan, all academic and research networks joined APAN, and has
the inter-continental links through APAN and on its own such as SINET.[13] In
Korea, the national testbed network is expected to link to APAN in addition
to national academic and research networks. In Australia and Singapore, national research networks are linked to APAN.AN. Other countries in Asia such
as Thailand, Hong Kong, and Indonesia have similar arrangements through Asia
Internet Infrastructure Initiative(AI3), the satellite-based research network.[14]
See Fig. 5 for the APAN member networks.

In Europe, the situation is similar to Asia-Pacific, but with more bandwidth.
TEN-34 is the primary regional high performance research network which serves
most of Europe.[15] See Fig. 4 for the member countries of TEN-34 consortium.
Nordunet, another regional academic and research network serves Scandinavian
countries.[16] Each country has its own national academic and research network
with links to the regional research network and North America.[17]

Countries in Latin America are moving toward establishment of their own
high performance research networks as well as interconnection of national academic and research networks.[18] Some of African countries such as Egypt and
South Africa are also moving toward the same direction as Latin America regarding domestic high performance networks.[19]

3   NETWORK TOPOLOGY and EXCHANGES

Regional and national research networks are being linked within each continent
as well as between continents. There are various coordination efforts to link these
networks. G7 GII/GIBN and CCIRN are some of the examples.

There are three models to link these networks to form the global research
network as discussed at GIBN Meetings.[20]

(1) Single global exchange point
(2) Distributed exchange in North America
(3) Exchange in each continent with intercontinental connections

See Fig.6 for diagrammatical description.

The first model is based on the single global exchange point such as STAR TAP in Chicago, which was proposed by NSF.[21] The second model, the distributed exchange in North America such as the exchanges in East Coast, West Coast, and North Border(and possibly South Border). The third model is the exchange in each continent with interconnection of the exchanges.

The first model based on the single global exchange point has the following advantages;

(a) It is workable now as implemented by NSF, called STAR TAP in Chicago.
(b) There are no "transit problems" since all cells packets are exchanged at one location. In particular, this approach solves Asia-Europe link optimally until we have the shortest Asia-Europe link, the trans-Siberia link.
(c) It may be most cost effective.

It also has the following disadvantages, too;

(a) It may cause additional delay. For example, the Asia-Chicago-California link may have much more delay compared with the direct Asia-California link, and it could be serious for some applications, and we need to study on this delay*throughput issue.
(b) It is not scalable compared with multiple exchange points.
(c) It is not robust as single failure at the exchange could cause substantial damage to the global research network.

The second model based on the distributed exchange in North America is opposite to the first model with respect to the advantage and disadvantage. The third approach of the exchange in each continent would be the long term issue if it ever be realized since we have to develop the exchange in each continent and come up with the funding for the intercontinental links.

CA*net 2 in Canada linked to vBNS and other US research networks at STAR TAP in Chicago in 1996. APAN and several national networks in Asia are connecting to STAR TAP now. In Europe, most regional and national academic and research networks connect to exchanges in East Coast. Some of them are extending their links to STAR TAP. These collaborative efforts with appropriate transit policy make these networks to form the global research network, some of which come with high performance capability. The second step is to establish the second and other global exchange points in North America, possibly starting from the one in East Coast. The global exchange point in West Coast may follow later. To progress to the third step, we need to establish the global exchange points in Asia, Europe and other continents. At APAN, we are working to make the exchange points in Tokyo and Seoul to be such a global exchange point.[22]

4 APPLICATIONS

With the global high performance research network being formed, we need to come up with the application infrastructure and user communities in addition to network management coordination and policy.

The following are considered some of the application infrastructure components for high performance research networks;

Cache
MBone
Security
Traffic Measurement

NLANR started the global cache hierarchy system project with collaboration of networks in Europe and Asia.[23] The global cache network is in place with appropriate software based on Squid. There is also the annual cache workshop with participants from these three continents.

vBNS operates high quality MBone with minimal packet loss now, and CA*net 2 collaborates on this matter.[25] CA*net 2 operates high performance MBone in Canada with 1 2 Mbps bandwidth now.[24] APAN and other networks plan to collaborate with these efforts to provide high quality and high performance MBone globally. Multicasting applications to other areas than video conferencing as well as more efficient multicasting are needed as the application infrastructure.

Security is another important area as stated in Next Generation Internet Initiative(NGI): Draft Implementation Plan;".....The security's essential role in the NGI is to support several goals: a secure and fair means of user access to and use of network resources(e.g., Quality of Service(QoS)), smart network management, internetwork peering(e.g., surety of routing updates), accounting/ costing for intercarrier as well as end user to carrier relationships, ensuring low latency control mechanisms, and nomadic/remote high speed access. A Public Key Infrastructure(PKI) that interacts with the industrywide PKI is paramount to the success of integrating and deploying security in the NGI. This subtask, Security will also develop ways for organizations or individuals to interoperate in the face of a rich and dynamic set of policies, for example, those that exist among different Federal agencies....."

Traffic measurement is also very important for any high performance and/or broadband networks. This is particular true to any long distance networks such as the global network. Long distance with many switches and routers tends to cause severe performance degradation. In order to optimize the performance, we need to be able to measure traffic on the networks. There are many measurement tools such as OC3Mon and Netflow.[11] We need to coordinate the deployment of these tools and traffic measurement globally. Several organizations are working in this area such as CCIRN and IETF as well as many high performance research networks.

5 ISSUES

There are many issues to be resolved to realize the global high performance research networks. Some of them are as follows;

> Routing
> Transit traffic
> Asia-Europe link
> Cost sharing
> GigaPoP

Routing for the high performance research networks poses a new problem; how to segregate different traffics; high performance research application traffic and commodity Internet traffic. All relevant institutions have both links; one for the high performance research network, and the other for commodity Internet. The routing proposed for vBNS and the network linked to it is the institution-based routing. If one institution route a high performance research application traffic to another institution over the high performance research network, all other traffics including commodity Internet traffic are also routed in the same research network. Since the traffic between these research institutions are less than 10institution, and would not flood the high performance research network with the commodity Internet traffic. We need to watch out how effective is this routing scheme compared other routing schemes.

Transit traffic is another hot issue among the high performance research networks, which tend to have rather tight acceptable use policies(AUP). In commodity Internet, the transit traffic is not the issue anymore since the backbone Internet service providers and others took care of the transit traffic among them. The transit traffic appears typically among inter- continental traffic in North America such as Asia-Europe traffic. There are several ways to solve the problem. One of them is to have the direct link between the relevant continents. The second approach is to have the single global exchange point as mentioned earlier. The third approach is to have the arrangement between the relevant exchange points. The first approach does not scale, and may be implemented in special cases where the traffic is substantial. The second approach is workable now once we agree on the single global exchange point. The third approach is of a longer term since we have to make various arrangement such as global exchange points and their interconnections.

Asia-Europe link is the issue coming up now, and DANTE in Europe is studying on this subject now.[25] Majority of inter-continental transit traffic is generated between Asia and Europe. To complicate the problem further, the optimal link between Asia and Europe is through North America now until the broadband trans-Siberia optical cable is installed in the next decade.

Cost sharing is always the major issue. In the global high performance research network, the biggest issue is who to pay for the network interconnection and the related matters. Traditionally, most research networks maintain a link to USA with most or all communication cost paid by the non-US networks. USA operates exchange points for interconnections of any research network. USA also subsidizes majority of the research and development work. There is also imbalance of the traffic; the traffic from USA is much larger than the traffic to USA. In the context of high performance research applications and commodity Internet, we have to coordinate the cost sharing globally to realize fair usage of the global high performance research networks. Discussion on this matter has been going on at various meetings; CCIRN, GIBN,... among the global global community as well as among commercial Internet service providers.

GigaPoP is the new concept, which may solve many problem of the high performance research networks. It was originally proposed in Internet 2, and other networks such as CA*net 2 and APAN are also implementing the concept now.[9] GigaPoP is the multi-organization network to access backbone networks such as the high performance research networks. One may consider the high performance research network as a set of GigaPoPs with their interconnections. Some of them function as exchange points to other networks. It has the translation capability of Layer 2 and Layer 3 networks. It has various servers for the research community covered by the relevant GigaPoP.

6 CONCLUDING REMARKS

Global high performance research networks are being formed now. Their Bandwidth will move up to Gigabps and beyond inevitably. The network topology and exchange will move to the single global exchange point to multiple global exchange points in North America, and possibly other continents. Optimal network interconnections with appropriate switches and routers are vital for efficient usage of these networks. In addition to high bandwidth, wireless capability on the network is becoming increasing important.

Global coordination on the research and development on the next generation network technologies as well as the development of the application infrastructure is very important in years to come. Major funding in each continent and country as well as its coordination is vital to success of the these networks.

The ultimate test on validity of the global high performance research networks comes from user communities who use these network to carry on their high performance research applications. Most applications are being carried out among science and engineering communities now. Increasingly, other disciplines such as social science and humanity are becoming important user communities to solve research problems in the next century. Participation from other continents such as Latin America and Africa are also very important to make the network truly global and solve the global problems.

References

1. Campos,I.:An External View, Proc.Cheyenne Mountain Workshop(1995)
   http://www.farnet.org
2. Chon,K.:The Internet; Next Step, Proc.KRNET'97(1997)
   http://cosmos.kaist.ac.kr
3. Chon,K.:Asia-Pacific Advanced Network(APAN), Proc.APII Workshop(1997)
   http://apan.net
4. Chon,K.:Global Networking from Asia-Pacific Perspective, Proc.INET'93(1993)
5. vBNS and other testbed networks in USA
   http://www.vbns.net
6. CANARIE National Testbed and CA*net 2
   http://www.canarie.ca
7. JAMES
   http://ww.labs.bt.com/profsoc/james
8. Proc.APII Testbed Forum(1996)
9. Internet 2
   http://www.internet2.edu
10. G7 GII/GIBN(Globally Interoperable Broadband Networks) Project
    http://www.ncsa.niuc.edu/General/GIBN
11. CCIRN(Coordination Committee for Intercontinental Research Networks)
    http://web1.hpc.org/ccirn
12. Next Generation Internet Initiative(NGI)
    http://www.ngi.gov
    http://www.ccic.gov
    http://www.cra.org/Policy/NGI
13. SINET
    httP://www/sinet.ad.jp
14. Asia Internet Infrastructure Initiative(AI3)
    http://www.ai3.net
15. TEN-34
    http://www.dante.net

16. Nordunet
    http://www.nordu.net
17. TERENA
    http://www.terena.nl
18. Chon,K.:Personal communications with Utreras,F. on ENRED and Taka-
    hashi,T.(1997)
19. African Network Symposium Proc., INET'97(1997)
20. Chon,K.:Cost sharing and Intercontinental Research Network Exchange - APAN
    Perspective, Contribution Paper to GIBN Meeting in Rome(1997)
21. STAR TAP
    http://www.startap.net
22. Chon,K.:Asia-Pacific Advanced Network(APAN), Draft Memo(1997)
    http://apan.net
23. NLANR
    http://www.nlanr.net
24. Chon,K.:Personal Communication with Bill St. Arnaud(1997)
25. DANTE, CAPE: Feasibility Study for Connecting Asia Pacific and Europe(1997)
26. Proc.Interop Conference(1997)
27. Proc.International Telecommunication Forum:ISS'97(1997).

Figures

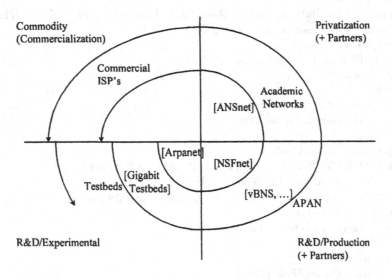

Fig. 1. Network Evolution Spiral

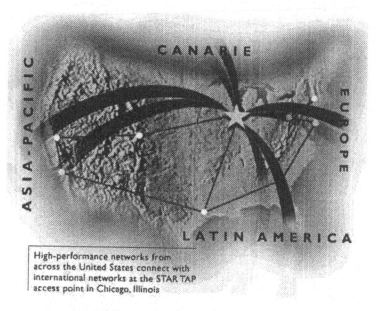

High-performance networks from across the United States connect with international networks at the STAR TAP access point in Chicago, Illinois

Fig. 2. STAR TAP

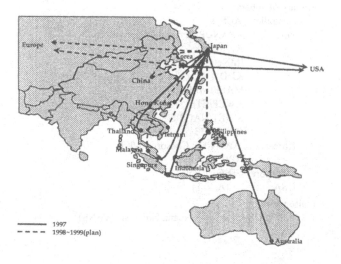

Fig. 3. APAN Network Topology

Fig. 4. Research Network - Europe(TEN-34)

Primary Members
    Australia: ACSys
    Japan: APAN-JP Consortium
                APII/CRL
                IMNet/STA
                KDD
                MAFFIN/MAFF
                RWCP/ETL
                SINET/NACSIS
                WIDE/AI3
    Korea: APAN-KR Consortium/KT
                APII
    Singapore: SINGAREN
    USA: (AT&T)
Liaison Members
        USA: Indiana University(vBNS)

Fig. 5. List of APAN Member Networks

6.1. Single Global Exchange Point

6.2. Distributed Global Exchange Point in North America

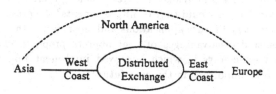

6.3. Global Exchange Point in Each Continent

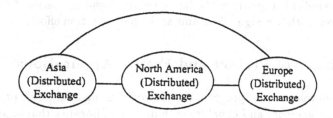

Fig. 6. Global Exchange Point Model

Java Applications and Implementations

Guy L. Steele Jr.

Sun Microsystems Laboratories
2 Elizabeth Drive
Chelmsford, Massachusetts 01824 USA

Abstract. The Java programming language has enjoyed great success in a variety of applications that include but are not limited to downloadable applets within the World Wide Web. Nevertheless, there have been some proposals for change. Would they be improvements? We present a sample range of current and future applications and then discuss the motivation, advantages, and disadvantages of a number of proposed changes. We also discuss some ways in which improved implementation techniques are likely to be important in the near future.

1 Introduction

Java is enabling many interesting and unusual applications. These applications require two kinds of support: in the language itself and in specific APIs. Each of these requires both a design effort and an implementation effort.

2 Examples of Present and Future Applications

Java allows developers to "program the network" using a full-scale programming language that is secure and capable, with dozens of libraries that support useful real-world application areas. Let us survey some examples of applications already in use and some that will be deployed very soon.

2.1 Front Ends for Databases

Many corporations have existing database systems that are very large, well-tuned and well-debugged, running on mature hardware platforms with mature operating systems. Typically, these databases have already supported the day-to-day operations of the corporation for many years. It would be foolish to risk the great instability of completely replacing these working systems, but there is a need to provide new functions and new access through the Internet, a corporate "intranet," or both.

Java provides a solution that has already been deployed many times: rather than rip out an existing system, Java can be used to wrap additional functionality around it:

– Interactive graphical user interfaces

- Translation between inquiry protocols
- Filtering of requests for security purposes
- Multiple views of the data for different purposes

A typical solution for a company that uses IBM mainframe computers would be a server/interface computer with two ports: one port speaks SNA, the other speaks TCP/IP; one communicates with the mainframe, and the other talks to the Internet. The server downloads Java interface software to client browsers, accepts requests from this downloaded software, translates and reformats the requests, queries the mainframe database, then translates and reformats the query results for display on the client.

An exciting development, now become widespread, is that companies can allow their customers to access information in the corporate database in a direct but regulated manner. This includes not just product information, for example, but inventory information: Is the item in stock? How soon can it be delivered? What is the price structure? Many companies go even further and allow customers to place orders or make reservations through the network.

It is possible to many of these things without Java, either with HTML forms or the scripting language known as JavaScript. Within their limited design, they function well; but Java, as a general-purpose programming language, allows the greatest flexibility. In practice, many interface applications use a combination of all three of these tools.

2.2 Telescopes

Two interesting recent applications of Java in the scientific community happen to involve large telescopes.

The Hubble Space Telescope. The Hubble Space telescope is monitored and controlled from the ground by its Control Center System (CCS). The CCS software is written in a variety of programming languages, but Java provides the "glue" and user interfaces. The CCS Java applets communicate with a middleware server, which in turn connects to the existing server system; this is very much the same arrangement as for corporate databases that we described in the previous section.

The control features of the CCS user interface allow authorized users to command the telescope to select new targets. The data visualization features, which Java uniquely enables, allow a user to view telemetry and engineering data either in real time, as it streams down from space, or from a data archive.

The original version of the Hubble software was implemented in FORTRAN, C, and X Windows on OpenVMS and was not easily distributed. In order to control the spacecraft or monitor data, engineers and scientists required direct network connections or had to be physically present at Goddard Space Flight Center in Maryland. The new Java-based CCS system allows engineers and scientists to view data from anywhere in the world, regardless of the hardware they use; all that is needed is a Java-capable browser. This saves both time and money by avoiding much of the need to physically transport personnel.

```
http://java.sun.com/features/1997/july/hubble.html
http://ccs.hst.nasa.gov/ccs.htm
```

Keck Observatory. The W. M. Keck Observatory, at the summit of Mauna Kea in Hawaii, has two of the world's largest optical and infrared telescopes. Java is being used for parts of the control software for the observatory's Adaptive Optics Project. The networking facilities of Java allow the Adaptive Optics user interface to be platform-independent and location-independent for remote access.

While the Keck telescopes are on the ground rather than out in space, they are still on a mountaintop that is fairly difficult to reach; while there is some air there, thin at that altitude. Most of the operation of the telescope is already controlled remotely from the Keck headquarters in Waimea, at a much lower altitude. The new Java-based GUIs will deliver remote and distributed access via browser, allowing authorized control from any location on the Internet. Remote operation allows the Keck software team to be on-call for immediate software support from the comfort of their own homes (which is a great convenience when you realize that the telescope operates all night long). Because Java is network-oriented by design, it makes it much easier to program distributed software for this kind of remote control.

The interface provides great flexibility through a combination of HTML, JavaScript, and Java applets. Each presentation screen may contain around 20 Java applets. Each applet has an associated JavaScript wrapper that generates the HTML code for placing the applet on the screen. This allows each presentation screen to be assembled dynamically, perhaps configured especially for that user according to his preferences, by executing all the relevant pieces of JavaScript to assemble an HTML page to present all the Java applets for that screen. (In a future version of the software, the Keck software group has plans to use the JavaBeans API for applet integration.)

```
http://java.sun.com/features/1997/nov/keck.html
http://www2.keck.hawaii.edu:3636/index.html
```

2.3   Sound and Multimedia

There are standards for transmitting audio and video on the Internet—*lots* of standards! I happen to be very fond of music, and one of my continuing frustrations since I first started using the World Wide Web is that no single browser seemed to be able to play all the music sample files that so many people have made available, because of all the different formats: `wav`, `au`, `aiff`, and multiple `midi` formats.

The Java Sound API, which should be available in 1998, provides a unified framework for audio playback and synthesis, including support for General MIDI.

I have great hopes that soon any music, any sound, will be playable on any browser.

The Java Sound API is part of an API suite for supporting multimedia applications:

- Java 2D API: two-dimensional graphics and imaging, including line art, text, and images, image compositing, and color space definition
- Java 3D API: an object-oriented scene-graph model designed for high performance as well as interoperability with existing three-dimensional graphics description formats such as VRML
- Java Media Framework API: a unified architecture, messaging protocol, and programming interface for media players, media capture, and conferencing
- Java Sound API: support for multiple audio formats, implemented by a software engine for high-quality 32-channel audio rendering and MIDI-controlled sound synthesis
- Java Speech API: a cross-platform API to support command and control recognizers, dictation systems, and speech synthesizers
- Java Telephony API: a cross-platform, object-oriented API for Java-based computer-telephony applications

Much of this technology has been done before in other contexts. The news here is in the integration these powerful enabling technologies with Java and Java-based software so that applications with rich, interactive multimedia interfaces can easily run on multiple platforms through Internet connections.

http://java.sun.com/products/java-media/

2.4 Smart Cards and Smart Jewelry

A version of the Java language has been specified for use in "smart cards" and other devices with limited memory. Previously, applications for smart cards have been written in assembly-code type languages using proprietary tools. The Java Card specification allows development of software for smart cards in Java using off-the-shelf Java development tools.

While many smart cards will contain fixed applications that exchange a limited amount of data with the outside world, the Java Card technology, like Java, supports the possibility of dynamic downloading of applet code to a smart card. This opens up a new range of possible functionality for smart cards.

The Java Card specification provides a subset of the full Java language because smart cards are not expected to have the memory, processor speed, or I/O connections of a desktop computer or workstation. For example, floating-point data and multiple threads are not required by the specification.

In a variation of the smart card, "smart jewelry" has been demonstrated in the form of a ring containing a smart card chip; the wearer need only wave the ring near a "lock" device to be allowed access to a computer or to open a door. I don't know whether this is a clever gimmick or the wave of the future, but it does demonstrate how small one can make a useful computer!

http://java.sun.com/products/javacard/index.html

2.5 High Performance Java

It has been proposed that an extended version of Java could be a convenient
vehicle for coding and sharing scientific applications that make heavy use of
floating-point arithmetic. Extensions are proposed because the original design
of Java emphasized portability and simplicity, not speed; as a result, correct
Java implementations deliver predictable floating-point results on every hardware platform, but nearly every hardware platform has some odd quirk that
makes it difficult for the implementor to produce the correct results efficiently
in every case.

Aside from the question of speed, some Java programmers want more expres-
siveness in Java to make numerical codes easier to code and to maintain.

It is not yet clear what extensions to Java would be necessary, but the design
of High Performance Fortran (a set of extensions to Fortran 95) might serve as
a model. We discuss this further in the next section.

3 Requirements for Language Design

In the previous section we have discussed some application areas for Java at
a fairly high level. These applications are supported by API specifications for
medium-level libraries. Some of these libraries support specific behavior, typically I/O behavior such as sound, video, graphics, or networked communication.
Other API specifications provide structured support for program organization,
for example:

- JavaBeans: support integration of separate application components
- Java RMI: communication and use of Java objects among distributed Java
  code
- JavaSpaces: sharing of persistent data among distributed Java code

But what about the low level? What is desirable in the Java language itself
to support these various high-level application areas?

One of the strengths of Java, as compared with C or C++, for example, is
that Java tends to catch certain common programming errors early, at compile
time, and catches certain other errors at run time by performing explicit checks
and reporting failures rather than allowing such failures to corrupt program
behavior.

Java catches programming errors at compile time principally by using a rigorous type analysis. If a variable is declared at compile time to have a certain
type, then the compiler guarantees the value of the variable at run time does
indeed belong to that type. As in C and C++, the programmer can insert a cast
operator to indicate conversion of an expression from one type to another, but if
the Java compiler cannot verify that the cast is always correct, then the generated code includes an explicit run-time test to make sure that type correctness
is maintained. If the test fails at run time, an exception is signaled.

Java catches errors at run time through the use of explicit tests at run time. It also avoids errors by making them impossible to commit in the first place. For example, a C program can get into trouble by explicitly freeing a piece of allocated storage and then (incorrectly) changing the content of that storage through a pointer that was retained (inadvertently or maliciously). Because Java uses automatic garbage collection, this cannot occur; there is no way to explicitly free storage, and a piece of storage is reclaimed only after there are no remaining references to it. (In effect, a garbage collector is a special-purpose theorem prover whose job is to prove theorems of the form, "There are no accessible references to such-and-so piece of storage.")

So far, these aspects of the design of the Java language have been fairly successful. But experience with the language so far has prompted many requests for extensions in three general areas: subsetting, parameterized types, and numerical computing. Let us discuss why some programmers consider the current Java language inadequate for their purposes, some of the proposals for change, and how well these proposals fit with the overall design philosophy of Java.

3.1 Subsetting

It is difficult to design a single programming language that solves all possible programming problems for all possible applications. Java does not try to be a good language for every possible purpose. Languages that do aspire to universal application usually suffer from what I call the "Arizona effect." This refers to an earlier time in the United States (I tell this story more as parable than as history), when certain persons with medical problems, such as allergies or asthma or other breathing difficulties, were recommended to move to Arizona, where there was a desert climate and very few plants to put pollen in the air. And so many persons from other parts of the country, especially the east coast, moved to Arizona. After living there for a while, they thought that the desert looked barren and began to miss what they had where they used to live. So they imported flowers and other plants, so that their new home would have all the favorite features of their old home. Soon they had all their old problems again and were as miserable and unhappy as they were before.

The designers of Java were relatively cautious and tried to avoid importing the difficult features of old programming languages. (They did not always succeed. My own judgment is that the switch statement is a difficult feature that perhaps should have been replaced by something like a case statement as found in Pascal. But this is a minor point, and the truth is that there may have been a social tradeoff here, because making the basic statements and expressions too very different from C might have made it harder for programmers to accept Java in the first place.) So Java is not too large a language and it is fairly easy for every implementor to support the complete language. This is very important: portability and platform independence are very important goals of Java, and they are possible only when every implementor supports the entire language.

But even Java is too big a language for some applications. A smart card, for example, has a rather small memory and does not have a display screen.

For both reasons, it would be absurd to require a smart card to support the complete Java AWT window software! On the other hand, other benefits of the Java language are very desirable for smart card programming.

This is not a new story. When I was a representative (briefly) to standards committee X3J11 (C programming language) in 1983–84, there were many debates about whether the I/O function printf should be a required part of the standard. On the one hand, it is a very familiar facility and is used by nearly every C programmer. On the other hand, it is a rather complicated piece of software and requires a certain amount of memory, as well as I/O support, and certain other representatives would always ask, "What about elevator controllers?" In other words, an important application area for C would be embedded systems, and it was desirable that such systems be coded in an official standard language but not be required to support facilities that make no sense in such embedded environments.

Such subsetting must be handled very carefully, lest the language definition become fragmented, which can produce portability problems. For now, Java-Soft has defined EmbeddedJava and PersonalJava, which provide subsets of Java language features for embedded environments and for "personal device" environments (such as network-based and mobile consumer electronics). So far, these seem to be fairly well-defined and separate application areas that will not cause any confusion for the arenas of browsers, database access, commercial applications, and systems programming that already use the full Java language. Nevertheless, caution is appropriate. Two or three distinct feature sets can be managed, but I believe it would be a mistake to define ten or fifteen distinct versions of any programming language! (We will return to this point later when we discuss numerical computation.)

http://java.sun.com/products/embeddedjava/
http://java.sun.com/products/personaljava/

3.2 Parameterized Types

For the most part, the current Java type system has been a success. It is powerful enough to enforce useful constraints on program behavior, to ensure the correctness of many program operations, and to detect and report many common programming errors at compile time rather than at run time (which means that the programmer sees the error message rather than the application user—a very desirable property!). On the other hand, the type system is simple enough for applications programmers (as opposed to programming language designers and theorists) to understand and use effectively on a day-to-day basis.

But there is one area that occurs frequently in Java programming where the Java type system does not do very well. This is in the use of "aggregate data structures"; the simplest example of this is the class Vector (in package java.util). A vector is a sort of expandable array with extra operations.

A vector can hold references to any Java object, but in practice the programmer often expects a vector to hold references only to objects of a particular type. For example, one vector might hold references only to strings; another might hold references only to threads. In the programmer's mind, it would be a programming error to try to store a reference to a thread into a vector of strings, and this would seem to be the sort of thing a type system ought to be able to prevent. Also, it would be convenient if the Java compiler could understand that whenever you fetch an element from a vector of strings, the result is in fact a reference to a string. Unfortunately, Java's current type system cannot do either of these jobs. As a result, the Java programmer is forced to use casts to solve the second problem, and to use either casts or great care to avoid the first problem. When fetching an element of a vector of strings, instead of

```
String s = myVectorOfStrings.elementAt(3);
```

the programmer must write

```
String s = (String)myVectorOfStrings.elementAt(3);
```

When storing an element into a vector of strings, the programmer must either write a cast:

```
myVectorOfStrings.setElementAt((String)aThing, 3);
```

or be very careful to ensure by other means that the value of aThing really is a reference to a string.

The problem with the use of casts is not the overhead at run time; that is the least of our worries. It is verbosity in the code and the possibility of failing to catch simple (and likely) errors at compile time.

As a result, a number of proposals have been put forward for extended type systems for Java (see the proceedings of such ACM conferences as 1997 POPL, 1997 PLDI, and 1997 OOPSLA). These fall into two main categories. *Virtual types* are very general and in an expert's hands are very flexible; there has been considerable experience with them in the Beta programming language, but they may be a bit too esoteric for general-purpose use. *Parameterized types* are perhaps a bit more familiar; C++ templates and the Ada generics facility fall into this category.

As of December 1997, there is still no consensus on whether to adopt parameterized types into Java, or on exactly what design to consider. The design constraints are formidable:

- It needs to be simple. It should be very easy to declare that a variable refers to a vector of strings; ideally, the declaration should consist only of the word Vector, the word String, and one or two characters of punctuation!
- It needs to solve the problem. Given a declaration such as, for example,

```
Vector<String> v = new Vector<String>(20);
```

then the compiler should be able to deduce that the type of

```
v.elementAt(3)
```

is `String`. Similarly, the compiler should be able to deduce in

`v.setElementAt(aThing, 3)`

that the type of `aThing` should be assignable to type `String`.

- It needs to fit cleanly into the rest of the Java language. For example, in the current Java language, the class `Stack` is a subclass of `Vector`. It would be sensible to expect `Stack<String>` to be a subclass of `Vector<String>`. Furthermore, the design needs to be compatible with "inner classes."
- It should not be too difficult to implement or require too much space or time.
- There should be a code-compatible upgrade path. Ideally, existing Java code using the existing `Vector` class could coexist with new Java code using the parameterized `Vector` class.
- There should be a JVM-compatible upgrade path. Ideally, there would be an implementation strategy that would allow code using parameterized types to execute in existing browsers. (This does not prohibit the possibility that an improved JVM implementation might provide even better error checking or better performance.)

It is not yet clear whether any single design can satisfy all these constraints in a satisfactory manner. Even if one can be found, the question still remains of whether it should be adopted. We must be sure that the "Arizona effect" will not haunt us.

3.3 Numerical Computing

There are four principal difficulties with using Java, as currently designed, for numerical computing:

- Performance. In the interest of insuring portability, Java requires all floating-point operations to have very specific, repeatable, machine-independent behavior. This behavior is consistent with the IEEE 754 floating-point standard, but in fact is more specific, more restrictive, because IEEE 754 in fact was intentionally unspecific on certain points (such as exactly which NaN value is produced for an invalid operation, as well as the exact precision to which intermediate values in an expression are calculated). As a result, while IEEE 754 has brought about 99% compatibility among hardware architectures, it has not achieved 100% compatibility, and that last 1% difference still creates great problems. The current design of Java is something of a compromise: it is simple, plausible, and easy to understand, but for every current popular hardware architecture, there is some aspect of the Java specification that is not directly supported by the hardware and therefore requires a tricky software emulation that has reduced performance.
- Functionality. There are certain operations specified by IEEE 754 that are not currently supported by Java. This includes access to "flag information" about whether overflow, underflow, or division by zero has occurred.

- Extensibility. Simple floating-point data is not the only kind of data manipulated by numerical programs. There are complex numbers, vectors and matrices, matrices of complex numbers, rational numbers, intervals, and many other kinds of numerical objects in common use.
- Notation. While general object-oriented method notation seems adequate, even convenient, for most purposes, we are used to using specialized infix operators (+, -, *, /, <, etc) for numerical computations. Java, like nearly all programming languages, provides built-in support for such operator notation for simple integer and floating-point arithmetic. The question arises as to whether such notation should be extended to other numerical and mathematical objects.

Let us now consider how each of these points might be addressed.

First, performance. Note that we have implicitly assumed that the use of interpreters is not the performance bottleneck. While many existing implementations of Java use bytecode interpreters, others are available that use either JIT ("Just In Time"—that is, load time) compilation technology or conventional static standalone compilers. Before the end of 1998, these compilers will surely produce code that is competitive in performance with, say, the best C++ compilers. No, the problem has to do with the mismatch between the definition of Java and current hardware architectures. There is currently a debate about which, if either, should give way:

- Position A: Java is the way of the future. Portability is crucial; correctness comes first. Therefore we should implement Java as defined, and future hardware designs may include changes to support Java efficiently as well as correctly.
- Position B: There are already millions of machines on the planet in use, today and every day, that have trouble supporting Java as currently defined. A slight loosening of the semantics (principally to allow certain computations to be *more accurate* than Java currently permits—which, for some programs, admittedly could cause later computations to be less accurate, or at least different in unpredictable ways) would probably not harm most programs and would let them run a lot faster, making much better use of the installed base of hardware, in which there is already a huge monetary investment. We shouldn't have to wait years, until this hardware base is replaced, to get good performance.
- Position C: Leave Java alone. Don't make every implementor support a lot of floating-point complexity. If you want high performance, use Fortran.

Next, functionality. On the one hand, certain kinds of code are difficult to write without the IEEE 754 features that Java currently omits. On the other hand, IEEE 754 presents a rather low-level, single sequential processor, assembly-language sort of programming model that depends on hidden state (side effects) and a trap mechanism whose control structure (and its relationship to the rest of a high-level programming language) is not specified. Certain aspects of this model, notably the hidden state, actually obstruct the goal of high performance on modern pipelined or parallel hardware architectures. While it is desirable to be able to detect such conditions as overflow, it is not obvious that the IEEE 754 programming model should be enshrined in Java.

Now, extensibility. "Arizona!" Surely it is not desirable to add a dozen new built-in data types to Java—it would add greatly to the implementation burden, and there would be a strong temptation to "subset" the language back to its current form by omitting the numerical facilities! Moreover, a proverb (well-known in the United States) runs:

> Give someone a fish, and he can eat for a day.
> Teach someone to fish, and he can eat for a lifetime.

Proposals are being studied that would allow such aggregate data types as vectors, matrices, complex numbers, and intervals to be user-defined as Java classes, with some features or keywords that would enable a good Java compiler to open-code operations on such data structures and perhaps to avoid heap allocation in many cases. Besides keeping the core language relatively simple, this approach would be compatible with existing Java implementations and would open up a market for third-party numerical support libraries. (It should also be noted that parameterized types might be relevant in coding such numerical libraries: such types as `Matrix<Interval>` or `Vector<Complex<Rational>>`[1] would be perfectly sensible.)

Finally, notation. This is technically the easiest of all—it is handled entirely at compile time, and therefore requires no special run-time support—and yet there are some technical subtleties. The designers of Java originally considered operator overloading and rejected it; it was their considered opinion that while operator overloading indeed made numerical code clearer, it made nonnumerical code much more difficult to read, and indeed had been badly abused by too many C++ programmers. Inasmuch as the intended application domain for Java did not include highly numerical code, omitting operator overloading seemed the conservative thing to do.

As for the technical subtleties: nearly everyone agrees that it is sensible for

```
a+b
```

to mean something like

```
a.plus(b)
```

—that is, an overloaded operator is merely an abbreviated form of method call. This makes sense when the type of a is a reference type; and when neither a nor b is of reference type, then both are of primitive type, and Java's existing built-in rules cover that case. But what if a is of primitive type, while b is a reference?

---

[1] I am, by the way, aware that in C++ one would need to write this with a space, as `Vector<Complex<Rational> >`. There are grammatical tricks for getting around this, however, so I felt free to omit the space in my hypothetical Java example.

- Proposal 1: Forbid that case. This is very simple, easy to explain, and makes sense. Unfortunately, it prohibits a very common mathematical convention: while sums are usually written with constants last (a + 3), products are typically written with constants first (3 * v). Old habits die hard.
- Proposal 2: Say that when a is a reference, then a+b means a.plus(b); otherwise, if b is a reference, then it means b.reversePlus(a) (except that a is evaluated before b). This is better, but fails to solve another problem. Suppose that a mathematical vector class has been defined, and now another programmer wishes to define a matrix class. This can include a method to multiply a matrix by a vector, because m*v means something like m.multiply(v). But what about multiplying a vector by a matrix? The multiplication is not commutative, so we can't insist on always writing m*v; v*m means something different. But the vector class isn't under the control of the programmer who is writing the matrix class. There needs to be a way for the matrix class to handle v*m—but what if the vector class does indeed try to handle v*m? (Maybe it purports to be able to multiply a vector by any object??)
- Proposal 3: This is my current favorite. If a is a reference and b is not, then a+b means a.plus(b). If b is a reference and a is not, then a+b means b.reversePlus(a). If both a and b are references, then a+b means *both* a.plus(b) and b.reversePlus(a); that is, exactly one of these two method calls should have a most specific applicable method—if they both do, then a+b is ambiguous and therefore a compile-time error.

There are certain points that these proposals do not address. For example, some machines support well some sort of "extended" (80-bit) or "quad" (128-bit) floating-point type. But to add such a type to Java as a required type would result in poor performance and implementation headaches on machines that don't support it; to add such a type as an option would destroy portability. What to do? What to do?

4 Implementation Strategies

Whether or not the Java language is changed or extended—perhaps, as some users urge, it is just fine the way it is, thank you very much—there remains a great deal of scope for improved implementation techniques and strategies.

Java has turned out to be so attractive a language design that different organizations want to use it for a very wide range of applications covering a very wide scale:

- High performance (whatever that means—supercomputers?)
- Servers, including multiprocessor clusters or SMPs
- Interface boxes
- Browsers (or other GUI) on the desktop or in kiosks
- Appliances and personal devices (cell phones, CD players)
- Smart cards and smart jewelry

Aside from the question of language subsetting—even if the same language were used uniformly at all scales—there is a need for a range of implementations with different performance and cost characteristics. Some have special requirements, such as soft or hard real-time response. A simple example is that multimedia delivery cannot tolerate the unpredictable, unbounded pause times inflected by many of the simpler storage management (garbage collection) algorithms; on the other hand, a small embedded system such as a smart card may not have enough memory to support the more sophisticated storage management techniques that avoid long pauses.

Another important area of research is "on-the-fly" compilation. By this term is meant not only JIT compilation (translating byte codes to native machine code when a class is loaded) but run-time compilation. There are two aspects to run-time compilation that may be important to best Java performance. First, a Java implementation can use run-time profiling feedback to decide the best strategy for allocating compilation resources. It doesn't make sense to use a great deal of effort to optimize code that is not executed frequently. Second, a Java implementation can use run-time information gathering and caching strategies to optimize compiled code for the behavior of that particular running instance of the code. For example, it might happen that a virtual method call could, in principle, invoke any of several method definitions, but during this particular program execution it nearly always invokes one particular definition. The compiled code can be customized to "play the odds" by using an in-line test for that case first; this can make the method dispatch much faster on average. As a result, Java code using an on-the-fly compiler might well run *faster* than code produced by the very best static standalone compiler.

A third area I would like to mention is parallelism. Java is relatively unusual among programming languages in explicitly providing for parallelism in programs in a portable manner. However, I would like to point out opportunities for parallelism in the infrastructure of the Java Virtual Machine.

Suppose a JVM has two (or more) processors as its disposal. Should they all be assigned to execute user threads? Maybe a processor should be dedicated, or at least made available, for compilation activities. And what about storage management? It may still be difficult to use truly *concurrent* garbage collection, in which the garbage collector executes at the same time as user processes, because without extremely carefully designed hardware support, the synchronization overhead is likely to be prohibitive. But it may not be too much trouble to design a *parallel* garbage collector, where user processes must pause during a garbage collection but the garbage collection algorithm itself makes use of many processors simultaneously.

5   Conclusions

I believe that Java has been successful, and continues to be widely used, because it successfully helps to manage complexity. By discarding some old programming paradigms and supporting a few carefully chosen new ones, it has simplified the process of coding and deploying applications.

It is worthwhile to examine a progression of languages used for systems programming.

1. Assembly language was very low level. You could do anything the machine could do, but the resulting code had little abstraction and was not portable. The basic data model was bits organized into words. The programmer had to code all the address arithmetic.

2. C was a great step forward in systems program. Lots of code, including an entire operating system, was *mostly* portable—let's call it "easily ported" rather than portable. The C language provided some useful data abstractions; the bits of assembly language were organized into an array of bytes, which could then be fairly automatically divided up into record structures (**struct**) and/or arrays whose elements were data items other than bytes. And, if you needed to, you could always get at the low-level bits. Just do a cast or two, and the compiler would let you access anything (but probably ruining portability). Of course, it was difficult to write code that would work properly on both big-endian and little-endian machines, and the language provided little help in maintaining the necessary discipline.

3. C++ built on record structures to support object-oriented programming. This allowed the construction of very high level abstractions and a disciplined programming style that lent itself well to true portability. But a cast or two still let you get at the underlying record structures, the underlying array of bytes, the underlying raw bits.

4. Java, having climbed up to a completely high-level object-oriented design, kicked the ladder out from underneath! In Java, it's all objects and a few disciplined primitive types. You're not allowed to see the raw bits of an object. Code is truly portable. Because the high-level abstractions are enforced by the type system—there are casts, but they are limited and cannot subvert the abstractions—code is safe and easy to maintain. Storage management can be automatic because the JVM can always tell whether a set of bits is a reference rather than an integer that accidentally looks like a reference. The behavior of a class can be described by an API that really means exactly what it says. Java has created a healthy competitive market in implementations of the APIs.

These are old ideas—abstract data types, objects, defined interfaces, automatic storage management—but with Java they have now found widespread acceptance and are in use in the real world, by hundreds of thousands of people, every day.

Back to Home: Where Computers and Networking Should Go

Mario Tokoro[1,2] *

[1] Sony Computer Science Laboratory Inc.
3-14-13 Higashi Gotanda, Shinagawa-ku,
Tokyo 141-0022 Japan
[2] IT Laboratories, Sony Corporation
6-7-35 Kitashinagawa, Shinagawa-ku
Tokyo 141-0001 Japan

Abstract. Revolutionary and profound changes have been observed quite recently, particularly in the arena of computer and communications. CPU power hungry applications, business applications and mass distribution (web-cast) are current beneficiaries of technology: Internet and image/graphic processing. It is the author's belief that home (domestic) applications and personal communication should deserve much more benefits derived from development of the technology in the upcoming generation, three years in Internet-standard-time. This paper describes the technical improvements required for the home and personal applications and also introduces the overview of a new technology which will help facilitate the implementation of the proposed applications.

1 Introduction

Computers are ubiquitous. So are Networks. True, at offices and labs. They are connected through the Internet. Distributed databases can be easily used for complicated query. Some people tried the deciphering contest and won the prize, connecting a huge number of computers over network. Web sites are exploding and flooding the network with stored information. Kids enjoy computer games, chat or e-mail over the Internet with "machine-gun" key strokes. It is true, current computers and networks provide excellent services for those computer comfortable people at offices and labs.

Computers are now part of the individual household more than ever. However, their dominant application is still limited to ones for, more or less, those comfortable with computers: Games, web-browsing, tax-return-application, portfolio management, personal check management, spread sheet and word processing. Our marketing experience tells that there are a lot more in the domestic(home) market who have hesitation with computers and networks but who at the same time expect benefit of technology.

Much has been done to the networking for offices and labs. It is time to come Back to Home. The author firmly believes that both academia and industry in

---

* e-mail: tokoro@itlab.sony.co.jp

computer and networking technology should contribute in a way the benefit of technology is made available to the majority of home users who deserve it.

2 Home Applications and Required Network Technology

Personal computers and the Internet are available almost anywhere in the advanced nations. Digital communication media is rapidly replacing conventional analog media. Most importantly, digital home appliances are also in much demand particularly among the Audio Video equipment. Equipment such as these brings about new applications for home users.

2.1 Personal Multimedia Communication

Video transmission over the Internet is technically available. But due to the intrinsic characteristics of the current Internet, quality of motion picture transmitted over networks is far below the expectation of the general public. Voice is interrupted. Picture halts suddenly and starts again, missing part of a scene. Once fiber optic networks provide the access to the home users and with the proper technology, digital AV equipment can become the source and destination of digital image(motion/still) transmission over the network without sacrifice in quality. Transmission can be either in bulk or real-time. Two-way multimedia communication is required along with one-way(broadcast) communication. One of the issue to be resolved is the guaranteed transmission of video data over network. The current Internet does not guarantee such continuous media transmission.

2.2 Home Network

Digital AV equipment are to be connected to each other in the home. Personal computers can also be connected. However, connection of each equipment is a big headache among home users. Too many wires and connectors in the back of the equipment end up in a "spaghetti." The desirable solution would be a single cable per equipment to carry computer data, audio-video(isochronous) data and control. The solution should also include a mechanism to identify the equipment and topology of connection.

Another key requirement for home network is the capability to transmit audio video data between AV devices and between AV devices and personal computers, again without sacrifice in quality. A digital still camera can send still image data to a printer. A digital camcorder can send video data for storage into a personal computer. Stored video data is edited and sent, for example, to grandpa living in a separate state over the network to deliver a happy birthday video message. Real-time video capture and transmission will also be a key requirement. Be reminded that man is a social animal. Communication is the integral part of social activity. Particularly, non-verbal communication made possible through multimedia transmission plays an equally important role as verbal communication.

2.3 Required Network Technology

The personal multimedia communication over network from home to home obviously requires two key capabilities.

- High bandwidth

  Applications for personal, interactive communication demand higher quality than regular office applications. For example, 2 to 6 Mbps of bandwidth is required for standard MPEG-2 video streams and 20 Mbps for DV video streams. Bidirectional, real-time communication is essential. Synchronization of video, audio, high-resolution still pictures, and text is also indispensable.

- Guaranteed QoS

  The multimedia data transmission requires the guarantee of bandwidth and constant delay. Thus the QoS services must be implemented on both WANs and Home Networks. Author proposes the AMInet architecture [1] for WAN and IEEE-1394 [3] for the Home Network since they satisfy this basic requirement. Overview is presented in the next section.

- Simple wiring

  Key importance of IEEE-1394 standard along with capability for Asynchronous and Isochronous transmission is the physical cabling. It requires only single cable assembly of three pairs of wire (six leads) and works as a high speed serial bus, allowing multiple data/control streams running simultaneously on it. An overview is presented in the following section.

- High-speed mobile communication

  Yet another key technology worthy of our attention is the high-speed wireless communication technology. IMT-2000, deliberations going on in ITU for instance, will provide 2 Mbps communication channel. Proposed LEO (Low Earth Orbitor) satellite systems will provide even higher speed of 2 Mbps to 155 Mbps. These wireless technologies will free multimedia applications to open a new way of personal mobile multimedia communication.

3 AMInet

AMInet(Advanced Multimedia Information network) is a fruit of the joint research activity among Sony Corporation/Sony Computer Science Laboratory Inc., Nippon Telegraph and Telephone Corporation, and Keio University. It incorporates a network/transport layer architecture designed for the transmission of continuous media (ex. motion picture) in real-time with guaranteed QoS(Quality of Service), overcoming the restrictions of the conventional IP network, while keeping upward and downward compatibility with it. The network architecture is primarily built on top of the ATM(Asynchronous Transfer Mode) technology [2] . However, the architecture allows the flexibility of underlying physical media such as xDSL(Digital Subscriber Line) and digital CATV.

3.1   AMInet vs RSVP

ASP(AMInet Setup Protocol) implements the resource reservation mechanism for guaranteed bandwidth. RSVP is a well known protocol to reserve bandwidth over IP networks. Primary difference between the two protocols is in the reservation set-up process and signalling protocol.

Bandwidth reservation process is initiated by the receiver in RSVP [4]. However, any party can start reservations in ASP. The difference in initiation comes from the target application. RSVP is presumably designed to fit for applications on the Mbone where transmission is receiver driven. However, in personal communication, reservation must be initiated by any associated party since communication is duplex in nature.

Both ASP and RSVP operate on the cell relay network. Both interact with ATM switch(s) to establish and release the VCC(Virtual Channel Connection) between originating and terminating end point. For this purpose, RSVP uses standard ATM signalling protocol (ATM Forum UNI [5] [6]). On the other hand, ASP uses IP to set up VCCs directly without need for a separate signalling mechanism. The reason for this proprietary protocol is the agility of signalling. Standard ATM signalling does not assume the frequent setup and tear-down of VCCs and these signalling process takes time. However in personal communication, VCCs are setup frequently and torn-down as users "surf" end points. ASP is designed to be light-weight and fast.

3.2   Continuous Media Transfer Extension

Once the bandwidth reservation is completed on a VCC by ASP, continuous media data is transmitted through the VCC using UDP-CMTE (UDP - Continuous Media Transfer Extension). The extension implements rate based flow control for continuous media. The sending side regulates traffic to the specified rate and forwarding ATM switch(s) guarantee the QoS of the VCC traffic.

3.3   Bulk Data Transfer Extension

Another extension was made to TCP/IT called TCP-BDTE (TCP - Bulk Data Transfer Extension). The extension is designed to transmit bulk data over AMInet. With the extension, bulk data can be transferred at maximum efficiency over the network. Packet loss seriously degrades the efficiency of the transfer. Congestion control and avoidance is also the important design criterion for the conventional TCP which does not assume underlying medium and has no knowledge of its bandwidth. The slow-start mechanism of TCP is smart mechanism for this purpose. As the name stands, transfer starts slow and continues on, gradually gaining its peek speed at the sacrifice of the efficiency during the initial part of the transfer. With the knowledge of bandwidth reserved for the VCC, TCP-BDTE starts transfer at the maximum rate without packet loss or its resulting congestion.

4   IEEE1394

IEEE 1394 standard is for high performance serial bus; Cable environment and Backplane environment. This section introduces primarily Cable environment. With its wire rate of 100Mbps, it is designed to carry asynchronous data and isochronous data simultaneously. (Faster rates of 400Mbps or even higher are under deliberation in the standardization body [7] .) The profile of home appliances is becoming smaller and smaller, leaving less room for connectors. The connection between appliances like VCR, TV, CATV box and so on are increasingly complex and sometimes even discouraging. The original concept "single cable carries all" is inevitable due to the requirement from home appliances.

4.1   Cable Environment

The standard specifies a simple six-lead cable medium. A pair for transmit, another pair for receive and the rest for the power supply. Physical topology of node(device) connection is in tree topology without closed loop. The cable medium allows up to 16 physical connections (cable hops).

The standard protocol provides an automatic mechanism for topology identification and unique node identification upon change in topology. This allows end users to plug and unplug appliances without need of addressing.

4.2   Isochronous Transmission

All nodes connected on a bus forms a single ring in the link layer protocol. In the Isochronous transmission, resource(bandwidth) is allocated in a way similar to the token bus. Specific timing signal called cycle-start rotates periodically at cycle of 125 micro-second. The cycle master on the bus guarantees the cycle. Specific portion of time(channels) after cycle-start is assigned for the isochronous transmission. The node assigned with a channel is permitted to transmit isochronous data for the duration of allocated time. The remainder of the 125 micro-second cycle other than assigned for isochronous transmission are allocated to asynchronous transmission.

5   Conclusions

Home users should deserve more benefit of high performance computing and networking technology. Personal multimedia communication will be the area where the next generation computer and networking technology can provide this benefit. The importance of high-bandwidth, continuous, real-time communications will increase. High-speed mobile communication should be integrated in the near future. Although there are still many issues that need to be worked out, the AMInet architecture and IEEE-1394 standard are the key technologies to affordable multimedia communication.

Acknowledgment

The author would like to thank Masami Furukori and Susumu Nakagawa of Sony IT Laboratories and Atsushi Shionozaki of Sony Computer Science Laboratory for their help and constructive comments in the preparation of this paper.

References

1. Shionozaki, A., Yamashita, K., Utsumi, S., and Cho., K., Integrating Resource Reservation with Rate-Based Transport Protocols in AMInet, *Proc. WWCA*, Tsukuba, March 1998.
2. http://www.atmforum.com/, ATM Forum.
3. http://www.1394ta.org/, The 1395 Trade Association.
4. Resource Reservation Protocol, RFC2205, IETF, September 1997.
5. ATM User-Network Interface Specification 3.1, af-uni-0010.002, ATM Forum, 1994.
6. ATM User-Network Interface Specification 4.0, af-sig-0061.000, ATM Forum, 199x.
7. IEEE 1394 Standard for a High Performance Serial Bus, IEEE Std 1394-1995, IEEE, 1995.

ObjectSpace Voyager – The Agent ORB for Java

Graham Glass

Chairman and Chief Technology Officer, ObjectSpace, Inc.

Abstract. ObjectSpace Voyager™ Core Technology (Voyager) is a simple yet powerful object request broker (ORB) for creating distributed Java applications. ObjectSpace Voyager is the first platform to seamlessly integrate fundamental distributed computing with agent technology. Voyager was designed from the ground up to support mobile objects and autonomous agents. The Voyager philosophy is that an agent is simply a special kind of object that can move independently, can continue to execute as it moves, and otherwise behaves exactly like any other object. Voyager enables objects and other agents to send standard Java messages to an agent even as the agent is moving. In addition, Voyager allows you to remote-enable any Java class, even a third-party library class, without modifying the class source in any way. Voyager also includes a rich set of services for transparent distributed persistence, scalable group communication, and basic directory services. This paper present a high-level overview of Version 1.0 of the Voyager Core Technology.

1 What Is Voyager?

ObjectSpace Voyager is the ObjectSpace product line designed to help developers produce high-impact distributed systems quickly. Voyager is 100% Java and is designed to use the Java language object model. Voyager allows you to use regular message syntax to construct remote objects, send them messages, and move them between programs. This reduces learning curves, minimizes maintenance, and, most importantly, speeds your time to market for new, advanced systems. Voyager's architecture is designed to provide developers full flexibility and powerful expansion paths.

The root of the Voyager product line is the ObjectSpace Voyager Core Technology. This product contains the core features and architecture of the platform, including a full-featured, intuitive object request broker (ORB) with support for mobile objects and autonomous agents. Also in the core package are services for persistence, scalable group communication, and basic directory services. The ObjectSpace Voyager Core Technology is everything you need to get started building high-impact systems in Java today.

As the industry evolves, other companies providing distributed technologies struggle as they try to adapt to the new Java language. These companies are required to adapt older object models to fit Java. This results in a series of compromises that together have a dramatic impact on time to market and development costs. Voyager, on the other hand, is developed to use the Java language as its fundamental interface.

One of Java's primary distinctions is the ability to load classes into a virtual machine at run time. This capability enables infrastructures to use mobile objects and autonomous agents as another tool for building distributed systems. Adding this capability to older distributed technologies is often impractical and results in difficult-to-use infrastructures. Voyager provides seamless support for mobile objects and autonomous agents.

1.1 CORBA Integration

Complete bidirectional CORBA integration was included in the 2.0 Beta 1 enhancement of Voyager, released early December 1997. This additional Java package allows Voyager to be used as a CORBA 2 client or server. You can generate a Voyager remote interface from any IDL file. You can use this interface to communicate with any Voyager or CORBA server. Without modifying the code, you can export any Java class as a CORBA server in seconds, automatically generating IDL for use by CORBA implementations.

As part of the 2.0 Beta 1 Voyager Core Technology, the CORBA integration is also free for most commercial use. For more information, read the ObjectSpace Voyager CORBA Integration Technical Overview paper or Part 4 of the ObjectSpace Voyager Core Technology User Guide, Version 2.0 Beta 1, on www.objectspace.com.

1.2 Developing with Voyager

Voyager was designed from the ground up to solve problems encountered in the development of distributed systems in Java. As the premier Java distributed systems architecture, Voyager is a technology that enables developers to solve these problems quickly and efficiently.

Consider the following issues.

– **Problem** Time to market is crucial and development time is expensive. Extra months spent in development mean extra months for competitors to gain market share.

Solution Voyager is the easiest way to build distributed systems in Java. Previous technologies require a tedious, clumsy, and error-prone multistep process to prepare a class for remote programming. A single Voyager command replaces this hassle and automatically enables any class for distributed computing and persistence in just seconds. Voyager does not require Java classes to be altered. You can remotely construct and communicate with any Java class, even third-party libraries, without accessing the source code. You can remotely persist any serializable object. Other technologies typically require the use of .idl files, interface definitions, and modifications to the original class, all of which consume development time and couple your domain classes tightly to a particular ORB or database technology.

– **Problem** Enterprise networks are usually composed of many hardware and operating system platforms. Systems built with legacy ORBs often require separate binaries for each platform. This increases developer load and system complexity and complicates system maintenance.

Solution Voyager is 100% Java. Voyager applications can be written once and run anywhere Java 1.1 is supported.

- **Problem** Resources in a distributed system need to be used wisely. When a machine is being overused, the load should be shifted to other, less used machines. Existing ORBs do not help developers solve this problem.

Solution Voyager is dynamic. Mobile objects and agents can be used to encapsulate processing and can migrate through the network, carrying their workloads with them. Instead of being limited to running only static processes on a given virtual machine, developers can now exploit the natural connection between agents and processing. The result is effortless, dynamic load balancing.

- **Problem** Information access needs vary. Sometimes information should be broadcast across the enterprise; sometimes it should be filtered based on the needs of the user. Sometimes information is transient, while at other times it is stored for future use.

Solution Voyager is comprehensive. It supports development of high-performance push systems using the built-in publish/subscribe technology. Voyager also supports distributed persistence, multicast messaging, and a rich set of message types.

- **Problem** Developers need to leverage JavaBeans(tm) components in a distributed context, but cannot afford to modify the architecture with wrapper code or spend time developing complex glue logic.

Solution Voyager is JavaBeans-enabled. It provides support for distributed JavaBeans events without requiring any modifications to the beans. No other ORB has such a seamless beans event distribution model.

- **Problem** Large systems and congested networks often result in sluggish software. Today's high-performance needs require responsive software.

Solution Voyager is fast. Remote messages with Voyager are as fast as other CORBA ORBs. Messages delivered by mobile agents can be up to 1,000,000 times quicker.

- **Problem** Today's embedded systems require small run-time footprints. Similarly, Web applets must be small to minimize download times.

Solution Voyager is compact. The entire Voyager system is less than 300KB, not including the JDK classes it uses. Voyager is a fully functional, agent-enhanced ORB and does not require any additional software beyond JDK 1.1.

1.3 Related Work

Voyager contains a superset of features found in other ORBs and agent platforms, including CORBA [3], JavaSoft's RMI [5], General Magic's Odyssey™ [4], IBM's Aglets™ [1], and Mitsubishi's Concordia [2]. Although Voyager can be used to supplement these technologies, it effectively replaces them with a single, easy-to-use platform.

ORBs that support fundamental distributed computing, such as CORBA, DCOM, and RMI, allow developers to create remote objects and send them messages as if they were local. They often include features such as distributed garbage collection, different messaging modes, and a naming service. However, none of them support object mobility or mobile, autonomous agents.

Agent platforms like Odyssey, Aglets, and Concordia allow developers to create an agent, program it with a set of tasks, and launch it into a network to fulfill its mission. However, they have minimal support for basic distributed computing and treat agents differently than simple objects. Aglets uses sockets, and Odyssey and Concordia use RMI to move agents between machines. But, none of these platforms allow sending a regular Java™ message to a stationary or moving agent. As a result, it is very difficult for objects to communicate with an agent after the agent has been launched and for agents to communicate directly with other agents.

2 Concepts

This section describes the concepts behind the ObjectSpace Voyager Core Technology architecture, using a mix of text, example code, and drawings.

2.1 Objects

Objects are the building blocks of all Voyager programs. An object is a software component that has a well-defined set of public functions and encapsulates data. The following object is an instance of the class Store with a public function to accept new stock.

```
Store store = new Store();
store.stock( "widget", 43 );
```

An object
(an instance store ← stock("widget",43)
of class Store)

2.2 Voyager-Enabled Programs

When a Voyager-enabled program starts, it automatically spawns threads that provide timing services, perform distributed garbage collection, and accept network traffic. Each Voyager-enabled program has a network address consisting of its host name and a communications port number, which is an integer unique to the host.

Port numbers are usually randomly allocated to programs. This is sufficient for clients communicating with remote objects and for creating and launching agents into a network. However, if a program will be addressed by other programs, you can assign a well-known port number to the program at startup.

```
Voyager.startup( 7000 ); // assign port number 7000 to this program
Store store = new Store();
```

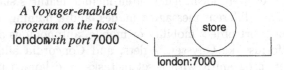

2.3 Remote-Enabled Classes and Virtual References

A class is remote-enabled if its instances can be created outside the local address space of a program and if these instances can receive messages as if they were local. Voyager allows an object to communicate with an instance of a remote-enabled class via a special object called a virtual reference. When messages are sent to a virtual reference, the virtual reference forwards the messages to the instance of the remote-enabled class. If a message has a return value, the target object sends the return value to the virtual reference, which returns this message to the sender.

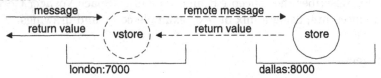

After remote-enabling a class, you can:

- Construct instances remotely, even if the class code does not exist on the remote machine.
- Send messages to remote instances using regular Java syntax.
- Connect to existing remote instances in other programs.
- Move remote instances to other programs, even if the class code is not already in the destination program.
- Make remote instances persistent.

2.4 Generating a Remote-Enabled Class

Use Voyager's vcc utility to generate a remote-enabled class from an existing class. The vcc utility reads a .class or .java file and generates a new virtual class. The virtual class contains a superset of the original class functions and allows function calls to occur even when objects are remote or moving.

The virtual class name is V plus the original class name. For example, if the file Store.java contains the source code for class Store, the compiled class file is Store.class. You can remote-enable the Store class by running vcc on either Store.java or Store.class to create a new, virtual class named VStore.

For more detailed information about remote enabling, refer to Chapter 5, "Fundamental ORB Features," of the ObjectSpace Voyager Core Technology User Guide, Version 1.0.

2.5   Constructing a Remote Object

After remote-enabling a class, you can use the class constructors of the resulting virtual class to create a remote instance of the original class. The remote instance can reside in your current program or a different program, and a virtual reference to the remote instance is created in your current program.

To construct a remote instance of a class, give the virtual class constructor the address of the destination program where the remote instance will reside. If the original class code for the remote instance does not exist in the destination program, the Voyager network class loader automatically loads the original class code into the destination program.

```
Voyager.startup( 7000 );
VStore vstore = new VStore( "dallas:8000/Acme" ); // alias is Acme
```

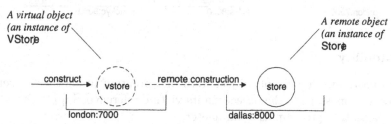

When a remote object is constructed, it is automatically assigned a 16-byte globally unique identifier (GUID), which uniquely identifies the object across all programs worldwide. Optionally, you can assign an alias to an object during construction. The GUID or the optional alias can be used to locate or connect to the object at a later point in time. This directory service is a basic Voyager feature. Voyager also includes an advanced federated directory service for more complex directory requirements. Refer to Chapter 16, "Federated Directory Service," of the ObjectSpace Voyager Core Technology User Guide, Version 1.0, for more information.

2.6   Sending a Message to a Remote Object

When a message is sent to a virtual reference, the virtual reference forwards the message to its associated remote object. If the message requires a return value, the remote object passes the return value to the virtual reference, which forwards it to the sender. Similarly, if the remote object throws an exception, the exception is caught and passed back to the virtual reference, which throws it to the caller.

```
vstore.stock( "widget", 43 );
```

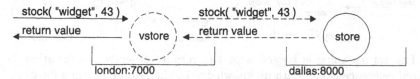

2.7 Connecting to an Existing Remote Object

A remote object can be referenced by any number of virtual references. To create
a new virtual reference and associate it with an existing remote object, supply
the address of the program where the existing remote object currently resides
and the alias of the remote object to the static VObject.forObjectAt() method.

```
// connect using alias
Voyager.startup( 9000 );
VStore vstore2 = (VStore) VObject.forObjectAt( "dallas:8000/Acme" );
int price = vstore2.buy( "widget" );
```

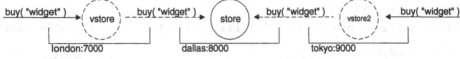

2.8 Mobility

You can move any serializable object from one program to another by sending
the moveTo() message to the object via its virtual reference. Supply the address
of the destination program as a parameter.

```
vstore.moveTo( "tokyo:9000" );
```

The object waits until all pending messages are processed and then moves
to the specified program, leaving behind a forwarder to forward messages and
future connection requests.

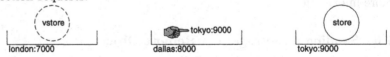

You can send a message to an object even if the object has moved from one
program to another. Simply send the message to the object at its last known
address. When the message cannot locate its target object, the message searches
for a forwarder. If the message locates a forwarder representing the object, the
forwarder sends the message to the object's new location.

```
int price = vstore.buy( "widget" );
```

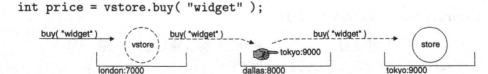

The return value is tagged with the remote object's new location, so the
virtual reference can update its knowledge of the remote object's location.

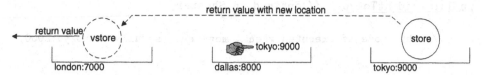

Subsequent messages are sent directly to the remote object at its new location, bypassing the forwarder.

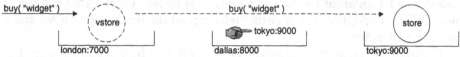

2.9 Agents

An agent is a special object type. Although there is no single definition of an agent, all definitions agree that an agent has autonomy. An autonomous object can be programmed to satisfy one or more goals, even if the object moves and loses contact with its creator.

Some definitions state that an agent has mobility as well as autonomy. Mobility is the ability to move independently from one device to another on a network. Voyager agents are both autonomous and mobile. They have all the same features as simple objects: they can be assigned aliases, have virtual references, communicate with remote objects, and so on.

To create an agent, extend the base class COM.objectspace.voyager.Agent and then use Voyager's vcc utility to remote-enable the agent's class. Use the resulting virtual class to instantiate an agent object and use virtual references to communicate with this object even if it moves.

Like all objects, an agent can be moved from one program to another. However, unlike simple objects, an agent can move itself autonomously. An agent can move to other programs, allowing the execution of distributed itineraries, or an agent can move to other objects, allowing communication using high-speed, local messaging.

An agent can move to another program and continue to execute when it arrives by sending itself moveTo() with the address of the destination program and the name of the member function that should be executed on arrival.

For example, an agent in dallas:8000 is told to travel. The agent sends itself a moveTo() message with two parameters: dallas:9000, the destination address, and atTokyo, the name of the callback function.

```
public void travel() // defined in Shopper
    {
    moveTo( "tokyo:9000", "atTokyo" );
    }
```

The agent then moves to tokyo:9000, leaving behind a forwarder to forward messages. After arriving at its new location, the agent automatically receives the atTokyo() message. The following code in the agent is then executed.

```
public void atTokyo() // defined in Shopper
    {
    // this code is executed when I move successfully to tokyo:9000.
    }
```

If an agent wants to have a high-speed conversation with a remote object, the agent can move to the object and then send it local Java messages. The easiest way for an agent to move to an object is by sending itself a variation of moveTo() that specifies both a virtual reference to the destination object and a callback parameter.

For example, an agent in dallas:8000 is told to buy from a store object. The agent sends itself a moveTo() message with two parameters: vstore, a virtual reference to the remote store object, and shop, the name of a callback function.

```
public void buyFrom( VStore vstore ) // defined in Shopper
    {
    moveTo( vstore, "shop" );
    }
```

After leaving behind a forwarder and moving to tokyo:9000, the agent receives the callback message shop() with a local native Java reference to the object store. The following code in the agent is then executed.

```
public void shop( Store store ) // defined in Shopper
    {
    // this code is executed when I successfully move to the store
    // note that store is a regular Java reference to the store
    int price = store.buy( "widget" );
    }
```

3 Advanced Concepts

3.1 JavaBeans Integration

Voyager is designed to integrate with the JavaBeans component model. Existing JavaBeans can be used in a Voyager system. Voyager extends the beans delegation event model by allowing all events to be transmitted across the network. This is possible without modifying the bean or event classes in any way.

Voyager also uses the beans event model for object- and system-level monitoring. Every remote Voyager object is automatically a source of events. Objects can listen to remote objects and monitor every aspect of the remote object's behavior. In particular, listeners are notified when the remote object receives messages, when it moves, when it is saved to or loaded from a database, and when the remote object dies.

Voyager allows system-level monitoring with the beans event model as well. Listeners can monitor when the system garbage-collects remote objects, when classes are loaded into the system, when messages are sent and received, and when agents and mobile objects arrive and depart.

Voyager extends the beans event model further by introducing persistent listeners. Typically, developers use standard beans listeners for transient listening. However, more complex systems often require listeners that can move with objects, or listeners that can automatically be stored to and retrieved from databases with the source objects. Voyager adds this critical piece of functionality to all listeners of Voyager events.

Voyager's integration with the JavaBeans event model allows developers to apply their bean knowledge and experience directly to their Voyager systems. The event system provides a wealth of information useful for monitoring, auditing, logging, and other higher-level, application-specific actions.

3.2 Dynamic Properties

Voyager allows developers to attach key value properties to remote objects. These properties are dynamically attached to any object without requiring modification to the object's source. This property mechanism is used by the publish/subscribe system to allow objects to specify what subjects they are interested in and can also be used to attach application-specific information to an object at run time.

```
myObject.addProperty( Subscription.SUBSCRIBE, "sports.basketball.*" );
```

3.3 Database-Independent Persistence

A persistent object has a backup copy in a database. A persistent object is automatically recovered if its program is unexpectedly terminated or if it is flushed from memory to the database to make room for other objects. Voyager includes seamless support for object persistence. In many cases, you can make an object persistent without modifying its source.

Each Voyager program can be associated with a database. The type of database can vary from program to program and is transparent to a Voyager programmer. Voyager includes a high-performance object storage system called VoyagerDb, but provides an interface layer to allow developers to drop in their own custom bindings to other popular relational and object databases.

To save an object to the program's database, send saveNow() to the object. This method writes a copy of the object to the database, overwriting any previous copy. If the program is shut down and then restarted, the persistent objects are left in the database. Any attempt to communicate with a persistent object causes the object to be reloaded from the database.

See Chapter 14 of the ObjectSpace Voyager Core Technology User Guide, Version 1.0, for more details about Voyager persistence.

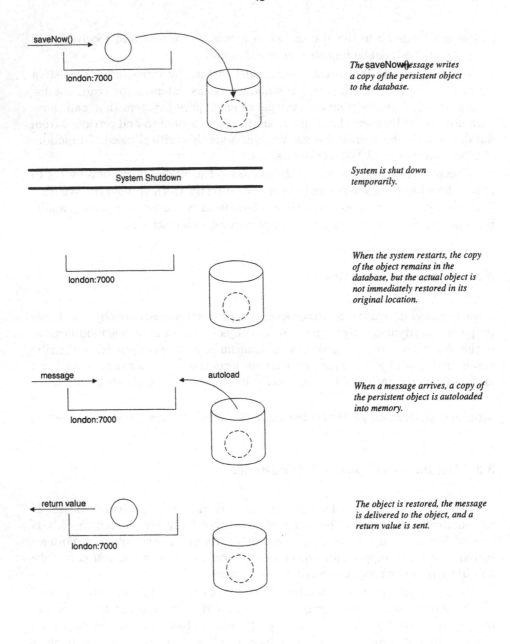

saveNow()

london:7000

The saveNow() *message writes a copy of the persistent object to the database.*

System Shutdown

System is shut down temporarily.

london:7000

When the system restarts, the copy of the object remains in the database, but the actual object is not immediately restored in its original location.

message → autoload

london:7000

When a message arrives, a copy of the persistent object is autoloaded into memory.

← return value

london:7000

The object is restored, the message is delivered to the object, and a return value is sent.

If a persistent object is moved from one program to another, the copy of the object is automatically removed from the source program's database and added to the destination program's database.

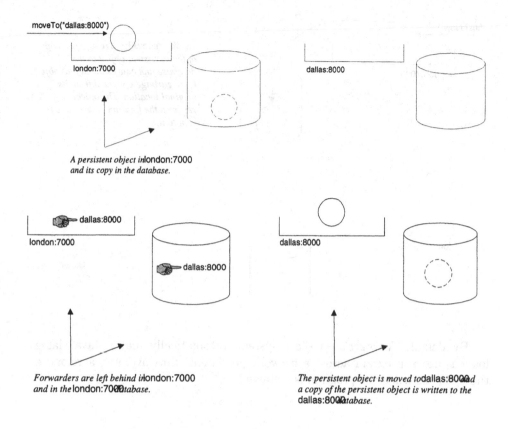

A persistent object in london:7000
and its copy in the database.

Forwarders are left behind in london:7000
and in the london:7000 *database.*

The persistent object is moved to dallas:8000 *and
a copy of the persistent object is written to the*
dallas:8000 *database.*

You can conserve memory by using one of the flush() family of methods
to remove a persistent object from memory and store it in a database. Any
subsequent attempt to communicate with a flushed persistent object reloads the
object from the database.

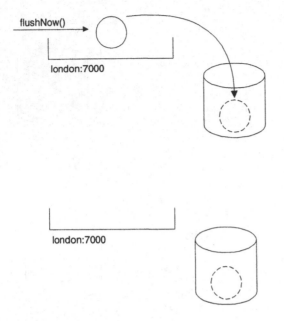

flushNow()

london:7000

The flushNow message *writes a copy of the persistent object to the database and causes the actual object to be garbage-collected from its original location. The object is restored the first time a message is sent to it..*

london:7000

By default, Voyager's database system automatically makes Java classes loaded into a program across a network persistent, thus avoiding a reload of these classes when the program is restarted.

3.4 Space — Scalable Group Communication

Many distributed systems require features for communicating with groups of objects. For example:

- Stock quote systems use a distributed event feature to send stock price events to customers around the world.
- A voting system uses a distributed messaging feature (multicast) to send messages around the world to voters, asking their views on a particular matter.
- News services use a distributed publish/subscribe feature so that broadcasts are received only by readers interested the broadcast topic.

Most traditional systems use a single repeater object to replicate the message or event to each object in the target group.

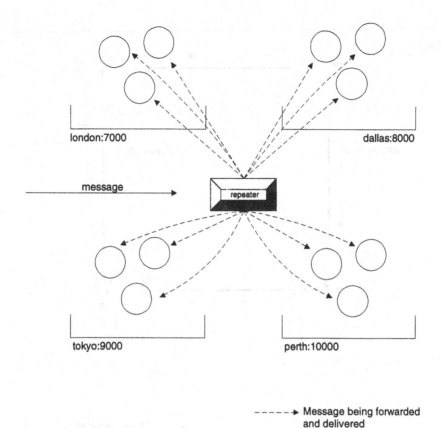

london:7000

dallas:8000

message → repeater

tokyo:9000

perth:10000

- - - - → Message being forwarded
and delivered

This traditional approach works well if the number of objects in the target group is small, but does not scale well when large numbers of objects are involved.

Voyager uses a different and innovative architecture for message/event replication called Space™ that can scale to global proportions. Clusters of objects in the target group are stored in local groups called subspaces. Subspaces are linked to form a larger logical group called a Space. When a message or event is sent into one of the subspaces, the message or event is cloned to each neighboring subspace before being delivered to every object in the local subspace. This process results in a rapid parallel fanout of the message or event to every object in the Space. A special mechanism in each subspace ensures that no message or event is accidentally processed more than once, regardless of how the subspaces are linked.

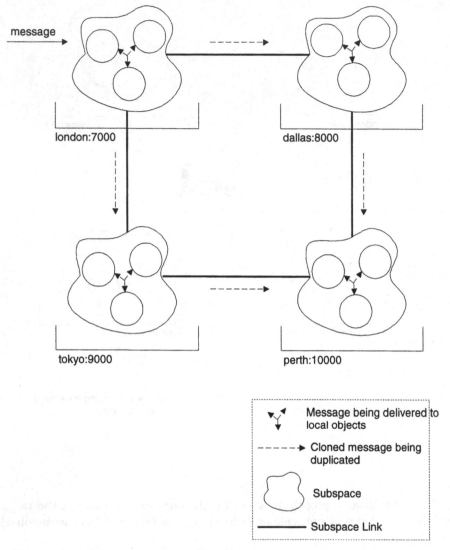

Voyager's multicast messaging, distributed events, and publish/subscribe features all use and benefit from the same underlying Space architecture.

3.5 Message Types

Unlike traditional ORBs, which use a simple, on-the-wire message protocol, Voyager messages are delivered by lightweight agents called messengers. Voyager has four predefined message types.

Synchronous Messages. By default, Voyager messages are synchronous. When a caller sends a synchronous message, the caller blocks until the message completes and the return value is received. You can use regular Java syntax to send a synchronous message to an object. Arguments are automatically encoded on the sender side and decoded on the receiver side.

```
int price = vstore.buy( "Killer Rabbits" );
```

One-Way Messages. Although messages are synchronous by default, Voyager supports one-way messages as well. One-way messages do not return a value. When a caller sends a one-way message, the caller does not block while the message completes.

```
vstore.buy( "Killer Rabbits", new OneWay() ); // no return
    ...
```

Future Messages. Voyager also supports future messages. When a caller sends a future message, the caller does not block while the message completes. The caller receives a placeholder that can be used to retrieve the return value later by polling, blocking, or waiting for a callback.

```
Result result = vstore.buy( "Killer Rabbits", new Future() );
    ...
int price = result.readInt(); // Block for price.
```

One-Way Multicast Messages. One-way multicast messages can be used to send one-way messages to all objects in a Space using a single operation.

```
VStore stores = new VStore( space ); // gateway into space
stores.stock( "video", 25 ); // send stock() to all stores in space
```

To send a one-way message to only certain objects in a Space, use a one-way multicast message with a selector.

Selective Multicast Messages. Multicast messages can be selectively broadcast to a subset of objects in a Space. For instance, Voyager supports traditional publish/subscribe multicasting where objects are selected based on whether or not they are subscribed to given subjects (defined as hierarchical strings). However, Voyager also supports a more general selection mechanism in that messages can be multicast to objects that meet any user-defined criterion.

```
VAccount accounts = new VAccount( space ); // gateway into space
Selector selector = new DelinquentSelector(); // select if delinquent
accounts.close( selector ); // close account if delinquent in payment
```

3.6 Federated Directory Service

Voyager provides a directory service for remote object lookup. Using the directory service, an object can get a reference to a remote or mobile object without advance knowledge of its location. Voyager's directory service avoids the single-server bottleneck/point-of-failure associated with monolithic directory services by allowing distributed directory services to be linked together to form a single, federated directory service.

All directories are completely integrated with Voyager's persistence mechanism, and like any object, can be saved to a database with a single command.

3.7 Dynamic Messaging

Voyager supports dynamic message construction at run time. The following code creates a synchronous message at run time using the Java virtual machine syntax for signature definition.

```
// dynamically create and execute a synchronous message
Sync sync = new Sync();
sync.setSignature( "buy( Ljava.lang.String; )I" );
sync.writeObject( "Killer Rabbits" );
Result result = vstore.send( sync );
int price = result.readInt(); // price
```

3.8 Life Spans and Garbage Collection

Each instance of a remote-enabled class has a life span. When an object reaches the end of its life span, the object dies and is garbage-collected. Garbage collection destroys an object, freeing the object's memory for reclamation by the Java virtual machine.

Voyager includes a distributed garbage collector that supports a variety of life spans.

- An object can live forever.
- An object can live until there are no more local or virtual references to it. By default, an instance of any class that does not extend Agent has this kind of reference-based life span.
- An object can live for a specified length of time. By default, an instance of any class that extends Agent lives for one day.
- An object can live until a particular point in time.

You can change an object's life span at any time.

4 Conclusion

Many people ask us, "If Voyager is free, then how will you make money?" We believe that, years from now, companies will not make much money by selling basic middleware. DCOM will be embedded and distributed everywhere. CORBA price points are already plummeting. In the not-too-distant future, the bulk of the features currently in the Voyager Core Technology will be freely available in several forms and locations. Your cost is in development time, and your revenues are increasingly dependent on time to market. ObjectSpace believes Voyager's

Java-centric binding, advanced mobile object features, and innovative services provide the best basis for rapid development of distributed systems in Java.

As the industry changes, we will continue to develop and sell partnerships, support, and other services, but we will also begin to unveil more and more next-generation, add-on features for the ObjectSpace Voyager platform. These add-ons will progress in areas of security, group communication, and persistence concurrency and will deliver the same time-to-market and rapid development advantages found in the Voyager Core Technology today. Unlike the Voyager Core Technology, these add-ons will not be free.

ObjectSpace is also pursuing several partnerships for the creation of technology integrations and enhanced development tools. Our relationships, based on the deployment of JGL, will enable the rapid distribution, adoption, and integration of the ObjectSpace Voyager platform.

As you look further into the future, you will see ObjectSpace using the Voyager technology base as the platform for its own next-generation product lines. As definite product release dates approach, we will announce these longer-term projects. Be assured that we will leverage Voyager's advantages, such as agent technology, to deliver products that, until now, you have only speculated about.

For additional information on Voyager, visit the ObjectSpace Web site at www.objectspace.com. You will find several additional white papers, customer stories, and of course, the complete Voyager Core Technology download. This download includes a comprehensive user guide that covers additional details on the Voyager 1.0 feature set. The Version 2.0 Beta 1 is also available for download.

References

1. Aglets by IBM. See www.ibm.com.
2. Concordia by Mitsubishi. See www.meitca.com/HSL/Projects/Concordia.
3. CORBA by OMG. See www.omg.org.
4. Odyssey by General Magic. See www.genmagic.com.
5. RMI by JavaSoft. See www.javasoft.com.

Worldwide Component Scripting with the PLANET Mobile Object System

Katsuya Matsubara[1], Takahiro Maekawa[2] and Kazuhiko Kato[3]

[1] Doctoral Program in Engineering, University of Tsukuba
[2] Master's Program in Science and Engineering, University of Tsukuba
[3] Institute of Information Sciences and Electronics, University of Tsukuba,
Japan Science and Technology Corporation,
Tsukuba Ibaraki, Japan

Abstract. Recently, component-based application developments to improve the software productivity and reusability have attracted our attention. The components are parts for building applications and for packaging program modules and they have increased reusability. Component-based software development is also useful for distributed cooperative software development since each component in an application can be developed by different developers independently. The authors are working on designing and implementing a distributed cooperative computing system for both local and worldwide networks. The system is called PLANET. One of the most notable features of PLANET is that it has been designed based on the mobile object concept, by which we mean objects are separable from a virtual address space. This paper describes scheme to implement a worldwide component scripting environment with PLANET . Some experimental results detained from prototype implementation are discussed to validate the design of the scheme.

1   Introduction

The present, computer software requires more functionalities, in proportion, such as GUI, WWW browsing, and DB connectivity as the performance of computers has improved and the number of computer users has increased. As a result, the scale of software is enlarged, and the complexity is increasing. Much academic and industrial research to increase software productivity and reusability has been done. Recently, component-based application building has attracted our attention in particular [6]. The components are parts for building applications and for packaging program modules and they have increased reusability. Component vendors supply reusable components, and application programmers can therefore build applications by assembling the components more efficiently.

Computer networks recently become more popular, so distributed and cooperative software development environments are going to be realized. Component-based software development is suitable for such cooperative software development since each component in an application can independently be developed by different developers. Most component-based software development systems support component developments, but distribution and sharing of the components rely on sophisticated human operations. In distributed and cooperative software development, it is important to integrate a mechanism for the distribution and sharing of components into the component-based system without imposing a burden on users.

1.1 PLANET Approaches

The authors are working on designing and implementing a distributed and cooperative computing system for both local and worldwide networks. The system is called PLANET [8, 9, 10]. One of the most notable features of PLANET is that it has been designed based on the *mobile object* concept. Most of the previously developed practical distributed computing systems were based on a message passing paradigm (including RPC) or they used the message passing mechanism as the key mechanism for implementation (see Reference [1] for a survey). To remove the limitations imposed by communication latency and to use restricted communication bandwidths more efficiently in worldwide networks, PLANET has adopted a paradigm of *object passing*, namely *mobile objects*, in its basic system design. The basic approaches of PLANET can be summarized follows.

- *Unified treatment of distribution and persistency.*
  In worldwide networks, it is unreasonable to assume that the receiver process for the mobile object is awakened whenever a sender tries to send an object and that the sender has to wait until the receiver becomes available. Worldwide distributed computing environments should give *persistency* as well as mobility to objects. In the PLANET system model, the objects are separated from a virtual address space and stored in a persistent space called a distributed shared repository (DSR for short), then they are put into a different virtual address space again.
- *Orthogonal protection domains.*
  We propose that the protection domain concept for mobile object systems should be *orthogonal* to the object encapsulation concept. That is, programmers only need to observe object encapsulation barriers during programming and they do not need to observe protection domain barriers. In PLANET, object interactions are specified in the same way whether the interacting objects are in the same protection domain at runtime or not.
- *Neutrality with respect to programming languages.*
  Most currently proposed mobile object systems have their own unique languages, and users cannot take advantage of mobile-object computing without using these new languages. In PLANET, mobile objects can be programmed in almost all programming languages since the protocols between language processors and the runtime system for object mobility are clearly defined.
- *Native mobile objects.*
  With respect to the program execution scheme, many currently proposed mobile object systems adopt a byte-code interpreter approach. There are several compelling reasons for adopting this approach. First, it is the most

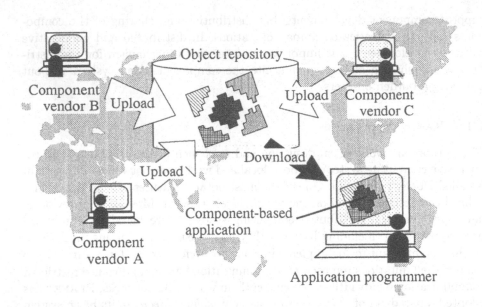

Fig. 1. Worldwide component scripting.

straightforward way to implement mobile objects. Second, the approach is undoubtedly suited to dealing with hardware (and even operating system) heterogeneity. Finally, the approach is suited to dealing with security issues. We pay in particular attention to the execution speed and aimed to make the execution speed of an object at distributed computer sites as fast as the speed in a single computer site. PLANET uses the approach of creating a novel execution mechanism, in which mobile objects are executed with native machine code, without sacrificing security issues.

1.2 Worldwide Component Scripting

This paper describes Worldwide component scripting (WWCS for short) with PLANET for distributed and cooperative software development. WWCS is a scripting environment that enables higher level programming in distributed and cooperative software development. A scripting environment has appeal for PLANET since scripting which has a higher descriptive power is suitable for rapid prototyping and iterative and incremental testing and debugging. Also, scripting makes it possible to use components developed in various programming languages in an application since each component is developed according to higher and restricted interfaces defined by the scripting system. PLANET is also a attractive platform for the scripting environment since it has many functionalities to support distributed and cooperative work in worldwide networks.

In WWCS, useful components developed by any software vendor in the world are stored in the object repository (see Fig. 1). Then, the stored components can be used from all over the world. An application programmer describes the combination of components by scripting. An application does computation by downloading the required components dynamically. Any component in an application can be downloaded and uploaded dynamically with its computational states during execution at all times. With this functionality, an application can be specialized in order to adapt it to the environment during execution. Downloading with component's computational states is able to implement functionality like a *mobile agent*.

WWCS makes it possible for each component to set the protection level flexibly at runtime. If a component object requires strict protection, such as when it is untrustworthy or unstable, all interactions from the component are indirect with strict access checking. If a component object requires no protection, the component can interact with other components directly and efficiently. Nevertheless, in both cases, component vendors do net need to be aware of the configurations for protection during programming.

1.3   Organization of the Paper

The rest of the paper is organized as follows. Section 2 briefly explains the system model for PLANET. Section 3 describes the worldwide component scripting with PLANET. Section 4 presents implementation strategies and prototype implementation of WWCS. Section 5 presents some experimental results of prototype. Section 6 discusses related work. Section 7 summarizes the paper and describes future work.

2   PLANET System Model

The system model for PLANET is described using four basic abstractions: *mobile object*, *place*, *protection domain*, and *distributed shared repository* (see Fig. 2).

- *Mobile object*
  A *mobile object* is an entity that may be encapsulated data, the program, and the computational state (so-called thread). As shown in Fig. 3, objects are classified into four types according to the data segments included in the objects. A basic-type segment includes data for basic data types such as integers, floating point numbers, strings, and bitmap image data. A structured data segment includes references (pointers) to data within the same segment. A program code segment includes codes that manipulate data in the objects. A computational state segment includes all the information required to maintain the state of computation, i.e., a program counter, CPU registers and other CPU-state materials, and a stack.
- *Place.*
  Place is an abstraction for computational resources, through which objects do their computation. A greatly simplified example of a place would be a

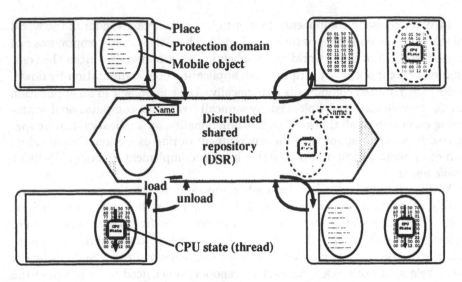

Fig. 2. PLANET system model.

computer host with one or more CPUs and memories. Another simplified example of a place is a LAN that has several computer hosts. A place, however, does not necessarily have persistent storage, such as that available through magnetic-disk devices, for storing objects since persistency is provided by the distributed shared repository (as described in the following).

– *Protection Domain.*
Since a place might be visited by a number of inherently enigmatic objects, it must have a protection mechanism. The protection mechanism should have at least two functionalities: the computational resources of a place must not be affected by accidental or intentional violations of access rights; and the objects and activities in a place must be protected against illegal access from one another. A *protection domain* is an abstraction for controlled object accesses. When an object is loaded into a place, at least one protection domain has to be specified; then if no access right violations are determined by the system, the object is *attached* to the protection domain. Any number of objects can be attached to a protection domain provided enough computational resources are available for that protection domain. The system grants access rights on a protection-domain basis, and the access rights granted to a protection domain are shared by all the objects within it. The level of protection is uniform within a protection domain, so object interaction within a single protection domain does not require domain-switching, thus permitting efficient execution. Sometimes we are required to give different access rights to certain objects in a protection domain. For this purpose, PLANET has a functionality that allows an object to be attached to several protection domains simultaneously, maintaining the coherency of the attached object with simple one-copy semantics.

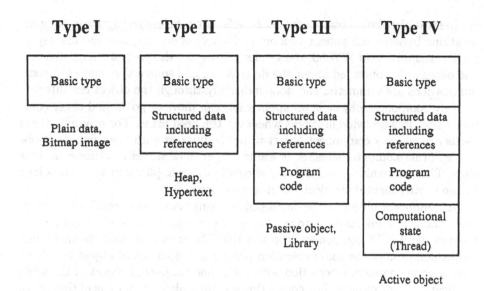

Fig. 3. Types of mobile object.

— *Distributed Shared Repository.*

The *distributed shared repository* (DSR for short) is an abstraction for the worldwide persistent object store, and it plays the central role in our object-passing mechanism. The DSR can be considered as a virtual medium spread throughout the world. Objects put on the DSR become accessible from places all over the world and they are guaranteed to persist until they are explicitly removed.

Object passing via DSR differs greatly from the object passing of other mobile-object systems such as Emerald [7], Telescript [14], and Obliq [3]. In these systems, object-passing is synchronous in the sense that both sender and receivers have to be aware that object passing is taking place; thus, the success of object sending depends on the state of the receiver. In PLANET, on the other hand, object-passing is asynchronous; that is, the sender and the receiver can communicate with objects independently of the other's state or lifetime.

3 Worldwide Component Scripting with PLANET

WWCS is a scripting system with PLANET for distributed and cooperative software development. In WWCS, a component is implemented by a mobile object of PLANET, and it is called a *component object*. A component object has four notable functionalities: symmetric communication, mobility, programming language neutrality, and execution with native machine code.

In most distributed component-based software development systems, communications between component vendors and application programmers are asymmetric and direct. In WWCS, the vendor's sites and the programmer's sites are not necessarily concerned about the destination and source sites since the communications are symmetric and done indirectly through the object repository.

Any component object in an application can move or go around other computer sites in worldwide networks whenever the need arises. For example, these needs are where a component object wants to interact with the component object at other computer sites, or it wants to get data stored at other computer sites. This mechanism is suitable for specializing an application so it can adapt to the environment dynamically during execution.

A component object can be developed by using many programming languages since the communication protocols between component objects are clearly defined in the WWCS component object model. The communication channel is one implementation of the communication protocol. A component object is able to have several channels. Interaction with the other component object in the same application is implemented by connecting a communication channel of the source component object with a communication channel of the destination component object. If a component object is going to interact with component objects at another computer site, the interaction is more efficient if the object is moved to the destination site through the object repository.

Each component object has a signature, which contains the vendor's information and method information such as method names, functionalities, and ways to invoke the method. The signature is encrypted because generally it has to be protected against modification and leaks.

For efficient execution, all component objects are executed with native machine code in WWCS. In most worldwide software development systems, applications are executed with a byte-code interpreter mainly because of heterogeneous computer environments and security issues. However, the almost all applications on a local computer and in local area networks are currently use native machine code. We believe that an application should be able to be executed with native machine code in both local area networks and worldwide networks if the heterogeneous and security issues could be solved. Currently, WWCS permits the native-code execution of component objects without sacrificing security, and in the near future it could be extended to deal with hardware heterogeneity.

The script language in WWCS is able to describe the downloading and uploading of component objects, the connection and disconnection between communication channels, thread management, and protection policies. In particular, the description of protection policies is a notable feature. There are four kinds of protection level in WWCS. There are:

NoTrust: All downloaded component objects are untrustworthy. All interactions between component objects and all access to the system are rigorously checked. If illegal access is discovered, it is annulled or the component object which is going to do the access is terminated by force. Although this protection level has heavier overheads for interaction and access it can be done safely.

AllTrust: All downloaded component objects are trusted. All interactions between component objects can be done without checking. However, all access to the system is checked since any action to the system may affect not only application but also other applications at the same computer sites. All interactions can be done even if they contain illegal interactions such as references to component object values without using communication channels. In the case of this protection level, interactions between component objects can be done efficiently and speedily but they are unsafe.

SomeTrust: Only component objects, which are able to satisfy the conditions specified in the script, are trusted. A component object is treated in the same way as *AllTrust* if it can be trusted, otherwise it is treated in the same way as *NoTrust*. This protection level is suitable for cases where untrustworthy component objects must form part of the application.

Inquiry: At this protection level, the application user is asked whether the component object can be trusted or not whenever a component object is downloaded into the application. This protection level is used if the application programmer is not able to judge whether downloaded component objects are trusted or not.

Additionally the scripting in WWCS can specify what kind of interaction, such as method invocation and variable reference into the component object, is permitted. Also, the arguments for each method invocation can be checked as to whether they are correct or not. The system can be guarded against illegal access since the kinds of permitted access to the system are specified in detail, such as each system call. Nevertheless, all descriptions of protection are only in the script but not in component objects. Component vendors may not be aware of the protection level on which the developed component object will be executed.

Figure 4 is a sample script in WWCS. The protection command sets up the protection policy for the script. In the sample script, the protection policy is SomeTrust, and the trusted component objects satisfy the condition specified. The Condition method in the next line defines the conditions required to decide whether a component object is trusted or not. The condition in the sample is that any trusted component object has the vendor's name in the Info table. The ActionOnException method in the third line decides the course of action when the system or component object is going to be accessed illegally. The DestroyComponent action indicates that the component object is to be destroyed whenever it is going to access the system or other component objects illegally. The download command instructs the system that the component object, which has a specified name, has been downloaded from the object repository.

4 Implementation

4.1 Implementation Strategies

The PLANET mobile object system is suitable as a platform for WWCS since it has helpful functionalities, such as the downloading and uploading of mobile

```
1   set prot = 'protection SomeTrust'
2   $prot.Condition("VendorName != NULL")
3   $prot.ActionOnException(DestroyComponent)
4
3   set disp = 'download "/graphical/gui/print_string"'
4   $disp.CreateWindow(200, 100, white)
5   $disp.SetFont(Times)
6   $disp.PrintString(20, 20, "Hello world!")
```

Fig. 4. Sample script.

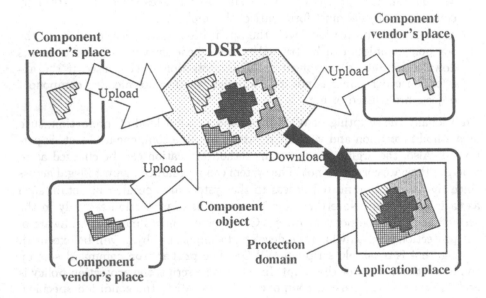

Fig. 5. Worldwide component scripting with PLANET.

objects dynamically, a physical location independent name space in the object repository, object execution with native machine code, and an orthogonal protection domain. Figure 5 shows the WWCS system model with PLANET. We will describe the our strategies when we are going to implement WWCS with PLANET.

Downloading a component object from DSR involves two strategies. The first strategy is to download all component objects in a single protection domain (see Fig. 6(a)). The interaction between component objects in the same protection domain does not require domain-switching and thus it can be efficiently executed. The other strategy is to create a new protection domain when a component object is downloaded (see Fig. 6(b)). The latter strategy is suitable when untrusted

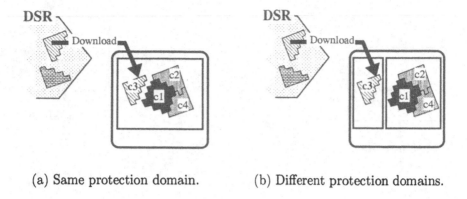

(a) Same protection domain.   (b) Different protection domains.

Fig. 6. Download a new component object from DSR into the application's place.

component objects must be downloaded into an application since all access to the outside of the protection domain is stringently checked. With the former strategy, the component objects are also prohibited from illegally accessing the system resources and other component objects in different protection domains. In both strategies, the component vendors do not need to be aware of the protection domains in the programming. All component objects can be assigned to any protection domain in response to the protection policy specified in the script.

Each component object in the script is executed with native machine code in WWCS. There are two solutions to script execution: interpreter-based and compiler-based. Interpreter-based execution makes it easy to test and debug programs since compilation is not required. However, the execution speed is restricted since the script is interpreted step by step during execution. In compiler-based execution, execution can be done at optimal speed since the script is translated into native machine code before execution. Also, interactions between component objects may be able to be optimized in compilation if the component objects are downloaded into the same application. We consider that WWCS has to provide both interpreter-based execution and compiler-based execution for the script.

4.2 Prototype Implementation

We are presently implementing a prototype system in order to verify the validity of WWCS.

The current prototype has several restrictions. In the WWCS component object model, the communication channels are divided into the input stream and the output stream like a UNIX pipe in the first prototype. The signature for the component object contains the vendor's name, his computer site name, the author's name, and the generated date, but not method information such

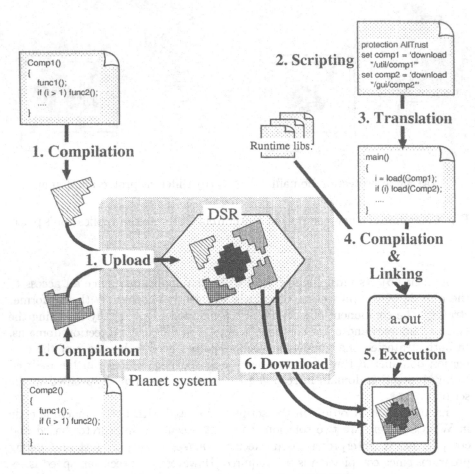

Fig. 7. Prototype system for WWCS.

as names, functionalities, and ways to invoke. The method information is useful in that an application searches component objects by using their functionalities, and that it wants to invoke the method of the unknown component object. The elimination of this restriction will be discussed in Sect. 7.

Figure 7 shows the flow for the distributed cooperative software development process in the prototype system. The following step numbers correspond to those in Fig. 7.

1. Each component developer describes the programs for component objects, compiles them, and then uploads them into DSR.
2. An application developer describes a combination of the component objects by scripting.
3. The translator translates the script into programs in a programming language, which is able to invoke PLANET primitives.

4. The resulting programs are compiled into an executable native code.

5. An application user executes the executable native code.

6. Then, the application computes by downloading the component objects specified in the script from DSR.

5 Performance of the Prototype

To examine the effect of the continuing implementation schemes with PLANET, we measured the performance of the prototype system using simple applications. The experimental environment had two Sun SPARC Station 20s with 64 MB of memory connected through a 10-Mbps Ethernet LAN and one Sun SPARC Station 20 with 128 MB of memory connected through the Internet. All component objects were about 113 KB, and each component object was transferred by the virtual memory page, whose size was is 4 KB which is similar to the virtual memory size in the SunOS, with using Remote memory-mapping mechanism [9, 11, 12]. The input/output stream between component objects had a memory buffer of 8 KB. The disk caches in PLANET and the memory caches in the operating system were flushed before each measurement. In the prototype implementation system, all component objects for an application were downloaded into the same protection domain. Measurement was done ten times under the same conditions, and the results were averaged.

We measured the overheads for downloading and executing the component objects in the prototype system. All component objects in the experiment did the same computation that is receiving text data from an input stream and then putting the received data into an output stream like a UNIX "cat" command. The object repository (DSR) was distributed to three computer sites, one of which was local, one was connected through the LAN, and one was connected through the Internet (see Fig. 8). The component objects stored at each computer site were called C_1, C_2, and C_3. The measurements were done using seven kinds of application (see Fig. 9). The first three applications were only constructed with C_1, C_2, and C_3, respectively (cases (a), (b), and (c)). Cases (d), (e), and (f) were only constructed with C_1 and C_2, C_1 and C_3, and C_2 and C_3, respectively. One of the component object's hands processes results to another component object's standard input stream in place of the standard output stream. The final application was constructed with C_1 and C_2 and C_3 (case (g)). Each application reads the text data file, which is 10 MB in size.

Figure 9 shows the response times for the applications. The horizontal axis indicates the application types and the vertical axis shows the response times. For cases (a), (b), and (c), the overheads for C_1 are larger than those for C_2 and C_3. In PLANET, a shadow file is created on the disk for caching. Compared with case C_1, writing to a shadow file in cases (b) and (c) parallels reading from an original file. Therefore, the difference in overhead between case (a) and cases (b) or (c) is the file copy overhead.

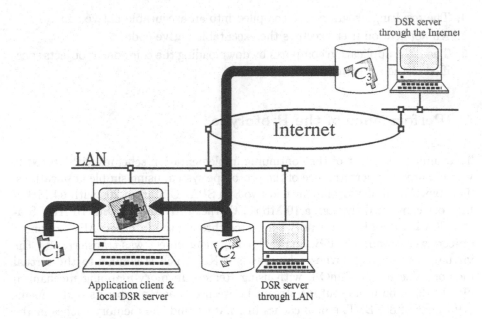

DSR server
through the Internet

Internet

LAN

Application client &
local DSR server

DSR server
through LAN

Fig. 8. Experimental Environment.

The interaction overheads between component objects in cases (d), (e), and (f) or case (g) are not the best since interaction in the prototype is simple and based on naive implementation. The overheads could be improved by implementing a more sophisticated interaction mechanism for WWCS. For example, double buffering may improve paralleliesm between component objects. If a few component objects are going to get the same data, it would be more efficient to sharing the buffer with their communication channels. The ad hoc retrying to obtain data from the communication channel would be unnecessary if each component object could notify when data was complete.

6 Related Work

Recently, several approaches have been proposed for building applications with components.

JavaBeans [2, 5] is a component-based software development system based on the Java object-oriented programming system. The component, called Bean, is made up of reusable software parts and it is able to be manipulated by the application builder visually. An application can be constructed with the components, which are under execution, since the components can be stored along with its computational states. Design signature and introspection provide a way of obtaining knowledge of a component's functionality and methods in the program. The sandbox, which contains the Java virtual machine (byte-code verifier,

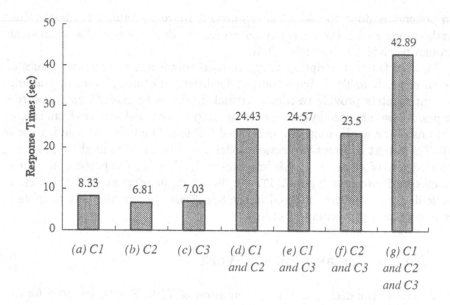

Fig. 9. Basic performance of the prototype system on simple applications.

class loader, and security manager) protects components safely. There are some similarities regarding the supply of persistency and protection for components between JavaBeans and WWCS. In WWCS, the components can be implemented in any programming language. All components in WWCS can be stored not only during building applications but also during execution. The protection mechanism is implemented by the memory management hardware (MMU), and it is able to check access outside the protection domain frequently. Furthermore, the application user can set up protection levels flexibly since the protection domain assignment can be decided dynamically during execution.

Active X [4] is a technology in which any application can download components, which are based on the component object model (COM for short) or the distributed component object model (DCOM for short). An application can invoke the methods in the components with "plugged-in" to Active X control. The Active X scripting interface implements the application builder by scripting in VBscript or JavaScript. The interaction between components in distributed environments is implemented by a mechanism based on remote procedure call (RPC). The components based on DCOM can use different functionalities for creating remote objects, for access to the remote objects, for authentication to guarantee safe access, and for access control. There are some similarities regarding implementation of the components in any programming language and interactions with remote components. In WWCS, interaction between distributed components is done to make the component move to remote computer sites. Furthermore, asynchronous communications are done to pass the components through persistent space called DSR.

Safe-Tcl [13] is a scripting language used to address the security issues on the Internet. Safe-Tcl is based on two facilities: *safe interpreters* and *aliases*. Safe interpreters provide restricted virtual machines to execute untrustworthy scripts. Aliases are used by untrustworthy scripts to request services from trusted portions of the application in a controlled fashion. The most notable feature of Safe-Tcl is that different protection policies can be implemented by providing different sets of aliases in a safe interpreter. In WWCS, the protection policies are classified into four types: AllTrust, NoTrust, SomeTrust, and Inquiry. In particular, the condition method in the SomeTrust policy makes it possible to set fine-grained protection policies.

7 Conclusions and Future Work

We described the design and implementation of WWCS with PLANET for distributed and cooperative software development. WWCS with PLANET provides component object mobility in worldwide networks, and it gives persistency to component objects with computational states. It also performs execution of the component object with a native machine code, and implements the protection mechanism separated from object encapsulation. Further, it permits the component object to be developed in any programming language. A distinguishing characteristic of WWCS is that it makes it possible to describe the protection policy easily in scripting.

The issues we will tackle in the future are as follows.

- *Designing a sophisticated component object model*
  The component object model in the prototype only defined the interface with the input/output streams. A sophisticated model must be designed enhance component reusability and connectivity.
- *Obtaining the functionality and way to invoke methods of downloaded components dynamically in the program*
  It is important for the application to obtain the functionalities and way to invoke methods of a downloaded component dynamically to the program even if it has no knowledge of the component's functionalities.
- *Searching component objects by using their functionalities*
  In worldwide networks, many component objects will be supplied from all over the world. Thus it is difficult for application developers to find the needed components by using the component name only. Searching components by using their functionalities is necessary when an application browser only has knowledge on the required functionalities.
- *Version management for component objects*
  In WWCS, the components have a long life since the component objects are stored and re-used repeatedly. Therefore, version management of long life

component objects is important. It is necessary for applications built into the previous version to be executed correctly even if a component vendor updates the components.

Acknowledgements

The authors wish to thank Professor Akinori Yonezawa and Dr. Kenjiro Taura at the University of Tokyo for kindly cooperating with us in performing the experiments described in Sect. 5.

References

1. Bal, H. E., Steiner, J. G., and Tanenbaum, A. S.: Programming languages for distributed computing systems. *Computing Surveys* **21**(3) (1989) 261–322
2. Brookshier, D.: *JavaBeans Developer's Reference*. New Riders Publishing (1997)
3. Cardelli, L.: A language with distributed scope. *Computing Systems* **8**(1) (1995) 27–59
4. Chappell, D.: *Understanding ActiveX and OLE*. Microsoft Press (1996)
5. Hamilton, G.: JavaBeans API specification. Sun Microsystems Tech. rep. (1997)
6. Jacobson, I., Griss, M., and Jonsson, P.: *Software Reuse*. ACM Press (1997)
7. Jul, E., Levy, H., Hutchinson, N., and Black, A.: Fine-grained mobility in the Emerald system. *ACM Trans. Computer Systems* **6**(1) (1988) 109–133
8. Kato, K.: Safe and secure execution mechanisms for mobile objects. J. Vitek and C. Tschudin, Eds., *Mobile Object Systems*, Springer-Verlag LNCS **1222** (1997) 201–211
9. Kato, K., Matsubara, K., Toumura, K., Aikawa, S., and Someya, Y.: Object passing and interaction mechanism of the PLANET mobile object system. In *2nd France-Japan Workshop Object Based Parallel and Distributed Computing* (1997) 147–161
10. Kato, K., Toumura, K., Matsubara, K., Aikawa, S., Yoshida, J., Kono, K., Taura, K., and Sekiguchi, T.: Protected and secure mobile object computing in PLANET. In *Special Issues in Object-Oriented Programming*, Dpunkt-Verlag (1997) 319–326
11. Matsubara, K., and Kato, K.: Implementation of distributed shared repository with distributed virtual memory technique. In *IPSJ Research Reports of System Software and Operating Systems*, **94**(64) (1994) 153–160 in Japanese
12. Matsubara, K., and Kato, K.: Implementation of the distributed persistent objects in PLANET system. In *IPSJ Research Reports of Database Systems*, **97**(113) (1997) 101–106 in Japanese
13. Ousterhout, J. K., Levy, J. Y., and Welch, B. B.: The Safe-Tcl Security Model. Sun Microsystems Laboratories Tech. rep. (1997)
14. White, J. E.: Mobile agents. In J. Bradshaw, Ed., *Software Agents*, MIT Press (1996)

Scalability in Object-Oriented Distributed Systems Environment OZ

Akihito Nakamura[1], Toshihiro Nishioka[2], Yoichi Hamazaki[1],
and Michiharu Tsukamoto[1]

[1] Electrotechnical Laboratory
1-1-4 Umezono, Tsukuba, Ibaraki 305, Japan
[2] Mitsubishi Research Institute, Inc.
2-3-6 Otemachi, Chiyoda-ku, Tokyo 100, Japan

Abstract. This paper presents the scalable architecture and implementation of object-oriented distributed systems environment OZ. OZ has the ability to transfer objects over networks and deliver the required classes automatically. To increase the scalability, OZ is designed totally from the language to application level services. Based on the object-oriented concept, programmers are free to share and reuse the programs independent of their locations since the system provides network-wide scope of class sharing. For efficient development of flexible and scalable distributed applications, various facilities including naming and trading services are provided. By using the object transfer function, the OZ trader provides flexible ways to access servers. Furthermore, to cope with interaction among objects across management domains, a basic mechanism for federal model using trader is provided.

1 Introduction

By significant advances of network and platform technologies, current information systems are based on distributed platforms and applications. Interconnection of local networks to the Internet forms worldwide computing environment. Transferring of Internet technologies to local computing environments, TCP/IP protocols and WWW-based applications are typical. As such, local and worldwide computing environments are seamlessly interconnected.

To effectively develop distributed applications that run on various environments, *scalability* of the distributed systems platform is considered important. Scalability is the capability of a system to scale up or down without changing structure of the system or algorithm of the application. The merits of scalable platforms are:

- possible to apply the system to various size of applications
- allows introduction of an application that will grow to unexpected size
- possible to use the same framework independent of the size of applications

Upward scalability is important in distributed systems, since extending a network by adding new computers or interconnecting networks is common. However, it is a problem if changing the size of the system brings about alteration of algorithms, application programs, or systems. The following features are the bases of scalable systems.

- *Flexibility* : The number of hardware and software components can be changed without affecting applications, while keeping the functionality and relative efficiency.
- *Interoperability* : To build large-scale systems, integration of legacy applications is necessary. Also, applications and systems that run on different platforms and are implemented using different programming languages should be interconnected and integrated.
- *Productivity and Extensibility* : Scaling up the stand-alone development process to the network environment one should be seamless. And result applications are independent of the size of the run-time environment. To encourage iterative and incremental growth of programs, extensibility ensures timely modification and enhancement of programs. Here, it is important to keep the consistency of old data and programs.

In this paper, we show the scalable architecture and implementation of *object-oriented distributed systems environment OZ* [13]. CORBA [11] introduces various kinds of facilities to build large-scale systems [12]. However, it is not applicable to small-size applications because of excessive overhead. On the other hand, Java [7] is started from programming language and now it has functions for remote object access. However, technical load map toward large-scale systems is not shown along with this approach. Several APIs are aimed to build larger systems, but it still lacks of objects and class management facilities.

As compared with other systems, the main advantage of OZ is its ability to share, transfer, and reuse objects and classes over networks. This feature is utilized to increase the scalability with respect to three aspects of the system: execution, management, and development. From the scalability point of view, the goal is that the OZ system scales from stand-alone computer to large-scale, wide area network environment. Here, "large-scale" means not only including large number of elements but also consisting of multiple authority domains in which local resources are managed by different policies. Before the OZ system, we developed the OZ++ system [14]. The basic concept of OZ was established in this system. OZ++ is enriched with management functions to cope with large-scale distributed environments like CORBA. However, OZ++ has less scalability due to its excessive management functions and implementation method. To solve these problems in OZ, we emphasized the following points:

- simple and portable run-time system
- flexibly configurable lightweight management systems
- seamless development and run-time environments to support network-wide scope of program sharing and reuse
- application level facilities for distributed service
- federation-based interaction and integration of management domains

The OZ run-time system has a minimum set of functions for object execution to work effectively in the small environment. The management subsystem to make a method invocation to remote objects, i.e. address resolution and class delivery, are implemented as supplementary modules to executor. This architecture increases downward scalability.

To share and reuse data and programs on a network environment, OZ development environment provides network-wide scope of class sharing and reuse. Also, by supporting multi-version classes, it helps incremental change of programs while keeping the interoperability of old data produced by outdated programs.

At the application level, we laid emphasis on *trader* and *federation* as essence of distributed services since they greatly contribute toward increasing flexibility and scalability of the system. Federation service helps interaction between management domains in large-scale systems. A few conceptual studies [2] have been done on this problem, but yet on mechanism and implementation. We provide simple federation mechanisms using traders.

The remainder of this paper is organized as follows. In Sect. 2, 3, 4, and 5, we discuss the scalability of OZ in terms of three system aspects: execution, development and management. In Sect. 2, scalability of the execution system and several management systems are described. In Sect. 3, we discuss the development environment which has network-wide scope of program sharing and reuse. Sect. 4 and 5 describe our trader and federation approach to build flexible distributed services and to integrate services in different management domains. Lastly, in Sect. 6, we make a comparative study of several systems.

2 Scalable Design and Implementation of OZ

OZ [13] is a distributed systems platform that is based on the object-oriented concept. To increase the scalability, we set the goal of design and implementation not only upward but also downward of OZ as to be efficient in a small-scale environment while flexible and sufficiently functional in a large-scale one. To achieve this goal, we set the subgoals as follows.

- simple and portable object execution system
- flexibly configurable lightweight management systems
- seamless development and run-time environments to support network-wide scope of program sharing and reuse
- application level facilities for distributed services
- federation-based interaction and integration of management domains

In this section, the points related to the first two are discussed. Others are discussed in the following sections.

2.1 Simple and Portable Object Execution System

We adopted a byte-code execution system in OZ for simplicity and portability. There are two types of execution systems with respect to codes.

- **Native-codes.** The compiler generates machine codes and is directly executed. Better performance is expected but there are many drawbacks: larger size, less portability, and difficulty in verification.
- **Byte-codes.** Architecture independent codes are generated and interpreted by the run-time system. Strong portability is provided but the performance may not be good.

In a large-scale environment, heterogeneity of computer architectures and operating systems cannot be avoided. Hence, portability of the system becomes important to utilize existing and emerging technologies to build large systems.

The OZ *executor* is an object execution system that runs on a Java VM (Fig.1). The OZ compiler generates Java byte-codes, i.e. Java classes, from OZ source programs. Now, the OZ executor is quite simple because the basic functions for object execution and class handling are already provided by the Java VM. This approach ensures portability of the OZ system and its applications in a heterogeneous environment.

The performance is one of the drawbacks of a byte-code interpreting system. As our policy, we use available Java VMs as they are, but did not attempt to modify or implement for reasons of compatibility and portability. Current challenges to just-in-time compilation technology will be a solution to this problem.

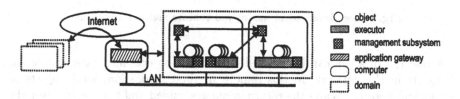

Fig. 1. OZ architecture

2.2 Two-Level Object Model to Increase Access Localization and Reduce Management Overhead

OZ provides two-level object model, global and local, as in Eden [1] and Argus [8], instead of the uniform object model as in Emerald [3]. In the uniform model, all objects have global identity and are accessible from other ones. In the two-level object model, only global objects have global identity and local objects are components of a global object. The object model in OZ is based on the following considerations.

- **Locality of access.** Objects have locality of access and the cost of access to objects on the same computer and objects on a remote computer differ considerably in large-scale distributed systems.
- **Management overhead.** All global objects should be identified and a mechanism to access global objects is required.

Also, there are several method invocation semantics concerned with transferring objects.

- **Call by reference.** Only the reference to the object is transferred and the object is accessed using the reference. The cost of transfer is low but the access cost is high in case of a remote object.
- **Call by value.** The contents of the object is transferred and copy is accessed. The cost of transfer is high but the access cost is low.
- **Call by move.** In Emerald, an object is moved to the computer where that object is accessed. The implementation is complicated and the cost is high.

For efficiency and scalability of an object management subsystem, we have introduced a two-level object model with combined object transfer semantics of call by reference and value (Fig.2). We refer to a global object as *cell*.

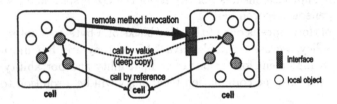

Fig. 2. Two-level object model and remote method invocation

A method of a cell can be invoked from other objects no matter where the cell exists in the network. In this remote method invocation, local objects as the method arguments and the return value are copied and transferred over the network by executors, i.e. call by reference. At this time, all the local objects that are directly or indirectly (recursively) referred from these local objects are also transferred. Programmers are not necessary to differentiate the class to be transferred or not. On the other hand, if an argument or the return value is a cell, only the reference to the cell is transferred, i.e. call by reference.

This object model is suitable for large-scale distributed systems, since only the objects which provide global services have global reference and method invocations to local objects are localized in a cell. Hence, management overhead of global resources is relatively small and the performance requirement is achieved.

In our old systems, we implemented global garbage collection (GC). However, the global GC was not cost-effective and degraded the scalability. In OZ, only the local object is a target of the GC and it is left to the Java VM.

2.3 Resolution of Global and Local Identities (Names)

Object Identity. There are two approaches to the object reference as follows.

- **Fixed length system dependent value.** The system is responsible for generating globally unique identifiers, e.g. OZ++ (64-bit) and Microsoft

COM (128-bit). This scheme introduces some management overhead and causes exhaustion problem in the future if each identifier is not reusable. If the identifier is used for resolution of the communication address, an object cannot be moved to any other computer. It decreases the flexibility and possibility of system reconfiguration.

- **Using existing schemes.** There are several name resolution schemes that are used in general. Domain Name Service (DNS) provides naming service on the large-scale, worldwide Internet at reasonable performance. For local computers, file path names are convenient for uniquely identifying resources.

We adopted the latter approach. To simplify the object referencing scheme and its management overhead in a small environment but to scale up to larger systems, we use the combination of file path name, user account, and DNS domain name for reference to cells dependent on the size of environment. This referencing scheme is simple in a small environment because it uses file path names. In a large-scale environment, references are rather long but sufficiently functional, even in the worldwide size, by using DNS.

OzHome is a directory to store deactivated (persistent) cells and other information owned by a single user (Fig.3). Each cell is serialized into an *object image file*, and is located in the *Global Object Directory* (GOD) — a directory in OzHome. Different cells are stored in different GOD so that a cell is uniquely identified by GOD in OzHome. A GOD is denoted by a dotted notation like **Servers.MyTrader**.

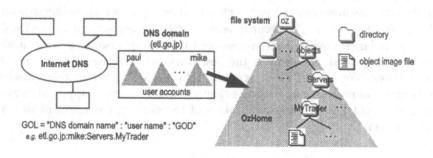

Fig. 3. GOL, OzHome, and GOD

A globally unique reference to a cell is called *Global Object Location* (GOL). It consists of three parts: *DNS domain name, user name,* and GOD. Domain name or both domain name and user name can be omitted based on the size of execution environment. In a single user environment, a GOD is sufficient. A domain name is required in the worldwide environment. This scheme is flexible and scalable because it is applicable to large-scale systems, even to the worldwide computing environment, as DNS demonstrates it.

Application Level Naming. To allow applications to name objects in its context, *name server* is used. Since only cells are accessible over networks, name server provides network-wide global naming service for cells (see Sect.4).

Language Level Identities. There are several names in the OZ language [17], i.e. instance variables, methods, and classes. To increase the run-time performance and type safety, the compiler resolves these names as much as possible. In the distributed environment, dynamic binding is highly expensive. Also, if classes are shared and reused in the distributed environment, modification of a super class or a referred class brings inconsistency. We introduce a multi-version class system for incremental and timely modification of classes (see Sect.3).

2.4 Flexible and Configurable Lightweight Management Systems

OZ has flexibility in configuring the execution environment in proportion to the size of the system. It scales not only upward but also downward.

No management subsystem is required for local computation in a single computer. The file system is used for persistent object storage and name resolution (Fig.3). If a network file system like NFS is used share GODs (i.e. object image files), name resolution of all the persistent objects in the shared file system is possible with only a short delay.

In LAN-based systems, several functions are required: *resolver, class transfer agent*, and *security server*. Resolver is implemented as an isolated subsystem and others as supplementary modules to the executor (Fig.1). A resolver converts a GOL to a communication address. If the executor finds the lack of classes required to the execution of an object, a class transfer agent is responsible to search and transfer the classes. The security server provides simple security service [5].

For more larger environment, across the Internet, *application gateway* is also necessary. In general, a firewall is the boundary between the Internet and the local network. We use HTTP proxy and WWW/CGI server to relay method invocations and return values because they are widely adopted application gateways and do not give rise to modification of the existing environment to scale up the system.

3 Seamless Development Environment to Support Network-Wide Scope of Program Sharing and Reuse

In addition to the scalability of the execution system, it is important to consider the scale of a development environment. OZ supports network development environments that seamlessly scale from stand-alone, single user environment to worldwide, independent multi-user environment while taking advantage of the object-oriented paradigm. As a provision for parallel and distributed development of classes, we provide three mechanisms: *class transfer, multi-version,* and *school*.

3.1 Class Transfer for Network Transparent Sharing and Reuse

In OZ, it is possible to inherit and refer classes over networks. The interface information of classes and implementation codes are delivered by the system. This is one of the most important features that contributes scalability. That is, the scope of sharing and reuse of programs is network-wide. Hence, locally developed classes that inherit or refer remote classes require no modification to share and reuse them in a network environment. Also, the code to serialize the objects for network transfer is not required because it is done by executor. Therefore, the programming in OZ is network transparent.

In other systems, share and reuse of classes that are distributed over the network are of hand-copy-basis. In CORBA, only the interface information can be shared using the interface repository. In Java, only a special class Applet can be transferred, but not in general.

3.2 Multi-Version Class System

Software is always upgraded and re-distributed. Even if a software is upgraded, data generated by the outdated version program cannot be wasted and it is impossible to re-compile all the programs and the related programs distributed over the network. There are the following solutions to cope with this problem.

- **Schema evolution.** Data are translated from old version to new [15].
- **Multi-versions.** Data of multiple versions are allowed to coexist without affecting to each other.

In OZ, we adopted the latter approach at the system level because the former approach is difficult to support in general and may fail if the change is drastic. It will still be able to provide objects to translate data at user level.

If a system is distributed and objects and classes are shared by independent users, a multi-version class system is required for timely modification and enhancement of programs, interoperability among old data generated by old programs, and co-development of implementation for the interface definition by different developers. We consider two phases that versions are taken into account.

- **Development phase.** Programmers want to change the version of developing programs in a small unit. A class may be a desired unit of versions because the unit of coding and compilation is a class.
- **Distribution and execution phase.** Programmers may want to distribute new versions of class libraries or application programs. In such case, a module is appropriate since a unit of class is rather small.

In OZ, a class is composed of two parts: *interface* and *implementation*. An interface defines the signature of public methods and an implementation defines the behavior (implementation codes). They are implemented as a Java interface and class, respectively. The OZ class identifier has the same naming scheme as GOL except user name, i.e. DNS domain name and file path are used. Two classes which have the same interface part but different implementation parts are versions of the same class, and mutually exchangeable.

We use a unit *subject*, a collection of closely related classes, to introduce the module concept (Fig.4). Once the development of the class is complete, related classes are combined as a set and written in a file for *release* to the network. For a single subject, there exist one *subject interface* that includes only the set of interface parts and multiple *subject implementations* including the set of implementation parts of different versions. That is, if the different version of implementation is desired, the subject implementation is replaced by another. Subjects are stored in a server called *catalog*.

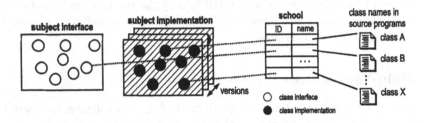

Fig. 4. Subject and school

3.3 School to Separate Development- and Execution-Time Class Name Space

In a situation that classes are shared and reused in a large-scale environment, class name conflicts may occur frequently and is difficult to change names of classes that are referred by other classes. Also, to allow multiple versions to coexist, different implementations for the same class should be distinguished. To solve these problems while keeping the freedom of programmer's naming policy, we distinguish development phase class names and execution time class identifiers.

School [10] is a mapping table between class names in source programs and the corresponding identifiers used in execution and management systems (Fig.4). The OZ development tools support the generation of globally unique identifiers for classes and maintenance of a school. To put it more precisely, a subject consists of a subset of a school entry and class codes. Programmers can use subjects in the catalog using the tools. At that time, the entries in the subject are merged into the school automatically.

4 Application Support Facilities for Distributed Services

4.1 Class Library for Distributed Management

In addition to the basic class library, provision of functions for servers is important in distributed application development. In OZ, *synchronization, security*

[5], *transaction*, and *replication* are provided as a class library. To increase the scalability, these functions are provided as a library, not a part of the executor, except the few parts of synchronization and security. CORBA specifies the same kind of services [12]. We implemented some of them in the executor since they are essential for an object execution, i.e. *object life cycle, persistency*, and *externalization*.

Replication and transaction are used to build highly available, safe applications. An object and service can be replicated and distributed to physically separated locations to increase the availability and balance access load in large-scale systems. Also, the service is replicated to meet the requirement of fault-tolerance.

4.2 Naming Service and Trader using Access Stub

The application level name and service resolution are provided by *naming* and *trading* services, respectively. These services contribute location transparency because the object or service required is accessed using location independent information — name of the object and name of the service or preference for service, respectively. Late binding and loose coupling of clients and servers make the system flexible. That is, binding between client and server is delayed until the request time using these services. Also, it is possible to utilize the services that are not available when a client is developed.

CORBA and ANSA [2] specify trader models. However, they still lack of flexibility in the selection of server and accessing mechanism from client to server after trading because matching is performed using simple values and the trader returns simple references to servers. The OZ trader model [9] provides a more flexible way to select and access the server by taking advantage of the object transfer facility (Fig.5). A server registers its service by sending a simple reference or an intelligent *broker* object to the trader. Before any actual service request, a client sends a service request to the trader to select a server which provides the most suitable service for the request. Brokers are used to make the matching and selection flexible.

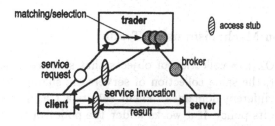

Fig. 5. OZ trader model

Details of an access mechanism is encapsulated in an *access stub* object. Since it is an object, flexible and intelligent access strategies can be included.

For example, fault-tolerant and load balancing algorithms can be implemented in access stubs.

5 Federation-Based Interaction and Integration of Management Domains

5.1 Problem

Federation deals with the heterogeneity of management policies in authorities. The problem appears when more than two authority domains are interconnected or merged into one domain and an object (client) requires interaction with another one (server) managed by the different domain. Here, the client does not know how to access the server and does not know how to utilize the service provided by the server. So far, the requirement of federal model is recognized [2] but there is no practical mechanism and implementation on this problem. In OZ, we provide federation mechanism using the trader.

We consider that the management policy of a domain is typically observed as its collection of servers because local resources in each domain are maintained using servers in a local context. For example, name server is shared by objects in the domain to have a common policy on naming. When an object wants to use the service provided by another domain, means to find the server and to utilize the service are necessary. There is a conventional approach to integrate multiple services provided by different domains using common service model.

- **Defining common service model.** A common service model is defined and a translation function is implemented between each local service and common service. It is difficult to define a common service model in general and implementation cost is high.
- **Using access stub (our approach).** Since the access method of the server is encapsulated into the access stub in OZ, it may be possible to utilize the service in another domain by switching the trader. Otherwise, modification of the access method is required but it is localized in the access stub.

5.2 Federation Mechanism using Trader

A federation in OZ is a collection of objects that shares a trader. That is, by using that trader, the same collection of servers are shared. In the interaction between cells in different domains, a client selects a trader, i.e. a collection of servers, based on its policy. If it works under the policy of the original domain, it uses the original trader. Otherwise, it uses the trader in another domain to follow the policy in that domain.

In OZ, a server search function and access method are provided by the trader and stub as shown in the previous section. There are two problems.

- The client object does not know how to access the trader in another domain.

- The client object does not know how to utilize the service provided by the server in another domain.

As a basic mechanism to solve these problems, we take advantage of the OZ trader and use a simple sequence of interactions to acquire the trader's reference in other domains. The required servers are reachable using the trader.

First, we consider a simple case that the client object accesses only servers in a single domain (Fig.6). Here, we assume that the local object has a method `imported()` and the cell has `getTrader()`, and every stub of trader is an instance of the same class.

1. The initial method `imported()` is invoked by the cell when an object is transferred.
2. The local object obtains the trader reference from the cell by calling back `getTrader()`.
3. As a result, a reference to the trader is obtained and the other servers can be reached using that trader.

If an object does not obey the policy of destination domain, it does not invoke `getTrader()`.

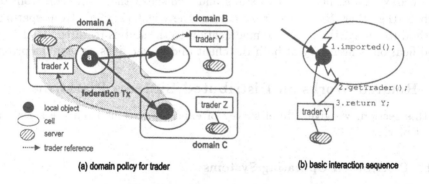

(a) domain policy for trader   (b) basic interaction sequence

Fig. 6. OZ federation (simple case)

Suppose that a local object a in federation T_x is transferred from domain A to B as shown in Fig.6. A reference to trader Y is obtained by the basic interaction sequence. Here, a belongs to another federation. Servers in domain B are used for the following computation of a in B. Conversely, in domain C, if a wants to retain the original trader X, it will not invoke `getTrader()` in `imported()`.

The problem is rather difficult if the client uses both servers in different domains at the same time and the type of stubs are incompatible. If a client directly interacts with servers, it is necessary to modify the client program and/or server programs to deal with two kinds of access methods. In OZ, a client uses a stub to access the server and the details of access method are encapsulated in the stub. Hence, it is possible to localize modification only into the stub. One solution to this problem is to replace the implementation part of the stub by a new one (Fig.7a).

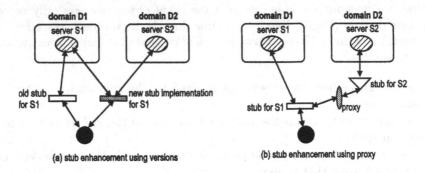

(a) stub enhancement using versions   (b) stub enhancement using proxy

Fig. 7. OZ federation (using access stub)

A proxy to delegate the interaction to the other stub can be another solution. The proxy resides between two stubs and translates the invocation from one stub to the other. Here, the proxy acts as the client (Fig.7b). By preparing a method to change the proxy, no modification to the stub is required. That is, no modification is necessary at both the client and server sides, except the proxy.

6 Related Works on Distributed Systems Platforms

In this section, we give a brief survey of existing systems from the scalability point of view.

6.1 Distributed Operating Systems

Distributed operating systems (DOSs) provide a distributed computing platform to cope with the network, fault, migration, replica, and scale transparency. Users and application programs are able to share computing resources, processors, memories, files, etc., distributed over the network, just as if they exist in the local computer. In the DOS approach, the functions to achieve the goals are implemented in the OS and tightly coupled. This approach forces all the computers to install the same DOS. In consequence, most of DOSs run in small-scale environments, LAN-based systems typically, and lack flexibility to add new functions and services. Hence, DOSs cannot scale to larger environments as well as to smaller ones because of excessive functionality.

Examples of DOSs which emphasize scalability are *Andrew File System* (AFS) [6] and *Coda* file system [16]. They are UNIX-based distributed file systems to provide scalability and security.

6.2 Object-Oriented Platforms

Instead of DOSs, object-oriented middleware is becoming the mainstream to provide distributed software platforms. Table 1 shows a comparative study of CORBA, Java, and OZ from the scalability point of view.

- **Java.** *Java* [7] is a object-oriented programming language which its execution system is based on the virtual machine (VM). The compiler generates byte-codes that are architecturally neutral, and the Java VM executes methods of objects by interpreting byte-codes. Because of this approach, Java provides strong portability.

  Current APIs support basic functions for distributed objects, e.g. remote method invocation (RMI) and object serialization. However, there is a gap between the development process of stand-alone applications and networked applications since the compilers are different and some installation work is required for RMIs. Also, Java lacks application level services and management functions for distributed objects and classes.

- **CORBA.** An *Object Request Broker* (ORB) is a common communication bus for objects. The *OMG Common Object Request Broker Architecture* (CORBA) [11] is an architecture for ORB aimed to specify a framework for transparent communication between application objects. By using a CORBA-compliant ORB, interoperable, network transparent applications can be developed based on a distributed object-oriented concept.

  An advantage of CORBA is the ability to integrate legacy applications using the *Interface Definition Language* (IDL). IDL is used to specify object interface. Applications written in various languages can be wrapped in IDL and they provide services to others as CORBA objects. Also, *inter-ORB protocols* and *bridges* enable to interconnect CORBA-compliant object environments developed by multiple vendors, and other non-CORBA environments.

  CORBA-based systems solve heterogeneity and interoperability in large-scale systems. However, CORBA run-time systems are relatively heavy and their performance are not good.

7 Concluding Remarks

In this paper, we described the scalable architecture and facilities of the OZ distributed systems environment. OZ is useful in implementing flexible and scalable distributed object systems. The OZ system is able to support various size of computing environments since it has been designed carefully from the language to application level (see Table 1). CORBA is one of the most suitable architectures to integrate legacy applications to build large-scale, interoperable distributed systems. Java is suitable for developing local applications or client-server type ones that requires no distributed management services since the language is well designed, with the exception of the fundamental management function.

Table 1. Comparison of distributed object-oriented systems platforms

	CORBA	Java	OZ
target system size	middle – large	tiny – middle	small – worldwide
integration of legacy systems	wrapping services by IDL	–	class library and application gateway
integration of management domains	–	–	federation mechanism
scope of interface sharing	same as the scope of interface repository sharing	local	worldwide
scope of class sharing	local	local	worldwide
distributed object management	naming, trading, etc.	– –	replication, naming, trading, etc.
global object reference	implementation dependent	URL (only with RMI registry tool and special programming)	GOL (DNS domain name + user name + file path)
distributed class management	interface repository	– –	class delivery and version management

For large-scale systems, loose coupling and late binding between clients and servers are necessary to build highly flexible and available applications. Also, to cope with heterogeneity of policies in management authorities, the federal model and supporting technologies are required. In OZ, the trader and federation service are provided. By using the federation mechanism, clients are able to switch the trader to access servers in other domains. Furthermore, merging of domains and utilization of services in multiple domains are possible with small overhead to modify access stubs.

Network transparent programming support is another important issue. To share and reuse programs on network environment, the OZ development environment supports multi-version classes to allow incremental change of programs. Also, it offers network-wide scope of class sharing and reuse. That is, programming in a stand-alone environment and the one on the network are seamless. Developed applications are free from the location of programs since they are delivered by the system at the run-time.

Downward scalability is also an important issue to cope with increasing requirements of mobile systems. It requires simple execution systems and performance optimization in a local environment. OZ supports small computers on the assumption of a file system and Java VM.

The OZ system 1.0α [13] is distributed as public domain software. This includes the smallest set of the functions. The next version 1.0β for the LAN environment and the final, worldwide version will be available at the end of 1997 and in the spring of 1998, respectively.

Acknowledgments

This research is conducted under the Advanced Software Enrichment project of Information-technology Promotion Agency, Japan (IPA). Design and implementation of the OZ system derived from the great contribution by researchers of the OZ project and the related organizations. We wish to thank these colleagues.

References

1. Almes, G. T., *et al.*: The Eden System: A Technical Review. IEEE Trans. Software Engineering, Vol.SE-11, No.1 (1985) 43–58
2. APM Ltd.: An Overview of ANSA. Architecture Report 000.00 (1993)
3. Black, A., *et al.*: Object Structure in the Emerald System. Proc. of OOPSLA'86 (1986)
4. Cardelli, L.: Obliq: A Language with Distributed Scope. Technical Report, Digital Equipment Corporation, Systems Research Center (1995)
5. Hamazaki, Y., Nishioka, T., and Tsukamoto, M.: The Security Mechanism of OZ: an Object-Oriented Distributed Systems Environment. to appear in Proc. of France–Japan Workshop on Object-Based Parallel and Distributed Computation (OBPDC'97) (1997)
6. Haward, J. H., *et al.*: Scale and Performance in a Distributed File System. ACM Trans. Computer Systems, Vol.6, No.1, (1998) 55–81
7. Gosling, J. and McGilton, H.: The Java Language Specification. A White Papaer, Sun Microsystems, Inc. (1995)
8. Liskov, B.: Distributed Programming in Argus. Comm. ACM, Vol.31, No.3 (1988) 300–312
9. Nishioka, T. and Tsukamoto, M.: A Framework to use Distributed Servers Based on Exchanging Objects. Proc. of SWoPP'96, Japan (1996)
10. Nishioka, T., Hamazaki, Y., and Tsukamoto, M.: Local Class Name Space Facility for Worldwide Object-Oriented Distributed Systems Environment. Proc. of the Int. Conf. on Worldwide Computing and Its Applications (WWCA'97), Lecture Notes in Computer Science 1274, Springer–Verlag (1996) 74–89
11. Object management Group (OMG), The Common Object Request Broker: Architecture and Specification. Revision 2.1 (1997)
12. Object Management Group (OMG), CORBAservices: Common Object Services Specification. (1997)
13. OZ: Object-Oriented Distributed Systems Environment. http://www.etl.go.jp/etl/bunsan/OZ_Proj/
14. OZ++: Object-Oriented Distributed Systems Environment. http://www.etl.go.jp/etl/bunsan/OZ/
15. Peney, D. J. and Stein, J.: Class Modification in the GemStone Object-Oriented DBMS. Proc. of the OOPSLA'87 (1987) 111–117
16. Satyanarayanan, M.: Scalable, Secure, and Highly Available Distributed File Access. IEEE Computer, Vol.23, No.5 (1990) 9–18
17. Tsukamoto, M., *et al.*: The Version Management Architecture of an Object-Oriented Distributed Systems Environment: OZ++. Proc. of OBPDC'95, Lecture Notes in Computer Science 1107, Springer–Verlag (1996) 310–328

Rapide: A Language and Toolset for Causal Event Modelling of Distributed System Architectures *

David C. Luckham **

Program Analysis and Verification Group
Computer Systems Lab
Stanford University

Abstract. This paper describes some of the features of Rapide, a language for modelling architectures of distributed systems. Rapide is an event-based architecture definition language. It has a semantics based on causally related events. Simulations of models in Rapide generate causal event histories which can be checked for correctness using event pattern constraints, or can be viewed and analysed by means of the Rapide toolset.

1 Introduction

Rapide-1.0 is a computer language for defining and executing models of system architectures. It is one of a new class of computer languages called *Architecture Definition Languages*, or ADLs.

The result of executing a Rapide model is a set of events that occurred during the execution together with *causal* and *timing* relationships between events. The production of *causal history* as a simulation result is, at present, unique to Rapide among event-based languages. Sets of events with causal histories are called *posets* (partially ordered event sets). Simulators that produce posets provide many new opportunities for analysis of models of complex systems, particularly those aspects involving distributed and concurrent behavior.

Rapide-1.0 is structured as a set of languages consisting of the Types, Patterns, Architecture, Constraint, and Executable Module languages. This set of languages is called the Rapide *language framework*.

The purpose of the framework is twofold: *(i)* to encourage multilanguage systems, *(ii)* to define language components that may be applied to, or migrated into, other event generating systems. Towards

---

* This project is funded by DARPA under ONR contract N00014-92-J-1928 and Air Force Rome Labs Grant F30602-96-2-0191, and by AFOSR under Grant AFOSR91-0354

** I am indebted to members of the Rapide project at Stanford who built the Rapide tools that are the topic of this paper: Marc Abramowitz, John Kenney, Walter Mann, Woosang Park, Alex Santoro, James Vera.

(i), we anticipate that the Executable Module, Constraint or Architecture sublanguages may be changed in fairly substantial ways, and that the Executable Module and Constraint sublanguages may be interchanged with other languages provided certain compatibility requirements are met. Towards *(ii)*, for example, the use of constraints expressed in terms of event patterns will have many applications to systems that generate events, not just the Rapide simulator. Such applications include monitoring distributed object systems based on CORBA ORBs or commercial publish-subscribe middleware such as information busses, for security, for conformance to standards, and for many other properties.

The Types language provides the basic features for defining interface types and function types, and for deriving new interface type definitions by inheritance from previous ones. Its semantics consists of the general rules defining the subtype (and supertype) relationship between types so as to allow dynamic substitution of modules of a subtype for modules of a supertype. The other sublanguages of the framework are extensions of the Types language. They assume the basic type definition features, and add new features in a way compatible with strong typing (i.e., every expression has a type). The architecture language extends the types language with constructs for building interface connection architectures. The Executable Module language adds modules, control structures, and standard types and functions. Standard types (i.e., data types available in many languages) are specified in a separate document as interface types. The Constraint language provides features for expressing constraints on the poset behaviors of modules and functions. The Event Pattern Language is a fundamental part of all of the executable constructs (reactive processes, behavior rules and connection rules) in the executable module and architecture languages, and also of the constraint language.

This paper will discuss some of the topics and issues surrounding Rapide. Specifically, we discuss :

1. the concept of *interface connection architecture*.
   The treatment of concepts of *architecture* given here is an extremely cursory and incomplete excerpt from one of our publications. It is included here because there is currently so much vagueness about "architecture", and so much use of the term without any attempt to define what it means. People mean many different things by "architecture". It is important that the reader or listener has some understanding of the concepts of architecture that have motivated the design of Rapide.
2. the Rapide concepts of *event, cause*, and *causal event history*.
   Rapide is an event-based language and simulation toolset. We give a short but quite detailed overview of *events*, causal histories of events, and Rapide computations.

3. tools for depicting and analyzing causal event histories.
   We give a short description of the present Rapide tools to support
   architecture modelling, i.e., building models of system architectures, simulating architectures and analyzing simulation results.
4. applications of Rapide and its toolset,
   both in modelling system architectures, and in the analysis of real-
   world distributed systems.

We will not have the time in this talk to deal with topics such
as different concepts of *system architecture*, the design of event-based
constraint languages that are specially suited to causal event behaviors,
or all the possible applications of the current Rapide toolset in *event
viewing* of real-world systems.

More information on Rapide and a suitable bibliography referencing our work and the work of others in the field of ADLs, can be found
in the Internet Web page:

> http://anna.stanford.edu/rapide/rapide.html

2   A Graphical Guide to Rapide

This section provides a top-down graphical summary of rapide. It
shows how the highest level language constructs, namely the constructs for modelling architecture, are composed of constructs from
the next lower level, and so on. Rapide has a very simple top-down
structure which is showing below.

2.1   Architectures

Figure 1 shows the main elements in architectures: an architecture
consists of components, connections between them, and constraints
on the architecture's behavior. [3]

So, if we want to build an architecture, we must first define the
types of its components, then some components, then connect them
up, and finally constrain the activity of the connections, e.g., by
adding, say, protocol constraints requiring connections to fire in particular orders.

A *Component* of an architecture is a module — i.e., an object of
an interface type. It is shown as being of three kinds: an interface
object (called simply an *interface*), an architecture that implements an
interface, or a module that implements an interface.

An interface defines a type of objects if it is used in a type declaration to define a type. However, an object can be declared by an
object declaration without any module implementation; in this case

---

[3] See Fig. 5 for the key to these diagrams.

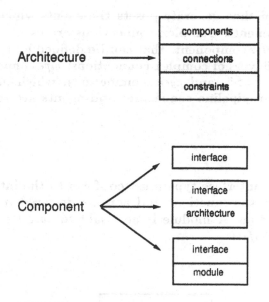

Fig. 1. Graphical Synopsis of Rapide: Architecture

we also refer to such an object as "an interface". In this case, the behavior part of the interface (below) acts as the module implementing the object.

The second and third kinds of components are really the same kind: an architecture is a restricted kind of module that contains only some of the constructs normally allowed in modules.

Connections are shown in Fig. 5. Connections in architectures are very similar to transition rules (in interface behaviors) and processes (in modules), so they are shown together in this figure. All three constructs are concurrent reactive rules. A reactive rule "reacts" when its pattern trigger is matched and then executes its body.

There are two kinds of connections, *basic* connections and *complex* connections. Basic connections define *identity* between pairs of interface features, e.g., a pair of functions, a pair of actions, or a pair of services. Identity is the strongest form of connection relationship. For example a basic connection between a required function of one component and a provided function of another defines the latter function as an alias for the former. Thus calls to the required function are replaced by calls to the provided function. Basic connections between functions and actions are essential to defining connections between components of an architecture.

Complex connections define more general connections between components. They may trigger on posets of events generated by some components and then generate posets the events which are received by other components. Complex connections are essentially syntactic sugar for *connector* components that can be defined by interface types. There are two flavors of complex connections: *pipe* connections, which use the syntax "=>", and *agent* connections, which use the syntax "|| >". Pipes are pipeline connectors and agents are multi-threaded connectors.

2.2 Interfaces

A module of an interface type must conform to the interface in that it must provide the functions and actions declared in the provides and actions section. A module is also said to *have the interface* or to *implement the interface.*

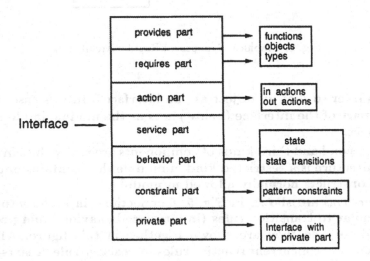

Fig. 2. Graphical Synopsis of Rapide: Interfaces

An interface can have up to seven parts, all parts being optional, see Fig. 2. The Provides part declares the names and signatures of functions, modules and types that modules of that interface type provide to other modules. The Requires part declares the names and signatures of functions, modules and types that will be required from other modules by modules of the interface type. A module can communicate synchronously with another module if it calls one of its interface required functions, and there is a connection that connects that function to a provided interface function of the other module.

The Action part declares the In and Out actions by means of which modules of the interface type can communicate asynchronously with other modules. Communication is by sending and receiving events that are generated by calls to those actions, and then "transported" by connections.

The Service part contains services (and Dual services). Services are like sub-interfaces that define plugs or sockets — i.e., bundles of functions and actions that must be connected to dual bundles, rather like, say an RS-232 port. Services are explained in Architectures LRM.

The Behavior part contains state (sets of objects) and transition rules that act on the state and also generate new events. Behaviors are rather simple kinds of modules that are defined in a very simple concurrent reactive language of pattern-triggered state-transition rules.

state transtions are shown in Fig. 5. They are used in behaviors and maps. A state transtion consists of a pattern or a boolean condition that triggers the execution of a sequence of operations on the state of a behavior, followed by the generation of a pattern of events.

The Constraint part contains constraints on the behavor of modules implementing the interface. Constraints may be input/output conditions on the parameters and return objects of functions, or they can be more general patterns of events that constrain the visible behavior (i.e., the sets of event visible at its interface) of the module.

The Private part can contain interface parts, but no other private part. The visibility of declarations in a private part is limited to modules with the same interface. The purpose of private parts is to allow modules with the same interface to be implemented differently and to inter-operate as if they were instances of the same module.

2.3 Modules

Modules implement interface types. As shown in Fig. 3 there are seven possible parts of a module, all optional. Note that all of the parts of an architecture are parts of a module. A module consisting of only these parts is called an architecture.

A module may also be an executable multi-threaded program, consisting of an initial part, executed first; then a process part, giving several processes that execute simultaneously; and a final part, to be executed when all processes have terminated. Constraints and exception handlers may also be parts of modules.

Processes (defined in modules) are shown in Fig. 5. A process can consist of a simple list of statements, to be executed once, as well as reactive statements such as the When statement, which repeatedly waits for a pattern of events and triggers the execution of a body of statements when a match of the pattern is observed.

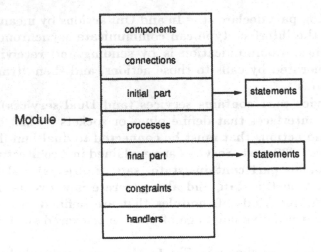

Fig. 3. Graphical Synopsis of Rapide: Modules

2.4 Maps

A map is a construct that defines mapping rules that transform the executions of one or more architectures (its domains) into an execution of another architecture or an interface (its range). The elements of maps are shown in Fig. 4. The mapping rules define how sets of events generated in the domain map into events in the range.

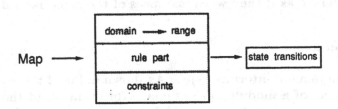

Fig. 4. Graphical Synopsis of Rapide: Maps

Mappings rules are very similar to state transition rules in interface behaviors. So the same concept of pattern-triggered transition rules are used to transform the events generated by one architecture into events defined in another architecture. A map can be the domain of another map, so maps can be composed transitively. Maps may contain constraints that restrict the order in which their rules can trigger.

Maps are an experimental language construct for relating different levels in a design heirarchy. Their main application is intended to be in defining conformance of detailed architectures to higher level, more abstract architectures. Compilation of maps allow them to be used as constraints to check conformance. Maps are defined in Architectures LRM.

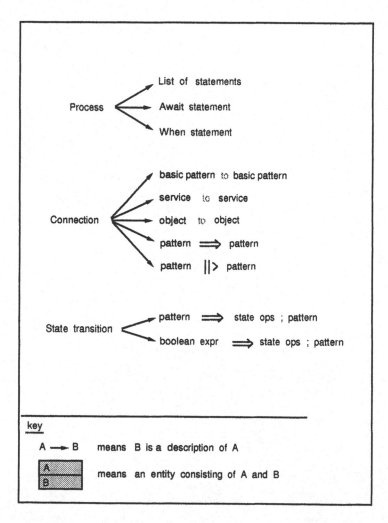

Fig. 5. Graphical Synopsis of Rapide: Other Constructs

3 Conclusions

Causality in event histories is critical in accurately representing behaviors of distributed systems. Rapide analysis tools can be applied not only to Rapide simulations, but also to the event histories generated by any system. At Stanford we are progressing towards integration of the Rapide toolset into many different enterprise viewing tools.

An Architecture of Software Commerce Broker over the Internet

Mikio Aoyama[1], Toshio Yamashita[2] and Shinsuke Kobori[2]

[1] Department of Information and Electronics Engineering, Niigata Institute of Technology, 1719 Fujihashi, Kashiwazaki, 945-11, Japan, mikio@iee.niit.ac.jp
[2] Advanced Information Technology Center, The Japan Research Institute, Limited, 16 Ichibancho, Chiyoda-ku, Tokyo 102, Japan, (yamasita, kobori)@tyo.aitec.jri.co.jp

Abstract. This article proposes an architecture of SCB (Software Commerce Broker) which aims at trading the software packages and components over the Internet. Component-based software engineering is coming into real development paradigm due to wide spreading of distributed objects environment and componentware. Since software can be distributed over the Internet, a Web-based commerce of software components and packages over the Internet is emerging. To realize Web-based commerce of software, we develop a prototype of SCB which collects information on software components worldwide over the Internet and provides a set of electronic catalogues of software components in a semi-formal specification language SCL (Software specification and Commerce Language). Furthermore, SCB provides play mechanism on which customers in remote locations can play the component through the Web. SCB is under evaluation in the Next Generation Software Engineering Program of Software CALS (Continuous Acquisition and Life-cycle Support) project in Japan.

1 Introduction

This article proposes an architecture of SCB (Software Commerce Broker) which aims at trading the software package and components over the Internet. The widespread use of the personal computers and Internet makes radical change of software development and distribution. Now, so-called CBSE (Component-Based Software Engineering) is coming into real development paradigm due to wide spreading of distributed objects environment and componentware [1, 5]. Since software can be distributed over the Internet, a Web-based commerce of software components and packages over the Internet is emerging [2]. On the other hand, practitioners are required to change the way of software development due to the rapid change to the requirements of software and their operating environment. Especially, customers and computer users require rapid development and change of new and existing applications due to keep up with the rapid change of business climate in the 1990s. To explore the CBSE technology from the practitioner's point of view, the NGSE (Next Generation Software Engineering) program of Software CALS (Continuous Acquisition and Life-cycle Support) project in Japan [13] is conducting the development and experiment of a variety of technologies for CBSE [2, 3]. Based on such experiment, the Software CALS project aims at providing a set of standards and guidelines for establishing the worldwide and open environment for software development over the Internet. One of the key technologies of NGSE program is SCB (Software Commerce Broker) which enables Web-based commerce of software over the Internet. We developed a prototype of SCB which collects information on software components worldwide over the Internet and provides a set of electronic catalogues of software components in a semi-formal specification language SCL (Software specification and Commerce Language) [4]. Furthermore, SCB provides play mechanism on which customers in remote locations can play the component through the Web. Currently, SCB is under evaluation in the NGSE Program of Software CALS project.

2 Component-Based Software Development and Commerce Broker

2.1 Component-Based Software Development

Although so-called CBSE environments are commercialized, there are few discussions on Component-Based Software Development model. To explore the CBSE, the NGSE program of Software CALS project proposed a model of Component-Based Software Development as illustrated in Fig. 1 [3]. As illustrated in Fig. 1, suppose Acquirer requests for proposals to SSIs (System/Software Integrators). One of the SSIs was awarded the application development. Then, the SSI subcontracts some parts of the application to, say, SDs (Software Developers) A and B. Furthermore, some parts of the application can be composed with the components from CVs (Component Vendors). We expect all the process above mentioned can be done over the Internet.

2.2 Commerce Broker

The emergence of component vendors is a driving force to make the whole software industry more structured similar to other modern manufacturing industries. That is, software industry could be structured into two sub-industries of component vendors and component integrators. However, the divide of work naturally requires a new sub-industry which coordinates the distribution and commerce of components between two sub-industries. We call it SCB (Software Commerce Broker). Fig. 2 illustrates a new structure of CBSE-based software industry which NGSE assumes. In NGSE program, we are exploring the following three major functions of SCB.

1. Collecting components information through the Internet,
2. Providing components information on the Web, and
3. Trading components over the Internet.

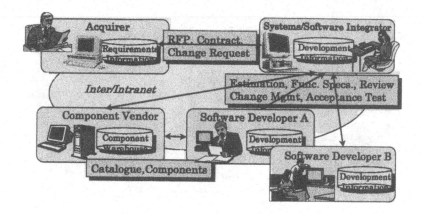

Fig. 1. Component-Based Software Development

3 Architecture Issue of Software Commerce Broker

To realize the SCB, we discuss the architecture of SCB in the following three levels.

1. Operation Architecture
2. Software Architecture
3. Information and Presentation Architecture

3.1 Operation Architecture

We expect the Internet, extranet and intranet as the underlying operation architecture.

3.2 Software Architecture

The software architecture of SCB needs to be network-centric since we expect SCB works on the Internet. Thus, the SCB run on Web server and provides information on the Web with HTML/HTTP. Furthermore, SCB needs to collect information on software components from other Web sites distributed all over the world. We adopted a network agent for automated search of component information over the Internet.

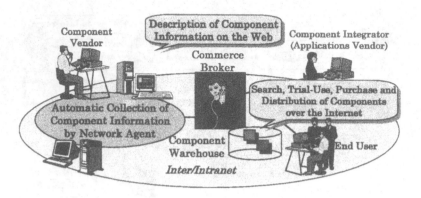

Fig. 2. Commerce Broker

3.3 Information and Presentation Architecture

Information and presentation architecture defines the internal and external presentation of component information. To specify the interface of objects, there are a few well defined IDLs (Interface Definition Languages) such as CORBA-IDL [10], IDL for DCOM (Distributed Component Object Model) [6], emerging CDL (Component Description Language) [11] and other ADLs (Architecture Description Languages) [16]. However, those IDLs are not able to describe information needed for trading components. To trade components, we need not only component specification but also various commerce information of vendors, purchase and license conditions, quality information and application examples. To provide such information on the SCB, .we propose SCL (Software specification and Commerce Language) which integrates both specification description and commerce description in a single language scheme [4].

4 Architecture of Software Commerce Broker

Fig. 3 illustrates an overview of SCB architecture which consists of the following three major subsystems.

1. Component warehouse stores component commerce information in SCL,
2. Agent collects component information over the Web and storing them into component warehouse in the form of SCL, and

3. Component player provides a mechanism on which component users can play components at the remote sites.

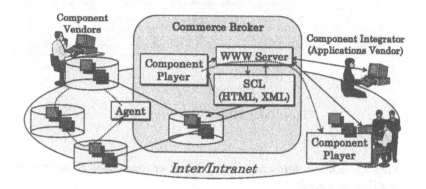

Fig. 3. Architecture of SCB

5 SCL: Software Specification and Commerce Language

Fig. 4 illustrates information structure of SCL which consists of two parts: commerce information and specification information. Each part also consists of a set of information modules. This structure aims at balancing the simplicity of description and rich description capability. Furthermore, this structure allows component vendors can describe a wide variety of information in an incremental way depending on the levels of abstraction and characteristics of information.

1. Commerce Protocol Specification
   This part describes commerce information of component. It consists of the following three modules. These modules are minimal and mandated except for evaluation module.
   - Abstract specification module includes name of component and its provided services (i.e. functions), category of services, version, abstract specifications. Service can be described in a natural language. Category de-

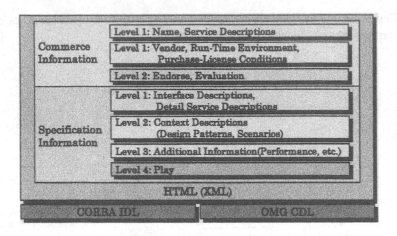

Fig. 4. Information Structure of SCL

fines application domains of component or functional classification with multiple keywords.

- Trading module includes vender information, purchase and licensing conditions.
- Evaluation module includes the evaluation report or recommendation by either third-party organization or component broker. This information can be useful in search of qualified components. Thus, the reliability of this information is critical. Commerce broker can differentiate its role by providing qualified evaluation information.

2. Interface Protocol Specification

This part consists of the following four modules.

- Interface description module One component can provide single or multiple interfaces (i.e. methods). Currently, we adopted an extended IDL upward compatible with CORBA-IDL. Therefore, signature rule and inheritance are completely compatible with those of CORBA-IDL. Component of SCL corresponds to module of CORBA-IDL and component of CDL.
- Context description module This module describes the static structure and dynamic behavior of a group of surrounding classes with which the component works. Static structure and dynamic behavior is respectively represented in class diagram and message diagram of UML (Unified Modeling Language) [14]. This information can help component acquirer to understand the context of component and select an appropriate one.

3. Additional information module This module provides the following information in order to make better understanding of components.

  - Performance: size of disk space for storing component, minimal memory size required for execution, and execution time.
  - Application: application examples, tips, FAQ (Frequently Asked Questions), and so on.

4. Play This provides interface invocation information and scenario for trial use of component.

6 Example of SCL Description

To explain SCL notation, we use FontDialogDirector which is an example of mediator pattern [7]. Boldface and italic respectively represents keywords and items which can be omitted. "//" leads comments.

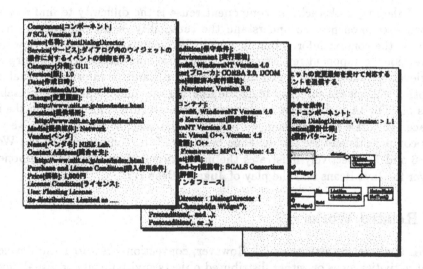

Fig. 5. An Example of SCL Description: FontDialogDirector

Fig. 6 illustrates a Web-based representation of the example.

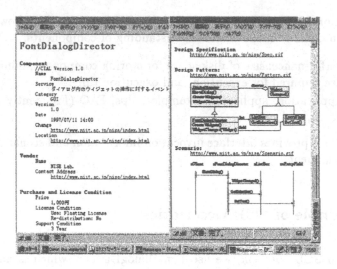

Fig. 6. Web Representation of FontDialogDirector

7 Component Player

One of the major obstacles to component reuse is the difficulty to find out appropriate components. To understand the reusability of components, we need to know the context information in which the component can work. However, conventional component repositories provide little information to such purpose. Retrieval mechanisms are based on only keywords and/or informal textual description which is not sufficient to decide whether the component can be reusable. IDLs of CORBA and DCOM also provide little semantic information on the interface. To tackle this problem, we proposes play mechanism on which we can play components and see the dynamic behavior of the components on the Web. Fig. 6 and 7 respectively illustrates the initialization of prototyped Component Player for Java Beans and the play of Juggler Bean [17].

8 Related Works

CBSE is attracting attentions [5]. However, conventional research and development activities focus on either distributed objects environments or visual development environments. Little works have been done on SCB. Among them, Ning proposed producer(i.e. vendor)-broker-integrator model of component-based software development organization [12]. This article first proposed the concept of SCB (Software Commerce Broker) and its architecture. Describing component

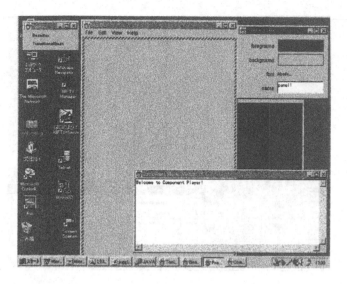

Fig. 7. Initialization of Component Player

specification is another important research topics. The ADLs (Architecture Description Languages) share the interests with component description languages since the ADLs need to deals with components as the elements of architecture. Representative ADLs include ACME [8], Rapide [9] and UniCon [15]. CORBA-IDL and IDL for DCOM also provide interface definition. High-level extensions of IDL include ASL [12]and CDL [11]. However, these languages lack commerce information. Since SCL is aimed at describing electronic catalogues of software components, SCL is designed to describe a wide variety of commerce information in a single presentation framework.

9 Conclusions and Future Study

This article proposed the concept of SCB (Software Commerce Broker) and its architecture. At the heart of SCB, we proposed SCL (Software specification and Commerce Language) to realize electronic commerce of software packages and components over the Internet. With SCL, we can describe both commerce and interface specification information in a single presentation framework. SCB can collect, present and distribute the information of software components through the Internet. SCB also provides component player. We developed a prototype of SCB and are conducting pilot project of component-based software development with the prototype of SCB. Currently we are working on the refinement of SCL by the feedback from the pilot development and development of translator

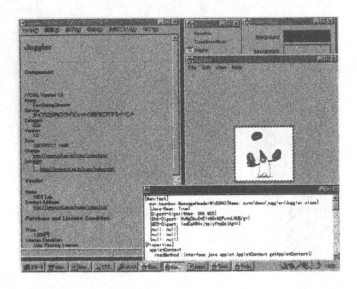

Fig. 8. Playing a Java Bean on the Web

mapping SCL to existing IDLs, and integration of SCB with Web-based CBSE environments.

Acknowledgements: The authors would like to thank colleagues in NGSE team of Software CALS consortium and Componentware WG of INSTAC for their cooperation in the development of SCB. This research is supported by IPA (Information technology Promotion Agency) and HITOCC (Hyper Information Technology Oriented Corporation Club) program of JISA (Japan Information Service Industry Association).

References

1. M. Aoyama: Componentware: Building Applications with Software Components. J. of Information Processing Society of Japan. **37-1** (1996) 91–97 (In Japanese)
2. M. Aoyama: Exploring Next Generation Software Development in Software CALS. JISA Bulletin. **44** (1996) 58-69 (In Japanese)
3. M. Aoyama: Process and Economic Model of Component-Based Software Development. Proc. 5th IEEE Int'l Conference on Assessment of Software Tools (SAST '97) (1997) 100–104
4. M. Aoyama, T. Yamashita and S. Kobori: SCL: A Software Specification and Commerce Language. Proc. of IPSJ SIG Software Engineering Workshop. (1997) 33–40 (In Japanese)
5. A. W. Brown: Component-Based Software Engineering. IEEE CS Press (1996)

6. N. Brown, et al., Distributed Component Object Model Protocol – DCOM/ 1.0, http://www.microsoft.com.
7. E. Gamma, et al:, Design Patterns. Addison-Wesley (1995)
8. D. Garlan, et al.: ACME: An Architecture Description Interchange Language. http://www.cs.cmu.edu (1997)
9. D. Luckham, et al.: Guide to the Rapide 1.0 Language Reference Manuals. The Stanford Rapide Project (1996)
10. OMG: The Common Object Request Broker: Architecture and Specification, Revision 2.0. http://www.omg.org (1995)
11. OMG Business Object Domain Task Force: Business Object Facility. Revision 1.0 (1997).
12. J. Q. Ning: A Component-Based Software Development Model. Proc. IEEE COMPSAC '96 (1996) 389-394
13. H. Nagano: Software CALS: Aims and Experiments. J. of Information Processing Society of Japan. **37-12** (1996) 1083-1088 (In Japanese)
14. Rational Software Co.: UML Notation Guide, Version 1.0 http://www.rational.com (1997)
15. M. Shaw, et al.: Abstraction for Software Architecture and Tools to Support Them IEEE Trans. Software Eng. **21-4** (1995) 314-335
16. M. Shaw and D. Garlan: Software Architecture, Prentice Hall (1996)
17. SUN Microsystems: Java Beans 1.0. http://java.sun.com/beans (1996)

Distributed Process Management System Based on Object-Centered Process Modeling

Makoto Matsushita[1], Makoto Oshita[1], Hajimu Iida[2] and Katsuro Inoue[1]

[1] Division of Software Science, Graduate School of Engineering Science,
Osaka University, 1-3 Machikaneyama, Toyonaka, Osaka 560-8531 Japan
[2] Information and Technology Center, Nara Institute of Science and Technology,
8916-5 Takayama, Ikoma, Nara 630-0101 Japan

Abstract. Most of process-centered software engineering environments and those languages focus on process-oriented software development process. However, recent software development tends to require to focus on product-oriented software development, because of emergence of various types of software developments; e.g., software reuse, component-based composition, and so on. To achieve this, we propose in this paper a new development environment named *MonoProcess/SME (Software process Management Environment)*, which is based on an object-centered software process model *MonoProcess* we also propose. MonoProcess consists of a set of objects which represent artifacts and resources in the software development. An object has attributes and methods, which represent characteristics and operations of the object, respectively. MonoProcess/SME is an software development environment for project management and development support, using the idea of MonoProcess modeling. MonoProcess/SME illustrates software development environment as it is, and provides an environment for software process execution, management, and improvement.

1 Introduction

Software process description and its enaction help the software development to proceed effectively and to produce high quality software[9, 10, 12]. However, most of process-centered software engineering environments tend to enforce specific types of development activities to the developer. Also, they require proprietary and exclusive systems/environments which are completely different from existing software development environment [3, 4, 5, 6, 13, 14, 15]. Therefore those systems are not yet widely used in real software development.

Recent software development methods such as object-oriented programming, software reuse, component-based programming mainly focus on product-oriented software process; i.e., artifacts in software development environment. However, most of these software process languages[2] focus on the description of process-oriented software process; i.e., a procedure of software development. In a process-centered software engineering environment, these product-centered idea of software development should be supported, to make more effective support for software development.

In this paper, we propose a process management system, MonoProcess/SME (Software process Management Environment), based on our product-oriented software process description model, MonoProcess. We have developed a prototype system of MonoProcess/SME, which contains essential features for representing and enacting ISPW-6 (The Sixth International Software Process Workshop) example problem[11]. The goal of MonoProcess is to illustrate software development environment as it is, and provide a framework for software process description, management, and improvement.

MonoProcess consists of a set of objects, which are artifacts and resources in the software development. An object consists of attributes and methods. An attribute represents characteristic of the object. A method is a function applied to the objects. MonoProcess provides a feature of grouping any objects, which enables to combine two or more objects into a single object. It also provides object inheritance to share information between objects. Messages to objects, which would activate the methods or attribute accesses are recorded automatically as the operation history of the object. With these features, the status of the software development environment is easily monitored, and thus MonoProcess/SME provides helpful information to the project manager. MonoProcess/SME assumes that it runs under network-based software development environment, and is also used by the developers to help their work.

The major contributions of MonoProcess and MonoProcess/SME are as follows:

- Activities in software development environment is collected.
- Granularity of the object representation is easily managed by using the object grouping and inheritance features. Multi-grained operations are established straightforward.
- Any partial information within an object is easily extracted.
- The representation of the objects is flexibly changed corresponding to the change of the project structure.
- MonoProcess/SME is easily installed to existing development environments.

This paper is organized as follows. In Sect. 2, we will describe the definitions and features of MonoProcess, and we compare our model to other software process description languages. In Sect. 3, we will explain an idea of MonoProcess/SME. Finally, we conclude our work in Sect. 4.

2 MonoProcess

In this section, we introduce our process model named *MonoProcess*. At first, the definition of MonoProcess object is presented. Then we will see how the software process is presented with this model. We also show the feature of MonoProcess.

2.1 Overview

All artifacts and resources in the software development environment are represented as *Objects*. Software development environment is defined as a set of objects. Object O is defined as $\{Ol, A, M\}$, where Ol is an object label, A is a set of attributes, and M is a set of methods. Ol is the unique name of this object, used to specify the object.

An attribute of an object is defined as $\{Al, Av\}$, where Al is an attribute label and Av is an attribute value. An attribute label is the unique name for attribute and it indicates what kind of information is needed to the object. Information itself is represented by the attribute value. The type of the attribute values is a number, string, label, or list of these types. Some attribute label is already defined in MonoProcess to specify object grouping, etc.

A method is defined as $\{Ml, Mv\}$, where Ml is a method label, and Mv is a method operation. The method label is a unique name for this method operation, showing what operation is done with this method. Actual operation is defined by the method operation: a mapping among sets of objects. Operations of the method operation are: to refer/change attribute values, to execute methods, to make new objects, to get a list of object in the environment, to get a attribute/method list of certain object, to search objects by attribute/method label/value, to invoke tools or operations to out of the model, to execute numeric/literal/collection operation found in common programming languages, and so on.

The object definition described above is similar to the one of object oriented programming languages. However, MonoProcess object definition does not specify any concept of object class, since it may difficult to define all of the classes needed for describing the whole objects and the real world may be too complex to classify as a class structure of object oriented fashion.

Figure 1 is an example of MonoProcess object. This description shows an object of a design document named ".Doc.Design".

In this example, four attributes (@Owner, @Type, @Input, and @Location) are defined to show the information about this object. For example, an attribute @Owner shows who is the responsible person of this document, is defined as the another object which represents the person. There are two methods, &Edit for editing this document, and &View for viewing this document.

2.2 Software Development Process

We introduce two types of derived objects, "partial object" and "status object", to describe software development process. These objects are similar to normal objects defined in previous section, however, these types of objects are not intended to describe artifacts in the software development environment.

The partial object Op can be defined with respect to a certain object O. Op contains an object label whose prefix is the same as O, and it includes subset of attributes and methods of O. Op contains partial information of the target object O, and it represents a typical characteristics of O, illustrating what we are interested in.

We can define a status object Os with partial objects, a *status* of software development environment. Actually, the status object is defined as a set of partial objects; the status object is intended to clarify the status itself as a single

```
Object .Doc.Design def
        Attribute @Owner .Person.Matsushita;
        Attribute @Type "Design Document";
        Attribute @Input (.Doc.Specification .Doc.Schedule);
        Attribute @Location .ShareDisk.Document
        Method &Edit def
                $editor = .caller&GetEditor(@Type);
                if ($editor) {
                        &View;
                        invoke($editor, @Location . "design.doc");
                }
        endMethod
        Method &View def
                $viewer = .caller&GetViewer();
                if ($viewer) {
                        invoke($viewer, @Input);
                }
        endMethod
endObject
```

Fig. 1. Object sample

element. We assume that a status in software development environment can be illustrated with artifacts in an environment. In MonoProcess, development process P is defined as a transition sequence of those status objects.

Consider a simple example of three MonoProcess objects, named .SPEC, .CODE, and .TEST, and these represent a specification, source code, and test result respectively. In this example, we assume each object has the same attribute label "@FINISHED", which indicates this object has been completed or not. When we define status object .SAMPLESTATOBJ as the set of three partial objects, including .SPEC.ISFINISHED, .CODE.ISFINISHED and .TEST.ISFINISHED, defined as "only contains attribute @FINISHED of .SPEC, .CODE, and .TEST, respectively", we can see the process as the transition of .SAMPLESTATOBJ. At first, three of all attributes are set to "false". Next, attribute of .SPEC is changed to "true", and then .CODE is changed to "true". Finally all attributes are set to "true". Such sequence of .SAMPLESTATOBJ instance is a process.

2.3 Features

MonoProcess has various features to support project management, software development, and cooperation for developers. In this section, we show these features with some examples.

Reference Scope and Access Control of Objects. In general, all objects can refer and/or can be referred to/from other objects. However, each object may set a scope of reference with object own attribute. In the MonoProcess framework, the reference scope from an object is specified as the access control definition of other objects, therefore following is focused on the access control definition.

Access control description of an object is defined by "group" and "permitted operation". Group specifies a set of objects, identified by group name. Each object can join the group, and it is represented as an attribute @GROUP. Objects which have no attribute @GROUP definition, or have an attribute but no values are defined, are considered not join any groups defined in other objects.

An attribute @ACCESS represents allow/deny operation to this object. There are four types of operations, "read attribute", "change attribute", "execute method", "allow inheriting". Attributes @GROUP and @ACCESS are the access control for the object itself. Moreover, MonoProcess provides par-attribute or par-method access control, in the same manner of above.

If the MonoProcess modeling follows object-oriented architecture strictly, these features are realized with the class hierarchy and/or associations. However, we think the use of object-oriented structure is not adaptable fully to the software process description. We set the MonoProcess model flexible and simple enough for illustrating the chaotic and complicated actual software development environment.

Operation History. An operation to an object such as referring attributes is processed by sending a message to the object and activating a method of the object. In the MonoProcess framework, any operation to all objects are recorded as a history[3]. Operation history is stored in an attribute, labeled @ATTRIBUTE.HISTORY or in a method, labeled &METHOD.HISTORY. The attribute history records a list of labels of the object which operates the attribute, operation time, and the contents of referenced value/changed value. The method history records a list of labels of the object which executes the method, beginning and ending time of the execution, and the results of execution.

These histories are automatically recorded, i.e., reading an attribute @X is really achieved after recording a history to an attribute @X.HISTORY. The execution of &Y is really achieved after recording a history to an attribute &Y.HISTORY.

Flexible Object Creation. Object creation is achieved by inheriting attributes and methods from .OBJECT, a pre-defined object template, or from any existed object. Any object creation is the same as object inheritance, therefore following explanation is focused on object inheritance.

Object inheritance is triggered by executing a method &FORK, which is already defined in template object. This method gets parameters which is used to

---

[3] This is possible under our assumption of the granularity of the MonoProcess description. The process descriptions are generally not so in fine granularity or they do not create and delete objects seriously as scientific calculation.

modify self-copied object. Redefine &FORK method allows to define object-specific initialization.

Assume that an object .A is already defined, and object .B inherits from .A. First, .B is created as a *copy* of .A but it does not have any attributes and methods which are not allowed to be inherited. Then, a modification and addition to .B is processed. In MonoProcess, inheritance is accomplished with a copy of existing object associated with newer definitions and additional definitions for the new object.

Arbitrary and Multi-Grained Object Definition. In this example (Fig. 2), each source code is defined as one object (.SRC1 and .SRC2), and these source codes are a part of one module (.MODULESRC).

In this example, objects .SRC1, .SRC2 and .MODULESRC have the same method named "&MAKEOBJ". However, the behavior is not the same; .SRC1&MAKEOBJ simply performs compilation and .MODULESRC&MAKEOBJ executes compilation of each source and also linking all the source. In MonoProcess, methods with same label could perform different activities. This means that MonoProcess supports grain sensitive operation.

If a developer decided that the source code represented as object .SRC1 should be divided into two source codes .SRC1.MAIN and .SRC1.SUB, he/she executes an object creation by .SRC1&FORK twice and makes new objects, which are managed by .SRC1 object.

Easy Information Extraction. We assume that object .FOO has an attribute .FOO@MAINTAINER, which represents the responsible person of this object. One day, the responsible person is changed from person A to person B. Later something wrong with .FOO, and we want to know which is the person in charge.

In MonoProcess, we may check an attribute .FOO@MAINTAINER.HISTORY, to catch up the transition of value .FOO@MAINTAINER, since if the responsible person of .FOO was changed, i.e., attribute value of .FOO@MAINTAINER was changed, .FOO@MAINTAINER.HISTORY was also changed.

Assume there is also object .BAR, which is the same type of object .FOO. If we decide to trace the change of responsible person, we may say:

```
StatusObject .MTSTATUSES def
        PObject .FOO.MTSTATUS;
        PObject .BAR.MTSTATUS;
endObject
PObject .FOO.MTSTATUS def
        Attribute @MAINTAINER;
endObject
PObject .BAR.MTSTATUS def
        Attribute @MAINTAINER;
endObject
```

In this description, two partial objects, .FOO.MTSTATUS and .BAR.MTSTATUS are defined, and using these objects we compose a new status object .MTSTATUSES.

```
Object .SRC1 def
       ...
       Attribute @Location "host/path/to/src1";
       Method &MAKEOBJ def
               invoke(.COMPILER@Location, @CompileFlags,
.SRC1.OBJ@Components)
       endMethod
       ...
endObject

Object .SRC2 def
       ...
       Attribute @Components "path/to/src2";
       Method &MAKEOBJ def
               invoke(.COMPILER@Location, @CompileFlags,
.SRC2.OBJ@Components)
       endMethod
       ...
endObject

Object .MODULESRC def
       ...
       Attribute @Components (.SRC1 .SRC2);
       Attribute @Location "host/path/to/module";
       Method &MAKEOBJ def
               foreach $Component (@Components) {
                       $Component&MAKEOBJ;
               }
               invoke(.LINKER@Location, @Components, @Location);
       endMethod
       ...
endObject
```

Fig. 2. Multi-grained objects

We can grasp the process by checking the transition of .MTSTATUSES object.

Mapping Between a Model to Real Environment. We need a mapping between described process model with MonoProcess and the real software development environment. The mapping is achieved by the MonoProcess/SME system, a software development management environment based on MonoProcess framework.

User interface of MonoProcess/SME provides the operation objects themselves. With this interface, the developers can operate objects easily and the activities are mapped into the MonoProcess framework. Periodical search mechanism is used to synchronize automatically between the model to the real environment. While a method is executed, files are modified/referenced or tools are invoked. The changes of the status in the model influence to the real environment.

3 MonoProcess/SME

3.1 System Design

Figure 3 illustrates MonoProcess/SME system. MonoProcess/SME works on a network-based environment, co-exists with existing environment, uses an open web technologies for accessing and operating the MonoProcess objects, and is for both developers and project managers.

There are three parts in MonoProcess/SME; repository part, user-interface part, and method engine part.

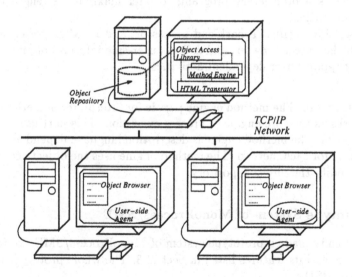

Fig. 3. MonoProcess/SME

Repository. The repository part is for object storage management. It handles object descriptions, and stores software development project information such as object operation histories, and is composed of the object repository and the object access library.

The object repository is a storage of objects. It contains the structure information defined in the objects, attribute values, and method descriptions. In the viewpoint of the object repository, MonoProcess/SME can be seen as an object-oriented distributed database system.

The object access library increases accessibility to the object repository. MonoProcess allows to use two or more languages for the method descriptions, and the object access libraries have to be prepared for each language. We currently use language such as Perl-based description language or UNIX shell script.

User-Interface. The user-interface part is for interactions between the system and the users. It provides the feature to browse object repository, execute a method, and so on. This part is composed of the object browser, user-side agent, and HTML translator.

The object browser is an user interface of MonoProcess/SME. We employ a HTML document browser as the object browser. Translating from information in the object repository to web-browserable form is done in HTML (HyperText Markup Language)[7] translator. It is embedded in the web server, performing as the interface to the other parts of the system. The object browser may be implemented as a proprietary program, to offer maximum strength of object repository operation.

The user-side agent is a back-end processor, and it exists per each user. It works with the object browser, and collects user-side information, invokes some tools, and supports user-dependent activities.

Method Engine. The method engine part is for interpreter of method description. It works as the core engine of process execution. This part uses/is used by other two parts. The method engine is description language dependent part, and it is activated for each method. The method engine uses the object access library to check/modify the object repository.

3.2   Prototype System of MonoProcess/SME

We have already made a prototype system of MonoProcess/SME, to implement MonoProcess and its features listed in Sect. 2.3. The whole prototype system is build on FreeBSD.

Since the MonoProcess/SME is used with existing software development environment, we should organize the whole system to be portable and flexible. This is why we employ the Perl language to implement the prototype system, the web browser for the user-side interface.

Repository. We simply apply the UNIX file system to the repository to enable easy operation, since the structure of the MonoProcess object can be mapped to file system directly. The object access library is written in Perl, since we think MonoProcess/SME should be portable. Using Perl language, we can port to the other operating system easily.

User-Interface. The object browser is just a web browser in this prototype. We use commonly used web browser for fast prototyping and for platform independent implementation of MonoProcess/SME. We do not hesitate to implement user-side agent in C for the speed and performance issue, since user-side agent should be environment dependent component of this system. The HTML translator is the module of Apache[1] web server, and do the conversion between the object and its attributes and methods to the URL (Uniform Resource Locator).

Method Engine. We employ Perl-based tiny description language for object description and implements the method engine in Perl. The object access library is used with the description. The Perl language is powerful, flexible and portable enough for our purpose of the prototype system.

Applying the Prototype System. We applied the prototype system to describe ISPW-6 process modeling example[11] (Fig. 4). We describe a detailed behavior of ISPW-6 example process to confirm that MonoProcess/SME provides the facility of software development support environment.

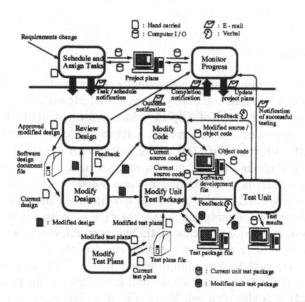

Fig. 4. ISPW-6 Process Modeling Example

The description is enacted and the resulting environment established a proper behavior of the ISPW-6 example[8, 16]. Figure 5 is an sample screen-shot about using with MonoProcess/SME environment; activities in software development, such as tool invocation, product passing from an activity to an another activity, and so on is executed within MonoProcess/SME environment.

118

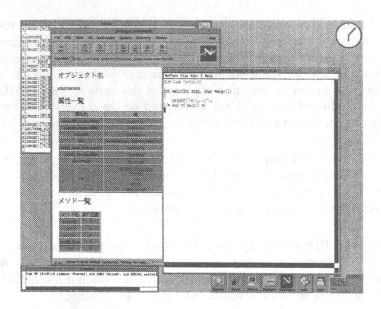

Fig. 5. Screen-shot of Prototype System

4 Conclusion

In this paper, we propose a new development environment MonoProcess/SME, based on an object-centered software process model MonoProcess.

MonoProcess is composed of *Objects* which represent artifacts in software development environment. In this model, software process is shown as a state transition of status objects. With this model, software process is illustrated clearly; that is powerful enough for the process management.

MonoProcess/SME is a MonoProcess-based software development environment. MonoProcess/SME can be used with existing development environment, and it provides product management and reactive activity execution support. A prototype system of MonoProcess/SME has been implemented and ISPW-6 example has been described and executed on the prototype.

For a further research topics, a full implementation of MonoProcess/SME has to be completed. Validation of our model and more support for process enaction based on validation is also planned. We also have a plan to extend the model to use the description of process improvement, to employ the meta-level framework shown in recent object-oriented architecture.

Acknowledgement

We are grateful to Tetsuo Yamamoto and Yutaka Fujiwara for their contribution of the development of a prototype of MonoProcess/SME.

References

1. Apache Project: Apache HTTP Server Project. <URL:http://www.apache.org/>
2. Armenise, P., Bandinelli, S., Ghezzi, C., Morzenti, A.: Software Process Representation Language: Survey and Assessment. Proc. of the 4th Conf. of Software Eng. and Knowledge Eng. (1992) 455–462
3. Bandinalli, S., Nitto, E.D., Fuggetta, A.: Supporting Cooperation in the SPADE-1 Environment. IEEE Trans. Software Eng. **22** (1996) 841–865
4. Bandinelli, S.C., Fuggetta, A., Ghezzi, C.: Software Process Model Evolution in the SPADE Environment. IEEE Trans. Software Eng. **19** (1993) 1128–1144
5. Bandinelli, S., Fuggetta, A., Grigolli, S.: Process Modeling in-the-large with S-LANG. Proc. of ICSP2 (1993) 75–83
6. Ben-shaul, I.Z., Kaiser, G.E.: A Paradigm for Decentralized Process Modeling and its Realization in the Oz Environment. Proc. of ICSE16. (1994) 179–188
7. Berners-Lee, T., Connolly, D.: Hypertext Markup Language – 2.0. RFC 1866 (1995)
8. Fujiwara, Y: Software Process Modeling with Objects and its Software Development Management System – Repository Implementation and its Application to ISPW-6 Example. Bachelor Thesis of Department of Information and Computer Sciences, Osaka University (1997)
9. Inoue, K.: Current Research Activities on Software Process. Japan Society for Software Science and Technology Technical Report **95** (1995) 1–10
10. Katayama, T.: Software Processes and Their Research Topics. Proc. of 11th JSSST Conf. (1994) 433–436
11. Kellner, M.I., Feiler, P.H., Finkelstein, A., Katayama, T., Osterweil, L.J., Penedo, M.H., Rombach, H.D.: Software Process Modeling Example Problem. Proc. of ISPW6 (1991) 19–29
12. Ochimizu, K.: Survey of Research Activities on Software Process. Journal of IPSJ **36** (1995) 379–391
13. Sutton Jr., S.M., Heimbigner, D., Osterweil, L.J.: APPL/A: A Language for Software Process Programming. ACM Trans. Software Eng. Methodology **4** (1995) 221–286
14. Tarr, P., Clarke, L.A.: PLEIADES: An Object Management System for Software Engineering. Proc. of the First ACM SIGSOFT Symposium on the Foundations of Software Engineering (1993) 56–70
15. Taylor, R.N., Belz, F.C., Clarke, L.A., Osterweil, L., Selby, R.W., Wileden, J.C., Wolf, A.L., Young, M.: Foundations for the Arcadia Environment Architecture. Proc. of third ACM SIGSOFT/SIGPLAN Symposium on Practical Software Development Environment (1988) 1–13
16. Yamamoto, T: Software Process Modeling with Objects and its Software Development Management System – Modeling and User-Interface Implementation. Bachelor Thesis of Department of Information and Computer Sciences, Osaka University (1997)

Systems Software for Multimedia Computing*

Ragunathan (Raj) Rajkumar

Real-Time and Multimedia Laboratory
Department of Computer Science
Carnegie Mellon University
Pittsburgh, PA 15213
USA
raj+@cs.cmu.edu

Abstract. In this paper, we take a macroscopic look and identify the emerging needs of the internet and worldwide computing domain driven by multimedia and instant communications. We then take a microscopic look at a few system software solutions that act as basic building blocks to satisfy end-user requirements. Specifically, we identify the application-level requirements expected by users in an interconnected world and then translate them to system-level requirements within the infrastructure. In the Real-Time and Multimedia Laboratory at the Department of Computer Science at Carnegie Mellon University, we are addressing a vertical range of problems, solutions to which will enable predictable and well-behaved interconnected systems. As illustrative examples, we provide an overview of the resource kernel approach and distributed real-time objects. Among the other solutions we have developed are analytical support for tradeoffs across multiple QoS dimensions, many-to-many communications services and scalable real-time kernels. These solutions serve as essential building blocks for flexible construction of the various layers in an interconnected world of computing and communications.

1 Introduction

1.1 Motivation

The explosive growth of the internet and the World-Wide Web is and will be a fundamental force in driving trends in computer science for many years to come. The ongoing tumultuous merger of telephony, television and computing capabilities is reflected in the new products supporting internet telephony, second-generation set-top boxes and palm-top devices. The supply of a seemingly unending customer/application base has ignited the demand for market share among industry titans in the computing, cable, networking, consumer electronics and telecommunications companies.

Interspersed in this base of worldwide computing, real-time and embedded systems are used in many application domains including feedback control

---

* This work was supported in part by the Defense Advanced Research Projects Agency under agreements E30602-97-2-0287 and N66001-97-C-8527.

systems, (manufacturing) process control, robotics, air traffic control, avionics, target-tracking, real-time object recognition, discrete assembly and vehicle navigation. According to a recent study[2], 90% of the world's microprocessors are used not in PCs, but are hidden inside electronics products. These systems typically employ multi-rate concurrent control of different actuators, interface with a variety of sensors such as radar, use multiple audio/video/data streams (for image/target tracking, human-to-human communications), and perform compute-intensive signal processing. Many of these systems such as air traffic control tend to be distributed in nature and also need to satisfy end-to-end timing requirements which span processor boundaries. Multimedia systems include on-line collaborative applications, and on-demand services such as information and education on demand. These systems require low latencies for interactive applications and jitter-free timing behavior for non-interactive applications.

Two fundamental roadblocks unfortunately remain in this global race towards establishing market share, standards, self-sustaining revenue streams and name recognition. First, the networking infrastructure in general and the "last mile" problem in particular limits the deliverable bandwidth to the end-user. Secondly, the computing and communications substrates continue to miss key ingredients such as predictable resource management, adequate tools and standards that can ensure interoperability and predictability, two fundamental ingredients of telephones and TVs. The first problem is perhaps just one of adequate investment in the infrastructure and exploiting existing wiring infrastructures in cable TV, telephone and electricity. The second problem is one that computer scientists must make rapid headway on with regards to the end-points and within the network.

1.2 Organization of the Paper

The rest of this paper is organized as follows. In Section 2, we identify requirements from the user perspective in an interconnected world of computers and communication devices. We then map these requirements to system-level requirements to motivate and illustrate the many aspects being worked at by our Real-Time and Multimedia Laboratory at Carnegie Mellon University. Section 3 presents a detailed overview of our resource kernel approach. Section 4 provides a brief overview of our Real-Time CORBA architecture. Finally, we present some concluding remarks in Section 5.

2 Requirements from the User and System Perspectives

In this section, we shall identify requirements from an end-user perspective, and then map them to requirements that must be satisfied by the systems software that supports the infrastructure.

---

[2] "Jet-Powered Computers" by David Kline in *Hot Wired* magazine, Issue 4.10, October 1996.

2.1 User-Level Requirements

Users in the modern age of communications have far-reaching expectations which open up a wide range of opportunities for vendors of hardware, software, and networking products. These expectations can be summarized as follows:

- **U1. Connectivity**: The growth of the internet and the WWW, by default, imposes the need to connect with servers on a global basis. While this requirement seems obvious, it must be noted that intranets and extranets are desirably accessible by only few authorized people but not by all. In other words, security and accessibility requirements can also be in conflict with one another. This requirement for connectivity also takes different forms in different industry segments. In a manufacturing enterprise, the corporate division may want real-time information from the factory floor, but these requests and resulting responses should not hurt the operations of the floor itself. Advanced weaponry, fighter aircraft and ships in use by national defense departments have significicant connectvity *and* security requirements. Networked medical systems and patient monitors must be interconnected and yet must be real-time and reliable. Process control systems like automated assembly systems benefit from connectivity but impose tight timing requirements. Automotive control systems must interface with navigation and entertainment aids for a car's occupants but have very different timing requirements. Distributed control systems, such as air traffic control systems and street traffic control systems, are also networked systems with real-time and high availability requirements.
- **U2. Lower costs**: While the costs of computing ($/MIPS) and storage ($/MB) have been dropping precipitously, the costs for connectivity ($/Kbps) have not dropped proportionally. This is primarily due to the lack of high-bandwidth connections to the end-user (the so-called "last mile" problem). While cable modems and xDSL technologies expect to relieve the strain here, they are yet to be widely deployed. In addition, the asymmetric bandwidths (higher downlink bandwidths compared to uplink bandwidths) can significantly impede "symmetric applications" such as collaborative video-conferencing. Needless to say, proposed solutions must be affordable for wide adoption.
- **U3. Interactive Appliances**: Devices in common use at work, at home and during transportation can and will become interactive in nature. TVs and telephones at home, computers at work and cellular phones on the road must be able (a) to interconnect for sending/receiving email and audio-visual communications, (b) to download email, news and financial information, and in addition (c) serve their native computing, entertainment, communication and notification capabilities. Traditionally simpler gadgets like refrigerators, lighting control and toasters can also become networked appliances for centralized control, but we believe that these are farther into the future than one may come to expect in these rapidly changing times.
- **U4. Notification and Discrimination Capabilities**: A user likes to be notified of events of particular interest such as dramatic changes in stock

prices, newsitems of value, calls in an emergency situation, etc. Since different notifications have inherently different priorities to a user based on his/her current context, the user must be able to specify different priorities to each of these notifications in terms of chargeable costs, search and computational time spent, etc.

- **U5. Predictability**: Consider a VCR playing a cassette, a live TV channel or a movie theater. The entertainment experience is enhanced by the continuous smooth motion seen on the display. Video-conferencing on the internet, internet telephony, etc. offer acceptable functionality for some cost-conscious customers. However, their lack of smooth progression due to network traffic limitations and insufficient processing power almost guarantee that they will not replace telephones and face-to-face meetings anytime soon. In other words, predictable quality of service is a major ingredient for interactive systems to be widely adopted in practice.

2.2 System Requirements

The user-level requirements above map into a wide range of requirements at the system level. Our group at the Real-Time and Multimedia Laboratory at the Department of Computer Science at Carnegie Mellon is addressing many of these requirements. Each of these requirements is listed below followed by a brief description of our effort along that aspect.

- **S1. QoS guarantees**: The predictability requirement U5 at the user-level requires that the system support quality-of-service guarantees within the infrastructure. We believe that as multimedia applications on desktops and internet appliances mature, users will come to expect smooth video frame changes, jitterless audio, and synchronized audio and video. It is to be noted that VCR/TV/satellite technologies have been delivering such guaranteed timing behavior for years. It seems rather illogical to expect anything less from computers at least when a user is willing to pay for it, particularly if virtual reality environments must seem real, or for applications such as tele-medicine and tele-surgery. Such QoS guarantees must be supported within the network as well as at the end-points. Since the end-points have computing resources, network interface, storage interfaces, and logically shared services such as filesystems and display systems, the end-points must be able to deal with multiple resource types.

  We have built a resource-centric kernel called resource kernel which understands, guarantees and enforces QoS requirements [14]. The resource kernel supports guaranteed access to multiple resources using a uniform resource specification model. A detailed overview of the resource kernel is presented later in this paper.

- **S2. Tradeoffs across multiple dimensions**: The connectivity requirement can sometimes impose conflicting requirements where accessibility and security requirements must be satisfied simultaneously with only a finite set of resources. Resource management techniques in real-time and multimedia systems are reasonably well-understood but tradeoffs at higher levels of abstraction are not. Many applications can provide better performance and quality of service given a larger share of system resources. For example, feedback control systems can provide better control with higher rates of sampling and control actuation. Multimedia systems using audio and video streams can provide better audio/video quality at higher resolution and very low latencies. Tracking applications can track objects at higher precision and accuracy if radar tracks are generated and processed at higher frequencies or if better, but more computationally intensive, algorithms are used. Real-time decision-making systems can receive, process and analyze larger amounts of data if more resources are made available. Interactive systems can provide excellent response times to users if more processing and I/O resources are made available.

We have developed an analytical QoS-based Resource Allocation Model (Q-RAM) to make tradeoffs across multiple resource types [13].

- **S3. Flexible Middleware services**: The communication capabilities created by connectivity mean that many persons may be able to communicate with each other. Support for many-to-many communications where a user can 'push' or 'pull' information to/from another must be available. Other services must support ease of evolution of deployed systems. Features supported would include the upgrading of software modules so that newer versions of modules can be released with little impact on the rest of the system. Fault containment will be supported in that failures will not be allowed to propagate. A direct implication of this feature is that spatial and temporal enforcement may often be desired.

We have developed a real-time publisher/subscriber communication model that supports many-to-many communications [12]. We have also developed two software abstractions specifically intended for the evolution of deployed systems [3]. An abstraction called a *replaceable unit* allows dynamic upgrading of a software subsystem or module even while the system is running. An abstraction called a *cell* allows a software module to define its boundaries as a fault-containment region within which external faults cannot propagate.

- **S4. Size and Scalability**: The cost requirement U2 implies that smaller memory footprints on potentially less powerful processors may be needed to make interactive appliances (U3) practical. Hence, smaller windowing systems with TV display interfaces must be supported. The connectivity requirement also imposes the need for configurable protocol stacks which are deployed only if needed. The size and cost requirements coupled with the range of interactive appliances offer a staggering number of configurations that must be supported. The underlying system infrastructure including the operating system kernel must be able to support multiple configurations ranging from single-processor configurations with no disk and memory management to multiprocessors with large disks and memory management support. However, the abstractions and application programming interfaces available to the developer must remain the same.

We are developing a functionally scalable kernel that can be used across a wide range of configurations while maintaining an identical programming interface across all configurations. We adopt the strategy that richer abstractions be supported fully in larger configurations may be supported with weaker semantics in smaller configurations but with the same interface.

- **S5. Distributed Object Architectures**: Object-oriented programming has proved its values and will be in use for a long time. With interconnected systems, architectures (such as CORBA and DCOM) for objects in distributed systems constitute a natural evolution. The underlying infrastructure would then enable interoperability with standard interfaces for utilities and applications.

  We have built a real-time CORBA system that allows the real-time requirements of clients to be encoded and transmitted to servers, which then honor these requirements using separate worker threads with appropriate scheduling attributes.

- **S6. Tools**: Tools are the key productivity ingredients for developers. Higher the integration and interoperability among tools, better is the productivity obtained by a developer. Such tools must include analysis and simulation tools, and integrated design environments.

  We have developed distributed analysis and simulation tools, visualization of distributed events from multiple targets and real-time visualization of resource consumption that work in conjunction with our resource kernel.

3　Resource Kernels

In this section, we present an overview and performance evaluation of resource-centric kernels we call resource kernels.

Resource kernels are aimed at dealing with the problem of OS resource management for real-time and multimedia systems where multiple activities with different timing constraints must be scheduled concurrently. Time on a particular resource is shared among its users and must be globally managed in real-time and multimedia systems. A resource kernel is meant for use in such systems and is defined to be one which provides timely, guaranteed and protected access to system resources. The resource kernel allows applications to specify only their resource demands leaving the kernel to satisfy those demands using hidden resource management schemes. This separation of resource specification from resource management allows OS-subsystem-specific customization by extending, optimizing or even replacing resource management schemes. As a result, this resource-centric approach can be implemented with any of several different resource management schemes.

The specific goals of a resource kernel are: applications must be able to explicitly state their timeliness requirements; the kernel must enforce maximum resource usage by applications; the kernel must support high utilization of system resources; and an application must be able to access different system resources simultaneously. Since the same application consumes a different amount of time on different platforms, the resource kernel must allow such resource consumption times to be portable across platforms, and to be automatically calibrated. Our resource management scheme is based on resource reservation [9] and satisfies these goals. The scheme is not only simple but captures a wide range of solutions developed by the real-time systems community over several years.

One potentially serious problem that *any* resource management scheme must address is that of allowing access to multiple resources simultaneously *and* in timely fashion, a problem which is known to be NP-complete [2]. This problem of simultaneous access to multiple resources can be practically addressed by resource decoupling and resolving critical resource dependencies immediately. The resource kernel's functionality and flexibility has been demonstrated in the context of multimedia applications which need processor cycles and/or disk bandwidth.

3.1 Real-Time Resource Management Principles

We summarize below three basic principles of priority-driven real-time scheduling below and we propose that these principles can be applied in multimedia systems with equal benefit.

- **P1. Discriminatory (prioritized) resource allocation**: Tasks, messages and bus transactions are assigned priorities and resources are allocated to the highest priority request. In general, as long as the total load on the resource is less than a threshold, all the requests are guaranteed to meet their deadlines [7]. Priority-driven scheduling allows a resource to be utilized at a rather high level even when the resource is loaded with requests with a wide range of timeliness constraints. If a resource is fairly under-utilized, priority assignment em may be an overkill. Put another way, if priority-based scheduling is not possible on a resource, under-utilization of the resource *may* be sufficient to meet the constraints.
- **P2. Bounded priority inversion**: Priority inversion, where a higher priority request is blocked by a lower priority activity, is unavoidable in many cases (such as non-preemptible bus transactions and finite size ATM cells). However, it is imperative that unbounded priority inversion be eliminated, as in the use of semaphores in a priority-driven system [11, 16]. Such durations of priority inversion must be bounded and if possible minimized. Priority inheritance protocols have also been extended to dynamic priority algorithms [1, 4]. This principle of bounded priority inversion also lends fundamental insight into how preemptible a multimedia/real-time operating system or its device drivers need to be.
- **P3. Bounded periodic framework**: A bounded periodic model is one which processes incoming requests periodically and only for a pre-defined bounded duration of time. The practical concern with priority-driven systems is that a runaway high-priority process can subsume all of a resource to the detriment of all other processes. Clearly, enforcement of the maximum

execution or transmission time of a processor or message would be very desirable [9]. Such a bounded periodic model allows aperiodic activities to be processed as incoming requests, and therefore can also be represented and manipulated in the same framework as periodic activities. This is the theme behind the notion of so-called *aperiodic servers* [5, 17]. Since periodic tasks are a degenerate class of aperiodics, aperiodic servers are also well-suited for use with periodic tasks. Our resource reservation model is designed to exploit this particular aspect.

3.2 The Resource Reservation Model

The resource kernel gets its name from its resource-centricity and its ability of the kernel to

- apply a uniform resource model for dynamic sharing of different resource types,
- take resource usage specifications from applications,
- guarantee resource allocations at admission time,
- schedule contending activities on a resource based on a well-defined scheme, and
- ensure timeliness by dynamically monitoring and enforcing actual resource usage.

The resource kernel attains these capabilities by reserving resources for applications requesting them, and tracking outstanding reservation allocations. Based on the timeliness requirements of reservations, the resource kernel prioritizes them, and executes a higher priority reservation before a lower priority reservation if both are eligible to execute.

Explicit Resource Parameters Our resource reservation model employs the following parameters: computation time C every T time-units for managing the net utilization of a resource, a deadline D for meeting timeliness requirements, a starting time S of the resource allocation, and L, the life-time of the resource allocation. We refer to these parameters, C, T, D, S and L as explicit parameters of our reservation model. The semantics are simple and are as follows. Each reservation will be allocated C units of usage time every T units of absolute time. These C units of usage time will be guaranteed to be available for consumption before D units of time after the begining of every periodic interval. The guarantees start at time S and terminate at time $S + L$.

Implicit Resource Parameter If various reservations were strictly independent and have no interactions, then the explicit resource parameters would suffice. However, shared resources like buffers, critical sections, windowing systems, filesystems, protocol stacks, etc. are unavoidable in practical systems. When reservations interact, the possibility of "priority inversion" arises. A complete family of priority inheritance protocols [11] is known to address this problem. All these protocols share a common parameter B referred to as the blocking factor. It represents the maximum (desirably bounded) time that a reservation instance must wait for lower priority reservations while executing. If its B is unbounded, a reservation cannot meet its deadline. The resource kernel, therefore, implicitly derives, tracks and enforces the implicit B parameter for each reservation in the system. Priority (or reservation) inheritance is applied when a reservation blocks, waiting for a lower priority reservation to release (say) a lock.

Reservation Type When a reservation uses up its allocation of C within an interval of T, it is said to be *depleted*. A reservation which is not depleted is said to be an *undepleted* reservation. At the end of the current interval T, the reservation will obtain a new quota of C and is said to be *replenished*. In our reservation model, the behavior of a reservation between depletion and replenishment can take one of three forms:

- *Hard reservations*: a hard reservation, on depletion, cannot be scheduled until it is replenished. While appearing constrained and very wasteful, we believe that this type of reservation can act as a powerful building block model for implementing "virtual" resources, automated calibration, etc.
- *Firm reservations*: a firm reservation, on depletion, can be scheduled for execution only if no other undepleted reservation or unreserved threads are ready to run.
- *Soft reservations*: a soft reservation, on depletion, can be scheduled for execution along with other unreserved threads and depleted reservations.

System Call	Description
Create	Create a reservation port
Request	Request resource on reservation port
Modify	Modify current reservation parameters
Notify	Set up notification ports for resource expiry messages.
Set Attribute	Set attributes of reservation (hard, firm or soft reservation)
Bind	Bind a thread to a reservation.
GetUsage	Get the usage on a reservation (accumulated or current).

Table 1. A subset of the reservation system call interface for each resource type.

System Call Interface to Reservations Our resource reservations are *first-class* entities in the resource kernel. Hence, operations on the reservations must be invoked using system calls. A select subset of the system call interface for the resource reservation model is given in Table 1. A reservation modification call allows an existing reservation to be upgraded or downgraded. If the modification fails, the previous reservation parameters will be restored. In other words, if an application cannot obtain higher resources because of system load, it will at least retain its previous allocation. A notification registration interface allows the application to register a port to which a message will be sent by the resource kernel each time the reservation is depleted. A binding interface allows a thread to be bound to a reservation. More than one thread can be bound to a reservation. Query interfaces allow an application to obtain the current list of reservations in the system, the recent usage history of those reservations (updated at their respective T boundaries), and the usage of a reservation so far in its current T interval.

3.3 Processor Resource Management

We shall now discuss and evaluate our implementation of the resource reservation model for the processor resource. The processor reservation scheme is evaluated by running different workloads with and without the use of reservations. All our experiments use a PC using a 120MHz Pentium processor with a 256KB cache and 16MB of RAM. We illustrate two basic points in these experiments:

1. the nature of the three types of reservations, and
2. the flexibility to upgrade and downgrade different reservations. dynamically.

Reservation Type	Initial Reservation				Upgraded to				Downgraded to			
	C_i (ms)	T_i (ms)	D_i (ms)	C_i/T_i	C_i (ms)	T_i (ms)	D_i ms)	C_i/T_i	C_i (ms)	T_i (ms)	D_i ms)	C_i/T_i
Hard	8	80	60	0.1	12	80	60	0.15	4	80	60	0.05
Firm	15	80	70	0.19	19	80	70	0.24	11	80	70	0.14
Soft	20	80	80	0.25	24	80	80	0.3	20	80	80	0.25

Table 2. The processor reservation parameters used for Figures 1 through 4.

In the experiments of Figures 1 through 3, three threads running *simultaneously* in infinite loops are bound to the three reservations listed in Table 2. In the experiment of part (a) of Figures 1 through 3, only these three threads are running. In contrast, in the experiment of part (b) of Figures 1 through 3, many

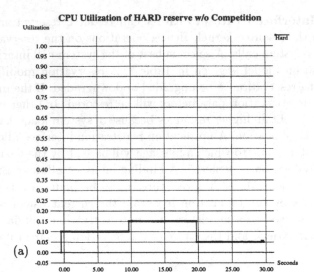

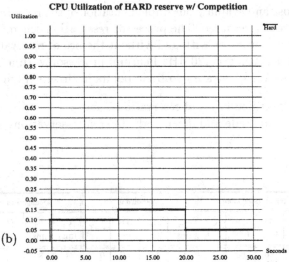

Fig. 1. Behavior of infinite loop threads using *hard* reserves (a) without unreserved competition, (b) with unreserved competition.

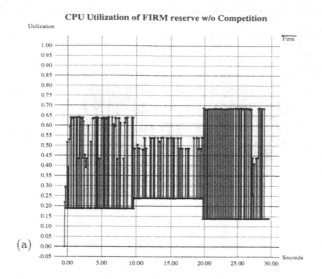

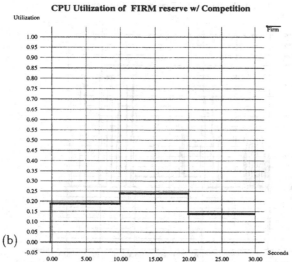

Fig. 2. Behavior of infinite loop threads using *firm* reserves (a) without unreserved competition, (b) with unreserved competition.

132

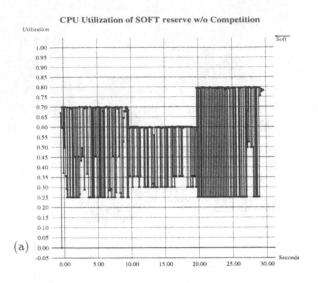

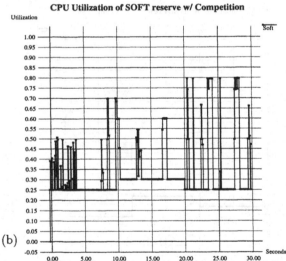

Fig. 3. Behavior of infinite loop threads using *soft* reserves (a) without unreserved competition, (b) with unreserved competition.

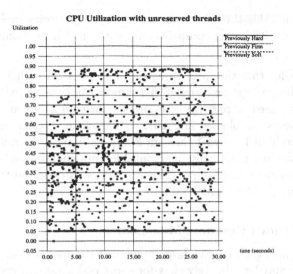

Fig. 4. Behavior of *unreserved* infinite loop threads *with* unreserved competition.

other unreserved threads in infinite loops are also running in the background and competing for the processor. The behavior of the three types of reservations is illustrated among these figures.

- The first reserved thread is bound to a hard reservation and should not consume more than its granted utilization which is initially 10raised to 15can be seen in (a), this thread, despite running in an infinite loop and the presence of many competing threads, obtains exactly this specified usage in *both* Figure 1-(a) and (b).
- The second reserved thread is bound to a firm reservation, and is allocated 19then downgraded to 142-(a), when there is no unreserved competition, this thread obtains a minimum of its granted utilization. In addition, it obtains "spare" idle cycles from the processor since there are no unreserved competing threads. However, in Figure 2-(b), when there is *always* unreserved competition, this thread obtains only its granted utilization. Thus, as intended, a firm reservation behaves like a hard reservation when the processor is *not* idle, and like a soft reservation when idle processor cycles are indeed available.
- The third reserved thread is bound to a soft reservation, which is allocated 25downgraded to 25cycles left behind by any threads with currently undepleted reserves. As a result, this thread obtains more cycles than its granted utilization in both Figures 3-(a) and 3-(b). It must be noted that the thread obtains a minimum of its granted utilization during all its instances. It can

also be seen that this thread obtains more processor cycles in Figure 3-(a) than in (b) since the former competes only with one thread bound to a firm reservation.

It must be recalled that the three threads of Figures 1 through 3 are running simultaneously. The completion times of this same set of threads (with the background competition used in part (a) of Figures 1 through 3) when run without using any reservations are plotted in Figure 4. The same threads which behave extremely predictably in Figures 1 through 3 now exhibit an enormous amount of seemingly random and practically unacceptable unpredictability. This demonstrates that our resource management scheme works as expected; without the scheme, resource usage is not predictable.

3.4   Disk Bandwidth Resource Management

Traditional real-time systems have largely avoided the use of disks. This is in part because they may be relatively slow for some real-time applications. However, many real-time applications can benefit from the use of disks to store and access real-time data (such as real-time database applications). Unfortunately, the use of a disk can (a) introduce unpredictable latencies, and even worse (b) the disk access requests must now be managed in conjunction with the processor scheduling. On the processor side, fixed priority algorithms allow a mix of tasks with different periodicity, and hence the disk subsystem must do too. Desktop multimedia systems also need to read from (or write to) disk storage relatively large volumes of video and audio data. In addition, these streams represent continuous media streams, and must therefore be processed by the disk subsystem in real-time. In other words, it would be practically very useful in practice if disk bandwidth can also be guaranteed in addition to managing processor cycles.

A simplistic disk scheduling algorithm with guaranteed access rates can be based on earliest deadline scheduling. An enhanced version exploits "slack" in the reservations to obtain a hybrid of earliest deadline scheduling and a traditional scan algorithm.

Filesystem Bandwidth Specification Our resource specification model for disk bandwidth is identical to that of processor cycles. In other words, a disk bandwidth reservation must specify a start time S, a processing time C to be obtained in every interval T before a deadline of D. The processing time C can be specified as # of disk blocks (as a portable specification) or in absolute disk bandwidth time in native-platform specification.

Admission Control Our simplest disk head scheduling scheme employs the earliest deadline scheduling algorithm [7]. The earliest deadline scheduling algorithm is an optimal scheduling algorithm for our scheduling model and can guarantee 100utilization under ideal conditions. In other words, a higher priority reservation must be able to preempt a lower priority preemption preemptively, and $D_i = T_i$. However, instantaneous preemptions are not possible in disk scheduling. An ongoing disk block access must complete before the next highest priority disk block access request can be issued. This introduces a blocking (priority inversion) factor of a single filesystem block access (as per [16]). Also, when $D_i < T_i$, the required earlier completion time (of $T_i - D_i$), must be added to the blocking factor. A detailed discussion of this admission control policy is beyond the scope of this paper and can be found in [10].

Performance Evaluation The capability of the disk bandwidth reservation scheme in our resource kernel to satisfy demands on disk bandwidth is illustrated in Figure 5. One disk bandwidth reservation of 12 disk blocks every 250 ms was requested in the presence of other unreserved accesses to the disk. As can be seen from the plot, this demand is satisfied by both the earliest deadline scheme and the just-in-time scheme; in fact, both lines are flat and coincide almost completely in the plot. However, the scan algorithm attempts to optimize disk throughput and pays for it by *not* delivering the needed throughput of 12 blocks every 250 ms. As a matter of fact, the bandwidth consumption varies widely.[3]

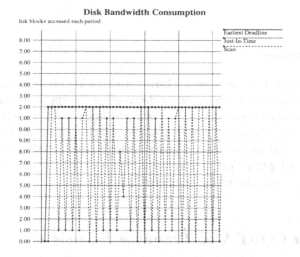

Fig. 5. Disk Bandwidth consumed (# of disk blocks read) by reserved thread. Our real-time schemes yield the (ideal) flat curves.

---

[3] The pattern is more dramatic in a zoomed out view with the x-axis ranging upto 400 periods, but the lines/points are not clearly legible in a relatively small black-and-white graph.

Requested throughput (KB/s)	Throughput with Scan (KB/s)	Throughput for Earliest Deadline Scheduling (KB/s)	Throughput Degradation (%)
1158.6	856.36	764.88	10.68%

Table 3. Scan and EDF real-time filesystem throughput comparison

We also imposed heavy disk traffic conditions and measured the throughput obtained under the scan and earliest deadline algorithms. This is shown in Table 3. As can be seen, the earliest deadline algorithm obtains only about 10price to be paid for the predictable and guaranteed disk bandwidth obtained by the earliest deadline algorithm (as shown in Figure 5).

Disk Throughput: The total disk bandwidth consumed in a similar experiment was 16,464 KBytes with the EDF and CPU reserve policy, and 17,750 KBytes with the Scan policy. This represents only a performance throughput loss of 7.25constraints and periodic bandwidth requirements are satisfied with the EDF/CPU reserves policy, while they are dramatically unsatisfied with the Scan policy.

3.5 Practical Issues

Other practical issues that our resource kernel approach address include the use of different reservations together, resource decoupling for applications which require the use of multiple resources, processor co-dependency (where the CPU must intercede in order to manage other resources such as disks and network interfaces), calibration of an application's requirements, the portability of resource specifications and adaptive QoS management. For a detailed description of this and other related issues, the reader is referred to [14].

4   Real-Time CORBA on Resource Kernels

In this section, we present a brief overview of CORBA and Real-Time CORBA followed by a summary of our Real-Time CORBA design and implementation.[4]

---

[4] This section is based on the Master's Thesis report of Min-Yu Yang and Ta-nien Lee, two students from our group.

4.1 CORBA

The Common Object Request Broker Architecture (CORBA) is an answer to the need for interoperability among the rapidly proliferating number of hardware and software products available today. It is a specification of an architecture and interface that allows an application to make request of objects (servers) in a transparent, independent manner, regardless of platform, operating system or locale considerations. The CORBA paradigm follows two existing methodologies, distributed client-server programming and object-oriented programming. The distributed computing is based on message-passing systems found in most UNIX systems. In CORBA, features of object-oriented programming such as encapsulation and inheritance are used. CORBA provides a flexible communication and activation substate for distributed heterogeneous object-oriented computing environments.

The construction of distributed real-time systems, however, is impeded by the lack of simple yet powerful programming models and the lack of making use of real-time software applications and components that have been implemented before. By integrating software components with real-time behavior, we believe that the time and difficulty of programming distributed real-time systems can be reduced. Moreover, with the capabilities and flexibility of CORBA serving to unify the infrastructure, we can focus more on providing solid solutions for higher-level real-time problems and worry less about how to make simple things work in our distributed heterogeneous real-time environments.

The CORBA specification includes three major components:

- **Interface Definition Language (IDL)** is a declarative language used to describe the interfaces that are called by client objects and provided by object implementations, including the signatures of all these impelementations. The IDL grammar is a subset of ANSI C++ with additional constructs to support the operation invocation mechanism.
- **Object Request Broker (ORB)** is the middleware that essentially enables seamless communication between a client and a server object. The ORB provides the mechanisms to find the object implementation for the request, to prepare the object implementation to receive the request, to communicate the data making up the request, to activate and deactivate objects and their implementations, and to generate and interpret object references.
- **Object Services** provided by CORBA includes a naming service for binding a name to an object, an event service for notification of named events, a concurrency control service for locking of resources to maintain consistency. A more complete list of the Object Services can be found in OMG's CORBA services: Common Object Services Specification.

In CORBA, essentially, all objects in the system talk to the common ORB interface, which is generated from the IDL defined by the application programmer. The underlying ORB is responsible for locating objects and transmitting messages and requests among those objects.

4.2 Real-Time CORBA

According to the OMG Real-Time SIG (Special Interest Group), the essence of
the definition of RT CORBA is:

> *"Real-Time CORBA deals with the expression and enforcement of real-time
> constraints on end-to-end execution in a CORBA system."*

This means that a Real-Time CORBA system must provide a way for client
objects to express its timing constraints on its requests, and that all CORBA
level software (including ORB and Object Services) must support enforcement of
the expressed timing constraints. This also means that the underlying operating
systems, along with the network that client and server use to communicate, must
support enforcement of real-time constraints. There are two main categories of
Real-Time CORBA requirements; one is with respect to the operating environment, the other is with regards to the CORBA run-time system. We summarize
some of these requirements next.

Operating Environment The operating environment must include the following:

- *Synchronized clocks.* To enforce timing constraints in a distributed system,
  the clocks on each node of the system should be synchronized to within a
  bounded skew of each other.
- *Use of real-time operating systems or resource kernels* that support priority-
  based or resource-demand-based queueing and scheduling where a higher
  priority task should be scheduled before a lower priority task.
- *Use of networks with QoS properties* that support guarantees and/or high-
  confidence estimates of latencies.

CORBA Run-Time System The run-time system components must include
the following:

- *Time type.* There should be CORBA types for timing constraints, time,
  scheduling information, and quality-of-service.
- *Transmittal of real-time and quality-of-service requirements with method invocation.* The standard should allow a client to specify its timing constraints
  either explicitly or implicitly in its method invocation. This information
  should be available to all the components involved in processing of the request in the system.
- *Consistent priority scheme.* There should be a globally consistent priority
  scheme in the system. The priorities of different tasks from different nodes
  should be set relative to each other so that their priorities make sense when
  they compete for system resources.
- *Priority queueing of all CORBA services.* All CORBA level software should
  use priority queueing to enforce the timing constraints in the end-to-end
  path of all requests.

– *Priority inheritance.* All CORBA level software should use priority inheritance if it queues one task while another is executing.
– *Real-time exceptions.* This allows the handling of violation of timing and quality-of-service constraints, including missed deadline and violated guarantee.

4.3 Overview of our RT-CORBA System

In our RT-CORBA system, whose implementation was led by Min-Yu Yang and Ta-nien Lee, we implemented part of the requirements listed above. We ported a CORBA compliant package named ILU from Xerox Parc onto the Real-Time Mach resource kernel. We also provided the means for transmitting the real-time constraints from client objects to server objects. In our real-time CORBA system, the timing constraints specified by the client are transmitted and enforced all the way to the execution of object implementation (server).

In order to invoke methods on a server, a client looks up a *Simple Binding Server* and gets the object handle of the server before it can request services. Hence, the very first thing a server object does before starting serving clients is to publish itself to the Simple Binding Server. Server objects are reactive. That is, a server object will not initiate any request. All the communications between the client and server starts at client's submitting requests. So, after initializing itself and registering itself with the Simple Binding Server, a server object will get into a "ready-serving" state and will wait for the connection requests from clients. If the server detects an interest in creating connection on a certain port, it then will create a direct connection between the client and itself as a dedicated communication channel. After that, it can provide services the client needs via this channel. One of the important things a server object will do during the initialization phase in order to provide real-time services is to create a real-time worker thread in charge of listening connection requests on a communication port.

In order to maintain the real-time properties of the client-side invocations, real-time attributes (such as priorities or resource requirements as specified in a resource kernel) are transmitted when a client object first connects to a server object. These attributes are used by the real-time worker thread created to service the client.

We have successfully implemented an audio-conferencing application which was originally written without objects and CORBA to use the RT-CORBA described above. While the overheads involved are higher than the native system as might be expected, our results indicate that the added overheads are quite acceptable.

5 Concluding Remarks

As processors become faster, networks become wider, and more people sign on to the internet, the demands and expectations imposed on this globally interconnected system will continue to grow. The complexity of these systems can and must only be tamed by the use of appropriate architectures comprising of interconnected structures and layers. Multimedia comprising of multiple data types including graphics, text, audio and video also forms the bulk of the current and expected workload. With audio and video exhibiting temporal requirements such as short end-to-end latencies and smooth playback, explicit resource management must be built into the infrastructure in order to satisfy these quality-of-service needs. At higher levels of abstraction, the limited resources in the system can be used for providing better application-level quality (such as better audio sampling rate), for providing security (e.g. by data encryption) or for enhancing end-to-end latencies (e.g. by processing smaller data chunks at a time). In other words, available resources must be traded off across multiple QoS dimensions. In order to interoperate with services available across the enterprise or across the internet, distributed object-based architectures such as CORBA must be used. These architectures, however, must continue to satisfy timing and other QoS requirements. In this paper, we have identified these and other requirements that arise at the user and system levels. Finally, we provided brief overviews of the various layers that are being addressed by the Real-Time and Multimedia Laboratory at Carnegie Mellon University. In particular, we have presented a resource-centric approach to building real-time kernels, and we call the resulting kernel a resource kernel. The resource kernel provides timely, guaranteed and protected access to resources.

Acknowledgements

The author would like to thank Kanaka Juvva, Anastasio Molano, Shuichi Oikawa, Min-Yu Yang and Ta-nien Lee for their contributions to the work described in this paper.

References

1. T. Baker. Stack-based scheduling of realtime processes. *Journal of Real-Time Systems*, 3(1):67–100, March 1991.
2. J. Blazewicz, W. Cellary, R. Slowinski and J. Weglarz. Scheduling under Resource Constraints – Deterministic Models. *Annals of Operations Research*, Volume 7, Baltzer Science Publishers, 1986.
3. M. J. Gagliardi, R. Rajkumar and L. Sha. Building Blocks for Designing Evolvable Real-Time Systems. In *The Proceedings of the IEEE Real-time Technology and Applications Symposium*, May 1996.
4. K. Jeffay. Scheduling sporadic tasks with shared resources in hard real-time systems. In *The Proceedings of the IEEE Real-time Technology and Applications Symposium*, December 1992.
5. J. P. Lehoczky and L. Sha. Performance of Real-Time Bus Scheduling Algorithms. *ACM Performance Evaluation Review*, Special Issue Vol. 14, No. 1, May 1986.
6. J. P. Lehoczky, L. Sha, and J. K. Strosnider. Enhancing aperiodic responsiveness in a hard real-time environment. *IEEE Real-Time System Symposium*, 1987.
7. C. L. Liu and Layland J. W. Scheduling algorithms for multiprogramming in a hard real time environment. *JACM*, 20 (1):46 – 61, 1973.

8. C. Lee, R. Rajkumar, and C. Mercer. Experiences with processor reservation and dynamic qos in real-time mach. *In the proceedings of Multimedia Japan 96*, April 1996.

9. C. W. Mercer, S. Savage, and H. Tokuda. Processor Capacity Reserves for Multimedia Operating Systems. In *Proceedings of the IEEE International Conference on Multimedia Computing and Systems*, May 1994.

10. A. Molano, K. Juvva and R. Rajkumar. Real-Time Filesystems: Guaranteeing Timing Constraints for Disk Accesses in RT-Mach. In *The Proceedings of the IEEE Real-Time Systems Symposium*, December 1997.

11. R. Rajkumar. *Synchronization in Real-Time Systems: A Priority Inheritance Approach*. Kluwer Academic Publishers, 1991. ISBN 0-7923-9211-6.

12. R. Rajkumar, M. J. Gagliardi and L. Sha. The Real-Time Publisher/Subscriber Communication for Inter-Process Communication in Distributed Real-Time Systems. In *The Proceedings of the IEEE Real-time Technology and Applications Symposium*, May 1995.

13. R. Rajkumar, C. Lee, J. P. Lehoczky and D. P. Siewiorek. A QoS-based Resource Allocation Model. In *The Proceedings of the IEEE Real-Time Systems Symposium*, December 1997.

14. R. Rajkumar, K. Juvva, A. Molano and S. Oikawa. Resource Kernels: A Resource-Centric Approach to Real-Time Systems. In *The Proceedings of the SPIE/ACM Conference on Multimedia Computing and Networking*, January 1998.

15. M. H. Klein, T. Ralya, B. Pollak, R. Obenza, and M. G. Harbour. *A Practitioner's Handbook for Real-Time Analysis: Guide to Rate-Monotonic Analysis for Real-Time Systems*. Kluwer Academic Publishers, 1993. ISBN 0-7923-9361-9.

16. L. Sha, R. Rajkumar, and J. P. Lehoczky. Priority Inheritance Protocols: An Approach to Real-Time Synchronization. *IEEE Transactions on Computers*, Pages 1175-1185, September 1990.

17. H. M. B. Sprunt, L. Sha, and J. P. Lehoczky. Aperiodic Task Scheduling on Hard Real-Time Systems. *Journal of Real-Time Systems*, June 1989.

Environment Server: A System Support for Adaptive Distributed Applications

Tatsuo Nakajima, Hiroyuki Aizu, Masaru Kobayashi, Kenji Shimamoto

Japan Advanced Institute of Science and Technology
1-1 Asahidai Tatsunokuchi Ishikawa 923-12 JAPAN

Abstract. Various new types of applications can be available in future computing environments such as mobile computing environments and ubiquitous computing environments. The applications may change our daily life dramatically since computers can be embedded in our daily necessaries such as televisions, microwaves, cameras, and air conditioners. In these environments, computing environments can be changed dramatically, and applications may be migrated among computers that have drastically different hardware configurations. Therefore, these applications should be adapted to various computing environments that may have dramatically different characteristics for their efficient executions, and the adaptation requires that the applications can access information about computing environments through a uniform interface.

In this paper, we propose an *environment server* that is important as a basic infrastructure for building adaptive applications for future computing environments. The environment server manages various information about computing environments in an integrated fashion, and applications can access these information through its well defined interface. This makes it possible to build adaptive applications with a systematic framework.

1 Introduction

Various new types of applications can be available in future computing environments such as mobile computing environments[FZ94, NH97] and ubiquitous computing environments[ACM93, Wei93]. The applications may change our daily life dramatically since computers can be embedded in our daily necessaries such as televisions, microwaves, cameras, and air conditioners.

In mobile computing environments, applications on mobile hosts can access servers on the Internet from anywhere at any time. Also, in ubiquitous computing environments where various physical objects become programmable by embedding computers into the objects.

For example, location information provided in mobile computing environments enables us to find the best and the nearest restaurant from us, or the best communication method with our friends according to our surrounding situations [SAW94, ST93]. Also, embedded computers into environments make it possible to monitor various information about us. For example, monitoring our behaviors helps us to extend human memory since a computer can give an advise to us by reminding us of our past behaviors[LF94]. The monitored information enables applications to change their behaviors according to user's behaviors. Therefore, applications can be executed efficiently since location information and monitored user's behaviors make the intension of users explicit.

Such advanced computing environments enable computers to help a user's work in various situations. Information provided to the users can be personalized according to the preferences and the current situations of the users. Also, various physical objects can be augmented by embedding computers into the objects, and the integration of physical reality and virtual reality provides us many powerful tools that we have not ever seen. For example, Harter proposed the active office that integrates physical objects in offices and information managed by computers in the office[HH94]. In a similar way, augmenting various environments enables us to build active homes, active universities, and active cities by embedding computers into various physical objects. One of the key issues realizing such wonderful future is to manage information about computing environments in an integrated fashion.

On the other hand, various computers that have different functionalities are connected to networks through various communication media by the dramatic improvement of hardware and network technologies. Also, mobile agents and mobile applications enable computer programs to be migrated among computers that have drastically different configurations[BRH94], and these applications may be executed on the computers that change their machine configurations dramatically[NH97, STW93, WB97].

In such environments, it is necessary to adapt applications to respective computing environments according to information about computing environments such as hardware configurations and system load. However, traditional operating systems provide information about computing environments in a very ad-hoc fashion since different types of information require to use different primitives to acquire the information. Also, such primitives are independently defined in respective computers. Thus, it is difficult to build adaptive applications in a systematic fashion.

In this paper, we propose an *environment server* that is important as a basic infrastructure for building adaptive applications that are important in future computing environments. The environment server manages various information about computing environments in an integrated fashion, and applications can access these information through its well defined interface. This makes it possible to build adaptive applications with a systematic framework. We implement a prototype of the environment server on Real-Time Mach[TNR90], and use it in several projects that develop adaptive software.

The remainder of this paper is structured as follows. In Sect. 2, we describe issues for building software that can be adapted to respective computing environments. Sect. 3 presents the design of the environment server, and we show its implementation in Sect. 4. In Sect. 5, we describe three projects that adopt the environment server for showing its effectiveness. Lastly, Sect. 6 summarizes the paper.

2 Adaptive Software

In this section, we describe some issues that are caused when building adaptive software. First, we describe what is information about computing environments. Next, we present why uniform primitives for acquiring information about computing environments are important for building adaptive software. Lastly, we show why a component that manages environmental information is important for building adaptive software in a systematic fashion.

2.1 Environmental Information

The recent progress of networks and distributed computing dramatically changes traditional computing environments. Distributed groupware systems need to acquire location information for sending data to the nearest computers of respective participants. Also, transmitting audio and video data requires to know the exact bandwidth, latency and error rate of currently used networks for ensuring the timing constraints of continuous media data. If such information about computing environments cannot be available, the performance of these applications can be degraded significantly, or these applications are inconvenient to use for naive users[HBBM96, ICPW97].

There are several types of information about computing environments that are required for adapting applications to respective computing environments. Some types of information are related to hardware resources. They include the bandwidth of networks, CPU power, battery capacity, and the characteristics of various devices. Also, other types of information are related to logical information such as location information and charges for communication media. These information is dynamically changed at every moment. We call such information about computing environments *environmental information*. We believe that such dynamically changed environmental information will become important for realizing mobile computing and ubiquitous computing environments, and applications should utilize such information for adapting their behaviors to respective situations.

2.2 Issues for Managing Environmental Information

As described in the previous section, it is necessary to exploit environmental information for adapting applications to respective computing environments. However, in traditional approaches, there is no uniform method for managing environmental information, since different systems provide different primitives for acquiring the information. Also, different types of resources may require different primitives for managing their information. Therefore, adding a new type of environmental information may require to change the structure of an application. This may require to modify a large part of the code of the application. Thus, it is difficult to extend the application for taking into account new environments in an incremental way. Also, if there is no uniform primitive for managing environmental information, it may be necessary to change the application's code for dealing with the environmental information according to its properties. Therefore, in this case, it is difficult to build adaptive applications systematically.

Thus, a system component that provides uniform primitives for managing environmental information is required for building adaptive applications in a systematic way. The component manages the environmental information in a uniform fashion, and it should provide the following three types of primitives.

- A primitive for acquiring environmental information.
- A primitive for updating environmental information.
- A primitive for notifying an event when environmental information is changed.

The primitives enable applications to deal with different types of information such as information about various types of devices, location information, and the current CPU utilization of an application in a uniform fashion. The component that manages environmental information in a systematic way makes it easy to add a new type of environmental information in the component. The component requires to change a small part of the code of an adaptive application when adding a new code for managing the new environmental information. Therefore, it is possible that adaptive applications are built by using a systematic framework.

2.3 Adaptive Applications and Environmental Information

This section describes the relationship between the component that manages environmental information and adaptive applications. The adaptive applications is required to make the tradeoff between several metrics that are not satisfied simultaneously explicit. A system determines which metric is currently important for satisfying a user's requirements, and resolves the conflicts between the metrics by using environmental information. For example, it is necessary to take into account the tradeoff between the consistency of data and the cost of communication in mobile computing environments. If the consistency of data is more important, the communication cost should be sacrificed. On the other hand, if a user requires to reduce the communication cost, the consistency of data may be sacrificed. Applications can determine the appropriate choices of the metrics according to environmental information and the requirements of users.

Applications can satisfy a user's requirements in a better way, if the applications can access context information such as the location of users and a user's recent behaviors. For example, a user can print out his document to the nearest printer if the location information of the user can be available. Also, a user can select the best communication method from a video conference system, a voice mail, a text mail, an internet telephone, and a traditional public telephone for communicating with his fiends. Monitoring user's behaviors enables us to personalize the system by leaning the user's daily habits.

3 Design of Environment Server

This section describes the *environment server* that manages environmental information in a uniform way. First, we describe the overview of the environment server. Next, we present how the environment server represents environmental information. Lastly, we show the interface provided by the environment server.

3.1 Overview of Environment Server

The *environment server* contains a database that manages environmental information in a uniform fashion. The interface of the environment server is well

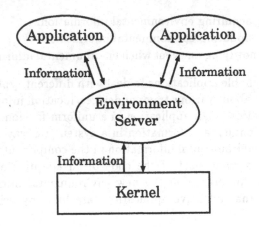

Fig. 1. Environment Server

defined, and an application can access environmental information by using its uniform interface as shown in Fig. 1.

In the environment server, respective environmental information is represented as objects, and the template of each object is represented as a class. The class contains a set of pairs of attribute names and attribute values, and a new class can inherit the attributes of parent classes. Also, the name space for the objects is defined using a hierarchical name space. In the name space, naming and query are integrated for making the query for attributes easy.

3.2 Representation of Environmental Information

It is preferable to group similar environmental information in order that users can deal with the environmental information easily, since the environment server needs to manage various types of information. The environment server enables us to define respective environmental information as hierarchically defined classes for managing environmental information without inconsistencies among them. As shown in Fig. 2, classes are managed in a hierarchical fashion according to the properties of information. One of unique features of our approach is to define three functions as an attribute value. The first function is called *acquire function* that is used for acquiring actual attribute values. The second function is called *update function* that is used for updating attribute values. The last function is called *initialize function* that is used for initializing attribute values. The function also starts a daemon for monitoring environmental information managed by other components and concerned with the attribute that is initialized by the function.

```
class Class Name: Super Class Name 1, .....
     (Attribute Name 1   (acquire func 1, update func 1, initialize func 1))
     (Attribute Name 2   (acquire func 2, update func 2, initialize func 2))
     (Attribute Name 3   (acquire func 3, update func 3, initialize func 3))
```

In the environment server, a new class can be defined by inheriting several classes. Since only attribute names can be inherited from super classes, a new class should define acquire functions, update functions and initialize functions for all inherited attributes respectively. The approach can prevent many problems caused by the traditional multiple inheritance schemes.

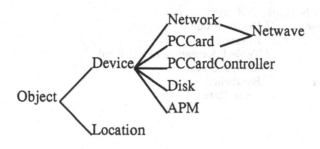

Fig. 2. Class Hierarchy for Environmental Information

Fig. 3 shows the definition of the Netwave class. The Netwave class inherits the PCCard class, then the PCCard class inherits the Network class. The Tuple attribute is inherited from the PCCard class, and the MACaddress, Bandwidth, ErrorRate attributes are inherited from the Network class. In the figure, the definition of acquire functions, update functions, and initialize functions are omitted, but these functions should be defined for all attributes inherited from the super classes.

Fig. 4 shows an object that is an instance of the Netwave class. These attribute values can be retrieved by using respective acquire functions for respective attributes. Also, the values can be changed by using update functions.

3.3 Name Space and Query

The objects representing environmental information in the environment server have a hierarchical name as shown in Fig. 5. The name space is drastically different from traditional hierarchical name spaces since the name space is integrated with queries for environmental information. In our scheme, each component in the hierarchical name space is the instance name of an object.

Fig. 5 depicts five objects, Device, PCslot, Netwave, EtherLink, and SunDisk. These objects are instances created by the classes defined in Fig. 3. The example contains two network device cards: Netwave and EtherLink, and a flash memory card: SunDisk, and these devices are inserted in PC card slots. If these devices are removed, the name of the object is disappeared under the lower name space of PCslot. Also, when the device is inserted again, the name of the object is appeared under the lower name space of PCslot. When an application needs to retrieve an attribute of the Netwave object, the name "/Device/PCslot/Netwave " indicates the object.

In the name space managed by the environment server, a node in the name space is a normal object that has one or more attributes. A node object aggregates all attributes of objects that are located below the node object in the name

```
class Network : device
     MACAddress       // MAC Address
     Bandwidth        // Bandwidth
     ErrorRate        // Error Rate

class PCCard : device
     Tuple            // Tuple Information of PC Card

class Netwave : Network, PCCard
     DeviceName       // Device Name
     Type             // Device Type
     Tuple            // Tuple Information of PC Card
     MACAddress       // MAC Address
     Bandwidth        // Bandwidth
     ErrorRate        // Error Rate
```

Fig. 3. Class Netwave

```
MyNetwave : class Netwave
     DeviceName       xnw0
     Type             "Xircom Netwave"
     Bandwidth        1Mbps
     MacAddress       xx-xx-xx-xx-xx-xx-xx-xx
     Tuple            "xxxxx"
     Error Rate       xx
```

Fig. 4. Netwave Object

space when acquiring attributes of the objects. In the example shown in Fig. 5, a node object whose name is "/Device/PCslot" aggregates all attributes of three objects: Netwave, EtherLink, and SunDisk. If an application retrieves the "size" attribute for "/Device/PCslot", the attribute value of the "size" attribute of the SunDisk object is returned.

However, the naming scheme that supports the aggregation of attributes needs to take into account a case when different aggregated objects have the same attributes. In this case, multiple attribute values may be returned. For example, when the "bandwidth" attribute is retrieved for "/Device/PCslot", two values are returned. The first one is returned from the Netwave object, and the second one is returned from the EtherLink object.

Therefore, the environment server allows an application to specify "Query-Type" that indicates how multiple attribute values are returned. Currently, an application can select one type from the following four choices. The first choice is *All*. When the choice is selected, all attribute values are returned. The second choice is *Best*. In this case, the best choice is returned. The third choice is *Worst*. The worst choice is returned when the choice is selected. The last choice is *Any*. One of multiple attribute values is selected randomly, and the selected attribute is returned to an application.

We show an example that specifies "QueryType" by using Fig. 5. The exam-

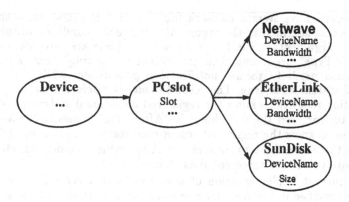

Fig. 5. Name Space and Query

ple queries the "bandwidth" attribute for /Device/PCslot. The returned value is enclosed by a parenthesis. The first element in the parenthesis is the object name that returns the attribute, and the second element is a pair of an attribute name and an attribute value. When *All* is specified, multiple values are enclosed by a square bracket.

Best: (EtherLink (Bandwidth 10Mbps))
Worst: (Netwave (Bandwidth 1Mbps))
Any: (Netwave (Bandwidth 1Mbps)) or (EtherLink (Bandwidth 10Mbps))
All: [(Netwave (Bandwidth 1Mbps)) (EtherLink (Bandwidth 10Mbps))]

If attribute values cannot be compared with each other, "Best" and "Worst" cannot be specified in the "QueryType" argument. If an application specifies "Best" and "Worst" as "QueryType" for such attributes, an error value will be returned.

3.4   Interface of Environmental Information

Applications can access the environment server through a uniform interface. In the primitives, "AttrName@ObjectName" is used as a syntax for accessing environmental information, where "AttrName" is an attribute name that is required to access the attribute, and "ObjectName" is an object that is represented as a hierarchical name. If the object name indicates a node in the hierarchical name space, the object name aggregates the attributes of objects below the node object in a hierarchical name space as described in the previous section.

The environment server provides the following three primitives for accessing environmental information.

error = **Get**(Attribute Name, QueryType, &Attribute Value);
error = **Put**(Attribute Name, Attribute Value);
error = **Register**(Conditional Statement, Callback Handler, Notification Type);

The *Get primitive* retrieves an attribute value by calling an acquire function corresponding to "AttrName@ObjectName". The *Put primitive* updates an attribute value by calling an update function of the specified attribute. The

Register primitive registers a callback function that is called when the conditional statement specified in the argument satisfies the condition of the "NotificationType" argument. In the *Register primitive*, there are three choices for the "NotificationType" argument. The first choice is "During" that is used when an application needs to receive notifications periodically while the registered conditional statement is true. The second choice is "Before" that is used when an application requires to know the registered conditional statement is changed from false to true, and the last choice is "After" that is used when an application requires to know the registered conditional statement is changed from true to false. In the above three primitives, attribute names, conditional statements, and attribute values are represented as strings.

In the current implementation of the environment server, the conditional statements specified in the *Register primitive* can use attribute names, standard data types such as integer and strings, conditional operators such as <, <=, >, >=, ==, and !=, logical operators such as & and ||.

The following shows some examples of conditional statements that can be specified in the *Register primitive*.

(1) [Bandwidth@/Device/PCslot/Netwave] < 1Mbps
(2) [Bandwidth@/Device/PCslot] < 1Mbps
(3) [BatteryCapacity@/Device/APM] < 10
(4) [Power@/Device/APM] == Battery

The conditional statement (1) defines the condition indicating that the bandwidth of Netwave is less than 1 Mbps. The conditional statement (2) means that the bandwidth of a network device currently inserted in PC card slots is less than 1 Mbps. The conditional statement (3) shows the condition that the capacity of a remaining battery is less than 10 %. The last conditional statement (4) indicates that the computer is currently driven by a battery.

If we allow conditional statements to represent the occurrence of an event, it is difficult to define the semantics of the & operator since the operator needs to take into account a condition that two events occur simultaneously in distributed systems, since it is difficult to know the exact times. Therefore, the environment server does not allow us to define the occurrence of an event in conditional statements. This means that the conditional statements represent all attribute values as states. Thus, for example, the insertion of a PC Card to a PC card slot is represented as "[slots@/Device/PCCard] ! = empty" and the "NotificationType " argument should be specified as "Before". A notification is delivered to an application when the environment server detects that "[slots@/Device/PCCard] ! = empty" changes from false to true.

4　Implementation of Environment Server

This section describes the implementation of the environment server. First, we describe the components contained in the environment server. Next, we present the attribute database storing the attributes of all objects in the environment server, and describe how the attributes are acquired and updated. Lastly, we describe a mechanism for notifying the changes of attributes to applications.

4.1 Structure of Environment Server

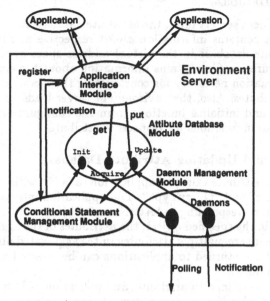

Fig. 6. Structure of Environment Server

Fig. 6 shows the structure of the environment server. The current version of environment server is implemented on Real-Time Mach[TNR90][1], and it consists of the following four components.

(1) **Application Interface Module**

The module manages the three primitives provided by the environment server, and forwards the requests from applications to other components.

(2) **Attribute Database Module**

The module manages attribute names and values in the attribute database that are stored in the memory space of the environment server. Each attribute contains an attribute name, an initialize function, an acquire function, and an update function for managing the attribute.

(3) **Conditional Statement Management Module**

The module manages conditional statements registered by the *Register* primitive. If the registered conditional statement satisfies the condition specified in the "NotificationType" argument, a notification is delivered to the application that registers the conditional statement.

(4) **Daemon Management Module**

The module manages daemons that monitor computing environments periodically, or that process events received from other components. The daemons are started in initialize functions as a new thread. They poll other components such as Real-Time Mach kernel or other components periodically with various protocols such as SNMP for acquiring environmental information, or wait for receiving events from other components.

---

[1] Since Real-Time Mach enables applications to acquire environmental information related to hardware resources, the operating system is suitable for building the environment server.

4.2 Attribute Database

When the environment server starts, the attribute database module reads a configuration file that contains information about respective attributes, and constructs the attribute database in the virtual address space of the environment server. The configuration file contains information about the class hierarchy of objects, and information necessary for constructing the hierarchical name space for respective attributes. Also, the environment server loads acquire functions, update functions, and initialize functions from the configuration file, and executes the initialization functions for respective attributes.

4.3 Acquiring and Updating Attribute Database

When acquiring an attribute value, an application calls *Get* with argument "Attr-Name@ObjectName" and "QueryType". The application interface module calls an acquire function corresponding to "AttrName@ObjectName". If the attribute cannot be defined in the specified object, the attributes of the aggregated objects are examined. If there are multiple attributes in the aggregated objects, attribute values that should be returned to applications can be selected according to the "QueryType" argument.

When we want to change an attribute, an application calls the *Put primitive* with "AttrName@ObjectName" and a new attribute value as arguments. The primitive calls an update function corresponding to "AttrName@ObjectName". If the attribute cannot be found in the specified object, an error is returned to an application.

4.4 Management of Conditional Statements

If an application requires to receive a notification when an attribute value is changed, the application calls the *Register primitive* with a conditional statement, a callback handler, and the "NotificationType" as arguments. When the registered conditional statement is satisfied, the callback handler specified in the argument is called. Conditional statements are stored in the conditional statement management module with its corresponding callback handlers. The module stores the conditional statements in a hash table, and a conditional statement can be searched by using an object name and an attribute name included in the conditional statement as keys for the hash table.

When one of daemons managed by the daemon management module detects a change of environmental information, an update function corresponding to the environment information is called. The function can also be called when an application calls the *Put primitive*. In this case, an object name and a modified attribute name are passed to the conditional statement management module, and the module searches all conditional statements that contain the object name and the attribute name by using the hash table. All conditional statements that are searched by using the hash table are examined, and if some of the statements satisfies the condition specified in the "NotificationType" argument, corresponding callback handlers are called in the applications that register the conditional statements. If the "NotificationType" argument is specified as "Before", the callback handler is called, when the conditional statement changes from false to true. When the "NotificationType" argument is "After", the callback handler is called when the condition statement changes from true to false. Also, when the "NotificationType" argument is specified as "During", the callback handler is called periodically, while the conditional statement is true. In this case, a thread is created when the conditional statement becomes true, and the thread invokes the callback handler periodically until the conditional statement will become false. When the statement becomes false, the thread is destroyed.

5 Example Scenarios

In this section, we describe three projects that adopt the environment server. In the first project, we are working on a toolkit for building adaptive mobile applications. Also, we are working on a continuous media toolkit supporting application mobility in the second project. In the last project, we are developing the mobile IP system that can select a suitable data link network according to computing environments.

5.1 Adaptive Mobile Applications

In the first project, we propose a framework for building adaptive mobile applications. In the framework[HKN96, HN97, NH97], a mobile application is constructed by composing small objects as a graph. We call the graph *object graph*, and the configuration of the object graph is changed if there is a change in computing environments.

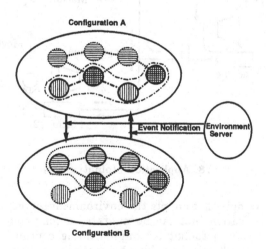

Fig. 7. Adaptive Mobile Applications

Fig. 7 shows an example of an adaptive mobile application that adopts the object graph framework. In this example, a mobile application has the configuration A when the application is executed in a normal mode. Now, let us assume that the environment server delivers a notification indicating that the application should be executed in an urgent mode. If the mobile application receives the notification, it changes the configuration from A to B. Examples of the urgent mode are cases when the capacity of a battery becomes very low, or a mobile host is disconnected from networks since a cheap communication media cannot be available. When the environment server delivers a notification again the computing environment is recovered to the normal mode, and the application receiving the notification recovers the configuration from B to A.

The environment server enables an application to use a uniform primitive for receiving notifications when there is a change in computing environments. If such a primitive cannot be available, the application needs to prepare respective daemons for monitoring respective environmental information. Also, the application may require to implement respective primitives for examining the conditions of respective environmental information. This makes the structure of the application complex, and it is difficult to maintain the application if it needs to be extended for taking into account a new computing environment. However, the environment server enables applications not to take into account the management of environmental information. Applications can focus on codes for managing the adaptations to respective computing environments. This improves the maintainability and the extensibility of applications significantly since the structure of the applications becomes very clear.

5.2 Application Mobility Support

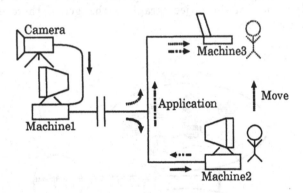

Fig. 8. Application Mobility Support

As a second example that adopts the environment server, we describe a continuous media application that can be migrated among computers. Our group is working on building a toolkit for implementing continuous media applications that support application mobility by extending continuous media toolkit CMT[Naka97]. Fig. 8 shows an application that a video stream captured by a camera displays to the nearest computer from a user. In the application, a computer that displays the video stream is changed according to the location of the user. In the example, we assume that a user is seated before the computer 2 currently. In this case, the video stream is captured on the computer 1 is delivered to the computer 2. The application on the computer 2 receives the video stream and displays it on a window. Now, let us assume that the user moves to near the computer 3. In this case, it is preferable to display the video stream on the computer 3 by moving the application that displays the video stream from the computer 2 to the computer 3.

However, a problem occurs if the application does not take into account the difference of machine configurations between the computer 2 and 3. For example, the display of the computer 3 may be smaller than one of the computer 2. If the difference is not taken into account, the automatic movement of applications is not practical. Also, we can assume that the computer 2 may have a color display, but the computer 3 has a monochrome display. In this case, the application needs to take into account the characteristics of display devices on the two computers. The environment server enables the application to adapt to computing environments by using the environmental information. For example, if an application can know the characteristics of a display device, the application can display a video stream in a suitable fashion.

Our continuous media toolkit enables an application to be constructed by connecting several modules. Thus, the application can be adapted to a different computing environment by changing the connectivity between modules. In other words, when an application is moved to a new computer, the application acquires environmental information such as the characteristics of a display device, and it changes the connectivity between modules for adapting to the new computing environment. Also, if the media data that are buffered in the computer 2 are not forwarded to the computer 3 when the application is moved, the quality of the video stream may be degraded significantly. Therefore, the buffered data should be forwarded to the computer 3 from the computer 2. However, the bandwidth between the computer 2 and the computer 3 may not be enough to transmit the buffered data without violating the timing constraints of the video stream. If the application acquires information about the effective bandwidth between two computers, the application can filter the media data according to the bandwidth between the two computers. Thus, the degradation of the quality of the video stream can become the minimum.

5.3 Extended Mobile IP System

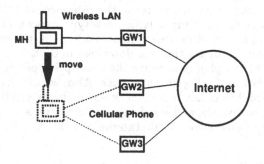

Fig. 9. Extended Mobile IP System

In the last example, we are working on building the mobile IP system that can select a suitable way for communicating with hosts on the Internet according to computing environments. The environment server enables us to extend the traditional mobile IP system in the following three points.

The first point is that a suitable data link network can be used for connecting to the Internet. In Fig. 9, mobile host MH is currently connected to GW_1, and GW_1 is the current foreign agent of MH. All packets from other hosts to MH are forwarded to GW_1. Now, MH goes out from the range of the wireless LAN, and the connectivity between MH and GW_1 is lost. MH accesses the environment server, and acquires information about networks that MH can be used currently. Let us assume that the environment server returns a cellular phone as the current best network. Then, a handoff occurs, and GW_2 is selected as a new foreign agent.

In the second point, the environment server selects the nearest foreign agent by using the current location of MH when MH uses a wireless phone as a current data link network. The environment server manages location information of MH by using GPS[2]. The information enables our system to select an access point with the cheapest cost.

In the last point, our mobile IP system customizes the TCP/IP protocol on wireless networks by using information from the environment server. In Fig. 9, an application uses TCP for connecting to a server on the Internet. The current implementation of TCP may cause several problems on low bandwidth networks, and networks with high error rate. Our system dynamically extends TCP by inserting a packet recovery algorithm which uses a selective acknowledgment between MH and GW_1 by snooping all TCP packets at GW_1[BSAK95], if the error rate of the wireless LAN becomes high. Also, since the bandwidth between MH and GW_2 is low, our system dynamically changes the implementation of TCP by incorporating the TCP header compression algorithm[DENP96], if GW_2 is selected as a foreign agent. Then, GW_2 compresses the headers of all packets, when the destination address of the packets is MH.

6 Conclusion and Future Work

In this paper, we described the *environment server* that manages environmental information in an integrated fashion. The environment server is a basic infrastructure for building adaptive applications systematically, and the adaptive applications are basic components for realizing mobile computing environments and ubiquitous computing environments. The paper described the representation and the naming of environmental information, the interface, and the implementation of the environment server. Currently, a prototype version of the environment server is being implemented on Real-Time Mach. Also, the environment server is used in the several projects that are described in Sect. 5.

In future, we have a plan to improve the description power of the conditional statements specified in the *Register primitive*. Also, we will investigate the order for invoking callback handler functions when multiple conditional statements are satisfied simultaneously, and the delay for delivering a notification when the condition of a registered conditional statement is satisfied should be taken into account.

References

[ACM93] "Special Issue on Computer-Augmented Environment", Communications of the ACM, Vol.36, No.7, 1993.

[BSAK95] H. Balakrishnan, S. Seshan, E. Amir, and R. H. Katz, "Improving TCP/IP Performance over Wireless Networks", In Proceedings of the 1st ACM Conference on Mobile Computing and Networking, ACM, 1995.

[BRH94] F.Bennett, T.Richardson, A.Harter, "Teleporting - Making Applications Mobile", In Proceedings of Workshop on Mobile Computing Systems and Applications, IEEE, 1994.

---

[2] We have a plan to use the location system provided by PHS in future.

[DENP96] M. Degermark, M. Engan, B. Nordgren, and S. Pink, "Low-Loss TCP/IP Header Compression for Wireless Networks", In Proceedings of the 2nd Conference on Mobile Computing and Networking, ACM, 1996.

[FZ94] G.H.Forman and J.Zahorjan:, "The Challenges of Mobile Computing", IEEE Computer, Vol.27, No.4, 1994.

[HH94] A.Harter, and A.Hopper, "A Distributed Location System for the Active Office ", IEEE Network, Jan/Feb 1994.

[HBBM96] R. Hayton, J. Bacon, J. Bates and K. Moody, "Using Events to Build Large Scale Distributed Applications", In Proceedings of SIGOPS European Workshop '96, 1996.

[HKN96] Akihiro Hokimoto, Kuniaki Kurihara, Tatsuo Nakajima, "An Approach for Constructing Mobile Applications using Service Proxies", In Proceedings of the 16th International Conference on Distributed Computing Systems, May, 1996.

[HN97] A.Hokimoto, T.Nakajima, "Robust Host Mobility Supports for Adaptive Mobile Applications", In Proceedings of the International Conference on World Wide Computing and its Applications'97, 1997.

[ICPW97] J. Inouye, S. Cen, C. Pu, and J. Walpole, "System Support for Mobile Multimedia Applications", In Proceedings of 7th Workshop on Network and Operating System Supports for Digital Audio and Video, 1997.

[IU97] H. Ishii, and B. Ullmer, "Tangible Bits: Towards Seamless Interfaces between People, Bits, and Atoms", In Proceedings of CHI'97, ACM, March, 1997.

[LF94] M.Lamming and M.Flynn, "Forget-me-not: Intimate Computing in Support of Human Memory", Rank Xerox, Technical Report EPC-1994-103, 1994.

[NH97] T. Nakajima, and A. Hokimoto, "Adaptive Continuous Media Applications in Mobile Computing Environments", In Proceedings of the international Conference of Multimedia Computing and Systems, 1997.

[Naka97] T. Nakajima, "A Toolkit for building Continuous Media Applications", In Proceeding of International Workshop on Real-Time Computing, Systems, and Applications, 1997.

[Naka98] T.Nakajima, "A Framework for building Adaptive Software", working memo, 1998.

[STW93] B. N. Schilit, M. M. Theimer, and B. B. Welch: "Customizing mobile applications", In *Proceedings of the 1st USENIX Symposium on Mobile & Location-Independent Computing*, August, 1993.

[SAW94] B.Schilit, N.Adams, R.Want, "Context-Aware Computing Applications", In Proceedings of Workshop on Mobile Computing Systems and Applications, IEEE, 1994.

[ST93] M.Spreitzer, and M.Theimer, "Providing Location Information in a Ubiquitous Computing Environment", In Proceedings of 14th ACM Symposium on Operating System Principles, 1993.

[TNR90] H.Tokuda, T.Nakajima, P.Rao, "Real-Time Mach: Towards a Predictable Real-Time System", In Proceedings of the USENIX Mach Workshop, October, 1990.

[Wei93] M.Weiser, "Some Computer Science Issues in Ubiquitous Computing", Communication of the ACM, Vol.36, No.7, 1993.

[WB97] G. Welling and B. R. Badrinath: "A Framework for Environment Aware Mobile Applications", In *Proceedings of the 17th International Conference on Distributed Computing*, Baltimore, Maryland, May, 1997.

Compiler-Generated Protection Domains and a Light Weight Runtime Protection Technique

Yo Furukawa and Etsuya Shibayama

Department of Mathematical and Computing Sciences
Tokyo Institute of Technology
2-12-1 Ohokayama Meguro Tokyo, Japan
{furukawa,etsuya}@is.titech.ac.jp

Abstract. Distributed applications consisting of various sorts of network loaded components potentially require fine-grained protection domains. Software based protection techniques allow cost effective fine-grained protection for those components. However, fine-grained protection is complicated for both the programmers and the runtime systems. We propose a compiler-based technique which automatically generates optimized protection domains from a simple description of protection policies. The *domain merging* technique is used to reduce the numbers of protection domains and cross domain calls. We also introduce a light weight protection mechanism for Java, based upon a code translation technique that can support low cost cross domain calls. Components are protected by the dynamic generated protection codes, so programmers do not have to write any protection codes. Most of the protection domains are statically resolved and only unresolved cross domain calls are checked by the dynamic checking mechanism.

1 Introduction

In recent, component technᴏᴌᴏgᴌᴇ᪐ ᴊuch as JavaBeans, DCOM and CORBA are used as infrastructures for distributed applications. We assume distributed applications here to consist of various network loaded components, each of which has its own birthplace, authority, privileges and directions of use. In addition to the distributed protection such as authentication mechanisms, local protection supports for those applications are essential. Consider the case of downloading or passing distributed components via the Internet. If some of these components were placed and executed in the same protection domain of the local system, they may be influenced by malicious components or unexpected interactions. The program user must be guaranteed that downloading components would never destroy or be the security flaws of their local machines. Besides, the program providers wish their components to work as they intended and not to be interfered by the other components from some other vendors.

Unfortunately, most of the existing systems don't have suitable solutions for this situation. Their mechanisms for protection are inefficient or inflexible. Protection domains in traditional operating systems are coarse-grained and thus inefficient to protect fine-grained distributed components with frequent interactions. In the distributed component systems with protection and frequent cross-domain calls, it is mostly important to reduce the cost per call and the number of calls themselves.

Java [GJS96] and its runtime system JavaVM provide a mechanism to protect the local systems from remote codes. They prevent the illegal memory access by the type safe language and the code verifier in the dynamic loading *ClassLoader*. By this mechanism and a centralized *SecurityManager*, all the potentially dangerous method calls from remote codes such as unlimited network accesses are intercepted and checked if the access is valid according to the local policy. However, this sand-box policy restricts all the downloaded components in a uniform way, which prevents the vendors providing 'real world' applications with full file system or network access.

Here, in this paper, we show a strategy to address this issue. First, we show the way to construct the protection domains automatically by mixing the cross-reference information of objects and the developer's and user's policy for their usage. Then, our static domain compiler merges these protection domains to reduce the cross-domain calls. We think that *protection domain merging* is one of the key techniques in the distributed environments. At second, we introduce a light weight runtime protection technique to support fine-grained and flexible protection. Original source codes don't have to be modified because protection codes are automatically inserted by our just-in-time domain compiler in the dynamic loader. The just-in-time compiler is also employed for the final optimization of the protection domain merging. To keep the problem simple and clear, we will present our system as an extension of Java, which replaces JavaVM's SecurityManager. These techniques are applicable to the dynamic loading systems which have multiple protection domains, including extensible softwares with plug-in features, mobile agent based systems, customizable and extensible system softwares.

The rest of this paper is structured as follows: Section 2 describes the generating flow of protection domains and the static merging of protection domains. Section 3 introduces our runtime techniques. Section 4 compares related works and Sect. 5 concludes our work.

2   Compiler-Generated Protection Domains

Two major costs in fine-grained protected systems are protection domain generation cost and runtime protecting cost. In this section, we present the domain generation and incremental merging techniques focusing on the local protection for the distributed component systems.

2.1   Software Based Extensible Protection

In distributed component systems, an application consists of multiple components with different sources and policies, and has multiple protection domains inside by nature. To support such an application, there are following demands on protection:

- **Efficient cross domain call**
  Frequent interactions between components need cost effective implementation of cross domain calls.
- **Customizable protection domain**
  Protection domain structures are application dependent. Resources to be protected should be decided by the policies of service providers and local machine users.

There are some implementations of language based protection, which are efficient than the traditional operating system level protection. SPIN's kernel extension mechanism [BS+95] employs a Modula-3 based language to guarantee the safety of extensions. Java and JavaVM provide protected environments for mobile codes by its type safe language and load-time verification. However, in those systems, the resources to be protected are fixed and the protection mechanisms are not extensible. Several extensions are proposed for Java's protection mechanism [WB+97, HC+97, Sun97]. The comparison of these extensions and our work is described in Sect. 3.5 and 4.

On the other hand, it is not easy for programmers to write an application with multiple protection domains. In the conventional protection model, an application belongs to a single protection domain. Programmers didn't have to care cross domain calls for usual applications. In the fine-grained protection model, relations among application components and protection domains are not unique. It is complex to map specific services to domains. In the following subsections, we present a compiler support for the fine-grained protection, which automatically generates and reduces domains to address the problem.

2.2 Defining Protection Policies

In our prototype implementation, the protection policy is a simple listing which denotes that who can do what operation. More sophisticated interfaces by language extension or compiler directives can be employed, but these issues are out of our current work. This protection description can emulate the security policy of JavaVM's SecurityManager. In addition, it can also describe principal based protection.

Figure 1 is a sample description of a local policy. In our prototype implementation, a policy file has two sections. The first section is the description of *guards* for protected methods. The first line in the table means that the NETCONN capability is needed to call net_conn() method. Note that these capabilities are employed for the description. As described in the Sect. 2.5, those capabilities are resolved statically and do not exactly match with the runtime capabilities. The net_conn_safe() in the second line is a secure interface or wrapper for the net_conn(). This line describes that net_conn_safe() will gain NETCONN capability. This method implements some specific security restrictions, for example,

# guard		
system.net_conn()	needs	NETCONN
system.net_conn_safe()	gains	NETCONN
system.file_open()	needs	FILEOPEN
system.file_read()	needs	FILEREAD
system.file_write()	needs	FILEWRITE
# inborn capability		
allow		system NETCONN
allow		NetSrv NETCONN
allow		system FILEREAD
allow		system FILEWRITE

Fig. 1. A policy description

such that the applet can connect to the host which it derives from. Unauthorized principals should not call net_conn() but net_conn_safe(). The second section of the policy file is a list of inborn capabilities. It enumerates the capabilities which are given to the principals by nature. In this example, an applet signed by the principal NetSrv can directly call net_conn() bypassing net_conn_safe(), which means that the applet from NetSrv can connect to any hosts.

2.3 Protection Domain as an Intermediate Representation

Protection domain in the narrow sense is a runtime abstraction which can be decided only by the relations between the participants and their runtime policies. For convenience, we informally define here a protection domain as the intermediate representation of the authorized resources for a participant according to the current policy.

In distributed component systems, a set of resources which an object accesses can be obtained from its cross reference information. We use the cross reference information as a starting point to construct the protection domains. A set of operations which are allowed or not allowed for a principal is described in an ACL (access control list). In addition to the ACL information, protection domain has to be presented with which capability one uses the interface. We use pACL (partial ACL) notation described below as an expression of a protection domain. pACL is a portable form of ACL with additional information on the usage of the object.

Figure 2 is an example of the pACL notation. This pACL denotes the protection domain of a simple DB access agent with a remote query feature. The *type* and *method* fields can be obtained from the cross reference information. The *resolve* field tells that the protection can be statically analyzed or should be checked dynamically. To allow someone to access remote machines via network is a static policy, because it would not change from the beginning to the end of the application execution. On the other hand, a dynamic policy should be

(type,	method,	resolve,	capability)
(import,	system.net_conn(),	static,	-NETCONN)
(import,	system.file_open(),	dynamic,	-FILEOPEN)
(import,	system.file_read(),	static,	-FILEREAD)
(import,	system.file_write(),	static,	-FILEWRITE)
(export,	db_agent.net_conn_unlimit(),	static,	+NETCONN)
(export,	db_agent.query(),	dynamic,	+FILEOPEN)
(export,	db_agent.query(),	static,	+FILEREAD)

Fig. 2. Sample of partial Access Control List

consulted in case of opening each files, because it may depend on the runtime context and file permissions. Here, static protection can be resolved when linking the objects, while dynamic protection needs dynamic checking for each call. The field *capability* shows which capability is needed to call the method. Details of the runtime capability system are described in Sect. 3.2.

2.4 Automatic Generation of Protection Domains

Figure 3 shows the generating flow of protection domains in our system. Protection domain can be generated automatically by the Java class files and the current policy. A program we call *static domain compiler* takes Java class files and the policy file as inputs and generates a digitally signed component. Generated protection domains described in pACL notation are encapsulated in the components.

From the policy file and class file, the compiler can generate a pACL automatically. Figure 4 is an example. The first line describes that the NETCONN capability will be needed for the system.net_conn() call and this restriction can be resolved statically. This is generated from the information of exporting methods in the net's class file and the description of the needed capability for system.net_conn() in the policy file. In the third line, because the method system.file_open() requires a file permission checking, the FILEOPEN capability is extended to perform dynamic checking of the executor's UID and its permission. The methods which need dynamically checked capability are marked as *dynamic*. For the static capabilities, the methods are marked as *static*.

2.5 Domain Reduction and Protection Level Selection

The size of protection domain can be scaled, trading the strength of protection and the runtime performance. It is important to find the suitable size and structure of protection domains specific to an application. Protection domain generated in the previous section is too fine-grained. It is not suitable for runtime protection because many cross domain (or cross object) calls with dynamic

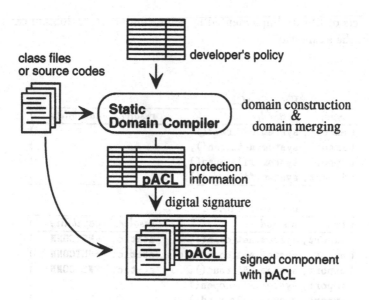

Fig. 3. Automatic generation of protection domains

net's pACL

(type,	method,		resolve,	capability	)
(export,	system.net_conn(),		static,	-NETCONN	)
(export,	system.net_conn_safe(),		static,	+NETCONN	)

file's pACL

(type,	method,	resolve,	capability	)
(export,	system.file_open(),	dynamic,	-FILEOPEN	)
(export,	system.file_read(),	static,	-FILEREAD	)
(export,	system.file_write(),	static,	-FILEWRITE	)

Fig. 4. Generated pACL

checkings will cause the significant slowdown of the application. Domain merging is an optimization or specialization technique under the current protection policy. The static compiler joins the protection domains together and removes needless protection according to the relations between the objects. Most of potential cross domain calls are resolved statically. In the distributed systems, however, the final structure of protection domain can be determined only at the loading time, because not all of the objects can be prepared previously. Necessary or unresolved protection is left in the protection domain information in the pACL notation. Cross domain calls between the objects with the same signature are resolved and implemented as ordinal method calls. Moreover, if one trusts objects or library implemented by some vendor, cross domain calls can be resolved in the same way.

URL's pACL

(type,	method,	resolve,	capability	)
(export,	system.URL_read(),			)
(import,	system.net_conn(),			)
(import,	system.file_open(),			)
(import,	system.file_read(),			)

net+URL's pACL

(type,	method,	resolve,	capability	)
(export,	system.net_conn(),	static,	-NETCONN	)
(export,	system.net_conn_safe(),	static,	+NETCONN	)
(export,	system.URL_read(),	static,	?NETCONN	)
(import,	system.file_open(),			)
(import,	system.file_read(),			)

net+file+URL's pACL

(type,	method,	resolve,	capability	)
(export,	system.net_conn(),	static,	-NETCONN	)
(export,	system.net_conn_safe(),	static,	+NETCONN	)
(export,	system.file_open(),	dynamic,	-FILEOPEN	)
(export,	system.file_read(),	static,	-FILEREAD	)
(export,	system.file_write(),	static,	-FILEWRITE	)
(export,	system.URL_read(),	static,	?NETCONN	)
(export,	system.URL_read(),	dynamic,	?FILEOPEN	)

Fig. 5. Merged pACL

Figure 5 is an example of a simple domain merging. The URL class is a system class which handles URLs. According to the scheme of the URL arguments (i.e. file:// or http://), system.URL_read() method will access local files or connect to the network. The *resolve* and *capability* fields for the URL class are blank, since the policy file (Fig. 1) has no decision for the URL class. In the case of merging the net class and the URL class, the third line is interesting. The question mark before capability denotes that the NETCONN capability may be needed to call the system.URL_read() though it is not checked in the system.URL_read() method. Callers of the method should acquire the capability in advance. This is because system.URL_read() may call system.net_conn(), which can be known from a simple analysis of the partial call graph.

In Fig. 6, the static compiler merges fine-grained protection domains of some class files, and generates a component with the protection domain information. When the Java dynamic loader requests, the component is passed over the net-

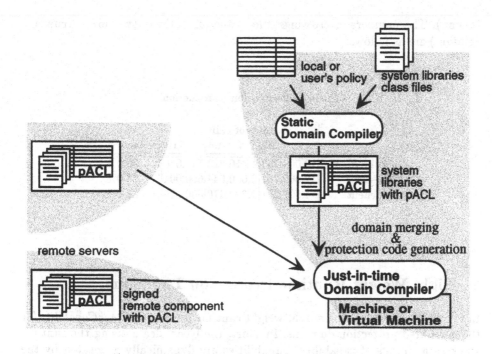

Fig. 6. Component transformation via network

works and just-in-time domain compiler resolves the runtime domains combined with the local components. The just-in-time compiler includes the same functions of the static one. In addition, it has the code generator and loading time optimizer described in Sect. 3.2. Though the just-in-time compiler includes the full functions of the static one, the static compiler is necessary to reduce the loading time analysis and reflect the developers' policy. This mechanism also allows incremental merging of protection domain, so the developers can save the loading time by pre-constructing the pACL in advance.

2.6 Estimation of Reduction

We estimate the effects of our mechanism by a simple experiment. We count the number of cross domain calls with various protection policies. Applications we used are a graphic editor and an ORB both implemented on Java. The graphic editor consists of three components: editor code, a GUI library subArctic [HS97] extending Java's AWT, and the Sun's Java class library. We used HORB [Hir96], a Java based ORB, and play 100,000 time ping-pong of a simple object between the server and client. First, we count the number of cross domain calls under the policy that each component does not trust each other (**vendor**). Second, we use the policy that Sun's class library trusts the downloaded GUI library and HORB (trust). The numbers of crossings and reduction ratios ((vendor - trust) / vendor) are as follows.

Table 1. Estimation of reduction

	num of calls			
	all	vendor	trust	reduction
graphic editor	10,008,763	1,416,813	144,070	90.0%
orb server	12,302,731	2,000,544	600,004	70.0%
orb client	4,802,251	1,300,470	500,015	61.6%

3 Light Weight Runtime Protection Technique

In this section, we describe a light weight runtime technique, *StackCapability* for the generated protection domains. In short, the basic idea is using the runtime stack as a storage of capability. Capabilities are dynamically generated by the inserted codes in the just-in-time domain compiler.

3.1 Extended Stack Introspection

The extended stack introspection is one of the light weight protection techniques for Java in [WB+97]. We share the idea of using the call-stack as the storage of capability, but the mechanism is slightly different. We first introduce the mechanism of the extended stack introspection for the explanation of our work. The original extended stack introspection uses two primitives `enablePrivilege()` and `checkPrivilege()` for protection. When an object wishes to use some resource with a specific privilege, it must explicitly *enable* that privilege by calling `enablePrivilege()`. In the `enablePrivilege()`, resource access is verified consulting the policy engine identifying which principals may access which resources in the system. If the access is permitted, a capability is recorded on the call-stack. Note that the call-stack in JavaVM is safe and secure area which can not be accessed illegally because of the type safe language. In the system code, before accessing the protected resource, `checkPrivilege()` must be explicitly called. `checkPrivilege()` searches the call-stack for the enabled privilege to the given resources, and throws an exception if not found.

An example of a stack trace is shown in Fig. 8. This illustrates the execution of the sample code in Fig. 7. This code restricts the network connection. In the `net_conn_safe()`, the default policy in the current Java implementation is employed, that is, network connections only to the host from which the applet originated are permitted. As in Fig. 8, an unprivileged code should call `net_conn_safe()` to get the privilege and make a network connection. It

```
// guard method
net_conn_safe(ip-address)
{
  if (ip-address is valid){
    enablePrivilege(NETCONN);
    net_conn(ip-address);
  }
}

// network connection
net_conn(ip-address)
{
  checkPrivilege(NETCONN);

  // actual connecting code
  ...
  ...
}
```

```
// network client
net_conn_unlimit(ip-address)
{
  enablePrivilege(NETCONN);
  system.net_conn(ip-address);
}
```

Code signed by authorized vendor

System library code

Fig. 7. Extended stack introspection: Sample code

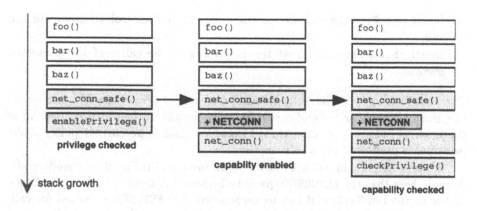

Fig. 8. Stack trace of extended stack introspection

cannot call net_conn() directly because it fails in the stack searching of the checkPrivilege(). A privileged code which is signed by an authorized vendor can directly call net_conn() by calling enablePrivilege() in advance.

Two major runtime costs for the extended stack introspection are the cost of a query to the policy engine in enablePrivilege() and the stack introspection cost in checkPrivilege() which is proportional to the current stack length. In addition, system codes should be modified to call checkPrivilege().

3.2 Code Generation and Dynamic Protection by StackCapability

For the extended stack introspection, both the system and application program-mers must explicitly insert the `enablePrivilege()` and `checkPrivilege()` primitives. Our approach, on the other hands, is to protect secure services by au-tomatically inserting the protection codes before every unresolved cross domain call. The generated protection domain information described in Sect. 2 is used to detect the cross domain calls. In dynamic loading systems, dynamic loaded codes are under the full control of the loader.

As described in Sect. 2.5, the final structures of the protection domains are determined at the loading time. The just-in-time domain compiler in the dynamic loader combines the protection domain of the loading components and those of already loaded components. If the compiler detects the unresolved cross domain call, protection codes are inserted into the caller and callee. Of course, most of the cross object calls which do not cross the domains will be implemented as an ordinary method call. We suppose here the dynamic code insertion by the just-in-time compiler, and applications without dynamic loading can also translate into the native code in advance and signed by the compiler. The usual method for code insertion is as follows:

1. Insert `markPrivilege()` in the caller before the unresolved cross domain call.
2. Insert `checkPrivilege()` at the beginning of the callee of the protected method.

The `markPrivilege()` method, differing from `enablePrivilege()`, just writes the name of the principal and capability without any authentication. Instead of the `enablePrivilege()`, `checkPrivilege()` consults the current policy if the principal is permitted to call the method.

We present here an example of the code insertion in Fig. 9 by pseudo code. Assume here that the `NETCONN` capability in Sect. 2.5 needs dynamic checkings. In the method of NetSrv, it can be recognized that `NETCONN` is needed for call-ing `system.URL_read()`. The `markPrivilege()` is inserted automatically before the call. The stack state indicates that `NETCONN` is requested to acquire by the NetSrv. This capability is checked in the `checkPrivilege()`. As shown in this case, this mechanism works in case of the indirect call of protected methods.

3.3 Domain Merging and Specialization

One of the most significant merit of the dynamic code generation is that it can make use of the information of the binding context. In addition to the statical reduction of protection domains, some of the dynamically checking code can be reduced by the static analysis under the current context and policy. For example, checking code which will always fail under the current context may be replaced by the specialized code.

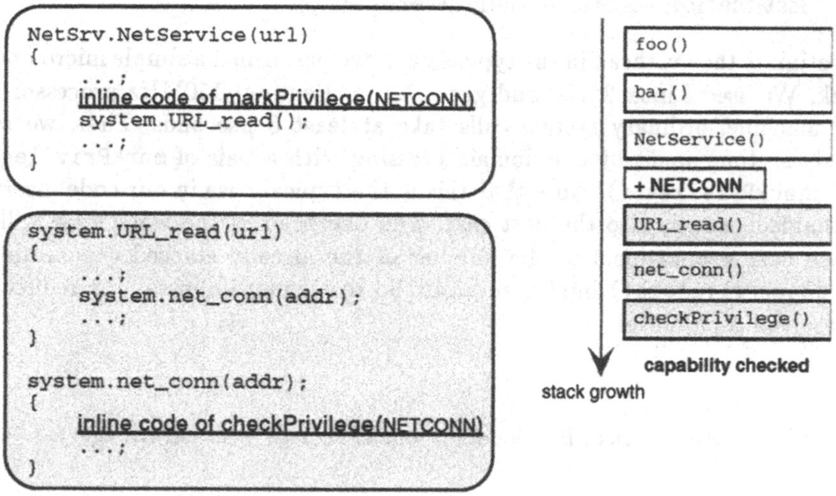

Fig. 9. Code insertion for StackCapability

3.4 Extensible Capability

Capabilities described above are static objects. Our capability system can be extended by programming the capability object. For instance, `markPrivilege()` and `checkPrivilege()` are the methods of capability objects which can be overloaded. Thus, system programmers can replace inlined protect code and extend the capability system using the runtime context, the system and user information.

3.5 Advantages against the Extended Stack Introspection

Finally, we summarize the advantages of our mechanism against the original extended stack introspection. There are two differences in the mechanisms.

- protection by dynamic code insertion
- automatic reduction of protection domain by static policy

We can accomplish the following advantages from the differences above.

- just fit and slim protection
- reuse of original program without any modification
  Developer does not need to insert `enablePrivilege()` or `checkPrivilege()` code explicitly.

3.6 Estimation of Mechanism Overhead

To estimate the overhead in the typical case, we performed a simple micro benchmark. We used Linux 2.0.30 and gcc 2.7.2 on Pentium 150MHz processor. On this machine, ordinary system calls take at least 6 μseconds. First, we measured the time spent by one domain crossing with a pair of markPrivilege() and checkPrivilege(). Note that this is the typical case in our code insertion mechanism, and is also the best case. The overhead in the worst case will increase near proportional to the number of the already stacked capabilities in our checkPrivilege() implementation. So it is again important to reduce the unresolved capabilities.

Table 2. Micro Benchmark of markPrivilege + checkPrivilege

null function	mark + check	crossing overhead
0.101	0.633	0.502 μsec

Again, in the same experiment in Sect. 2.6, we measured the execution time and the numbers of domain crossings. By the frequency of crossing and the benchmark above, we can estimate the runtime overhead of our mechanism.

Table 3. Estimation of runtime overhead

	time	crossings	trust crossings/sec	overhead
orb server	87.5 sec	600,004	6,857	0.34%
orb client		500,015	5,714	0.27%

4 Related Works

Extensible Kernel

SPIN [BS+95] has the extensible kernel with dynamic loading feature. Precompiled modules written in Modula-3 are loaded in the kernel. Extension modules co-locate in the kernel and can access the kernel interfaces with low overhead. Memory protection is guaranteed by the loading time checking of extensions and the type safety of Modula-3. SPIN intends the low-level kernel extension and does not support multiple domains in an application by itself. Our user level implementation of protection can co-exist with this approach. For example, the domain merging technique can be adopted to support secure interactions between extensions.

Software Based Protection

Type hiding is another software based protection approach for Java proposed in [WB+97]. They protect secure services from untrusted codes by hiding type (Java class). The specified class loader `PrincipalClassLoader` for each principal throws an exception or returns a specified subclass for requested class in case of the untrusted applet. One of the drawbacks stated in the paper is that it cannot change the protection policy after loaded. In addition, restricted versions of classes must be prepared in advance, which may differ for each security configuration. In our system, the protected codes can be automatically generated by the compilers and the policy file.

SLK (Secure Language Kernel) [HC+97] shares our motivation of protecting multiple domains in an application. Their mechanism *TypeCapability* is similar to that of type hiding. They statically check the capabilities when resolving the type at link-time. Dynamic checkings are done by prepared *wrapper* classes. They also do not have systematic way for automatic protection.

Sun Microsystems, Inc. has recently announced their future plan for protection in Java [Sun97]. Protection is implemented in user level and provides the fine-grained customization with table-based configuration. However, proposed protection model, which they call *Java Protected Domains*, seems to be a conventional one like those of the traditional operating systems. All resources are protected in the *System Domain*. Protection domains must remain distinct from each other and interactions among domains are permitted only through the trusted system code. This fixed model of protection domain will prevent flexible implementations of user level protection.

Operating System Specialization

Synthetix [PA+95] is an operating system specialization research. Their RPC case study [VMC96] employs component-coupling and session-oriented information for compile-time and runtime specialization of invariants and constants. Our work is a kind of specialization focusing on protection using the information of relation between components.

5 Conclusion

Distributed applications which consist of many network loaded components have many potential protection domains. To optimize the protection, we proposed a protection domain compiler. The compiler takes components and the policy, and generates protection domain automatically. To reduce the cross domain calls, we introduced a domain optimizing technique by simple analysis of call relations.

We also showed an optimized runtime protection technique for Java using the generated protection domain information.

In this paper, we concentrate our work on the simple description of policies and automatic protection mechanism to reduce the administration cost. A high level description of protection policy and compromise protocols of local and remote policies are our future works.

References

[BS+95] Bershad, B., Savage, S., Pardyak, P., Gun Sirer, E., Fiuczynski, M., Becker, D., Eggers, S., Chambers, C.: Extensibility, Safety and Performance in the SPIN Operating System. Univ. of Washington Tech. Report (1995)

[EKO94] Engler, D., Kaashoek, M., O'Toole Jr, J.: The Exokernel Approach to Operating System Extensibility. Proc. USENIX Sympo. on Operating Systems Design and Implementation (1994)

[TY97] Taura, K., Yonezawa, A.: Fine-grain Multithreading with Minimal Compiler Support – A Cost Effective Approach to Implementing Efficient Multithreading Languages. Proc. ACM Conf. on Programming Language Design and Implementation (1997)

[PC97] Plezbert, M., Cytron, R.: Does "Just in Time" = "Better Late than Never"? Proc. ACM Conf. on Principle of Programming Languages (1997)

[WB+97] Wallach, D., Balfanz, D., Dean, D., Felten, E.: Extensible Security Architectures for Java. Proc. ACM 16th Sympo. on Operating System Principles (1997)

[WL+94] Wobber, E., Abadi, M., Burrows, M., Lampson, B.: Authentication in the Taos operating system. ACM Transactions on Computer Systems 12, 1 (1994) 3-32

[PA+95] Pu, C., Autrey, T., Black, A., Consel, C., Cowan, C., Inouye, J., Kethana, L., Walpole, J., Zhang, K.: Optimistic Incremental Specialization: Streamlining a Commercial Operating System. Proc. ACM 15th Sympo. on Operating System Principles (1995)

[VMC96] Volanschi, E., Muller, G., Consel, C.: Safe Operating System Specialization: the RPC Case Study. Workshop on Compiler Support for System Software (1996)

[Fer95] Fernandez. M., Simple and Effective Link-Time Optimization of Modula-3 Programs. Proc. ACM Conf. on Programming Language Design and Implementation (1995)

[GJS96] Gosling, J., Joy, B., Steele, G.: The Java Language Specification. Addison-Wesley (1996)

[Yel96] Yellin, F., Sun Microsystems, Inc.: Low Level Security in Java. http://java.sun.com/sfaq/verifier.html (1996)

[Sun97] Sun Microsystems, Inc.: Secure Computing with Java: Now and the Future. http://www.javasoft.com/marketing/collateral/security.html (1997)

[TL+96] Adl-Tabatabai, A., Langdale, G., Lucco, S., Wahbe, R.: Efficient and Language-Independent Mobile Programs. Proc. ACM Conf. on Programming Language Design and Implementation (1996)

[HC+97] Hawblitzel, C., Chang, C., Czajkowski, G., Hu, D., Eicken, T.: SLK: A Capability System Based on Safe Language Technology. Cornell Univ. Tech. Report for Department of Computer Science (1997)

[JR86]   Jones, M., Rachid. R.: Mach and Matchmaker: Kernel and Language Support for Object-Oriented Distributed Systems. Proc. ACM OOPSLA'86 (1986)

[EF+97]   Eide, E., Frei, K., Ford, B., Lepreau, J., Lindstrom, G.: Flick: A Flexible, Optimizing IDL Compiler. Proc. ACM Conf. on Programming Language Design and Implementation (1997)

[PEK97]   Poletto, M., Engler, D., Kaashoek, M.: tcc: A System for Fast, Flexible, and High-level Dynamic Code Generation. Proc. ACM Conf. on Programming Language Design and Implementation (1997)

[AP+96]   Auslander, J., Philipose, M., Chambers, C., Eggers, S., Bershad, B.: Fast, Effective Dynamic Compilation. Proc. ACM Conf. on Programming Language Design and Implementation (1996)

[Hir96]   Hirano, S.: HORB: Distributed Execution of Java Programs. Proc. Conf. on World-Wide Computing and Its Applications (1997)

[HS97]   Hudson, S., Smith, I.: subArctic. http://www.cs.gatech.edu/gvu/ui/sub_arctic/ (1997)

Complete Computing *

Vipul Gupta, Gabriel Montenegro and Jeff Rulifson

Technology Development Group
Sun Microsystems, Inc.
901 San Antonio Road, MS UMPK15-214
Palo Alto, California 94303
Email: {*vgupta, gab, jeffr*}*@eng.sun.com*

Abstract. Our objective is to enable nomadic and mobile computing, as
well as telecommuting, small-office, and branch-office computing. These
areas have been dealt with extensively in the literature. However, they
have been treated as separate problem spaces and current solutions focus
on solving specific problems in one area while ignoring – or even exacer-
bating – those in another area. These problem spaces must be viewed as
being closely related, and must be addressed in a coherent fashion.
We call this unified vision and architecture *Complete Computing*.

1 Vision

As people navigate or relocate throughout the ocean of information that sur-
rounds them (Figure 1), they wish to maintain logical availability of some subset of their computing environment. We use the term computing environment
to include both a user's applications (*e.g.* document editor) and data (*e.g.* files,
mail, *etc.*). Maintaining this logical availability may require a combination of
several mechanisms including caching, replication, redirection, repackaging or
even prediction.

A mobile client is able to connect using a variety of schemes (serial, LAN,
wireless, WAN, through firewalls [5], etc) and is adept at operating in disconnected mode. This flexibility gives its user the illusion that information is always
close at hand, and that it follows him or her and presents itself for consumption
independently of the client's physical or logical location. An important corollary
is that this network model supports both user and terminal mobility, because
the objective is for the information to be available to the user at all times –
though perhaps in varying degrees depending on prevalent networking and environmental conditions.

In this paper, the term *Mobile Computing* represents the ambitious objective
of retaining a user's static computing environment (including all existing connections), even while the user and his portable device are moving. It attempts to

---

* This work was partly funded by the Ministry of International Trade and Industry
of Japan through the *Advanced Software Enrichment Project* of the Information
Technology Promotion Agency.

shield the user from the effects of physical or topological movement throughout the networking fabric.

In some instances, preserving a user's computing environment during movement may not be necessary. Instead it may be sufficient to ensure that the user's computing environment can be recreated wherever the user moves. This may require re-initiating network connections and/or reestablishing session state. We use the term *Nomadic Computing* for these situations.

Remote Computing or *Branch Office Computing* have similar requirements to the previous two, in that they involve access to a user's private computing environment (*e.g.* firewall-protected corporate resources) across a potentially hostile – or at least untrusted – public network. Nevertheless, the static – hence, stable – nature of this kind of computing translates into better resource availability and richer services.

Finally, *Small-Office/Home-Office Computing* assumes there are no private user environments beyond those available locally. The objective is to enable small, independent work groups. Since they do not belong to a parent organization, they lack assistance from system administrators and technical support personnel. Therefore, ease of use is of utmost importance. However, there is still a need for rich networking and application support.

The diverse areas mentioned above have been dealt with extensively in the literature but not as a cohesive whole. Our objective is to enable all of these forms of computing using a common set of tools and solutions. We call this unified vision and architecture *Complete Computing*.

By designing similar mechanisms for all these areas, we wish to prevent further fragmentation of proposed solutions. Our vision of complete computing has technology implications in several areas: hardware and software platforms, data persistence, caching and synchronization, configuration and management, applications, services, networking, and security.

In this paper we focus primarily on networking and the concomitant security issues. We identify the outstanding technical challenges, review proposed solutions, and discuss their applicability in different situations.

2   Elements of a Solution

For the following discussion, a mobile user is one who needs to access information and applications "on the road", i.e. from different locations (or even while changing locations) and under varying conditions. Access may be read-only or read-write and the access device may be personal (*e.g.* a portable, personal notebook or PDA) or communal (*e.g.* a kiosk at an airport).

2.1   Challenges of Mobility

Mobility imposes certain fundamental constraints which affect all aspects of computing.

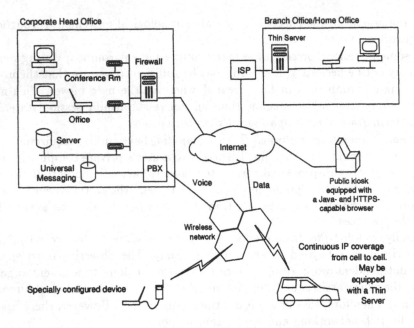

Fig. 1. An overview of the Complete Computing environment

1. Portable devices, as compared to their stationary counterparts, are "resource poor" (*e.g.* less powerful CPU, fewer I/O devices, smaller screen), and must manage their resources carefully. Power management is critical for battery-operated devices. Screen size and keyboard (or lack thereof) may influence the user interface.

2. Network characteristics like bandwidth and latency fluctuate widely. Therefore, mobile systems must deal with communication uncertainty – including complete disconnection – and adapt gracefully to these and other changes.

3. Mobility requires different forms of security.

   (a) *Network Security*. Traffic may at times pass through links with questionable security characteristics. New alternatives may be required for some traditional security mechanisms that use location information to distinguish between authorized and unauthorized users. As an example, many packet-filtering firewalls disallow certain kinds of traffic if it arrives on an interface facing the general Internet. Such firewalls may need to be enhanced with strong cryptographic mechanisms so legitimate traffic from authorized mobile users is allowed irrespective of the interface.

   (b) *Data and Device Security*. As opposed to large, stationary devices safely locked up in an office, lightweight, portable devices are frequently used in public places. Hence, they are prone to being destroyed, lost or stolen. Consequently, encryption and secure backups are used to prevent subversion or loss of data.

2.2 Agile Networking

In today's fast-paced information society, it is inconceivable to think that a mobile user can always carry all the information he needs on the local storage of his personal computing device. Typically, the information of interest will be distributed across a multitude of other hosts connected to a network. This immediately highlights the need for a mobile user to attach to a network, establish a communication path to the desired server and exchange information under a variety of conditions.

Consider a salesperson who, over the course of a few hours, uses a portable notebook in different networking modes — wireline LAN at his office, a different wireline LAN in a conference room, wireless LAN at the company cafeteria, wireless WAN at the airport, and a POTS modem connection at a hotel. Typically, each situation requires reconfiguration of the device. These configuration parameters may include IP address, network mask, default router, DNS server name, local printer, etc. In an ideal situation, most (if not all) of the necessary changes would be transparent to the end user and occur with minimal disruption. Newer protocols like DHCP [7], Mobile IP [21] and SLP [24] hold great promise for solving this challenge.

2.3 Disconnected Operation

Of course, there will be periods when a mobile user may not have access to any network or the cost of connecting to a network may be prohibitively high (as in an airplane). Support for disconnected operation is imperative for such situations. The user should be able to cache applications and data [2] in his current "working set" onto local, non-volatile storage and, at a later point, reconcile any changes made locally against other copies on the network. While a number of research groups have made encouraging progress in this particular area [16], mature industry-wide standards are still lacking.

2.4 Adaptivity

We anticipate the development of several classes of mobile computing devices differing in their CPU power, display size, screen resolution, input devices etc. While these characteristics do not change during the lifetime of a device, others such as network bandwidth and latency, remaining battery power, and available storage are more dynamic and applications could benefit from adapting to such changes. A web browser could turn off automatic downloading of in-line images when available network bandwidth drops. Such applications would benefit from a framework that supports adaptivity. This requires at least two essential components: (i) a database which contains current values of various system parameters, and (ii) mechanisms by which applications can either poll these values or subscribe to events corresponding to parameter changes.

---

[2] Java, with its ability to abstract away CPU and OS-specific differences holds great promise for realizing a vision in which applications, not just data, can be exchanged freely between all kinds of devices.

2.5 Firewalls and Virtual Private Networks

Corporate employees comprise a significant proportion of the mobile user community so allowing their access to corporate resources from remote locations is an important requirement. At present, access over PSTN (*e.g.* using PPP [23] with PAP/CHAP) is by far the most popular choice. In the near future, remote access mechanisms that use the Internet (rather than PSTN) for their transport are likely to become popular. These mechanisms offer significant savings in infrastructure costs and toll charges by tunneling packets between the end user and the corporate network through the Internet. Clearly, security is an important concern in this situation. Strong cryptographic mechanisms are required to ensure that only authorized users gain access to company resources and all sensitive information is hidden from eavesdroppers. Tunneling service may be provided at Layer 2 or Layer 3 and both avenues are being pursued within the IETF.

Many organizations deploy firewalls between their network and the Internet. Firewalls use filtering rules and/or cryptographic mechanisms to selectively block network traffic. Internet-based remote access mechanisms must accommodate the presence of firewalls at a corporate network's periphery. Here again, several efforts are underway within the IETF to address the issue of firewall traversal [6, 9, 18, 19]. The first internet-draft on the list [6] outlines how mobile hosts can establish Virtual Private Networks (VPNs) with their corporate networks using IP Security (IPSec) [13, 14, 15, 12, 17, 20]. Other proposals on the list add mobility support using Mobile IP and can be used to create Mobile VPNs (MVPNs). The additional mobility support allows transport level connections to be maintained across moves. The three MVPN mechanisms differ in the key-management protocols they use [2, 12], the requirements they impose on firewalls, and packet header overhead. Unlike TSP [18], the proposals described in [9, 10, 19] do not require firewalls to understand Mobile IP registrations. On the other hand, by requiring firewalls to understand Mobile IP registrations, TSP is able reduce the header overhead on network traffic.

2.6 Web Based Remote Access

All of the above firewall traversal mechanisms are aimed at providing IP level access to all applications even when the mobile host is outside its corporate network. For situations where access to specific applications is sufficient, SSL [8] due to its wide availability may provide a better alternative. The basic idea involves an application-specific proxy at the firewall. The proxy replaces direct communication between a client applet and a server with two separate connections: (i) one between the applet and the proxy, and (ii) another between the proxy and the server. Communication between the applet and the proxy is secured using SSL as the underlying transport. Since the applet can be downloaded from the same host as the proxy, communication between them may use a proprietary protocol without introducing interoperability problems. For instance, this proprietary protocol may be specially tuned for low-bandwidth links. Communication between the proxy and server still utilizes regular, well established protocols, *e.g.* IMAPv4, SMTP, HTTP, telnet, etc so no changes are required on the server side. A major advantage of this architecture is that the near-ubiquity of Java- and SSL-capable browsers eliminates the need to carry a personal device. A salesperson can walk up to any host, a kiosk or even a client's workstation, and use its browser to gain secure access to specific applications on his corporate network. The server is authenticated through SSL's certificate exchange mechanism and one-time passwords can be used to authenticate the user to the proxy host.

Whatever mechanism is chosen for secure, Internet-based access, it is important that existing applications be able to benefit from it with minimal changes. The Java application environment supports the notion of a socket factory which can be used to isolate applications from specific details of the packet processing required for firewall traversal.

3 Lightweight Devices and Personal Mobility

Our objective is to enable *people* to access their network resources independent from any of the following:

1. Physical location,
2. Internet access method,
3. Device used.

The last item will grow in importance with the deployment of internet kiosks, web-enabled hotel rooms, public internet terminals and similar devices. Device independence – besides being a desired objective – is sometimes necessary. For example, the user may not have authorization to connect any device he may be carrying to the existing network infrastructure: one company's employee may be forced to use existing devices at another company's premises.

3.1 Minimum Set of Platform Requirements

This mode of access must make very few assumptions about the underlying platform. We have arrived at the following elements which we believe are ubiquitous or nearly so, and enable remote access mechanisms at the transport layer and above.

1. HTML
2. HTTP and HTTP over SSL (HTTPS)
3. Java Virtual Machine (JVM)

An important consideration in arriving at this minimum set of requirements is that, prior to arriving at the remote site, no client software installation is required. Instead, any necessary client-side software is downloaded and executed dynamically on the JVM. Given that client platforms are notorious for their lack of reliability, modifying the configuration in any significant manner dramatically increases the possibility of software conflicts, lock ups and panics. It is generally recognized that executing Java byte code within the confines of the JVM is very effective in safeguarding the client against rogue software. What is not generally recognized is that, by virtue of leaving drivers and kernel code untouched and by limiting the capabilities of the code to those allowed by the JVM, bytecode execution also protects the machine from its own unreliability.

Another objective in arriving at a minimum set of platform requirements is that security must not be compromised. Thanks to Java's ability to dynamically download and execute code, basic SSL (HTTPS) services become the foundation for secure remote access mechanisms.

3.2 Distributed Cryptographic Infrastructure

With Java, it is possible to engage in international secure transactions and networking without contravening any laws.

Regulations concerning cryptographic technology vary from country to country. For example, in the U.S. strict export controls must be abided by. In France, use of cryptography by individuals is severely limited. Furthermore, governments may express these policies in ambiguous terms as a further deterrent to the dissemination of cryptography. Given this confusing landscape, it is obvious that for international corporations – particularly those implementing virtual private networks on the Internet – and for security-conscious travelers, divining the set of regulations valid in any given situation, and complying with it is a daunting task. Traditionally a user installs security software onto his laptop. As this user travels across international borders, he may have to uninstall and subsequently reinstall the software. Besides being cumbersome, this negatively affects the stability of the portable device, precisely at the time when the user is traveling and system administration resources are not available.

Java allows the *just-in-time* downloading of the – potentially digitally signed – cryptographic software, and its subsequent installation and execution under the watchful vigilance of the JVM. Having done this, the client is able to establish secure communications with its corporation's public server, and use it as a gateway into its private network. Notice that thanks to digital signatures, the client need not download the cryptographic software from the same machine that it then uses as a gateway into its network.

For example, suppose a U.S. user travels to Switzerland. and then accesses his corporation's world wide web site using the *https* protocol. The ensuing SSL negotiation selects a cipher that is common to the server and the client in order to encrypt the traffic. Assuming that the remote user is a law-abiding individual, the list of ciphers available at the client does not include strong encryption. For example, instead of RC4 encryption with a 128-bit key, the client may only have export-grade RC4 encryption with a 40-bit key. At this point, the client may choose to download a stronger cipher. However, it does so from a server in Switzerland, completes the SSL negotiation, and is able to secure the communications with the gateway in the U.S. using RC4 encryption with a 128-bit key.

Since the gateway machine in the U.S. never supplies the cryptographic code, export restrictions do not apply. At the same time, the local cryptographic code server in Switzerland enforces whatever *local* policies may apply. Currently, the U.S. government does not restrict encrypted traffic with off-shore sites, it only restricts exporting the technology to encrypt the traffic. [3]

Of course, the local government might impose additional restrictions on the use of cryptography. For example, if the visitor happens to be in France, his client will have no preinstalled ciphers, and any attempt to download them from a local "security" server would allow the latter to impose local regulations. The user might be informed that cryptography is disallowed, and that any traffic exchanged with the gateway for the U.S. corporation would be in cleartext. At this point, the gateway could impose its own policies and reject the request for remote access from the visitor in France. Alternatively, it could limit the remote user's access rights for the duration of the session.

As can be seen, these security servers take on the responsibility of enforcing local cryptographic policy, thus relieving the users from this onerous task. This constitutes a perfectly legal, distributed cryptographic infrastructure to secure traffic across international borders.

3.3 Configurable Socket Factory and RAFT URLs

There is no standard for internet remote access into corporate or private networks. The task of traversing the corporate firewall may be accomplished in several ways: specific gateway software, IP security (as it is being defined by the IETF), SSL mechanisms, HTTPS tunneling, SOCKS, etc. However, none of the firewall traversal mechanisms will prevail completely. RAFT (Remote Access and Firewall Traversal) URLs recognize this fact, and provide a naming and encapsulation scheme that shields applications from particularities.

RAFT URLs have the following formats:
raft:<raft-type>://<traversal-point>:[<other-info>]
raft:generic-url
Where the different parts have this meaning:

raft: This indicates that the URL that follows is a handle into a registry of remote access schemes.

raft-type: The name given to a specific firewall traversal or remote access method. Raft types denote very specific methods. For example, the use of IP layer 3 tunnels with SKIP, using an extended mobile registration protocol for dynamic tunnel set-up might be one such scheme. Another one might be a mechanism based on HTTPS tunneling.

traversal-point: This is a firewall, gateway or remote access server with which the system must negotiate access. Discovery of the traversal point is beyond the scope of this note.

---

[3] However, the cipher downloaded from the Swiss site must have been implemented without any aid from the U.S.

other-info: This is a scheme-specific initialization string. The scheme may imply further round-trip times before access is granted. This string is just a first step. It does not necessarily have to be used. The format of this parameter is defined by the scheme.

generic-url: Any possible URL as defined in [3].

A RAFT URL does not designate a data object, but rather a means to negotiate access through a traversal point to establish contact with private resources.

RAFT URLs are useful because no one method of remote access is likely to dominate. RAFT enables the specific form of remote access to be abstracted away from the applications that need the connectivity. It now becomes a two-part process:

1. Discovery of a RAFT URL.
   This may be accomplished, for example, by any of these methods:

   (a) The user visits a special web page and as part of the login process, authenticates itself to the gateway or firewall by any of these mechanisms:

       i. Client-side SSL authentication.
       ii. Hardware-assisted authentication using challenge-response schemes.
       iii. One-time passwords.

       The web server grants access by sending some relevant information to the client. A RAFT URL may be part of this information sent by the web server. The code that implements the mechanisms called for by the RAFT URL may be pre-installed on the device. Otherwise, the client may, at this time, download the code necessary to interpret and carry out the necessary operations for firewall traversal under the specified RAFT URL.

   (b) The appropriate RAFT URL is produced by querying a directory service such as LDAP, Service Location Protocol or DNS.

   (c) The possible RAFT URLs (and relevant code to execute them) are preconfigured into the mobile device. The system is set up for the current environment by choosing among the possible RAFT URLs. This may happen direct by the user's choosing from a menu among the possible RAFT URLs, or by some event notification mechanism informing the system.

2. Once the RAFT URL is discovered, it must be used by the system to set its default firewall traversal mechanisms accordingly. The implementation of this step and its transparency to applications is, of course, highly dependent on the system's software platform. As an example, a system may use the RAFT URL to set its socket factory appropriately. Applications built to the standard Java socket interface in package *java.net* need not be aware of the exact mechanisms involved.

Notice that from the point of view of the applications, the socket factory itself does not change, rather its internal behavior does.

Introducing this abstraction allows any type of firewall traversal or remote access scheme to be integrated into the platform, separately from the applications that use the network connection.

At this time, the gateway or firewall becomes a proxy so the remote client can access the private network.

3.4 Personal Mobility

Since the mechanisms outlined above rely on very widely deployed technologies (Java, HTTP, SSL), they also enable *personal mobility*. For example, a user can walk up to any public Internet terminal, and after properly authenticating himself to the relevant gateway, gain access into his private network.

Some words of caution are in order. This technology only secures the link between the client and the gateway machine. Once the data arrives at the client it is presented in cleartext for the user's consumption. A trojan horse client can easily collect the data at this point.

4 Specially Configured Devices

This section examines the "road warrior" or "power user" scenario which is distinguished by a user's ability to carry a specially configured portable device. The user is no longer bound by the constraints of communal devices, like kiosks, which generally offer minimal functionality. In what follows, we present a list of software solutions we consider important for power users.

Perhaps the most basic requirement of mobile users is the ability to change their point of attachment to the Internet with minimal disruption. Doing so typically involves changing several network configuration parameters. This task can be greatly simplified by a piece of software we call *network switcher*. It allows users to specify multiple "network profiles" (*e.g.* one for their office and another for their ISP at home) and switch to a pre-stored profile quickly and conveniently. The software can also initiate DHCP and gather necessary configuration parameters that way rather than through pre-specified profiles.

Whenever the IP address of a device changes, previously established transport-level connections are normally lost. Mobile IP allows a mobile device to be reachable at a fixed IP address (called its home address) irrespective of its current point of attachment to the Internet. Transport level connections established with the home address are preserved across moves. However, unlike PPP and DHCP, Mobile IP is a fairly new protocol and the required infrastructure (comprising mobility agents and client-side software) is not widely deployed.

When a mobile host is moved to a new network, it may need to discover resources like network printers or HTTP proxies in its immediate vicinity. The Service Location Protocol (SLP) is ideally suited to this task. In some situations, LDAP [25] which is more widely deployed may provide adequate functionality.

Connecting to the Internet and finding local resources is just one part of the overall challenge. Mobile users should also be able to access remote resources within firewall-protected private networks, *e.g.* a corporate network. This requires setting up a secure communication channel across a public network like the Internet, *i.e.* a Virtual Private Network (VPN). The concept of tunneling is central to VPN solutions. It refers to the practice of encapsulating one protocol in another. This might be necessary in order to carry non-IP traffic (*e.g.* IPX or Appletalk) across the Internet, or even to carry an encrypted packet within another packet directed at an intervening firewall. Tunneling service may either be provided at Layer 2 or at Layer 3. Layer 2 tunneling mechanisms (*e.g.* L2TP [11]) transfer PPP packets (encapsulating IP, IPX etc) across the Internet or other transport media. Layer 3 tunneling mechanisms, on the other hand, directly encapsulate network layer packets (*e.g.* IP, IPX) in IP. A number of Layer-3 tunneling protocols have been proposed (TEP [4], TSP [18]) that extend the basic Mobile IP protocol to allow chaining of multiple tunnel segments. All of these tunneling proposals ([11, 4, 18]) rely on IPSec to provide confidentiality, integrity and authenticity when the transport medium is the Internet. Currently, L2TP seems to have captured the largest mindshare among VPN technologies. Nevertheless, we feel that Layer 3 tunneling offers a superior solution especially when the underlying transport is the Internet. These advantages include:

- Better bandwidth utilization. Running protocol X over PPP over UDP (as with L2TP across the Internet) is less efficient than running protocol X directly over IP. (X may be IP, IPX etc)
- Greater reliability. With layer-two tunneling, each end point maintains a PPP state machine (including timers and retransmission logic) across a "simulated serial line". Unlike a real serial line, end points of the simulated line are often separated by large distances and/or many hops with only best effort delivery. As such, the PPP connections are prone to timeouts and frequent resets.

If multi-protocol support is considered unimportant, IPSec alone can go a long way in solving the secure, remote access problem. From a deployment perspective, it is perhaps easier to establish secure tunnels that extend from a corporate network's periphery to an ISP rather than all the way to the end-user device. The latter requires IPSec software on the portable device but offers the following advantages:[4]

- End-users are free to connect to their corporate network irrespective of the ISP used to "get on to the Internet".
- Corporations do not need to establish a trust relationship with ISPs, they only need to trust their own employees. A corporation in may be willing to trust an ISP based in the same country but may not be willing to trust an ISP based in another country even if the two ISPs are members of a roaming consortia. One can also think of several situations where an employee may connect to the Internet through a "provider" that has no prior agreements with the user's corporation. Examples of such "internet providers"

---

[4] As IPSec standards mature, we expect operating system vendors to bundle this functionality, greatly alleviating the deployment challenge.

include universities or temporary "terminal rooms" provided at academic and industry conferences.

IPSec based remote access requires an IPSec-capable node within the corporate firewall complex. Filtering and access control rules should be set up so that IPSec packets, and others necessary for establishing security associations, can be exchanged freely between this node and the general Internet. The address of this "IPSec gateway" must be known to external mobile hosts. The exact discovery mechanism is irrelevant to the subsequent discussion. Manual configuration and DNS lookup (*e.g.* using KX records [1]) are just two of the possible alternatives.

Very often, corporate networks use private addresses that are not advertised to the general Internet. Furthermore, internal routers are generally unaware of external addresses and return "ICMP unreachable" messages for such destinations (assuming they do not use default routing). This creates the challenge of ensuring end-to-end delivery between a host with an internal address (*e.g.* corporate file- or mail-server) and a host connected to the Internet using an external address. There are two basic approaches to this problem:

1. The first approach adds Network Address Translation (NAT) functionality at the IPSec gateway. After authenticating arriving packets, and before injecting them into the private network, the gateway does a NAT operation, replacing the external source address with its own IP address (the gateway may be assigned a range of internal addresses). This way when an internal host responds, it uses a destination address that is "valid" inside the corporate network. The response packet reaches the IPSec gateway, undergoes a reverse address translation, and IPSec processing before it is sent to the remote host [6].

   Inserting NAT in the communication path can "break" certain applications. Some applications carry network address information (IP address and/or TCP/UDP port) as part of the their payload and performing NAT for such packets can get complicated, *e.g.* replacing the IP address or port information in the application payload may require adjustments to the IP packet length. Certain NAT implementations go to great lengths to accommodate these applications while others simply let them fail silently. Similarly, applications in which an internal host must initiate connections (rather than the external host) are also harder to support and may require workarounds, *e.g.* FTP's passive mode may need to be turned on.

   In spite of these limitations, this approach is quite attractive as it requires nothing more than IPSec on the portable device. Even the internal hosts do not require any changes.

2. Another option for preventing the exposure of external addresses to internal routers is to use an extra level of IP-in-IP tunneling between the IPSec gateway and the internal host. This requires the internal host (or a proxy such as a Mobile IP home agent) to support IP-in-IP encapsulation and decapsulation. The principal advantage of this approach is that it transparently enables all applications and can be easily extended to work with Mobile IP [9, 10, 18, 19].

The portable device must also be responsible for securing the private network, because it extends its periphery. Therefore, it must implement some firewall capabilities, otherwise, any malicious individual that gains access to it will have gained access to the private network as well.

5 Enabling Groups of Users

We have also been investigating mechanisms to support small teams of mobile users traveling together. Disaster recovery teams offer an excellent example of this scenario. Another example may be a sales team traveling together that wishes to set up a "temporary branch office" of their corporation at a convention center. These situations call for "thin servers" around which a small network can be quickly established. This network may be based on either wireless or wireline LAN technologies. We have prototyped such a device and call it a Remote Site Server (RSS). An RSS can fulfill the booting, configuration, security, and routing needs of an assortment of connected clients. It offers DHCP, DNS, Mail, web-caching, file-sharing and firewall services. It also acts as a router to the outside world and can provide both network address translation (NAT) and secure communication capabilities. The NAT feature is handy for hiding multiple hosts on a private network behind a single ISP-provided IP address. All communication involving any of the hosts behind the thin server appears to originate from the thin server. This communication can either be in the clear or secured through IP-level or higher-level encryption and authentication, when necessary. The same VPN technologies that were described earlier (see Section 4) for connecting individual remote hosts to private networks are also applicable here. A variety of Internet connectivity options are supported including ethernet and dial-up PPP. Since the task of establishing Internet connectivity, negotiating network access across firewalls, and warding off hackers is off-loaded to the thin server, individual clients behind it need not concern themselves with any of the associated complexities. One may think of the RSS as a power-device (see Section 4) enhanced with server software to support protected workgroups.

The RSS feature-set is also a good match for small-office or home-office (SOHO) computing. These offices can be viewed as less volatile, or smaller, variations of "temporary" branch offices. These situations can benefit from most of the capabilities of the RSS but may not need the VPN capabilities. For example, a small, independently owned flower shop may not have a "parent" office with which it may need to establish secure channels.

One possible use of our remote site server is in supporting multiple satellite offices of a corporation. In any large deployment of these systems, ensuring that each is installed correctly and with the latest software packages is a major undertaking. We have addressed these issues in several ways.

We have developed a framework for automating the installation, upgrade and configuration of software packages on the thin server This framework organizes different software packages into distinct clusters. Each cluster can be independently installed and, if an older version of the cluster is detected, it can be automatically upgraded with a newer version. The framework stores configuration information separately from the software. This allows a pre-existing configuration to be reused with the newly updated software and eliminates the overhead of unnecessary reconfiguration. The thin server offers an HTML form-based administrative interface. As such, there is no need to connect a monitor to the thin server, and it can be managed from any device equipped with a web browser. In some cases, troubleshooting or special administration tasks may require complete shell access to the thin server. Our prototype offers telnet access (through a Java applet) to administrators on the local network and Secure Shell (SSH) login for remote administrators.

6 Conclusion

We have presented our vision of a *Complete Computing* environment. We leverage a common set of mechanisms to enable *mobile, nomadic, remote, branch office* and *small office* computing, hitherto addressed as disparate problems. From a user-centric point of view, the important distinctions are not directly related to any of the aforementioned modes of computing, but to the characteristics of the device used. Table 1 correlates the type of device to the user experience it affords. In all cases, the first step is to establish a communication path to the private network by (1) *hopping* on the internet, and (2) negotiating access past the corporate firewall. Having done this, the user (or the device on the user's behalf) has obtained access to the resources within the private network. However, the level of service with which these resources are now available reflect the characteristics of the device used by the remote user.

Using a Java and HTTPS enabled device allows the maximum degree of nomadicity. The user is able to use almost any portable computing device, and may not, in fact, carry one with him. These devices allow personal mobility in addition to nomadicity. However, the task of hopping on the internet is typically done by dialing into an ISP. This does not constitute automatic network configuration, as the user still has to worry about phone numbers, baud rate, and similar parameters.[5] Similarly, the firewall traversal is an explicit phase in which the user has to authenticate itself before gaining access to the private resources. Having accomplished this, the user is able to access but a handful of applications from the private network.

Specially configured devices also use ISP accounts to hop on the internet. Using IPSec mechanisms may make it easier to negotiate access past the firewall, but this step still exists. However, the level of application support improves considerably. Using these types of devices, it is possible to establish network level connections with the application servers within the private network. Full mobility is now possible.

Finally, devices that provide group support shield their clients from direct internet usage. Group support devices, such as our *Remote Site Server* create

---

[5] Strictly speaking, it is possible to establish internet presence by completely automatic means such as DHCP. However, typical ISP accounts do not yet allow this.

a protected workgroup safely ensconced away from the intimidating internet. A device within the protected workgroup benefits from automatic network configuration via DHCP support at the thin server. Likewise, the latter performs any required firewall negotiation on behalf of its clients. Given that the connection mechanisms used by the thin server to access servers in the corporate network are identical to those used by specially configured devices, the clients in the protected workgroup also enjoy a very high level of service.

Table 1. Modes of access when away from the the home network

Device Requirements	User Experience				
	Establishing a communication path		Level of Service		
	Auto. network config.	Implicit firewall traversal	Some apps (web based)	All or most apps (nomadic mode)	All applications (mobile mode)
Java and HTTPS enabled browser	N	N	Y	N	N
Specially configured devices	N	N	Y	Y	Y
Group support	Y	Y	Y	Y	Y

References

1. Atkinson, R.: Key Exchange Delegation Record for the DNS, *RFC 2230*, (Nov. 1997).
2. Aziz, A., Patterson, M.: Design and Implementation of SKIP, available on-line at *http://skip.incog.com/inet-95.ps*. A previous version of the paper was presented at INET '95 under the title *Simple Key Management for Internet Protocols (SKIP)*, and appears in the conference proceedings under that title.
3. Berners-Lee, T., Masinter, L., McCahill, M.: Uniform Resource Locators (URL), *RFC 1738*, (Dec. 1994).
4. Calhoun, P., Perkins, C.: Tunnel Establishment Protocol, Internet draft *draft-ietf-mobileip-calhoun-tep-00.txt* – work in progress, (1997).
5. Chapman, D. B., Zwicky, E.: *Building Internet Firewalls*, O'Reilly & Associates, Inc., (1995).
6. Doraswamy, N., Moskowitz, R.: Implementation of VPNs with IP Security, Internet-draft – work in progress, (1997).
7. Droms, R.: Dynamic Host Configuration Protocol, *RFC 2131*, (Mar. 1997).
8. Frier, A., Karlton, P., Kocher, P.: The SSL 3.0 Protocol, Netscape Communications Corp., (Nov. 1996).
9. Gupta, V., Glass., S.: Firewall traversal for Mobile IP: guidelines for firewalls and Mobile IP entities, Internet Draft *draft-ietf-mobileip-firewall-trav-00.txt* – work in progress, (Mar. 1997).

10. Gupta, V., Montenegro, G.: Secure and Mobile Networking, to appear in the ACM Journal on Special Topics in Mobile Networking and Applications (MONET), (special issue on Mobile Networking in the Internet).

11. Hamzeh, K., et al.: Layer Two Tunneling Protocol (L2TP), Internet Draft *draft-ietf-pppext-l2tp-08.txt* – work in progress, (Nov. 1997).

12. Harkins, D., Carrel, D.: The resolution of ISAKMP with Oakley, Internet Draft *draft-ietf-ipsec-isakmp-oakley-05.txt* – work in progress, (Nov. 1997).

13. Kent, S., Atkinson, R.: Security architecture for the Internet Protocol, Internet Draft *draft-ietf-ipsec-arch-sec-02.txt* – work in progress, (Nov. 1997) (a previous version appears as *RFC 1825*).

14. Kent, S., Atkinson, R.: IP authentication header, Internet Draft *draft-ietf-ipsec-auth-header-03.txt* – work in progress, (Nov. 1997) (a previous version appears as *RFC 1826*).

15. Kent, S., Atkinson, R.: IP encapsulating security payload, Internet Draft *draft-ietf-ipsec-esp-v2-02.txt* – work in progress, (Nov. 1997) (a previous version appears as *RFC 1827*).

16. Kistler, J. J., Satyanarayanan, M.: Disconnected Operation in the Coda File System, *ACM Transactions on Computer Systems*, 10, No. 1, (Feb. 1992) 3–25.

17. Maughan, D., Schertler, M., Schneider, M., Turner, J.: Internet Security Association and Key Management Protocol (ISAKMP), Internet Draft *draft-ietf-ipsec-isakmp-08.txt* – work in progress, (Jul. 1997).

18. Montenegro, G.: Tunnel Set-up Protocol (TSP), Internet Draft *draft-montenegro-tsp-00.txt* – work in progress, (Aug. 1997).

19. Montenegro, G., Gupta, V.: Firewall support for Mobile IP, Internet Draft *draft-montenegro-firewall-sup-02.txt* – work in progress, (Nov. 1997).

20. Orman, H.: The OAKLEY Key Determination Protocol, Internet Draft *draft-ietf-ipsec-oakley-02.txt* – work in progress.

21. Perkins, C., (Editor): IP mobility support, *RFC 2002*, (Oct. 1996).

22. Rekhter, Y., Moskowitz, B., Karrenberg, D., de Groot, G. J., Lear, E.: Address allocation for private internets, *RFC 1918*, (Feb. 1996).

23. Simpson, W.: The Point-to-Point Protocol (PPP), *RFC 1661*, (Jul. 1994).

24. Veizades, J., Guttman, E., Perkins, C., Kaplan, S.: Service Location Protocol, *RFC 2165*, (Jun. 1997).

25. Yeong, W., Howes, T., Kille, S.: Lightweight Directory Access Protocol, *RFC 1777*, (Mar. 1995).

Compact and Flexible Resolution
of CBT Multicast Key-Distribution

Kanta Matsuura[1], Yuliang Zheng[2], and Hideki Imai[1]

[1] IIS, Univ. of Tokyo, Roppongi 7-22-1, Minato-ku, Tokyo 106, JAPAN
kanta@iis.u-tokyo.ac.jp, imai@iis.u-tokyo.ac.jp
[2] School of Comp. & Info. Tech., Monash Univ., Melbourne, VIC 3199, AUSTRALIA
yuliang@mars.fcit.monash.edu.au

Abstract. In an open network such as the Internet, multicast security services typically start with group session-key distribution. Considering scalability for group communication among widely-distributed members, we can find a currently-leading approach based on a CBT (Core-Based Tree) routing protocol, where Group Key Distribution Centers (GKDCs) are dynamically constructed during group-member joining process.
In search of practical use of it, this paper first analyzes the CBT protocol in terms of its efficiency as well as security management. Then the paper proposes several improvements on the protocol with an aim to solve the problem identified. In particular, (1) an overuse of encryption and signatures is avoided and (2) a hybrid trust model is introduced by a simple mechanism for controling the GKDC distribution. A comprehensive comparison among the costs of several implementations is also carried out.

1 Introduction

Multicast-oriented applications require a sufficient security infrastructure especially when implemented in an open and global network. A good example is the Internet, where the next-generation protocol IPv6 (Internet Protocol version 6) considers security services for multicast as one of the central issues [1], [2]. The basic starting-point is secure and authenticated distribution or agreement of group session-keys.

A simple strategy is to assign the key-distribution function to a trusted single entity or Key Distribution Center (KDC). This strategy, however, very unlikely scales for multicast communication among widely- or sparsely-distributed members. Scalable approaches would be combined with multicast routing protocols since

- there exist routing protocols which provide dynamic and scalable properties,

- routing mechanisms are typically in close relation to group structures,

and

- combining two pre-processes (routing preparation and key-distribution) potentially saves bandwidth.

Looking at the Internet, we can find IGMP (Internet Group Management Protocol)[3] used in the final delivery of a multicast packet between a local router and a group member on its directly-attached subnetworks. IGMP delivery services can be jointed by a number of different multicast routing and delivery mechanisms among distributed routers.

For groups with dispersed or sparse membership, most scalable are Shared-Tree techniques such as PIM-SM (Protocol-Independent Multicast – Sparse Mode)[4] and CBT (Core-Based Tree) routing protocol[5]–[7]. The main differences between these two techniques are that

- CBT maintains its characteristics as scalable as possible by not offering the option of shifting from a Shared Tree to a Shortest Path Tree

and that

- CBT has fewer entries in the routing tables[8].

Thus, although not devoted to any specific implementation, a dynamic key-distribution protocol in conjunction with CBT[9] is currently considered as a strong candidate for a scalable multicast key-distribution scheme. This protocol uses Group Key Distribution Centers (GKDCs) which are dynamically constructed during group-member joining process.

This paper first overviews the CBT mechanism in Sect. 2, where several problems or questions are subsequently discussed, and finally four implementations are evaluated in terms of their computational costs and communication overhead. A more compact and yet more flexible resolution is then proposed in Sect. 3 with a function of controlling GKDCs, followed by the evaluation of four implementations. After discussion in Sect. 4, Sect. 5 gives conclusions.

2 Core-Based Tree

2.1 Routing Protocol

In the CBT routing protocol[5]–[7], a single shared delivery tree is built around several core routers. When a host wishes to join the multicast group, it casts an IGMP group membership report across its attached link. On receiving this report, a local CBT-aware router explicitly joins the delivery tree by generating a JOIN_REQUEST message, which is sent to the next hop on the path towards one of the group's core routers. In reply to this JOIN_REQUEST message, a JOIN_ACK message is generated by the core or another router which has already joined the tree on the path between the core and the host. This JOIN_ACK message traverses the reverse path of the join and thus a new branch is created. Routers along the new branch are called non-core routers, and there exists a parent-child relationship between adjacent routers along the branch. The resulting tree is a bidirectional and acyclic graph that reaches every member host. Once the tree is established, packets are forwarded in a simple way: when a node receives a multicast packet, it forwards copies of the packet on all branches of the group's tree except for the branch on which the packet arrived.

There are two significant differences between the CBT and other network-layer multicast routing protocols such as DVMRP (Distance Vector Multicast Routing Protocol) and M-OSPF (Multicast extensions for Open Shortest Path First) [10]. First, different from DVMRP and M-OSPF, CBT messages have their own protocol headers, which allow the protocol to make explicit provision for security. Second, CBT is a Shared-Tree technique; there exists one shared delivery tree per group, not per sender. By contrast, the other protocols use Source-Based Tree architecture, which is less scalable than Shared-Tree architecture.

2.2 Security Mechanism

The CBT architecture complements security by secure joining process [9]. This complementation assumes the presence of an internetwork-wide asymmetric cryptosystem[3]. In particular, join-process messages such as IGMP group membership reports, `JOIN_REQUEST` messages, and `JOIN_ACK` messages are equipped with security parameters by the use of the asymmetric cryptosystem.

We describe an example of secure CBT joining by using a sample tree shown in Fig. 1[4]. The main terms used in the description are as follows.

C: An elected primary core which takes on the initial role of GKDC.

TKN-X: Token of an entity X, typically containing recipient's identity, a time-stamp denoted as TS-X, and a pseudo-random number to help a recipient with verification procedures; the time-stamp demonstrates message freshness, and the random number demonstrates message originality. If X is a host, recipient's identity is omitted.

$SIG_X(\cdot)$: Signature with the secret key of X.

$ENC_X(\cdot)$: Encryption with the public key of X.

KM: Key materials to be delivered. A group key and a key-encrypting key are contained. The former is used for encrypting group data traffic. The latter is created by the primary core and used for re-keying the group with a new group key just prior to an old key exceeding its lifetime.

ACL: Group access control list created by a CBT group initiator.

SAp: Security Association parameters pre-negotiated through ISAKMP (Internet Security Association and Key Management Protocol) [13] or Photuris Key Management Protocol [14].

GAP: Group access package sent from an already-verified node to a joining node.

The format of GAP is

$$SIG_{\text{sender}}\left(\text{TKN-sender}, SIG_C\left(\text{ACL}\right), SE_{C\rightarrow\text{host}}, SE_{C\rightarrow\text{next-hop}}\right),$$

---

[3] Public-key management systems can be globally provided, for instance, through extended DNS (Domain Name System) [11] or WWW (World Wide Web) [12].

[4] This tree has only one core for simplicity, but typically a CBT tree comprises several.

where $SE_{X \to Y} = ENC_Y \left(SIG_X (KM, SAp) \right)$.

ACL is assumed to have been already sent from the initiator to the primary core. It is also assumed that the primary core has already participated in Security Association establishment to hold KM and SAp. These pre-processes are carried out by using a unicast protocol such as ISAKMP [13] or Photuris [14].

Join-Request: First, the host h sends an IGMP group membership report

$$\left(SIG_h (TKN\text{-}h), \text{MEMBERSHIP\_REPORT} \right)$$

to the local router A. On receiving this report, A authenticates the h's token which is digitally-signed. If successful, A generates a CBT join-request

$$SIG_A \left(TKN\text{-}A, SIG_h (TKN\text{-}h), \text{JOIN\_REQUEST} \right)$$

and unicasts it to the next-hop router B on the path to the core C. Next, B verifies A's signature. If successful, B relays the request to the core C by unicasting

$$SIG_B \left(TKN\text{-}B, SIG_h (TKN\text{-}h), \text{JOIN\_REQUEST} \right).$$

Finally, the core C verifies B's signature and also h's signature. If this is successful and the host h is found to be included in the group access control list ACL, C generates a group access package GAP.

Join-Acknowledgement: The core router encapsulates the group access package GAP in a join-acknowledgement, and digitally signs the whole message:

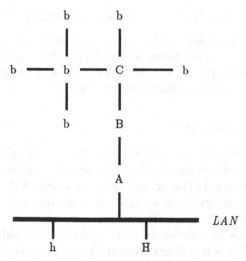

Fig. 1. An example of Core-Based Tree. C is the primary core. A, B, and b's are non-core routers. h is a host which wishes to join the multicast group. The LAN (Local Area Network) where h resides is under its local CBT-aware router A. Another host H is on the same LAN.

$$SIG_C\left(SIG_h\left(\text{TKN-h}\right), \text{GAP}, \text{JOIN\_ACK}\right).$$

This is sent to B. Then C's signatures on the whole message and on GAP are verified by B. If both successful, B extracts the encrypted information $SE_{C\to B}$ from GAP and decrypts it. Then B verifies C's signatures on this information and on the access control list ACL. If successful, B subsequently stores the ACL in an appropriate table, encrypts the information (key materials and security-association parameters) with a local key, and also stores it. Next, B encrypts the key information with the next-hop router A's public key to reform GAP. The resulting whole acknowledgement message

$$SIG_B\left(SIG_h\left(\text{TKN-h}\right), \text{GAP}, \text{JOIN\_ACK}\right)$$

is sent to A. On receiving this message, A follows the same verification and storage process. Subsequently, A generates an IGMP group membership report

$$\left(SIG_h\left(\text{TKN-h}\right), SE_{C\to h}, \text{MEMBERSHIP\_REPORT}\right),$$

where $SE_{C\to h}$ is extracted from the received GAP and just forwarded. The host h receives this report and identifies it by its signed token. Finally, h decrypts and verifies the key information. Thus h securely obtains the key materials and the security-association parameters, and the routers A and B become GKDCs[5].

Once the above process is successfully completed, the router A, which is now available as GKDC, directly responds to the request

$$\left(SIG_H\left(\text{TKN-H}\right), \text{MEMBERSHIP\_REPORT}\right)$$

from another host H by sending

$$\left(SIG_H\left(\text{TKN-H}\right), SE_{C\to H}, \text{MEMBERSHIP\_REPORT}\right)$$

back to H. $SE_{C\to H}$ can be generated by A, since A knows $SIG_C\left(\text{KM}, \text{SAp}\right)$. H then identifies it by its signed token and decrypts $SE_{C\to H}$. Finally, if the core's signature on the decrypted information is successfully verified, the report is accepted. The whole process is summarized in Fig. 2.

2.3 Problems and Questions

Security: First, information on key can be distributed widely, which might provide less security for the system; uncontrollable scalability could be a threat. The system trusts each router's behavior according to the spirit of the Internet, but this trust does not automatically mean that the data-storage systems of the routers are sufficiently protected against attackers.

Second, GKDCs store key materials in encrypted form, but without any freshness parameters. This is less secure than storage with freshness parameters such as time-stamps or nonces, which are deterrents to replay attacks.

---

[5] When any process failure occurs or an invalid signature is found, a JOIN_NACK message is returned toward the local router A. The host h is then notified of the failure by a resultant IGMP membership report. It initiates a join-request again if it wishes.

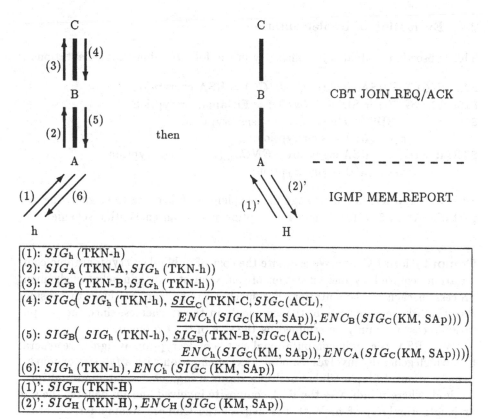

Fig. 2. Process description of secure joining to the sample Core-Based Tree. After the joining process of host h, another host H makes a join-request.

Efficiency: First, sender's signature on GAP (highlighted by underlined fonts in Fig. 2) is redundant and unnecessary. This is because GAP is carried by a join-acknowledgement message which is signed as a whole by the sender.

Second, the first signed and encrypted information, which is underlined in Fig. 2, might be also redundant; the same information is contained in the following part. If really redundant, this underlined part is considered to cause a waste of bandwidth; in general, simultaneous use of digital signature and public-key encryption leads to large communication overhead.

Digital signature and public-key encryption cost a lot not only in bandwidth but also in computation. The cost depends on cryptographic algorithms, which motivates us to evaluate the efficiency of specific implementations[6].

---

[6] No specific implementation is discussed in the Internet RFC (Request for Comments)[9] which proposes the CBT-based key-distribution protocol.

2.4 Evaluation of Implementation

This subsection evaluates the efficiency of the following four implementations[7]:

RSA: $SIG(\cdot)$ = RSA signature, $ENC(\cdot)$ = RSA encryption.
ElGamal: $SIG(\cdot)$ = SDSS, $ENC(\cdot)$ = ElGamal encryption.
SC: $SIG(\cdot)$ = SDSS, $ENC_{router}(\cdot)$ = signcryption,
       $SE_{C \to host}(\cdot)$ = signcryption.
SC_RSA: $SIG(\cdot)$ = RSA signature, $ENC_{router}(\cdot)$ = signcryption,
       $SE_{C \to host}(\cdot)$ = signcryption.

Since signcryption cannot change the recipient with keeping the signer, the last part of GAP in SC/SC_RSA uses signcryption just as an encryption scheme.

Computational Cost: We estimate the cost of public-key cryptographic computation required by one execution of join-request and join-acknowledgement process in each implementation. For specific comparison, we have to consider the currently-required size of the exponents in those schemes, since the computational cost is mainly determined by the size of the exponent.

With RSA, the main computational cost is in decryption or signature generation which generally involves a modular exponentiation with a *full size* exponent, namely about $1.5|n|$ modular multiplications using the "square-and-multiply" method, where n indicates the RSA composite involved and $|n|$ denotes the size or length (in bits) of n. With the help of the Chinese Remainder Theorem, this cost can be reduced to be $1.5|n|/4 = 0.375|n|$. On the assumption that $|n| = 1536$, which is recommended to be used for long-term security (say, more than 20 years), we compute the total cost of the implementation RSA.

Next, ElGamal requires (1) one modular exponentiation for generating a signature, (2) two for verifying a signature, (3) two for encrypting, and (4) one for decrypting. Resulting numbers of modular multiplications are (1) $1.5|q|$, (2) $1.75|q|$, (3) $3|q|$, and (4) $1.5|q|$, respectively, where q is the order of the subgroup used in SDSS. Assuming that $|q| = 176$, which provides long-term security quite similar to that considered in the case of RSA, we compute the total computational cost of ElGamal.

Likewise, we compute the costs of SC and SC_RSA; (1) one modular exponentiation for signcrypting and (2) two for unsigncrypting result in (1) $1.5|q|$ and (2) $1.75|q|$ modular multiplications. Signature generation and verification cost the same as in ElGamal and in RSA, respectively.

Those costs are given as a function of the number of non-GKDC routers, as shown in Fig. 3. SC_RSA is the most efficient and ElGamal is the least efficient. The cost of SC_RSA is about 74% of that of ElGamal when there exist non-GKDC routers.

---

[7] Since signcryption is a relatively new cryptographic primitive, we overview it in Appendix. The readers can consult textbooks (for example, [15]) about the other well-known encryption/signature algorithms.

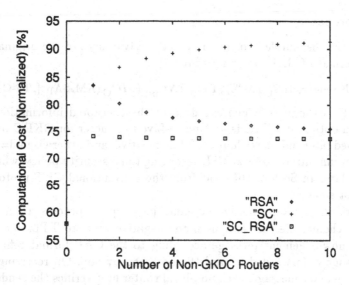

Fig. 3. Computational cost (normalized by the cost of ElGamal) of the conventional CBT scheme with $|n| = 1536$ and $|q| = 176$.

Table 1. Communication overhead of SC represented by the ratios to those of RSA, ElGamal, and SC_RSA.

	$(h \rightarrow A)$ or $(H \rightarrow A)$	$(A \rightarrow B)$ or $(B \rightarrow C)$
vs. RSA	17.2%	17.2%
vs. ElGamal	100.0%	100.0%
vs. SC_RSA	17.2%	17.2%

(a) during join-request process

	$(C \rightarrow B)$ or $(B \rightarrow A)$	$(A \rightarrow h)$ or $(A \rightarrow H)$
vs. RSA	15.0%	11.5%
vs. ElGamal	39.7%	25.6%
vs. SC_RSA	22.5%	29.3%

(b) during join-acknowledgement process

Communication Overhead: Assuming the same security level as in the evaluation of computational cost, we use $|p| = |n| = 1536$ and $|hash(\cdot)| = |q|/2 = 88$, where p is the order of the multiplicative group and $hash(\cdot)$ is the one-way hash function used in SDSS-based schemes. The evaluation result is shown in Table 1. Since SC is estimated to be the most compact, this result is represented by the ratios of the overhead of SC to those of the other implementations.

3 An Efficient Resolution

To solve or answer to the issues identified in Sect. 2.3, this section describes an efficient resolution of secure CBT key-distribution.

3.1 Protocol

The resolution is simple enough to keep the advantages of the original scheme; just the format of GAP is changed into

$$\left(\text{TKN-sender}, SIG_C\left(\text{ACL}\right), \text{TTL}, ENC_{\text{nd}}\left(SIG_C\left(\text{KM}, \text{SAp} \left[, \text{TS-C}\right]\right)\right)\right)$$

where "nd" is the node which can decrypt the encrypted information next. [ ] denotes an option and TTL is a Time-to-Live parameter for GKDC permission; as described later, nd=next-hop if TTL is positive, and otherwise nd=host. The core assigns an initial value to TTL according to its security policy, which will be discussed later in Sect. 4. Different from the conventional CBT protocol, GAP itself is not signed.

In particular, after exactly the same join-request process as in the original CBT scheme, the core assigns a non-negative value to TTL, and generates a join-acknowledgement message according to the GAP format refined above. This message is forwarded toward the host hop by hop. On receiving the join-acknowledgement message, each non-local router first verifies the sender's signature on the whole message[8]. If successful, one of the following three procedures occurs, depending on the value of TTL[9]:

(TTL>1) The router decrements the TTL and subsequently decrypts or unsigncrypts the information contained in the last part of GAP. Then the core's signatures on this information and on ACL are verified. If successful, the router encrypts (or signcrypts) the information with the public key of the next-hop (and additionally with the router's own secret key in the case of signcryption). The resultant acknowledgement message as a whole is signed with the router's secret key and forwarded. The router stores KM, SAp, and ACL in a signed and encrypted form to become GKDC. This stored information optionally includes the time-stamp generated by the core, depending on the security policy.

(TTL=1) The router decrements the TTL and subsequently decrypts or unsigncrypts the last part of GAp. Then the core's signatures are verified. In addition, the host's signature on the token is verified with the public key consistently derived from the CBT routing information. If everything is successful, the router encrypts (or signcrypts) the information with the public key of the host (and additionally with the router's own secret key in the case of signcryption). The resultant acknowledgement message is forwarded in a digitally-signed form. The storage process occurs in the same way as in the case of TTL>1.

(TTL=0) The router is not qualified as GKDC; neither key materials nor ACL is stored. The router just signs the whole message and forwards it to the next-hop.

---

[8] When any joining-process failure occurs or an invalid signature is found, a JOIN_NACK process is provoked in the same way as in the conventional scheme.

[9] If an attacker changes the value of TTL, it can be detected by the verification of the sender's signature on the whole message.

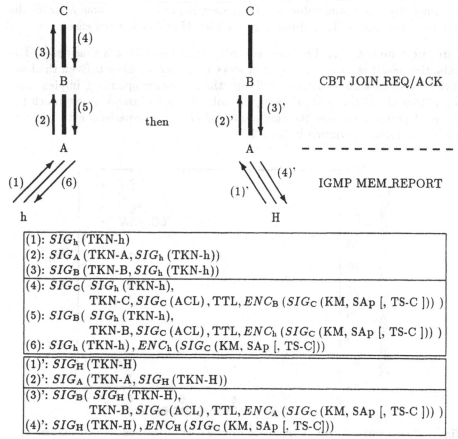

Fig. 4. Process description of the proposed secure joining to Core-Based Tree when the initial value of TTL is 1. The joining process of host h qualifies router B as a GKDC, and then that of host H qualifies A.

The local router follows the same process, except that the resultant message is not a join-acknowledgement message but an IGMP group membership report

$$\big(SIG_h\,(\text{TKN-h})\,,ENC_h\,\big(SIG_C\,(\text{KM},\text{SAp}\,[,\text{TS-C}\,]\,)\,\big)\,\big)\,,\texttt{MEMBERSHIP\_REPORT}\big)\,.$$

The whole process is exemplified in Fig. 4.

3.2 Evaluation of Implementation

This subsection evaluates the proposed protocol considering four implementations in a similar way as in Sect. 2:

RSA*: $SIG(\cdot)$ = RSA signature, $ENC(\cdot)$ = RSA encryption.
ElGamal*: $SIG(\cdot)$ = SDSS, $ENC(\cdot)$ = ElGamal encryption.
SC*: $SIG(\cdot)$ = SDSS, $ENC(\cdot)$ = signcryption.
SC_RSA*: $SIG(\cdot)$ = RSA signature, $ENC(\cdot)$ = signcryption.

For simplicity, the initial value of TTL is assumed to be large enough for all the routers to become GKDCs through one joining (Fig. 4 is not the case).

Computational Cost: The same security level as in Sect. 2 is considered. The evaluation result is shown in Fig. 5; SC_RSA* is the most efficient. Even the least efficient one, ElGamal*, is more efficient than the corresponding implementation (ElGamal) of the conventional protocol. Figure 6 illustrates how much the proposed protocol reduces the computational cost in comparison with the conventional protocol reviewed in Sect. 2.

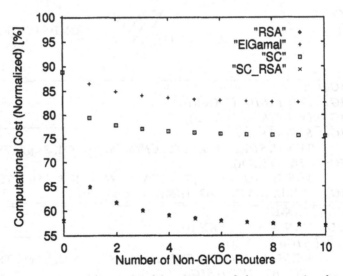

Fig. 5. Computational cost (normalized by the cost of the conventional ElGamal) of the proposed scheme with $|n| = 1536$ and $|q| = 176$.

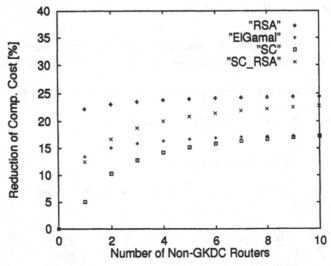

Fig. 6. Computational-cost reduction by the proposed protocol ($|n| = 1536$, $|q| = 176$).

Table 2. Communication overhead during join-acknowledgement process of SC* represented by the ratios to those of RSA*, ElGamal*, and SC_RSA*. Considered parameters are: $|p| = |n| = 1536$ and $|hash(\cdot)| = |q|/2 = 88$.

	$(C \rightarrow B)$ or $(B \rightarrow A)$	$(A \rightarrow h)$ or $(A \rightarrow H)$
vs. RSA*	17.2%	17.2%
vs. ElGamal*	50.9%	38.4%
vs. SC_RSA*	20.6%	23.7%

Communication Overhead: There is no difference between the conventional and the proposed protocols, in the overhead during join-request process. Table 2 shows the communication overhead during join-acknowledgement process, where the same security level as in previous discussion is assumed. Since SC* is estimated to be the most compact, the comparison result is represented by the ratios of the overhead of SC* to those of the other implementations.

In comparison with the original protocol, the proposed protocol requires shorter communication overhead during the join-acknowledgement process; assuming $|TTL| \ll |KM|$, $|TS\text{-}C| \ll |KM|$, and the same security level as in the previous discussions ($|p| = |n| = 1536$ and $|hash(\cdot)| = |q|/2 = 88$), the overhead reduction of the messages between routers is estimated as follows:

$$\text{RSA* vs. RSA:} \quad \frac{3|n| + |KM| + |SAp|}{8|n| + |KM| + |SAp|} > 37.5\%,$$

$$\text{ElGamal* vs. ElGamal:} \quad \frac{2\left(|hash(\cdot)| + |q|\right) + |p| + |KM| + |SAp|}{6\left(|hash(\cdot)| + |q|\right) + 2|p| + |KM| + |SAp|} > 44.3\%,$$

$$\text{SC* vs. SC:} \quad \frac{2|hash(\cdot)| + 2|q| + |KM| + |SAp|}{7|hash(\cdot)| + 7|q| + |KM| + |SAp|} > 28.6\%,$$

and

$$\text{SC_RSA* vs. SC_RSA:} \quad \frac{|n| + |q| + |hash(\cdot)| + |KM| + |SAp|}{5|n| + 2|q| + 2|hash(\cdot)| + |KM| + |SAp|} > 21.9\%.$$

4 Discussion

4.1 A Question of Trust

The CBT security architecture assumes that all the routers on a delivery tree are trusted and do not misbehave. In reply to the question whether this assumption is reasonable in internetworking, the original RFC (Request for Comments) [9] makes two remarks:

(A1) Depending on the security requirement and perceived threat, the presented model may be acceptable.

(A2) A higher level of security can be provided by imposing all the join-request authentication on a core router.

In our scheme, the latter (A2) can be provided by assigning the minimum initial value to Time-to-Live parameter, *i.e.*, TTL=0. The flexibility of this kind of control with the help of TTL will be discussed in the next subsection. It should be noted that even this "only one GKDC" situation is still more scalable than protocols with "only one KDC"; different groups can use different GKDCs in CBT-based protocols.

The proposed scheme provides another improvement on security by optionally including an authenticated time-stamp in the key-material container. Such a use of a time-varying quantity convinces the entities that the session-keys are *fresh*. As well-known in the research community of information-security technologies, freshness of the keys contributes to the protection against replay attack. This time-stamp can be replaced with other freshness parameters such as nonces.

4.2 Controlling GKDC Distribution

A need for controlling GKDC distribution or expansion is suggested by the higher-level security modification (A2) mentioned in the previous subsection. This control should be viewed not only from security requirements, but also from load distribution/concentration and traffic efficiency. A large initial value of TTL precludes too much burden from concentrating on a small number of GKDC routers, but might provide insufficient security. By contrast, a small initial value of TTL provides us a high level of security, but might cause too heavy load on GKDC routers and traffic flood. One practical solution to this balancing problem is to offer a flexible controlling mechanism *with a cost as small as possible*; we propose the use of a Time-to-Live parameter TTL, which permits the recipient router to become GKDC when positive. Both computational cost and communication overhead caused by the deployment of TTL are negligible.

The use of TTL implies a hybrid trust model; the trust tree is no longer the same as the distribution tree. The core assigns an initial value to TTL to show the region of the routers which the core itself trusts. Suppose that the router B receives a join-acknowledgement message with TTL=1 from the core C, which tells B that B is trusted by C but that farther downstream routers are not trusted by C. This acknowledgement process does not allow the farther routers to become GKDCs this time. When the next join-acknowledgement process occurs as a result of the next join-request, B assigns an appropriate initial value to TTL to show the region of the routers which B trusts; if the next-hop router A is trusted by B, B can assign a positive initial value without consulting the core C. Thus the trusted region can be expanded request by request.

4.3 Sender-Specific Keys

After completion of the proposed key-distribution, each member can easily multicast a sender-specific key by signing it with his/her own secret key and encrypting the result with the obtained group key. This message includes necessary Security Association parameters.

Non-member senders can also distribute a sender-specific key. They first negotiate with the primary core to establish the Security Association parameters and their session key. Thereafter, by using the group's current session-key, the core multicasts the sender-specific session-key together with the sender's security parameters to the group.

5 Conclusions

This paper analyzed and improved a scalable multicast key-distribution based on CBT.

In the analysis, four implementations were compared: RSA-based scheme (RSA), ElGamal-based scheme (ElGamal), signcryption-based scheme (SC), and signcryption-with-RSA scheme (SC_RSA). In cryptographic computation, SC_RSA costs least and ElGamal costs most. The computational cost of SC is moderate, and its communication overhead is by far the shortest. The computational cost was examined in detail as a function of the number of non-GKDC routers between the joining host and the core router of the group.

Likewise, in the proposed protocol, four implementations were compared: RSA*, ElGamal*, SC*, and SC_RSA*. The result was quite similar to that of the conventional protocol; SC_RSA* gives the smallest computational cost, and SC* gives the shortest communication overhead. In each implementation, the proposed protocol is more efficient than the conventional one. The computational-cost reduction depends on the number of non-GKDC routers and saturates to be approximately 24% (RSA* vs. RSA, or SC_RSA* vs. SC_RSA) and 17% (ElGamal* vs. ElGamal, or SC* vs. SC). The overhead is also reduced significantly; at least 37.5% saving in the case of RSA*, 44.3% in the case of ElGamal*, 28.6% in the case of SC*, and 21.9% in the case of SC_RSA*. These advantages of the proposed protocol are due to the deployment of a cheaper Group Access Package than the conventional one.

To summarize the issues on efficiency, the combination of RSA and signcryption is the best implementation in terms of the computational cost and the signcryption-based implementation is the best way in terms of the communication overhead, both in the original protocol and in the proposed protocol. For each implementation with more than two non-GKDC routers, the proposed protocol saves at least 13% of the computational cost and 22% of the communication overhead.

In addition to the efficiency, the proposed scheme provides two improvements. The first one is a function of controlling the expansion or distribution of GKDCs. This contributes to protocol flexibility in balancing security requirements and traffic efficiency or load concentration. The second one is a freshness parameter optionally included in a returned key-material container. This contributes to the protection against replay attack.

References

1. Atkinson R. J.: Toward a More Secure Internet, IEEE Computer **30** (1997) 57–61
2. Oppliger R.: Internet Security: Firewalls and Beyond, Comm. ACM **40** (1997) 92–102
3. Fenner W.: Internet Group Management Protocol, Version 2, RFC2236 (1997)
4. Estrin D., *et. al.*: Protocol Independent Multicast-Sparse Mode (PIM-SM): Protocol Specification, RFC2117 (1997)
5. Ballardie T., Francis P., and Crowcroft J.: An Architecture for Scalable Inter-Domain Multicast Routing, Proc. of ACM SIGCOMM (1993) 85–95
6. Ballardie A.: Core Based Trees (CBT version 2) Multicast Routing — Protocol Specification —, RFC2189 (1997)
7. Ballardie A.: Core Based Trees (CBT) Multicast Routing Architecture, RFC2201 (1997)
8. Billhartz T., *et. al.*: Performance and Resource Cost Comparisons for the CBT and PIM Multicast Routing Protocols, IEEE Journal on Selected Area in Communications **15** (1997) 304–315
9. Ballardie A.: Scalable Multicast Key Distribution, RFC1949 (1996)
10. Moy J.: Multicast Routing Extensions for OSPF, Comm. ACM **37** (1994) 61–66
11. Eastlake D. 3rd and Kaufman C.: Domain Name System Security Extensions, RFC2065 (1997)
12. Berners-Lee T., *et. al.*: The World-Wide Web, Comm. ACM **37** (1994) 76–82
13. Maughan D., *et. al.*: Internet Security Association and Key Management Protocol (ISAKMP), (work in progress).
14. Karn P. and Simpson W. A.: Photuris: Session-Key Management Protocol, (work in progress).
15. Stinson D. R.: CRYPTOGRAPHY: Theory and Practice, CRC Press (1995)
16. Zheng Y.: Digital Signcryption or How to Achieve Cost(Signature & Encryption) << Cost(Signature) + Cost(Encryption), Lecture Notes in Computer Science 1294, Springer-Verlag (1997) 165–179

Appendix: SDSS and Signcryption

To avoid forgery and ensure confidentiality of the contents of a letter, for centuries it has been a common practice for the originator of the letter to sign his/her name on it and then seal it in an envelope, before posting it. In a secure and authenticated communication over an open and insecure network, the same two-step approach has been followed; before a message is sent out, the sender of the message would sign it using a digital signature scheme, and then encrypt the message (and the signature) using a private-key encryption algorithm under a randomly chosen message-encryption key. The random message-encryption key would then be encrypted by using the recipient's public key. We call this two-step approach *signature-then-encryption*.

In general, the sum of the cost for signature and the cost for public-key encryption is computationally expensive. Originating from questioning whether it is absolutely necessary for one to spend the sum of the costs to achieve both confidentiality and authenticity, the author of [16] proposes a primitive called *signcryption*.

Intuitively, a digital signcryption is a cryptographic method that fulfills both the functions of secure encryption and digital signature, but *with a cost smaller than that required by signature-then-encryption*. This paper uses an implementation of signcryption based on a Shortened Digital-Signature Standard (SDSS). By using the notation listed in Table 3, Fig. 7 shows an SDSS which is referred to as SDSS1 in [16]. The signcryption based on this SDSS1 is illustrated in Fig. 8.

Table 3. Notation.

Parameters public to all:
p — a large prime
q — a large prime factor of $p-1$
g — an integer with order q modulo p chosen randomly from $[1, 2, \cdots, p-1]$
Keys of the sender and the recipient:
$SK_{Alice} \in [1, 2, \cdots, q-1]$ — secret key of Alice
PK_{Alice} — public key of Alice where $PK_{Alice} = g^{SK_{Alice}} \bmod p$
$SK_{Bob} \in [1, 2, \cdots, q-1]$ — secret key of Bob
PK_{Bob} — public key of Bob where $PK_{Bob} = g^{SK_{Bob}} \bmod p$
Operations and functions:
$KH_k(\cdot)$ — a one-way hash function key-ed with k
$hash(\cdot)$ — a one-way hash function
(E_k, D_k) — encryption and decryption algorithms of a private key cipher (attached subscrypts indicate the keys)
$\|$ — Concatenation
$\in_R$ — Random picking (ex.: $x \in_R [1, 2, \cdots, q-1]$ indicates that x is randomly picked from $[1, 2, \cdots, q-1]$.)

Generation of signature (s_1, s_2) on a message m	Signature verification
$x \in_R [1, 2, \cdots, q-1]$ $k = g^x \bmod p$ $s_1 = KH_k(m)$ $s_2 = x/(s_1 + SK_{Alice}) \bmod q$	$k = (PK_{Alice} \cdot g^{s_1})^{s_2} \bmod p$ Accept m if and only if $KH_k(m)$ is identical to s_1.

Fig. 7. Example of SDSS (SDSS1).

Signcryption by Alice		Unsigncryption by Bob
$x \in_R [1, 2, \cdots, q-1]$ $(k_1, k_2) = hash(PK_{Bob}^x \bmod p)$ $c = E_{k_1}(m)$ $s_1 = KH_{k_2}(m)$ $s_2 = x/(s_1 + SK_{Alice}) \bmod q$	$(c, s_1, s_2) \Rightarrow$	$(k_1, k_2) =$ $hash\left((PK_{Alice} \cdot g^{s_1})^{s_2 \cdot SK_{Bob}} \bmod p\right)$ $m = D_{k_1}(c)$ Accept m if and only if $KH_{k_2}(m)$ is identical to s_1.

Fig. 8. Example of signcryption based on SDSS1.

Integrating Resource Reservation with Rate-Based Transport Protocols in AMInet

Atsushi Shionozaki[1], Kei Yamashita[3], Shusuke Utsumi[2], Kenjiro Cho[1]

[1] Sony Computer Science Laboratory Inc.
Shinagawa-ku, Tokyo 141 Japan
{shio,kjc}@csl.sony.co.jp

[2] IT Laboratories, Sony Corporation
Fujisawa-shi, Kanagawa, 251 Japan
utsumi@sm.sony.co.jp

[3] NTT Optical Network Systems Laboratories
Yokosuka-shi, Kanagawa 239 Japan
kei@exa.onlab.ntt.co.jp

Abstract. This paper presents a resource reservation scheme that integrates transport protocol extensions to support continuous media and bulk data transfer. Specifically, our resource reservation protocol maps IP flows onto ATM VCs and end nodes support extensions to TCP/UDP so that the reserved bandwidth can be fully used. These modules have been implemented as part of the first phase of the AMInet Project dedicated to providing advanced integrated services as fiber to the home and high speed backbone networks become reality. Performance figures of our implementation are given to show that our mechanisms can support services beyond TCP/IP and to prove the effectiveness of our system.

1 Introduction

Fiber to the home (FTTH)[24] is a reality that is just around the corner. Other ways of bringing high speed networking closer to the home such as xDSL technology [16] have also been proposed and are regionally being introduced. By simply supporting constant high bandwidth network accessibility to the home, such technological advancements can bring forth new lifestyles. However, the most popular worldwide network, the Internet, will not be able to support user demands of such high quality because it lacks support for high speed processing and integrated services (IS). As a result, many improvements and extensions, even new architectures have been proposed to countermeasure such new technologies. One approach that has been taken to attack issues in the continuous media application domain in the Internet is resource reservation. With resource reservation, the network can provide quality of service to users that require IS, but at the same time, it must be efficiently used so that network resources are not wasted. When integrated with the appropriate transport mechanisms at the end nodes, the effective usage of a high bandwidth large-scale network can be pushed to its maximum capabilities.

This paper focuses on the effective use of resource reservation in such high speed large-scale networks by integrating it with rate-based transport mechanisms. Though it seems straightforward to utilize dedicated connections set up via resource reservation, filling up the reserved pipe is not trivial. Such effective use of networking resources is one of the main goals of the *AMInet* project. We describe the *AMInet Set up Protocol* or *ASP*, our resource reservation protocol, that supports fast ATM VC set up without ATM signaling and our implementations of TCP and UDP extensions that can exploit the reserved resources. As a result, from our performance evaluation, we show that AMInet can support guaranteed reservations that require 4Mbps to 100Mbps, that is, from MPEG2 video streams to super high definition image data at the same time filling the pipe to effectively use network resources.

The paper is organized as follows. Section 2 presents an overview of the AMInet project, its relation to TCP/IP, and the focus of this paper. Section 3 outlines issues that arise in resource reservation schemes and transport protocols and their implementations. Section 4 describes the design and implementation of our system. Performance figures and evaluation are given in Sect. 5. Section 6 presents related work. We conclude the paper with Sect. 7.

2 AMInet Overview

The AMInet project, a joint project between Sony Computer Science Laboratory Inc., NTT Optical Network Systems Labs., and Keio University, was started in April 1996 to build a new wide area network that can support rigorous user demands when FTTH or xDSL becomes available. The AMInet project not only focuses on wide area networks but also on networks in the home as depicted in Fig. 1. The AMInet network consists of *Backbone Routers* and *Edge Routers* that have switching and routing capabilities. The backbone routers provide high throughput interconnections and the edge routers installed at the telephone local exchanges or network operation centers (NOC) maintain subscriber information. Currently ATM is used in the backbone to provide high speed communication. In AMInet, each household is constantly connected, without the need for dialup, by ATM via optical fibers or xDSL technologies via copper lines. The *Home Router* interconnects computers and audio/video appliances in the home to the outside network. The Home Router supports several types of networks for internal use such as 100BASE-TX and IEEE1394.

The AMInet protocol architecture includes the basic Internet protocols such as TCP, UDP, and IP for compatibility with the Internet. Some of the three types of routers described previously might be equipped with a switching engine for fast data transfer, but all incorporate an IP engine, and thus are called routers in AMInet. Although AMInet makes use of the ATM technology in its backbone, the AMInet protocol architecture is media-independent, so ATM is simply regarded as a data link like Ethernet or IEEE1394, just as in IP. However,

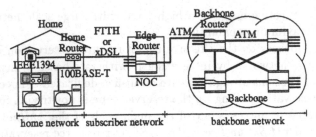

Fig. 1. AMInet network

in contrast to the Internet architecture and the OSI reference model, AMInet dynamically configures the optimal protocol stack through negotiations. Thus, some layers even the IP layer may be bypassed during data transfer. Negotiations are not the focus of this paper, and will be presented in a future paper. Another important feature of the AMInet protocol architecture is that signaling or connection set up for QoS support runs on IP even if the end nodes are connected to an ATM network. This is because IP can be more robust and flexible when used as the basic transport for resource reservation and also has performance advantages as described in Sect. 5.

The first phase of the AMInet project focused on multimedia communication and fast bulk data transfer through software implementations. Multimedia communication such as teleconferencing and video broadcasting will be a typical application in wide area networks. Although many attempts have been made at experimenting with and implementing multimedia communication, there are few actual running systems that span a large scale and are used on a general purpose high speed networking platform. On the other hand, bulk data transfer is attracting considerable attention as an application in wide area networks, e.g., transfer of entire video movie files and high definition medical images. This paper shows that when resource reservation schemes and rate-based transport protocols are combined in AMInet, effective multimedia communication and fast bulk data transfer can be supported.

3   Issues

3.1   Resource Reservation

Resource reservation is now a prerequisite of packet networks, mainly the Internet, to support IS. It introduces the need for connection oriented services at lower layers, thus ATM or IEEE1394 is appropriate as a data link. AMInet currently focuses mainly on ATM VCs for reservations, though IEEE1394 is planned. Current IETF standards or proposals that deal with reservations assume the use of ATM SVCs, mostly for integration with RSVP[34, 12, 4]. This means that ATM signaling is required to set up VCs. However, ATM signaling has been the focus of many studies as it is complex and time consuming[22, 19, 1]. Some have taken the approach of differentiating the time consuming tasks involved in signaling for optimizations or parallel processing[32, 17]. Using multiple paths for reserving resources to save crank-back operation time[10] has also been proposed. But still most ATM switches available from vendors today report poor set up times as the signaling mechanisms were originally designed assuming human users initiate each call. Another key disadvantage of current signaling is that it does not support dynamic changes in QoS. This is a major drawback.

In AMInet, we integrate the flexibility of IP as a transport for signaling and the advantages of ATM VCs for guaranteed connections. They are integrated in ASP which will be detailed in Sect. 4.1.

3.2 Transport Layer

TCP has incorporated many extensions [6, 23] from its inception. However there is an inherent limit to how well it can perform in networks that consist of long fat pipes, because of the lack of explicit knowledge of how much bandwidth is available for a particular flow. TCP performs congestion control by detecting packet loss. TCP incorporates many mechanisms to perform in unpredictable internetworking environments, however, in a long fat pipe, packet loss can lead to unused bandwidth, in addition to the necessity of having a large window at the end nodes. TCP may also send packet bursts exceeding the network capacity during slow start, fast recovery, or by ack compression[26, 25]. These issues can all be averted if a resource reservation scheme is incorporated and available bandwidth is guaranteed, so that we can restrict TCP's sending rate to observe the maximum link bandwidth parameter for the reservation.

To illustrate our point we measured the behaviour of TCP in a long fat pipe. Figure 2 shows data throughput and Fig. 3 shows the packets dropped by an ingress router between a sending and receiving node. In both figures the X axis shows elapsed time of data transfer in seconds. We adjusted the rate at which the ingress router sends packets downstream to 40Mbps, while the sender sends data at full speed on its 155Mbps ATM link. In other words, this configuration introduces a bottleneck in the network. For this experiment, RTT was set to 20ms by using a hardware delayer box and both buffers on the sending and receiving sides were set to 160KB. The packet buffer on the router was 32KB(4 times the MTU). In Fig. 2, TCP slow start can be observed at the beginning followed by a relatively steady peak at 35Mbps due to fast recovery. However, packets are lost throughout the entire transmission, and at time 85sec, pipe drain occurs and is repeated several times later on.

We can see that traffic shaping plays a very important role in high speed networks. We claim software shaping is necessary even if hardware shaping is provided. In ATM, usually the NIC or switch in the data path supports shaping in hardware. Such hardware shapers can precisely control the rate at which each cell is sent out onto the fiber (on an OC3 link 1 cell every $2.7\mu sec$). However, in an internetworking environment one cannot assume that traffic shaping mechanisms will be provided in hardware all the time. Even if a backbone network incorporates ATM, it is highly likely that end nodes are connected to legacy data links such as Ethernet. In such cases, even if it is possible to set up dedicated

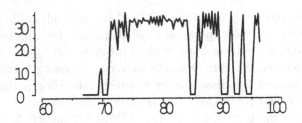

Fig. 2. TCP Throughput (RTT: 20ms)

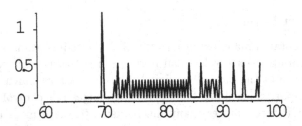

Fig. 3. TCP Packet Drop (RTT: 20ms)

VCs within the ATM backbone to support hardware shaping, current TCP/IP may not be able to fill the reserved pipe as is clear from Fig. 2. A similar phenomena can be observed within the sending node. If TCP sends packets to the NIC at a rate that exceeds reserved bandwidth, it is possible to flood the NIC and device driver buffers resulting in packet loss.

For continuous media applications that do not require reliable transport one can choose UDP, however, it can over-saturate the pipe. Thus again, some kind of shaping mechanism is necessary. The IETF has proposed RTP[28] that provides application oriented real-time features in conjunction with UDP. RTP provides features for multiplexing flows and synchronization, however does not support flow control mechanisms. So traffic shaping is left up to the application. This is one way of attacking the problem, but transport layer traffic shaping can provide finer grain shaping and can sustain more flows than at the application layer. It turns out that transport level shaping is necessary for our target applications as will be shown later.

4 Design and Implementation

4.1 ASP

The AMInet Set Up Protocol (ASP) is a signaling or set up protocol used to establish reservations in a widely distributed computing environment. It runs on top of IP and sets up fast reservations[7] on routers in an internetwork. The reservations can be abstractions for virtual circuits as in ATM or relations to some kind of packet queueing class architecture. That is, one can utilize ASP in place of normal ATM signaling to directly set up ATM VCs on AMInet routers. ASP supports its original switched virtual circuit scheme. In other words, what is generally known as ATM SVCs that require ATM signaling are not used, but instead, what we call VCs-on-demand can be set up and deleted across the network. Although, many set up protocols or signaling mechanisms have been proposed, ASP is different in that it provides many alternative set up variations that can be selected accordingly to meet application and router needs. It also supports dynamic change of QoS without need for setting up an alternate VC. ASP maintains compatibility with IP and data transfer uses normal IP packets. These IP packets are mapped to specific reservations depending on the source and destination IP address pair, source and destination port numbers, and protocol id field. Best effort traffic flows through default best effort VCs and coexist with reserved flows without effecting them at all. It supports real-time data transfer in the TCP/IP framework so that legacy applications can easily be ported along with multicasting capabilities.

Many types of applications run in the Internet framework or isolated ATM LAN situations: multicasting types such as the mbone, teleconferencing, remote diagnosis, and video-on-demand. In any case, mapping of the QoS parameters onto lower level resources such as ATM VCs should be done efficiently and in a scalable manner. For instance, in a video-on-demand application VCs need not be set up in both directions between the server and client. Only a one way VC is necessary, unlike bidirectional VCs. In such a case, if the application or higher level transport protocols, or even ASP itself needs to send a message for inter-action between the server and client, they can be sent on VCs dedicated to best effort IP traffic or ASP messages. ASP messages can be transmitted on either VCs for best effort traffic or dedicated VCs[30]. In such a case dedicated VCs are set up in the same topology as the best effort VCs. However for conferencing applications bidirectional VCs need to be set up. Either case is supported by ASP. Furthermore, it is also easy to specify different QoS parameters for the downstream and upstream traffic when VCs are needed in both directions.

ASP, not unlike RSVP or ST-2+[2], supports both receiver and sender initiated set up. In either case, the VCs and QoS parameters can be specified in one direction or both directions with different values. Also, depending on the application or situation, the sender or receiver might not have the necessary QoS information, or this information can be isolated to the peer node. In such cases, ASP supports one pass reservation with QoS parameters for both directions.

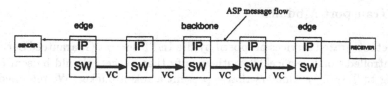

Fig. 4. ASP receiver initiated set up

In Fig. 4, a typical situation is depicted: a reservation request is issued by the receiving node. This case illustrates what might happen in a video broadcasting application where reservations are only needed for data flow from the sender to receiver. The receiver interprets QoS parameters, determines the new VPI/VCI for use in this connection, sets this information if it is equipped with an ATM NIC, and creates an ASP message. It sends this ASP message to the edge router, that is the ATM ingress router, using normal IP routing. This router sets output VPI/VCI parameters on its switch towards the receiver. Input VPI/VCI parameters are also set for the VC incoming from the next hop upstream. Consequently, the VC created for this session is for data forwarded in the reverse direction compared to this reservation request flow. Upon receipt of the request at the sending node an acknowledgment message may be forwarded back to the receiving node. This is not shown in the figure. After reservation completes, a VC is created for this session. It cuts through, or bypasses IP processing on the routers in the backbone.

Figure 4 only illustrates one example of set up by ASP. The same VC can be set up in the second pass if only the sender has QoS information necessary to establish the reservation. Also, if specified, VCs in both directions can be set up in one pass. If an application decides to upgrade its service level from best effort to IS, the data flow can be re-mapped to the newly established VC in the figure from the default best effort VC.

ASP has been implemented as a daemon processes on FreeBSD. It integrates a switch control library and a VC mapping mechanism in the PCI ATM card drivers. Currently, three types of routers are supported. The home router is equipped with a normal 100Base-T Ethernet interface and an ATM interface. The edge router is equipped with multiple ATM interface cards. Finally the backbone router consists of a PC that runs FreeBSD for the IP engine and an ATM switch. The PC in the backbone router controls the ATM switch. In our current implementation, we use Adaptec and Efficient Networks PCI ATM interface cards and Fore ASX-200WG ATM switches. The backbone router incorporates the switch control library that uses SNMP messages to set up VCs on the corresponding switch. When ASP is used, reservations are implemented as VCs-on-demand. ASP currently supports one to many multicast by setting up multicast VCs within the ATM switches. It supports leaf node joins and reservations. Bandwidth parameters are interpreted from the QoS parameters passed from the application and are set on the UPC corresponding to the VC. Thus, real-time IP flows are mapped onto CBR VCs.

4.2   Transport Modules

Internet integrated services proposed by the IETF such as Guaranteed Service[29] or Controlled Load Service[33], both specify that packets should be sent out according to TSpec parameters that represent a token bucket. We modified TCP and UDP in the FreeBSD kernel (version 2.2.1) to support token bucket. Our extensions maintain compatibility with normal TCP and UDP implementations. For TCP, code was inserted to check the token bucket before a packet is given to IP. For UDP, a packet buffer was added resulting in a very different implementation.

Since we use ASP to reserve VCs for a particular TCP session, congestion control through window size adjustment is not necessary. In other words, the congestion window can be ignored and only the advertised window need be considered. Thus, a congestion control flag is introduced so that congestion control can be set on or off to use or ignore the congestion window. The TSpec parameters and toggling the use of TCP congestion control can all be set through setsockopt(2) calls.

We are targeting our system to applications that send data in the 4Mbps to 100Mbps range, so if we assume the existence of hardware shapers in the NIC or ingress routers equipped with several 10K byte buffers, granularity for software shaping of 10ms is not sufficient (a 40Mbps flow requires approximately 50K bytes). The FreeBSD kernel timer used for the shaping timer in our implementation defaults to a value of 10ms, so we changed the kernel clock to support 1ms traffic shaping (a 40Mbps flow now only requires approximately 5K bytes).

5 Evaluation

Various experiments were performed to evaluate our implementation on PC-AT compatibles equipped with Pentium processors (200MHz). Our transport extensions are denoted as TCP Bulk Data Transfer Extensions or simply, *TCP-BDTE*, and UDP Continuous Media Transfer Extensions as *UDP-CMTE*.

5.1 ASP Performance

Figure 5 shows the breakdown costs for ASP for establishing a new reservation (`asp_open`)and deleting a new reservation (`asp_close`) with one router equipped with a switch between the sender and receiver (just unicast). The sender and receiver nodes are both equipped with ATM NICs and the time for ASP includes setting the flow maps on the NICs. `swctl_lib` denotes the time taken in the switch control library and `switch` signifies the time taken to communicate with the ATM switch hardware via SNMP when the library is used.

From this graph, we can see that the most of the overhead lies in our switch interface that uses SNMP to set up VCs within the ATM switch. It takes an average of 40 to 50msec to add a new VC using this interface. However, depending on the switch hardware, adding a VC can take anywhere from 40 to 110 msec. We could not pinpoint what causes this instability within the switch for lack of internal specifications. Rough estimates from our performance measurements conclude that without using ATM signaling, we can establish VCs per intermediate switch at a rate of 20 to 25 VCs/sec. However, this is again due to the switch internal processing overhead. We plan to replace these switches with our own hardware modules that implement ASP processing, at switching speeds in the order of 100 VCs/sec. PCC [32] supports such figures but our integration with IP can support a more robust network.

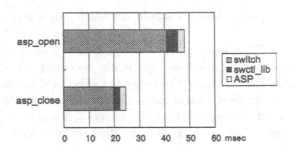

Fig. 5. ASP Performance breakdown

5.2 Comparison with TCP

Figure 6 shows TCP BDTE throughput for the same experiment for TCP as in Fig. 2. Token bucket size was set at under 2 times the MTU, so even if the window size is large, buffer overflow does not occur, thus packets are not dropped.

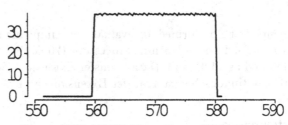

Fig. 6. TCP BDTE Throughput (RTT: 20ms)

In Fig. 7, we compared throughput of TCP and TCP BDTE by varying the packet buffer size at the sending and receiving nodes in the same network configuration. For TCP, a second curve is shown that shows the performance of a modified TCP with a retransmission timeout (RTO) of 50ms instead of the default 500ms. When the window size is set over 160KB, the need for excessive retransmissions decreases TCP throughput. This happens regardless of the RTO value. In other words, for TCP to perform better, a larger packet buffer is needed at the bottleneck. If sufficient packet buffer is not available, not only does TCP throughput decrease, but router queues will fill up increasing latency, potentially influencing data for other connections in a negative way. With TCP BDTE, we can effectively shape traffic to fill the pipe up to 40Mbps. Furthermore, it is possible to increase throughput with minimal packet buffers, decreasing the probability of effecting other connections.

Another potential bottleneck might be found in the sending node itself. In the FreeBSD TCP implementation, data is passed from TCP/IP to the NIC by using normal TCP flow control mechanisms, so this presents the same problems as if there were a bottleneck in the network when RTT is high. To demonstrate

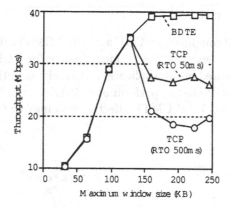

Fig. 7. TCP Throughput Comparison (Net RTT: 20ms)

our point, 2 PCs connected to each other via only the hardware delayer were set up to compare the throughput of TCP and TCP BDTE.

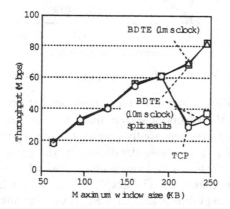

Fig. 8. TCP Throughput Comparison (NIC RTT:20ms)

In Fig. 8, we can see that when TCP window size is increased, the buffers in the NIC and device driver (total of 96KB) of the sending node overflows, resulting in a decrease in throughput. TCP throughput drastically decreases when the window is above 192KB. For TCP BDTE, when the shaping timer period is 1ms, throughput continues to increase compared to TCP. However, when the shaping timer is set at 10ms, throughput above 192KB becomes very unstable flapping between 70Mbps and 30Mbps. This happens because the 10ms case requires a larger token bucket, increasing possible buffer overruns.

It can be concluded from these results, that traffic shaping at the transport layer is effective and can defeat problems TCP sometimes faces when there are buffer bottlenecks in the network or even on the sending node. Furthermore, the timer granularity used for shaping traffic influences throughput considerably and justifies our reason for implementing a 1msec shaping timer.

5.3 Comparison with UDP

Figure 9 shows the throughput for UDP and UDP CMTE. The kernel clock was configured at 1msec to support fine grained shaping for UDP CMTE. For UDP, shaping was implemented in the application. It can be seen that even when there is no system load, UDP cannot perform over 50Mbps, the limit for application level shaping. However, UDP CMTE effectively shapes traffic until 100Mbps.

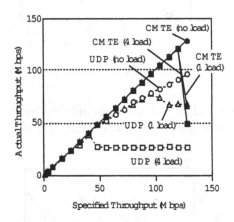

Fig. 9. UDP Throughput Comparison

Since our fine grain shaping mechanism does present overhead on the system, we also investigated the effects of system load. In this load experiment, we ran a background process that repeatedly executes bcopy operations. As shown in Fig. 9, UDP throughput decreases drastically in the presence of this load but UDP CMTE is not effected. This is even more clear when we ran 4 background processes to simulate more load. The graph also shows the hardware limitations of the PC used in the experiment as UDP CMTE throughput tapers off at around 128Mbps. In other words, UDP CMTE effectively sends out shaped traffic as long as there are enough CPU resources available. On the other hand, application level shaping cannot sustain the target rate in the presence of load.

5.4 Shaping Accuracy

Tables 1 and 2 show performance figures to illustrate the accuracy of our shaping extensions in TCP BDTE. They were taken with an ATM traffic analyzer that probes AAL5 frames sent from a PC. Hardware shaping on the ATM NIC was turned off. Table 1 shows the ratio between the specified and observed rate and Table 2 shows the ratio of packets that violated the specified token bucket parameters to all packets sent. The shaper timer period was set at 1ms.

When the total specified rate (per VC rate multiplied by number of VCs) was very high (128Mbps) the rate observed did not meet the specified rate. However, in all other cases, the observed rate is within 1 to 5 percent of the specified rate.

Table 1. Rate ratio: observed rate/specified rate

VCs	Mbps per VC							
	1	2	4	8	16	32	64	128
1	1.009	1.008	1.006	1.011	1.006	0.994	0.968	0.922
2	1.009	1.008	1.006	1.007	1.005	0.989	0.954	NA
4	1.007	1.005	1.003	0.995	0.978	0.769	NA	NA
8	0.992	0.976	0.945	0.889	0.734	NA	NA	NA

Table 2. Violated packet ratio: # of packets that violated/all packets

VCs	Mbps per VC							
	1	2	4	8	16	32	64	128
1	0.008	0.008	0.008	0.008	0.008	0.008	0.009	0.000
2	0.008	0.008	0.008	0.008	0.007	0.008	0.013	NA
4	0.004	0.002	0.007	0.013	0.005	0.006	NA	NA
8	0.003	0.003	0.006	0.005	0.004	NA	NA	NA

Only under 1 percent of the packets violated the specified rate most of the time. These results show that even our simple implementation can provide accurate traffic shaping. The same results were observed for UDP CMTE.

5.5 System Overhead

Finally, the figures for the overhead incurred by traffic shaping is given. We measured the decrease in throughput of the bcopy benchmark program, while sending traffic using UDP, UDP CMTE, TCP, and TCP BDTE. From these results we can get a feel for how transport level shaping and shaping granularity influences the system. For UDP, shaping was implemented in the application and results are shown in Fig. 10. TCP results are shown in Fig. 11.

We could not measure throughput above 64Mbps for UDP because the PC could not provide enough processing power. Figure 10 illustrates the overhead incurred by UDP CMTE when compared with UDP. Until 48Mbps, traffic shaping performed by UDP CMTE decreases throughput of the benchmark program on the average of about 7.5%. Over 48Mbps, since UDP cannot meet its target rate, the slope of the line gets steeper and likewise effects the benchmark program throughput. However, UDP CMTE is able to shape traffic consistently until 128Mbps. Even though the benchmark program is effected, high network throughput service with shaped traffic can be supported by UDP CMTE. In addition, the two measurements for UDP show little difference as the kernel timer granularity is changed to implement our fine grain shaping timer. For the TCP comparison in Fig. 11, it can be observed that both TCP and TCP BDTE reach a performance limit around 50Mbps to 64Mbps similar to UDP. The overhead involved for TCP and TCP BDTE is on the same order as UDP and UDP CMTE, however, TCP BDTE reaches its throughput limit a bit faster than TCP.

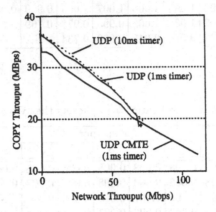

Fig. 10. UDP and UDP CMTE: Effect on System Load

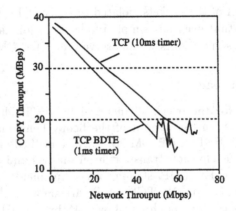

Fig. 11. TCP and TCP BDTE: Effect on System Load

We conclude from these results that the system overhead incurred by the traffic shaping mechanisms is on the average less than 7.5% of normal TCP/UDP. Even though there is an overhead, the transport extensions support consistent data output even when high network throughput is required.

6 Related Work

Our approach is not entirely new and most of the ideas were derived from previous work. Our main contribution was to demonstrate a simple but effective system built from off the shelf hardware and to confirm its applicable range of applications.

ASP suppports fast reservations and was designed to be used in conjunction with bulk data transfer and continuous media transport protocols. Its main purpose is to integrate flexible IP routing and VCs-on-demand. We have pointed out other work that have tried to efficiently deal with and optimize signaling in Sect. 3. ASP is most closely related to RSVP and ST-2 or its variants. ASP is basically an extension of ST-2+ that is integrated closely with ATM. One of the key assumptions is that in the AMInet cloud, all routers are equipped with VC switching technologies (as is usually assumed in most label switching environments). This makes it easier for us to design the protocol and make flexible but fast signaling or set up possible. That is, we can cut through below IP at any point in the network, pass point of reservation failure information to the routing module for effective QoS routing, or dynamically change QoS without creating new VCs. The main difference between ASP and label switching technology is that ASP focuses on supporting IS, that is carrying QoS information during set up and how fast this set up takes place. RSVP and ST-2 are under more constrained as they have to assume a more general environment. ASP also does not require multiple VCs to support different levels of QoS[3], though it supports capabilities for switching a data flow map between different VCs, usually for aggregation. As a drawback, we need integrate ASP with efficient multipoint to multipoint multicast schemes[15]. ASP is also not soft state like RSVP.

As for TCP over ATM, many have reported on the its performance problems [27, 20, 25]. TCP over ATM often exhibits poor performance, since they each have their own traffic control mechanism[5] and their granularity differs in several orders of magnitude in both time and space. Our approach tries to bridge the gap by implementing software shaping in the transport layer.

Attempts have been made to extend TCP for high-speed networks[6, 23, 8]. However, as long as TCP relies solely on window-based control, it may not always be able to fill up the long fat pipe. With our extensions, TCP becomes rate-controlled at its peak rate but still remains window-controlled at lower rates.

On the other hand, a variety of protocols have been proposed to challenge transport issues concerning high speed networks[11, 21, 31, 9]. The most difficult challenge shared by these protocols is to dynamically determine available bandwidth for flows. The ATM ABT-DT service [18] can likewise be categorized into this group. The inherent limitation of adaptive schemes is that, if traffic fluctuates rapidly compared with the feedback latency as often happens in a long fat pipe, it becomes difficult to manage. However, we can avoid complex adaptive flow control issues for a long fat pipe by incorporating resource reservation. Some of the early simple rate-based approaches that were once abandoned for lack of rate-guarantee mechanisms have once again become feasible as ATM becomes widespread. Others[14] have proposed similar ideas through simulation, investigating the effect of token bucket and fine grain timers. Our experience with a real system in part confirms their simulation results.

7 Conclusion and Future Work

In this paper, we presented our integrated reservation scheme and traffic shaping transport extensions in AMInet. Together they support efficient continuous media and bulk data transport. ASP, our reservation protocol supports switched VCs in a flexible way so that VC resources are efficiently used and QoS can be changed dynamically. On the other hand, our software shaping extensions to TCP and UDP are accurate within 5% of specified rate and provides these benefits at the expense of only 7.5% on system performance.

We have plans to incorporate ASP into our own switch hardware to prove its efficiency and to integrate it with QoS routing to show that it can provide a more flexible resource reservation platform.

Acknowledgments

The authors would like to thank Dr. Mario Tokoro, Dr. Tomonori Aoyama, and Dr. Sadayasu Ono and the members of the AMInet project from Sony Computer Science Lab. Inc, Sony Corp., NTT Optical Network Systems Labs, and Keio University for their comments.

References

1. N. Anerousis. Signaling System Performance in ATM Networks. In *Proceedings of Workshop on Open Signaling* (1996)
2. L. Berger and L. Delgrossi. Internet STream Protocol Version 2 (ST2) – Protocol Specification – Version ST2+. RFC 1819 (1995)
3. S. Berson. "Classical" RSVP and IP over ATM. In *Proceedings of INET'96* (1996)
4. S. Berson and L. Berger. IP Integrated Services with RSVP over ATM. Internet draft. Work in Progress.
5. F. Bonomi and K. W. Fendick. The Rate-Based Flow Control Framework for the Available Bit Rate ATM Service. *IEEE Network* (1995) 25–39
6. D. Borman, R. Braden, and V. Jacobson. TCP Extensions for High Performance. Request for Comments (Proposed Standard) RFC 1323 (1992)
7. P.E. Boyer and D.P.Tranchier. A Reservation Principle with Applications to the ATM Traffic Control. *Comp. Net. and ISDN Sys.*, Vol. 24 (1992) 321–334
8. L. S. Brakmo and S. W. O'Malley. TCP Vegas: New techniques for Congestion Detection and Avoidance. In *Proceedings of SIGCOMM'94* (1994) 24–35
9. D. R. Cheriton. VMTP: A Transport Protocol for the Next Generation of Communication Systems. In *Proceedings of SIGCOMM'86* (1986) 406–415
10. I. Cidon, R. Rom, and Y. Shavitt. Multi-Path Routing combined with Resource Reservation. In *Proceedings of Infocom'97* (1997)
11. D. D. Clark, M. L. Lambert, and L. Zhang. NETBLT: A High Throughput Transport Protocol. In *Proceedings of SIGCOMM'87* (1987) 353–359
12. E. Crawley, L. Berger, S. Berson, F. Baker, M. Borden, and J. Krawczyk. A Framework for Integrated Services and RSVP over ATM. Internet draft. Work in Progress.

221

13. L. Delgrossi. *Design of Reservation Protocols for Multimedia Communcation.* Kluwer Academic Publishers (1996)
14. W. Feng, D. Kandlur, D. Saha, and K. Shin. Understanding TCP Dynamics in an Integrated Services Internet. In *Proceedings of NOSSDAV '97* (1997)
15. M. Grossglauser and K. K. Ramakrishnan. SEAM: Scalable and Efficient ATM Multipoint-to-Multipoint Multicasting. In *Proceedings of NOSSDAV'96* (1996)
16. G. T. Hawley. Systems Considerations for the Use of xDSL Technology for Data Access. *IEEE Communications Magazine*, Vol. 35 No. 3 (1997)
17. G. Hjalmtysson. Lightweight Call Setup. In *Proceedings of 15th International Teletraffic Congress* (1997)
18. *ITU-T Recommendation I.371 Traffic Control and Congestion Control in B-ISDN* (1995)
19. C. Kalmanek. What's Hard about ATM Signaling? In *Proceedings of Workshop on Open Signaling* (1995)
20. S. Kalyanaraman, R. Jain, S. Fahmy, R. Goyal, F. Lu, and S. Srinidhi. Performance of TCP/IP over ABR. In *Proceedings of IEEE Globecom'96* (1996)
21. S. Keshav. A Control-Theoretic Approach to Flow Control. In *Proceedings of SIGCOMM'91* (1991) 3–16
22. S. Keshav. *An Engineering Approach to Computer Networking.* Addison-Wesley (1997)
23. K.Fall and S.Floyd. Simulation-based Comparisons of Tahoe, Reno, and SACK TCP. *Computer Communication Review*, Vol. 26, No. 3 (1996)
24. T. Miki. Toward the Service-Rich Era. *IEEE Communications Magazine*, Vol. 32, No. 2, (1994)
25. P. P. Mishra. Effect of Leaky Bucket Policing on TCP Over ATM Performance. In *Proceedings of ICC'96* (1996)
26. V. Paxson. Measurements and Analysis of End-to-End Internet Dynamics. Ph.D. Thesis, University of California Berkeley (1997)
27. A. Romanow and S. Floyd. The Dynamics of TCP Traffic over ATM Networks. In *Proceedings of SIGCOMM'94*, (1994) 79–88
28. H. Schulzrinne, S. Casner, R. Frederick, and V. Jacobson. RTP: A Transport Protocol for Real-Time Applications. Request for Comments (Proposed Standard) RFC 1889 (1996)
29. S. Shenker, C. Partridge, and R. Guerin. Specification of Guaranteed Quality of Service. Internet Draft. Work in Progress.
30. A. Shionozaki and M. Tokoro. Control Handling in Real-Time Communication Protocols. In *Proceedings of SIGCOMM '93* (1993)
31. T. W. Strayer, B. J. Dempsey, and A. C. Weaver. *XTP - The Xpress Transfer Protocol.* Addison-Wesley Publishing (1992)
32. M. Veeraraghavan, G. L. Choudhury, and M. Kshirsagar. Implementation and Analysis of PCC (Parallel Connection Control). In *Proceedings of Infocom'97* (1997)
33. J. Wroclawski. Specification of the Controlled-Load Network Element Service. Internet Draft. Work in Progress.
34. L. Zhang, S. Deering, D. Estrin, S. Shenker, and D. Zappala. RSVP: A New Resource ReSerVation Protocol. In *IEEE Network* (1993) 8–18

Experiences with a Mobile Testbed

Kevin Lai, Mema Roussopoulos, Diane Tang, Xinhua Zhao, Mary Baker

Stanford University

Abstract. This paper presents results from an eight-day network packet trace of MosquitoNet. MosquitoNet allows users of laptop computers to switch seamlessly between a metropolitan-area wireless network and a wired network (10 Mbit/s Ethernet) available in offices and on-campus residences. Results include the amount of user mobility between the wired and wireless networks, the amount of mobility within the wireless network, an examination of application end-to-end delays, and an examination of overall packet loss and reordering in the wireless network. We find that the average mobile host switches between the wired and wireless networks 14 times during the trace and moves within the wireless network five times. Round trip latencies in the wireless network are very high, with a minimum of 0.2 seconds. Even higher end-to-end delays, of up to hundreds of seconds, are due to packet loss and reordering. These delays cause users to change their usage patterns when connected to the wireless network. We conclude that latency is a critical problem in the wireless network.

1 Introduction

The popularity of portable computers combined with the growth of wireless networks and services has led to many efforts to make mobile computing an everyday reality. To achieve this goal, designers need information about the behavior of mobile hosts (portable computers) and the characteristics of the networks they use. Although existing studies of the characteristics of local-area wireless networks are helpful for investigating in-building mobile environments [9] [19] [23], there is currently little packet-level information available about wide-area wireless networks. This information is important if we are interested in mobility outside of small areas such as homes and offices. Understanding wide-area wireless network performance in terms of latencies, packet rates and packet loss will help us design, model, simulate and optimize protocols and applications to perform well in this environment, while information about the day-to-day behavior of mobile hosts and their usage patterns in real systems will help us choose which protocols and applications to tackle.

This paper presents the results from an eight-day trace of a network of mobile hosts that incorporates a wireless system available throughout our metropolitan area. The network, called MosquitoNet, allows users of laptop computers to stay connected to the wireless network while moving around our area, and to switch seamlessly between the wireless and a wired network. Switching seamlessly means that all ongoing network applications continue working when a host's network connection changes.

Our results include the amount of user mobility between the wired and wireless networks, the amount of mobility within the wireless network, a comparison of usage patterns between the wired and wireless networks, an examination of application end-to-end delays, and an examination of overall packet loss and reordering in the wireless network. To summarize our findings:

- Mobility: On average, a mobile host switches between the wired and wireless networks 14 times during the eight days (with a minimum of three times and a maximum of 34). On average, a mobile host moves within the wireless network five times during the eight days (with a minimum of one move and a maximum of 14 moves). We found seven distinct locations at least one-half mile apart in the wireless network that were visited by mobile hosts. The widest spread locations were 70 miles apart.
- Latencies: Round trip latencies in the wireless network are high, with a minimum of 0.2 seconds. Much higher end-to-end delays (up to hundreds of seconds) result from packet retransmissions due to loss and reordering. High latencies and the rate of packet loss and reordering prevent hosts from fully utilizing the available bandwidth of the wireless network.
- Optimizations: Simply changing telnet from character mode to line mode improves its interactive response by requiring 50% fewer round trips. Batching NFS meta-data requests can reduce them by as much as 20%, but NFS still suffers from lack of data prefetching.

Many other wide-area wireless networks will also have high latencies relative to local-area technologies, so we conclude that contending with latency presents a critical challenge for making wide-area mobile data networks successful. Some simple techniques for improving the behavior of applications sensitive to high end-to-end delays, such as using local line editing in telnet, can vastly improve users' perceptions of network behavior. Additionally, it is clear that file systems such as NFS that use a request/response (RPC) model will not survive in the wireless environment unless they are optimized to prefetch data or combine multiple operations into single requests (such as looking up information for a whole directory at once).

The remainder of this paper is organized as follows. Section 2 describes the project goals and the environment studied. Section 3 describes the tracing and analysis tools. Section 4 describes the overall and per-application usage patterns of hosts on the wired and wireless networks, as well as end-to-end delays, packet loss, and packet reordering in our wireless network. Section 5 looks at some possible optimizations for telnet and NFS in the wireless network. Section 6 describes related work, and Sect. 7 presents conclusions and some future work.

2 The System Under Study

This section describes the goals of the MosquitoNet project and the hardware and software that make up our testbed.

2.1 Goals

The goal of the MosquitoNet project is to work towards providing "anywhere, anytime" Internet connectivity for mobile hosts. A host should be allowed to remain continuously connected to the Internet. If cost or battery power are concerns, then the mobile host may disconnect as appropriate, but it should be able to reconnect seamlessly whenever desired. If users have control over when to disconnect, then they can choose to do so gracefully, perhaps by synchronizing file caches or unlocking locked files.

For continuous connectivity, a mobile host must be able to switch to the best network available in its current location. The metric for choosing the network, if more than one network is available, could be performance, cost, available resources in the network, security, or some combination of the above and other features. We do not believe that a single, globally available wireless network will provide mobile hosts with the best performance or cost. Instead, we believe users will want the generally better performance of wired networks where they are available. They may also choose local-area wireless networks over wide-area wireless networks when available. While it is not yet possible for mobile hosts to find a practical wireless network in all locations, we believe the recent growth of wireless services is evidence that this is a direction worth pursuing.

2.2 Hardware

The MosquitoNet testbed currently consists of eight laptop computers (our mobile hosts), a router, and two networks. The laptops are IBM Thinkpad 560's, Samsung SensLite 200's and a Panasonic ProNote CF-11. The router is a 90MHz Pentium. The laptops and the router all run Linux. The two networks are 10 Mbit/s Ethernet and packet radio. We picked the packet radio network for two reasons. First, it is available throughout our metropolitan area, so it allows us to experiment with continuous wide-area mobility. Second, it is sufficiently different in characteristics from Ethernet to bring forth the problems and challenges that arise for applications, protocols, and users when connectivity switches between such extremes.

The packet radio network consists of Metricom spread-spectrum, frequency-hopping radios [17]. These operate in the 902-928 MHz band of the unlicensed spectrum allocated by the FCC for low-power devices. Each laptop is equipped with one such radio connected via the serial port. We consider the Metricom network to be one large wireless IP subnet. Radios may communicate with each other peer-to-peer when within range, but otherwise they communicate through Metricom's packet-switched, geographically routed network, which forwards packets between "poletop" transceivers spread around our metropolitan area. Packet forwarding within the wireless network is done at the link level and is invisible to higher-level protocol layers.

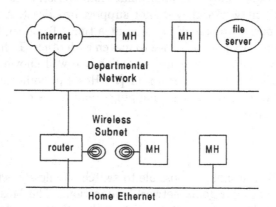

Fig. 1. This figure shows the layout of the MosquitoNet testbed. The router forwards packets between the wireless subnet, the "home" Ethernet of the mobile hosts, and the departmental Ethernet. Mobile Hosts (MH) can connect to their home network, or they can connect to ("visit") the wireless subnet or other Ethernet subnets available around the Internet. Note that the file server is on the departmental Ethernet, so all file server traffic to the mobile hosts runs through the router.

The layout of the MosquitoNet testbed is shown in Fig. 1. The router forwards packets between three networks: the wireless subnet, the mobile hosts' "home" Ethernet subnet, and the building-wide departmental Ethernet. Packets sent by mobile hosts visiting "foreign" networks such as the wireless subnet pass through the router (Sect. 2.3). Also, any packets from mobile hosts on their home Ethernet will go through the router when accessing hosts or services outside that network, such as our file server.

Although the radios are sold as Hayes AT modem emulators, we have written a device driver in the Linux operating system that uses their lower-level packet switching interface. This allows the one radio on our router to communicate with multiple client radios. Otherwise, we would need to run a SLIP or PPP service and attach a bank of radio modems to our router to support its point-to-point connections with multiple laptop clients. The router would require one radio per concurrently active client.

Compared to local-area networks, wide-area packet radio networks generally have lower bandwidth and higher latencies for the same level of power. Metricom radios are no exception. Their air transmission speed is 100 Kbits per second. We run our serial ports at 115,200 bits per second to allow for the full bandwidth of the radios. The radios are half-duplex, which means that data traveling through an intermediate radio has its bandwidth cut to half the air transmission speed. Per-packet latencies are very high, with a minimum round trip time of 200ms.

The Metricom radios have one additional characteristic that is not common to all packet radio networks: they do not support broadcast. A Metricom radio can only send a packet to one other radio at a time. To do so, the radios must tune their frequency hopping sequence to match each other. To handle broadcast protocols such as ARP, we currently establish one well-known radio hardware address as the address of an ARP server [1]. Hosts periodically let this server know their hardware-to-IP address mappings, and hosts can query this server for other hosts' mappings.

2.3   Software

To support mobility, it must be possible to switch seamlessly between networks, i.e., without disrupting ongoing network connections. The MosquitoNet proto-type uses a mobile IP protocol [22] to achieve this. With mobile IP, connection-oriented protocols such as TCP can continue to use the "home" IP address of the mobile host, even if it switches to a network interface with a different IP address. Our mobile IP protocol supports the use of "foreign agents" if they are found in the networks to which a mobile host connects, but we prefer the extra flexibility that is provided when a mobile host acquires its own "care-of" IP address in the networks it visits [2].

Mobile IP uses encapsulation of network packets, and the size of the extra header reduces the maximum transmission unit (MTU) available when a mobile host is connected to a "foreign" network (any network, including the wireless, that is not its home Ethernet subnet). The radios have a small MTU to begin with (1024 bytes), which is further reduced to 1004 bytes with encapsulation.

3   Data Collection

This section describes how we gathered and analyzed our network traces. To gain a general picture of how mobile hosts are used, and to gather data to compare wired and wireless usage, we set aside eight days (from 4:00am one Saturday morning until 4:00am on Sunday morning) during which our research group used only our laptops as display and input devices.

We record two types of information for our traces: a tcpdump record of all packets sent over the network interfaces, and a record of the radio network status. We use tcpdump to trace IP and ARP activity on both the radio and Ethernet interfaces of each laptop, as well as on the radio and home Ethernet interfaces of our router. The radio status information includes the list of visible poletops and their signal strengths. We use this information to determine the physical location of the mobile host within the wireless network.

4 Users, Latencies and Packet Loss

We received feedback about the usability of the wireless network from all of our users. The overwhelming consensus is that high end-to-end delays are the biggest problem. Even typing a single character in telnet or doing a directory listing in NFS can incur a frustrating delay. Users report that X11 and NFS are unusable. They also report that telnet can be painful, but they use it anyway, since there are no better alternatives. However, all users reported web browsing (HTTP) to be acceptable on the wireless network. We believe this is the case for two reasons. User expectation allows for longer delay of operations while web browsing, since this can be slow even on wired networks when accessing sites over the Internet. Also, many web browsing operations do a more satisfying amount of work per user request than do more interactive applications such as telnet, which incurs a round trip delay for a single character echo.

In the rest of this section, we examinine host mobility and telnet and NFS behavior. We present evidence that high end-to-end delays cause users to change their behavior. These delays are due to the high per-packet round trip time of the wireless network and to packet loss and reordering in the network.

4.1 Host Mobility

We investigate the mobility of hosts in these networks. We are interested in answering questions such as whether users take advantage of the wireless network when the wired network is not available, how often they switch between the wired and wireless networks, and how much they move around geographically within the wireless network.

The first data column of Table 1 shows the number of times each host switches between the wired and wireless networks over the eight days. A host switches to the wired network when its user inserts an Ethernet PCMCIA card that is connected to the network. The movement between networks varies significantly across hosts, with the average number of switches being 14, the minimum three and the maximum 34. The host that switched networks 34 times also had the most traffic overall. Since users often leave the radios on even when they are using the Ethernet, we do not count the wireless network as being active if the Ethernet interface is active as well.

The second data column of Table 1 shows that users take advantage of the wireless network at many locations. The table presents the number of times a host uses the wireless network, moves by at least a half-mile, and then uses the wireless network in the new location. The average number of moves is five, with a minimum of one and a maximum of 14. There are seven distinct locations represented in this data. Known visited locations include the Computer Science department, the student campus residence area, the home of a faculty member, a cafe on the south side of Palo Alto, Fremont, San Francisco, and the beach in Santa Cruz. San Francisco and Santa Cruz are about seventy miles apart.

Table 1. This table shows the number of times a given laptop switches between the wired and wireless networks and the number of times it changes its physical location within the wireless network. Note that this is not a count of the number of user sessions, as these may extend across network switches.

Host Name	ant	bee	butterfly	dragonfly	junebug	midge	termite	weevil
Num. of Network Switches	11	8	12	34	16	3	13	18
Num. of Moves	2	5	5	5	8	3	1	14

Unfortunately, using poletop information alone, we are not able to detect movement within a one-half mile radius. For instance, we are unable to distinguish between a laptop user using his laptop in his office and at a nearby library. Thus, this data represents a lower bound on the amount of mobility while using the wireless network.

4.2 End-to-End Delays in the Wireless Network

In this section, we look at end-to-end delays experienced in the wireless network by telnet (over TCP) and NFS (over UDP), two of the applications users reported as being slow. We find that the high delays have two causes. The first cause is the high minimum round trip latency of the wireless network. The second cause is a high level of packet retransmissions, due to loss and reordering in the network.

We calculate the end-to-end delays for telnet and NFS in a manner that reflects what the users actually experience with these applications. For telnet, the delay is the difference between when data is sent and when the first acknowledgment for that data is received. For NFS, the delay is the difference between when the first packet for an NFS request is sent and when the first reply is received.

Figure 2 shows the distribution of round trip times seen for telnet and NFS traffic. These results show delays in the wireless network ranging from 0.2 seconds to several hundred seconds. Note that even the minimum latency is noticeable to users, since previous reports show that users begin to find interactive response time slow when it exceeds 100 to 200ms [12]. The median delays are painful, but not hopeless: the telnet median is 0.97 seconds and the NFS median is 0.6 seconds. Sixty percent of telnet delays are 1.3 seconds or less, and sixty percent of NFS delays are 0.7 seconds or less. However, the high end of the scale is clearly intolerable.

From the figure, we see that telnet and NFS delays differ in distribution. This is because TCP and NFS retransmission strategies and parameters differ. NFS uses a fixed exponential backoff starting at 0.7 seconds. However, TCP in general waits longer than NFS to retransmit, and so its overall delays will be larger. To set its retransmission timer, TCP uses an adjustable mechanism based on its estimate of the average round trip time and the average deviation of round trip

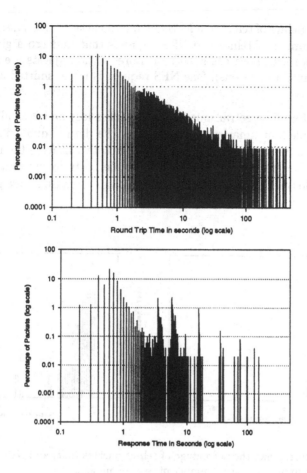

Fig. 2. This figure shows the percentage of telnet packets (top) and NFS request packets (bottom) versus response time for the wireless network.

times [13]. For TCP's retransmission timeout to be as small as NFS's, it would have to calculate the deviation in round trip times as being less than 125ms. However, even under ideal conditions, TCP's average estimate of the deviation is 225ms. (This result was measured by pinging packets peer-to-peer between nearby radios on two otherwise inactive hosts. There was an average round trip time of 335ms over the 1800 samples.) TCP's adjustable mechanism also causes the smoother distribution of telnet delays, while NFS shows two peaks (of about three percent) between one and ten seconds, which correspond to its retransmission timeouts.

Although NFS delays are generally shorter than telnet delays, we find that users are more frustrated with NFS than telnet. We believe this is because a user can see what progress telnet is making, even if it is slow. In contrast, when NFS is slow, users cannot see what is actually happening.

The very long delays of telnet and NFS are due to packet retransmissions. Figure 3 shows the number of telnet and NFS requests that undergo a given number of retransmissions. In both cases, 80% or more of the requests are transmitted only once (no retransmissions). One NFS request is retransmitted 26 times!

The reasons for these retransmissions are packet loss and a small amount of reordering. Table 2 summarizes these results. The data is divided into packets sent from the router to the mobile hosts and packets sent from the mobile hosts to the router. For transmissions from the mobile hosts to the router, we see a 25.6% packet loss rate. This is clearly high enough to cause severe performance degradation in the network.

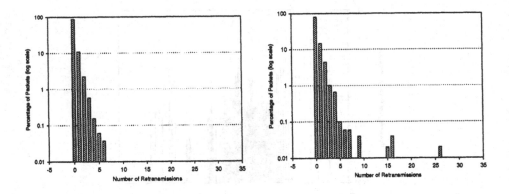

Fig. 3. This figure shows the percentage of telnet packets (left) and NFS request packets (right) that undergo a given number of retransmissions.

It is interesting to note that packet loss is much lower in the reverse direction, from the router back to the mobile hosts (3.6%). This is because a mobile host will retransmit requests until network conditions are good enough (the mobile host is within range of a poletop, or a temporary condition of network interference or congestion has eased). When conditions are good, the mobile host's packets will get through to the router. Because the responses to these packets follow quickly, they will usually experience the same good conditions and will successfully reach the mobile host on the first try.

Table 2 also shows packets arriving out of order. One of the reasons for this is that packets can take multiple routes from a source to a destination in our radio network. Since a Metricom radio is usually in range of several poletops through which it could send packets, packets sent later through a faster route will arrive before packets sent earlier.

Table 2. This table summarizes the characteristics of the wireless network. We classify packets into two categories: packets sent from the mobile hosts to the router and packets sent from the router to the mobile hosts. The numbers in parentheses give the actual number of packets involved.

Network Characteristic	Mobile Hosts to Router	Router to Mobile Hosts
Packets lost	25.6% (13,232)	3.6% (2,143)
Packets received in order	72.3% (37,380)	91.3% (53,832)
Packets received out of order	2.1% (1,103)	5.1% (3,059)
Average out-of-order distance	3.04	3.9

We are able to calculate packet loss and reordering by matching packet "signatures" on the hosts and the router. The packet signature is a 32 bit CRC. A packet sent by a host is considered lost if its signature does not appear in the router's trace, and vice versa. Packet A is considered to be received out of order if it arrives at the destination after some packet B that was sent later. The out-of-order "distance" of a packet A is the number of packets sent after it but received before it.

This packet reordering can contribute to retransmissions in protocols, such as TCP, that are sensitive to it. TCP normally accounts for minimal out-of-order delivery of packets, but treats packets as lost if they are delivered at an out-of-order distance of three or more. Each out-of-order packet causes a duplicate ACK to be sent, and three duplicate ACKs cause the sender to perform a fast retransmit [26]. Unfortunately, the average out-of-order distance in MosquitoNet is greater than three, so some of these packets are treated as lost and will thus contribute to the total number of retransmissions.

5 Application Optimizations for the Wireless Network

In this section, we consider some optimizations for telnet and NFS over the wireless network. Since we are unable to reduce the latency of the wireless network, we look for ways to avoid and hide end-to-end delays. We can avoid delays in telnet by batching together as many characters as possible into a packet. For NFS, we can hide delays by prefetching data and avoid delays by batching together lookups of files in one directory into a single request.

Telnet handles long end-to-end delays poorly because users must suffer the round trip time for every character they type. In addition, placing only one character in a packet is inefficient use of the network and router. With Nagle's algorithm, which sometimes batches together characters in interactive traffic, this problem would not be as severe [18]. However, telnet applications sometimes turn off this algorithm because it increases the end-to-end delay for terminal keystrokes that generate multiple characters [25]. Our telnet traffic does not use Nagle's algorithm.

One possible optimization is to use "line mode telnet" [5]. This allows an entire line to be typed and possibly edited before a packet is sent. For a line 10 characters long, line mode telnet would use 2 packets sent and received, while regular telnet would use 22 packets sent and received. More importantly, the user would only suffer the round trip delay once instead of 11 times (once for each character and once for the return key). This optimization is more effective for users than Nagle's algorithm, because it gives users immediate feedback for what they have typed and allows them to edit without suffering any network latency.

We compared the trace of one of our heavy telnet users using line mode telnet for one day with the same user's trace (using regular, or "character mode" telnet) during our eight-day period. Table 3 summarizes the TCP payload sizes of packets sent from the mobile host to the router. We omit TCP ACKs because they are not sent as a direct result of user actions.

Table 3. This table compares the payload size for packets sent from the mobile hosts to the router using character mode telnet and line mode telnet.

Telnet Mode	Number of Samples	Minimum Size	Median Size	Average Size	Maximum Size	Total Size
Character	650	1 byte	1 byte	8.52 bytes	698 bytes	5544 bytes
Line	302	1 byte	4 bytes	18.44 bytes	697 bytes	5571 bytes

Although the total payload bytes sent from the mobile host to the router for line mode telnet is approximately the same as for character mode, the line mode trace has 54% fewer packets. This means that the router had about 50% less incoming load on it and the user suffered the round trip time 50% less frequently for the same amount of data typed. All the users who have tried this mechanism report that it makes telnet acceptable on the wireless network. As a result of this experiment, we are developing a mobile shell that uses this technique but is more sophisticated about operations such as file editing that do not work well in line mode.

We also look at possible optimizations for NFS. Overall, the request/response (RPC) nature of NFS is awkward in a network with high per-packet latencies. A new request will not be started until the previous one has received a reply. The key to improving NFS performance is to reduce the number of end-to-end delays seen by users. We can do this by caching and prefetching more data, pipelining requests, or batching requests into single packets when possible.

NFS would benefit from techniques such as prefetching, as indicated by Fig. 4, which shows the distribution of NFS request types on the wired and wireless

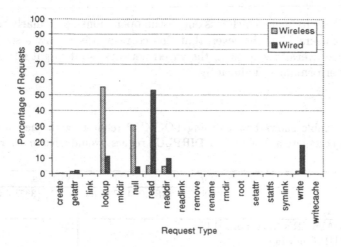

Fig. 4. This figure shows the distribution of NFS request types on the wired and wireless network.

networks. Users tend to decrease dramatically the number of data requests they make when switching from the wired network to the wireless network (from 185,014 to 357). As a result, techniques to improve data transfers, by prefetching, and to reduce needed transfers, by more aggressive caching, are essential in making file system performance tolerable on the wireless network.

Batching together multiple requests into single packets might also help reduce end-to-end delays. For example, we could speed up listing large directories if all the directory information could be transferred in one READDIRPLUS operation, rather than in many LOOKUP operations as is currently the case. This optimization is in the NFS version 3 specification [7]. To determine the possible benefit of the READDIRPLUS operation, we look at how many associated LOOKUP requests follow a READDIR request. The READDIRPLUS request would return attributes in addition to filenames, which is equivalent to batching the READDIR and LOOKUP requests. Given the 1004-byte MTU of the radios (including encapsulation overhead), we can fit the attributes and filenames for a maximum of six files in a packet. Thus, if six or fewer LOOKUPS follow a READDIR, they can be batched into one request packet.

Table 4 shows the results of batching. The number of batchable LOOKUP and READDIR operations is reduced by a factor of six (from 18,527 to 3,015 requests in the wired case), and the number of original meta-data operations is reduced by over 20% (from 73,704 to 58,192 requests). This would somewhat improve the speed of directory listings, which was one of the operations particularly reported as slow by our users. Note, however, that this corresponds to only a six percent improvement in overall requests on the wired network, so it might not improve overall NFS performance significantly.

Table 4. This table shows how batching LOOKUP requests with their associated READDIR requests into a single READDIRPLUS request would affect our NFS workload.

Type	Wired	Wireless
Original Requests: total, (data;meta-data)	258,718, (185,014; 73,704)	5,031, (357; 4,674)
Number of READDIR's with more than 1 LOOKUP following	1,070	164
Number of LOOKUPs following READDIR average, (minimum; maximum)	16.3, (1; 307)	15.25, (1; 20)
Number of original LOOKUP and READDIR requests that we can batch together	18,527	2,665
Number of batchable LOOKUP and READDIR requests after batching	3,015	438
Resulting number of requests after batching originals: total, (data; meta-data)	243,206, (185,014;58,192)	2,804, (357; 2,447)

6 Related Work

We have found little literature about packet-level studies of wide-area networks, although [11] includes a latency measurement of 15 seconds on average for a round trip TCP/IP packet over CDPD [8]. Also, a study of asymmetry on TCP performance [4], found the mean end-to-end round trip delay through a Metricom packet radio network to be 2.5 seconds, vastly larger than our measured mean of 0.97 seconds for telnet over TCP. While their measurements were made from a bulk TCP transfer, rather than collected over the course of days, the reason for this significant difference in mean delays remains unclear.

In contrast, there are several packet-level studies of local-area wireless networks. Work by [9] and [19] looks at the types of packet errors found in these environments, and [23] also reports throughput. More recent work by [21] gives an extensive study of the packet loss, latencies, and bandwidth of the Wave-LAN network as seen by a host moving between buildings (but within the line of sight of their WavePoint basestations) and within buildings. Packet loss between buildings reaches as high as almost 40%, and corresponding latencies reach almost one second. In another scenario, while in an elevator, packet loss reaches 100%. Otherwise, packet loss seems to be quite low, averaging from less than one percent to about five percent, and latencies seem to hover around 10ms. We can conclude that the behavior of this wireless network depends greatly on the location of the mobile host, but that it generally shows an order of magnitude better latency, packet loss and bandwidth than the wide-area network in our study.

Besides measurements of the WaveLAN network, [19] and [21] also present a method to observe and predict the behavior of applications in a wireless network in a repeatable manner. The authors first measure end-to-end behavior of round trip packets in a local-area wireless network (WaveLAN). This information is distilled into a model of packet loss and delays. A modulation layer is then placed between applications and the wired network, and this layer drops and delays packets according to the model. The results of running several workloads on the wired network using this modulation technique closely predict the behavior of those workloads when run in the real wireless network. It would be very useful to repeat this effort in a wide-area wireless network.

There are many efforts to adapt applications and protocols to networks with weak connectivity. Coda [16] uses a technique called hoarding to cache copies of needed files on a laptop so they will be locally available during periods of poor connectivity. This form of aggressive caching and prefetching, along with cache consistency protocols, allows mobile hosts to avoid issuing many requests over a poor link. Rover [14] uses queued, non-blocking remote procedure calls to allow applications to continue processing even if the remote procedure call must wait until network connectivity is reestablished. Thus Rover's queuing techniques can help hide the poor connectivity and high latencies found in a wireless network environment.

The concept of proxies has been used to improve performance of many protocols such as X, HTTP and TCP in low-bandwidth and high-latency environments [15] [27] [3]. As seen in [3], this technique is particularly helpful for avoiding TCP's backoff and retransmission features, which were developed for wired networks in which packet loss indicates congestion [6]. Unfortunately, there are many networks a mobile host might visit (particularly networks not under the control of the mobile host's own administrative authorities) in which it may not be possible to place proxies in useful positions. Nonetheless, our experiences in MosquitoNet lead us to believe that proxies should be adopted where possible.

7 Conclusions and Future Work

The high latencies and rate of packet loss and reordering prevent hosts from fully utilizing the available bandwidth on the wireless network. Other wide-area wireless networks, such as CDPD, also have high or even higher latencies. Unfortunately, network manufacturers currently tend to focus on increasing bandwidth rather than reducing latency [24]. We need to convince network manufacturers that reducing latency is just as crucial to the success of wide-area wireless networks as increasing bandwidth.

We must also search for ways to optimize the behavior of applications sensitive to high end-to-end delays. We have at least two options. The first is to avoid latency from applications. The local line editing technique we tried for telnet was simple, yet effective enough to change users' perception of telnet performance on the wireless network. We will soon switch to using our mobile shell, which incorporates this optimization and other features. The second option is to hide end-to-end delays. NFS, for example, will not survive in the wide-area wireless environment without techniques such as prefetching data. We must either fix NFS, or we must switch to a more sophisticated file system (such as Coda [16]) that provides these techniques.

We plan to incorporate into MosquitoNet several other techniques that will improve the performance of our wireless network. For instance, we are currently experimenting with adding more than one radio onto our router. We do this by creating a virtual radio device that actually uses one or more radios for incoming packets and one or more radios for outgoing packets. To the outside world, all the radios appear to be functioning as one single device. This way, we can minimize some of the latencies caused by the router's single radio switching between incoming and outgoing traffic.

8 Acknowledgements

We would like to thank the USENIX Association, Daimler-Benz Research and Technology and the Xerox Palo Alto Research Center for supporting the student authors of this paper. This work was also supported in part by MITI (Ministry of International Trade and Industry) through the "Advanced Software Enrichment Project" of IPA (Information-technology Promotion Agency, Japan).

References

1. Armitage, G.: Support for Multicast over UNI 3.0/3.1 based ATM Networks. Internet Request for Comments 2022, November 1996.
2. Baker, M., Zhao, X., Cheshire, S., Stone, J.: Supporting Mobility in MosquitoNet. Proceedings of the 1996 USENIX Conference, San Diego, CA, January 1996.
3. Balakrishnan, H., Padmanabhan, V., Seshan, S., Katz, R.: A Comparison of Mechanisms for Improving TCP Performance over Wireless Links. Proceedings of SIGCOMM'96, August 1996.
4. Balakrishnan, H., Padmanabhan, V., Katz, R.: The Effects of Asymmetry on TCP Performance. Proceedings of Mobicom'97, September 1997.

5. Borman, D.: Telnet Linemode Option. Internet Request for Comments 1184, October 1990.
6. Caceres, R., Iftode, L.: Improving the Performance of Reliable Transport Protocols in Mobile Computing Environments. IEEE Journal on Selected Areas in Communications, vol. 13, no. 5, June 1995.
7. Callaghan, B., Pawlowski, B., Staubach, P.: NFS Version 3 Protocol Specification. Internet Request for Comments 1813, June 1995.
8. Cellular Digital Packet Data Specification. Release 1.0. July 19, 1993.
9. Eckhardt, D., Steenkiste, P.: Measurement and Analysis of the Error Characteristics of an In-Building Wireless Network. Proceedings of SIGCOMM'96, August 1996.
10. Fulton, J., Kantarjiev, C.: An Update on Low Bandwidth X (LBX); a Standard for X and Serial Lines. Proceedings of the 7th Annual X Technical Conference, January 1993,
11. Housel, B., Lindquist, D.: WebExpress: A System for Optimizing Web Browsing in a Wireless Environment. Proceedings of Mobicom'96, November 1996.
12. Jacobson, V.: Compressing TCP/IP Headers for Low-Speed Serial Links. Internet Request for Comments 1144, February 1990.
13. Jacobson, V.: Berkeley TCP Evolution from 4.3-Tahoe to 4.3-Reno. Proceedings of the 18th Internet Engineering Task Force, p. 365, September 1990.
14. Joseph, A., deLespinasse, A., Tauber, J., Gifford, D., Kaashoek, M.: Rover: A Toolkit for Mobile Information Access. Proceedings of the 15th ACM Symposium on Operating Systems Principles, December 1995.
15. Kantarjiev, C., Demers, A., Frederick, R., Krivacic, R., Weiser, M.: Experiences with X in a Wireless Environment. Proceedings of the Usenix Mobile and Location-Independent Computing Symposium, August 1993.
16. Kistler, J., Satyanarayanan, M.: Disconnected Operation in the Coda File System. Proceedings of the 13th ACM Symposium on Operating Systems Principles, October 1991.
17. Metricom, Inc.: URL: http://www.metricom.com.
18. Nagle, J.: Congestion Control in IP/TCP Internetworks. Internet Request for Comments 896, January 1984.
19. Nguyen, G., Katz, R., Noble, B., Satyanarayanan, M.: A Trace-Based Approach for Modeling Wireless Channel Behavior. Proceedings of the 1996 Winter Simulation Conference, 1996.
20. Noble, B., Nguyen, G., Satyanarayanan, M., Katz, R.: Mobile Network Tracing. Internet Request for Comments 2041, October 1996.
21. Noble, B., Satyanarayanan, M., Nguyen, G., Katz, R.: Trace-Based Mobile Network Emulationr. Proceedings of SIGCOMM'97, September 1997.
22. Perkins, C.: IP Mobility Support. Internet Request for Comments 2002, October 1996.
23. Reynolds, N., Duchamp, D.: Measured Performance of a Wireless LAN. Proceedings of the 17th Conference on Local Computer Networks, September 1992.
24. Satyanarayanan, M.: Keynote Address to ACM Mobicom'96. November 1996.
25. Stevens, W.: TCP/IP Illustrated, Volume 1. Addison-Wesley, 1994, p. 269.
26. Stevens, W.: TCP Slow Start, Congestion Avoidance, Fast Retransmit, and Fast Recovery Algorithms. Internet Request for Comments 2001, January 1997.
27. Watson, T., Bershad, B.: Local Area Mobile Computing on Stock Hardware and Mostly Stock Software. USENIX Symposium on Mobile and Location-Independent Computing, August 1993.

Design and Implementation of Mobile IP System with Security Consideration

Masahiro Ishiyama, Atsushi Inoue, Atsushi Fukumoto, Toshio Okamoto

Communication and Information Systems Research Lab.
Research and Development Center, Toshiba Corporation.
1, Komukai Toshiba-cho, Saiwai-ku, kawasaki 210, Japan

Abstract. As the commercial use of the Internet is becoming common and the demand for mobile computing over the Internet is emerging, it is necessary to construct a secure mobile environment. This paper presents an implementation example of such a system which employs a secure mobile IP protocol on stationary security gateways and mobile hosts. The IETF standard Mobile IP protocol is modified with IP security primitives, which control the packet flow from a mobile host through multiple security gateways. Using IP security primitives, the packet going into a corporate network and the packet going out of the visiting network are both securely processed. This IP security based packet control allows transparent mobile access from anywhere on an IP network even with sufficient security support by encrypting and authenticating IP packets. The current implementation status and the performance evaluation are also reported.

1 Introduction

Security support is one of the key feature for wide commercial use of the Internet. Demands for mobile computing are also emerging as smaller PCs and PDAs become more commonly used. Users of such equipment want to communicate from remote IP connection points through various communication media. For example, even when an office worker is away, he/she may need to access proprietary information inside the company from a satellite office. In order to realize such mobile application of the Internet, security mechanisms for mobile environment are necessary.

This paper proposes an approach with IP layer security/mobility support to meet this need. The IP-layer processing provides a generic security/mobility solution because it does not affect existing upper layer application software.

IP security (IPsec) and Mobile IP are proposed by IETF (Internet Engineering Task Force) as standard IP technologies. On IPsec, the standard protocol for packet authentication and encryption are proposed. Mobile IP is a protocol for supporting transparent access from/to mobile hosts using tunneling technology. Combining these protocols, we are developing a prototype system, in which secure Mobile IP is implemented on gateway servers and mobile hosts. This paper presents the design policy of the prototype system, focusing on how the packets from remote mobile hosts can securely traverse the security gateways using IPsec primitives. The current implementation status and the preliminary performance evaluation are also reported.

2 Key Technologies

2.1 Mobile IP

Mobile IP [1] is a protocol for supporting transparent IP mobility. With Mobile IP, users can use a fixed (home) address assigned to the mobile host even when the mobile host changes location on the IP network. Mobile IP supports host mobility as follows:

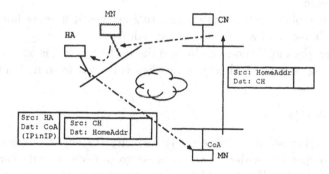

Fig. 1. Mobile IP operation.

- A fixed home address is assigned to a mobile node. The mobile node can continue to use this home address even when it changes the location on the IP network.
- A Care-of-Address (CoA) is an address which is used by the mobile node on the visited network. A CoA is given from a foreign agent or assigned directly to the mobile node (by DHCP or other methods). The latter case is called "co-located care-of-address".
- A home agent is placed on the home network where the mobile node is originally connected. The home agent receives information from the mobile node and maintains mobile information (such as the CoA). When the mobile node moves from its home network, the home agent receives packets in place of the mobile node, and then forwards the packets to the mobile node's current location.
- A foreign agent is placed on the visited network to which the mobile node has moved. The foreign agent specifies a CoA for the mobile node. It receives the packets from the home agent and forwards them to the mobile node. When the mobile node uses a co-located CoA, the foreign agent is not necessary.

- When a mobile node moves, it acquires a CoA on the visited network. After that, the mobile node sends a "Registration request message" containing the care-of-address to its home agent. After the "Registration request message" is accepted, packets destined for the mobile host's original address (home address) are received by the home agent. Then the packet is encapsulated in IPinIP [2] destined for the registered CoA and forwarded.
- When the mobile node uses a co-located CoA, the packets from the home agent are directly transmitted to the mobile node. The mobile node decapsulates the forwarded packets and extracts the original packets destined for its home address (see Fig. 1).
- When there is a foreign agent, the packets from the home agent are transmitted to the foreign agent. The foreign agent decapsulates the forwarded packets and forwards the original packets to the mobile node by link-layer transmission.
- When the mobile node sends packets to someone, it uses its home address, not the Care-of-address, for the source address.
- Therefore, the mobile node exchanges the packets as if it is on the home network (using its home address), even when it is away from its home network.

2.2 IP Security

In order to satisfy security concerns, IP security (IPsec) is proposed[3]. IPsec proposes two specific headers that are used to provide security services. One is the Authentication Header (AH) [4], which provides data integrity and authentication. The other is the Encapsulating Security Payload (ESP) [5], which provides integrity, authentication, and confidentiality for IP datagrams.[1]

Various authentication/encryption algorithms can be used for AH/ESP. The "Security Association" decides what algorithms are actually used. The Security Association is a set of parameters, such as authentication/encryption algorithms and keys. A Security Parameter Index (SPI) is given as a parameter of AH/ESP. The combination of a given SPI and Destination Address uniquely identifies a particular "Security Association". Therefore, when an entity uses IPsec, it must negotiate a Security Association with the correspondent IPsec entity in advance. The management of the Security Association is the role of key management protocol[2].

Using IPsec, the security is guaranteed on the IP layer without any impact to the upper layer applications. Between the gateways and/or hosts which implement IPsec, a virtual private network (VPN) can be constructed with sufficient data secrecy, even on a low security network like the Internet.

---

[1] When integrity and authentication are only required, either AH or ESP can be used. If the performance is critical, AH might be better (because hash is faster than encryption). If the traffic must be hidden on the intermediate path, ESP should be used.

[2] Our current prototype system uses SKIP proposed by Sun Microsystems, for the key management protocol. See [6] for detail.

3 Security Issues on Mobile IP

Mobile IP provides transparent IP mobility support for mobile terminals. However, when Mobile IP is used for accessing a corporate network from a remote site, there might be several security flaws.

- **Packets going into a corporate network**
  On Mobile IP, the mobile node sends the packets with the source address set as its home address. Looking from the inside of the home network, a mobile node's packet cannot be distinguished from IP address spoofing attack packets coming from the outside with Inside address listed as the source address. The firewall at the entrance to the corporate network can detect that and refuse to pass the packet. If this packet can enter the corporate network, the network is a potential victim of an IP address spoofing attack, and that is too dangerous.
  For regulating Mobile IP, some kind of authentication is performed between the home agent and the mobile node. Therefore, it is difficult for an impostor to adopt the guise of the mobile node. The home agent processes the packet destined to the mobile node's home address, but it has no way to check the packet coming from the outside with the source address set to the home address. Therefore, the issue of IP address spoofing attack cannot be resolved within the Mobile IP framework.
- **Packets going out from the visited network**
  The packet from the mobile node might conflict with the firewall on the visited network, because the firewall protects the visited network by restricting the outgoing packet flow.
- **Confidentiality of communication**
  When a network is protected by a firewall, it is assumed that the network inside is secure, and send/receive the proprietary information without any protection (such as encryption).

However, when a mobile node goes out of the protected network, and tries to gain access to the network from a remote site, the proprietary information is moved outside the protected network and might be subject to eavesdropping. Therefore, we have to guarantee the confidentiality of the information sent to the mobile node.

As described above, when a protected network is accessed using Mobile IP, a mechanism is needed which makes it possible to,

Issue 1 provide protection from IP packet forgery
Issue 2 secure traversal of firewalls
Issue 3 guarantee communication confidentiality

3.1 Combining IPsec and Mobile IP

The above issues are all resolved by IPsec. In IPsec, the integrity of the IP datagram is guaranteed by AH and ESP, and the confidentiality is guaranteed by ESP.

For Issue 1, AH's integrity property can be employed, confirming that the received packets are actually sent by the mobile node. For Issue 2, AH can also be used between the mobile node and the firewall, which guarantees that the packet received by the firewalls comes from a mobile node with the privilege of traversing the firewall, and that the packet is not altered between them. For Issue 3, ESP's confidentiality property can be employed for protecting the IP datagram. When the packet goes toward the outside mobile node, ESP can be used between the firewall and the mobile node to avoid eavesdropping.

All the above issues between the mobile node and the firewall are resolved by introducing IPsec. As IPsec and Mobile IP are designed independently, they have no impact on each other, even when used simultaneously.

4 Issues on Combining IPsec and Mobile IP

However, when Mobile IP and IPsec are combined, a new issue arises. As the mobile node moves over the IP network using IPsec, the correspondent IPsec entity might change depending on the IP connection point. For example, consider the case when the mobile node communicates with host H1 in Fig 2. If the mobile node is at position A, it has to go through the firewall FW. But when it moves to position B, it does not go through FW. When the mobile node talks with host H2, the situation is reversed.

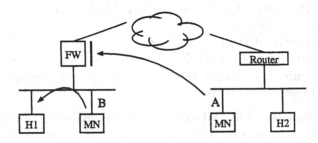

Fig. 2. The change of traversed firewalls on Mobile Node's movement.

Therefore, the mobile node must identify which firewalls (on the path toward the correspondent node) have to be traversed every time it changes location on the IP network. Since we assume there are nested firewalls (inside one network), there might be multiple firewalls to be traversed in general.

5 Proposed System

A typical system configuration is shown as Fig. 3. An IPsec-processing firewall is called a "Security Gateway (SGW)". We assume that all firewalls in the system are SGWs with IPsec-processing capability. A SGW is typically placed on the boundary between the inside network of a certain organization and the Internet (just like an ordinary firewall). Also, a SGW can be placed inside the organization in order to protect the network of a specific division.

On the home (sub)network of a mobile node, there is a home agent (HA). The correspondent node (shown as CN) can be anywhere in the system as far as the SGW's policy allows.

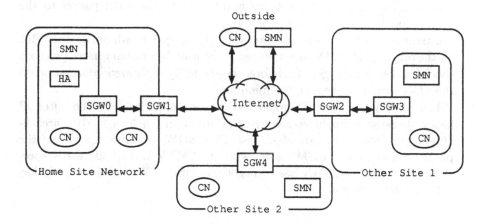

Fig. 3. Typical system configuration.

5.1 Security Gateway

As described before, the SGW provides security services (including IPsec) to the hosts of its protected network. We assume that each SGW is properly maintained by skilled system administrators, who can decide the security policies for the SGWs considering the various demands from the organizations. Therefore, if communication between two networks is allowed, the SGWs know each other and exchange the necessary information with each other.

5.2 Secure Mobile Node

A mobile node has to process IPsec by itself. This IPSEC-processing mobile node is called a "Secure Mobile Node (SMN)". SMN uses co-located care-of-addresses. Therefore, SMN can decapsulate the packets from the home agent, and no foreign agents are needed.

5.3 Assumption for the Proposed System

We assume the following about the system configuration, the operation of system components, and the maintenance conditions.

- There are no IP address collisions on the proposed system. That means, when one IP address is specified, one host uniquely corresponds to the address.
- The correspondent node with which SMN can communicate using Mobile IP, can be reached from the home network of the SMN. That means, when the SMN moves anywhere in the system, the communication between the correspondent node and the home agent (which relays the packet to the current location of SMN) is guaranteed.
- We assume that SGWs are maintained by skilled system administrators. But on the other hand, SMNs are assumed to be used by ordinary users (without special skills/knowledge). Therefore, the statically registered information on the SMN should be kept to the minimum.
- When SMN uses IPsec, it should use the care-of-address for the outer IP header because it might receive error information (such as ICMP unreachable) forwarded to the care-of-address. Each SGW has to recognize that the packet comes from the SMN even with the SMN's care-of-address is specified. Therefore, the SMN has to negotiate with SGWs in advance via key management protocol.

5.4 Dynamic SGW Discovery

When a SMN moves on an IP network, the path toward the correspondent node changes. This means that the SGWs to be traversed also change. However, the approach of installing all the information about all SGWs and their protected network sets onto a SMN does not meet the demand to limit the information on the SMN to the minimum possible level. Therefore, it is necessary to investigate the method of dynamically discovering SGWs to be traversed for a given correspondent node.

The basic strategy is that when the packet traverses the SGW, the SGW reports to the SMN that a kind of authentication is necessary.

When receiving packets, an ordinary firewall decides whether it receives/forwards or discards the packets. This decision is based on the firewall's security policy. An SGW's security policy is that "before a packet is allowed to go through, a kind of authentication is necessary". When the SGW receives packets on which no authentication has been done, the SGW notifies the source address that authentication is necessary for the received packets (usually the SMN). For this authentication request message, a UDP or ICMP packet with some specific format can be used.

All SGWs must allow the authentication request packet to traverse in order to let SMN be able to receive the packet. This authentication request might be returned to the SMN's home address, not SMN's care of address. Therefore all SGWs know IP routes to any point of network.

Let's consider the case that the Mobile Node MN communicates with host H traversing SGW S1 (see Fig. 4). S1 is on the path between MN and H. First, MN sends a plain IP packet to host H. S1 gets the packet and judges that an authentication code is necessary for forwarding this packet to H, so S1 returns the authentication request to the source address of the packet (MN). MN receives this request and appends S1 to the list of SGWs to be traversed.

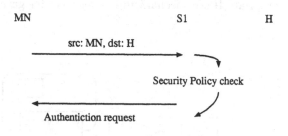

Fig. 4. Dynamic gateway discovery.

5.5 Dynamic Discovery and Outside Network

When an organization employs an SGW, it is common that it does not expose the internal IP network path information to the outside world. The dynamic SGW discovery described above assumes that the packet surely arrives at the intermediate SGW along the path toward the destination correspondent node. Therefore, a path from the mobile node's current location to the destination must exist. But when the mobile node goes to an outside network and tries to access an internal host, this assumption might not be valid.

To avoid such a situation, we define a "default border gateway". A border gateway is a SGW placed on the border between inside/outside networks for an organization. A mobile node has to have at least one entry of the following information.

(border gateway, All internal networks)

All internal networks is a set of all network addresses which are used in the organization. All such networks are protected by one border gateway (not necessarily the specified border gateway). For example, three networks (Home Site Network, Other Site 1, Other Site 2) correspond to this *All internal networks* in Fig. 3.

We call the border gateway specified above a *default border gateway*. When a mobile node detects that its care-of-address is not included in the *All internal networks* set and the address of CN is included in *All internal networks*, then it uses this *default border gateway* as the Next-hop SGW (without doing dynamic SGW discovery). Even if the mobile node is not in *"All internal networks"*, we assume that the ability to reach the default border gateway is guaranteed.

The SMN's default border gateway might be the incorrect border gateway. That is, even though the default border gateway receives the packet and has processed the IPsec (such as authentication and decryption), the destination of the packet is not included in the SGW's protected network. In such a case, the default border gateway has to forward the packet to another border gateway, employing an appropriate IPsec mechanism between border gateways (see Fig. 5)

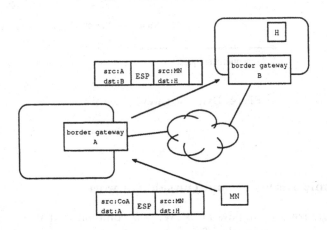

Fig. 5. Transmission between border gateways.

The advantage of using a default border gateway is as follows:

First, it makes possible for a mobile node to securely communicate from an external network to an internal network without registering the information about all border gateways (and their protected networks). If all SGWs support the dynamic discovery method, the only information a SMN needs to know is this pair *(border gateway, All internal networks)*.

Many people think that a firewall should not expose its information to the outside world. The firewalls must be "calm" and should not send unnecessary packets to the outside. The border gateways should be especially calm because they can be attacked from everywhere over the Internet. On the other hand, a SMN assumes reception of a response from the SGW in order to realize the dynamic SGW discovery, and this conflicts with the previous "SGW should be calm" principle. So, it is necessary to find the balanced solution.

On this system, we stipulate that all SMNs know (at least one) default border gateway. The SMN and the default border gateway do not exchange messages as in the case of the dynamic SGW discovery scheme. Therefore, when the SMN moves out of the organization, we can limit the packet flow between the SMN and the default border gateway to a minimum, and the border gateway can be maintained more securely.

5.6 SGW to Be Discovered

There are two paths along which SGWs to be traversed need to be discovered. One is the path from the current location of the mobile node to the home agent. The registration request/reply messages and IPinIP packets from HA flow on this path. Once the mobile node moves, it maintains this path and sends Mobile IP registration message to the home agent.

The other is the path from the mobile node to the correspondent node. The packets from the mobile node flow on this path. As we assume that the path from the correspondent node to the mobile node (via home agent) is already guaranteed (as the correspondent node is reachable from the mobile node's home network), there is no need to care about that.

5.7 Security Issues on Authentication Request

All SGWs have to forward authentication request packets. But SGWs also act as firewalls, and so there might be some cases where the fact that all authentication request packets are allowed to traverse without permission is considered to be a security problem. In this case, SGW can use IPsec to send/forward authentication request.

We assume that the information about Next-hop SGWs are registered to all SGWs in advance. Next-hop SGW means the nearest SGW on the route to a final destination. Next-hop SGWs are used for the IPsec routing, just like Next-hop routers for the IP routing. When an SGW sends/forwards authentication request, the SGW applies IPsec to authentication request with Next-hop SGW to protect it. If there are no more Next-hop SGWs, the SGW examines the final destination of the authentication request packet whether it is in the network protected by the SGW. If the final destination is in the protected network, the SGW simply forwards it. If not, since the final destination must be a moving mobile node, the SGW can use IPsec with the node to forward it.

In this way, the SGW can confirm that the authentication request packet is from the neighbor SGW. Although the SGW cannot confirm the packet from the claimed originator in IP header, this scheme can let the SGW forward the authentication request more securely. And the mobile node can also confirm that the authentication request packet is from the neighbor SGW.

6 Communication Examples

We will explain the example communication scheme using Fig. 6. In Fig. 6, S1, S2 and S3 are SGWs. M1 is an SMN. m1 is a home address of M1. c1 is a

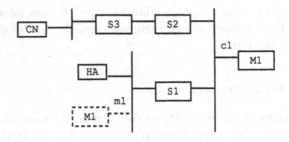

Fig. 6. Sample configuration.

Care-of-Address in the visited network. HA is a home agent of M1. CN is a the correspondent node of M1.

In IPsec, there are two protocols: AH and ESP. We assume that all SGWs and M1 use AH in the following examples, although SGWs and SMNs can choose these protocols for suitable security level.

6.1 Registration Phase

We will explain an example in which M1 sends a registration toward HA using Fig. 7.

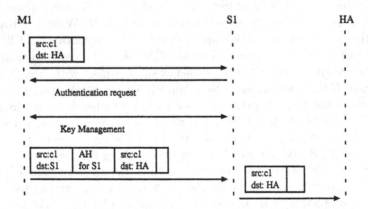

Fig. 7. Packet flow on registration phase.

Once M1 moves, it sends a registration request packet to HA. This packet arrives at S1 on the route from M1 to HA. S1 checks this request packet and sends back the authentication request to M1, because this registration request is not protected by IPsec. Since the source address of this registration request is c1, the authentication request from S1 goes directly to M1 (not via HA). Then, M1 appends S1 into the gateway traversal list for destination HA, and M1 tries to establish a Security Association (SA) for S1. Though we don't discuss the key exchange method here, a key management protocol, such as SKIP[6] or ISAKMP[7], can be used for that purpose.

Now M1 sends registration request using IPsec for S1. S1 receives this packet, decapsulates and forwards the result. Then HA receives the decapsulated registration request packet from M1. HA processes this and sends back its reply to M1 (IP-address:c1). S1 receives this reply and forwards it to M1 using IPsec because S1 already established SA for M1.

6.2 Communication Phase

After the registration, M1 can communicate with other hosts using Mobile IP protocol. We will explain the example in which M1 communicates with CN using Fig. 8.

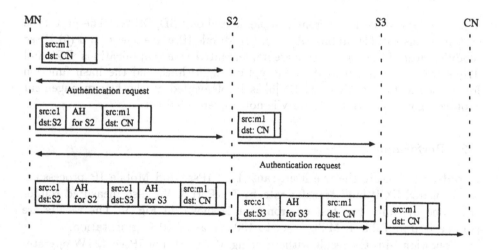

Fig. 8. Packet flow on communication phase.

M1 sends packet to CN. This packet arrives at S2 first on the route to CN. S2 sends back authentication request to M1. Since the source address of this packet is m1, this authentication request goes to M1's home network. HA intercepts this packet, encapsulates the packet using IPinIP, and forwards it to M1 on the visited network. The packet arrives at S1. S1 forwards the packet to M1 using IPsec. Then M1 appends S2 to the gateway traversal list for the destination CN, and establishes a SA with S2.

Now M1 can use IPsec for S2, M1 sends packet to CN using IPsec with S2. S2 receives this packet and decapsulates it and forwards the result. The packet arrives at S3. This time, S3 sends back the authentication request packet to M1 in the same way. All the intermediate SGWs, such as S3, perform the same processing as S2.

After setting SA for each SGW, the IPsec mechanism is used for each SGW based on the SA. The M1 processes the packet (destined for CN) by AH (with S3's SA), and then processes the packet (destined for S3) by AH (with S2's SA). When S2 receives this packet, it decapsulates the packet and forwards the result packet. The forwarded packet is sent to S3. Then S3 processes the packet (in just the same way), and forwards the decapsulated packet. That packet is forwarded to CN.

Both S2 and S3 can authenticate that the sender of the packet is M1 as M1 sends the packet including AH for S2 and S3.

7 Implementation Status and Evaluation

7.1 Implementation Status

The prototype system is currently implemented on BSD/OS 2.1. The prototype system consists of (1) Mobile IP node, (2) Mobile IP home agent, and (3) IPsec module. Most of the components are implemented as user applications. DES and Triple-DES are implemented as encryption algorithms, and the hash function for authentication is MD5. SKIP [6] is implemented as the key management protocol. Dynamic SGW discovery is not implemented yet.

7.2 Performance

In order to measure the overhead caused by IPsec and Mobile IP processing, we measured TCP bulk transfer rate by NetPerf [3]. We also measured round-trip time by ping. The test environment is shown in Fig. 9. The results are summarized in Table 1. MTU is set to 1300 to avoid IP fragmentation.

Condition I-i is the result without using Mobile IP nor IPsec. SGW operates as a router (no IPsec processing). On Condition I-ii, only Mobile IP is used. SGW works as a router also. Condition I-iii and I-iv use SKIP as the key management protocol. We measured both AH-only and AH+ESP cases. IPsec is used between the SGW and SMN. Condition I-v and I-vi use both Mobile IP and IPsec simultaneously.

Comparing Condition I-i and I-ii, the performance from CN to SMN is worse. The packet from sender to receiver contains the payload, but the packet in the reverse direction contains ACK only. On transmitting from CN to SMN, the packet with large payload is encapsulated on the HA, and then forwarded to the SMN. Therefore, the packet passes the CN's link twice, and it consumes

---

[3] URL: http://www.cup.hp.com/netperf/NetperfPage.html

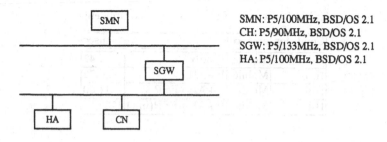

SMN: P5/100MHz, BSD/OS 2.1
CH: P5/90MHz, BSD/OS 2.1
SGW: P5/133MHz, BSD/OS 2.1
HA: P5/100MHz, BSD/OS 2.1

Fig. 9. Environment for performance measurement.

Table 1. Results of performance measurement.

Condition	protocol	From→ To	Mbit/sec	msec
I-i	Plain IP	SMN→ CN	7.04	1.24
	Plain IP	CN →SMN	7.09	1.25
I-ii	Mobile IP	SMN→ CN	6.28	2.39
	Mobile IP	CN →SMN	3.85	2.34
I-iii	IPsec (AH only)	SMN→ CN	3.19	4.95
	IPsec (AH only)	CN →SMN	2.43	4.83
I-iv	IPsec (AH+ESP)	SMN→ CN	2.00	5.89
	IPsec (AH+ESP)	CN →SMN	1.81	6.08
I-v	Both (AH only)	SMN→ CN	3.11	5.49
	Both (AH only)	CN →SMN	2.33	5.33
I-vi	Both (AH+ESP)	SMN→ CN	1.94	6.63
	Both (AH+ESP)	CN →SMN	1.67	6.50

more (almost double) bandwidth. From the result for Condition I-iii, the IPsec overhead is also very high.

Comparing Condition I-iv and I-vi, even when using Mobile IP and IPsec simultaneously, the result is almost the same as for IPsec only. The reasons are:

- The processing on each host for the packet from the SMN does not change from the case when only IPsec is used.
- The Mobile IP packet processing is done on the HA, and the IPsec processing is done on the SGW separately. On the SMN, only the processing for IPinIP decapsulation is appended. Therefore, we think that the overhead coming from the IPsec decryption processing might be more dominant than the portion of overhead from the Mobile IP.

In order to evaluate the overhead of Mobile IP registration, we measured round-trip time of Mobile IP registration request/reply. The test environment is the same as Fig. 9. The results are summarized in Table 2.

Table 2. Results of registration measurement.

Condition	protocol	msec
II-i	Mobile-IP only	4.42
II-ii	Mobile-IP+AH	10.72
II-iii	Mobile-IP+AH+ESP	11.60
II-iv	Mobile-IP+AH+ESP(init)	1732.77

From the result for Condition II-i, II-ii and II-iii, the registration overhead is very small and it seems that registration overhead will not degrade the communication quality. Condition II-iv is the result which includes key exchange overhead of IPsec. We used SKIP protocol as key management protocol for IPsec. SKIP uses Diffie-Hellman computation to generate the shared secret key at the initial phase of communication. Since mobile node sends a registration request packet first when it moves to a visited network, this overhead will degrade the registration performance, because Diffie-Hellman computation is very time-consuming. But once the shared secret key is calculated, SGWs and SMNs can store and use it in the cache. Therefore this calculation occurs only once for each destination of IPsec, and the impact of this overhead is small.

As this prototype implements most of the modules as user applications, a great deal of overhead seems to come from the data copy between the kernel and user spaces. We can expect better performance with kernel implementation.

8   Concluding Remarks

This paper proposes a system with secure mobile computing support, in which two IETF standard protocols, IPsec and Mobile IP, are effectively combined. The proposed system consists of security gateways placed on each organization, mobile nodes which can move freely on the Internet, and home agents which maintain the host mobility. When a mobile node moves to any IP connection point, it can automatically discover the security gateways along the path to the correspondent node. Since an IPsec mechanism operates on each security gateway, the packets from the mobile node can be securely passed over each SGW.

A prototype system is implemented on BSD/OS. On the prototype, we have measured the performance. The results are also presented. The processing overhead is high on a high-speed LAN environment, but on a low-speed WAN or serial line communication, the performance will be feasible.

A number of topics are candidates for future work, including the implementation of dynamic SGW discovery, a detailed mechanism for certificate distribution, route optimization and cooperation with existing firewalls.

Acknowledgement

This work has been sponsored by MITI(Ministry of International Trade and Industry) through "Advanced Software Enrichment Project" of IPA(Information-technology Promotion Agency, Japan).

References

1. C. Perkins. IP Mobility Support. RFC 2002, October 1996.
2. C. Perkins. IP Encapsulation within IP. RFC 2003, October 1996.
3. R. Atkinson. Security Architecture for the Internet Protocol. RFC 1825, August 1995.
4. R. Atkinson. IP Authentication Header. RFC 1826, August 1995.
5. R. Atkinson. IP Encapsulating Payload. RFC 1827, August 1995
6. A. Aziz, T. Markson, H. Prafullchandra. Simple Key-Management For Internet Protocols (SKIP), (I-D draft-ietf-ipsec-skip-07.txt), August 14, 1996
7. D. Maughan, M. Schertler, M. Schneider, J. Turner. Internet Security Association and Key Management Protocol (ISAKMP), (I-D draft-ietf-ipsec-isakmp-08.txt), July 26, 1997

A Network Architecture for Continuous Mobility

Keisuke Uehara[1], Takamichi Tateoka[2], Yasuhito Watanabe[1], Hideki Sunahara[3]
Osamu Nakamura[1] and Jun Murai[1]

[1] Keio University,
5322 Endo, Fujisawa-shi, Kanagawa 252-0816, Japan
[2] The University of Electro-Communications,
1-5-1, Chofugaoka, Chofu, Tokyo 182, Japan
[3] Nara Institute of Science and Technology,
8916-5 Takayama, Ikoma, Nara 630-01, Japan

Abstract. A system architecture for continuous mobility of Internet-connected computers is designed and proposed. The architecture considers network transparency, geographical location transparency, and performance transparency, with strong support for mapping between an identifier space of the Internet and geographical location information. The architecture is defined by 1) identifier space support functions, 2) continuous Internet connectivity functions, and 3) performance transparency functions. Two experimental systems are implemented based on the architecture and are tested. The systems achieve continuous mobility in practical environments for automobiles connecting to the Internet, and in classrooms with about 40 roaming students.

1 Introduction

Many issues arise ranging from the hardware level to the application level to construct an actual mobile computing environment. For example, at the hardware level, a computer must be small and portable. At the data link level, wireless communication technologies for both the local area and the wide area must be established. At the network level, seamless connectivity from/to mobile nodes must be provided. At the application level, new applications specific to a mobile environment must be developed.

As of today, most of the problems at the hardware level have been solved. Computers are small and light enough for users to carry them. The PC card technology allows dynamic reconfiguration of network interfaces of a computer, e.g., from a 10BASE-T interface to a wireless LAN interface.

Some problems for mobility support have been solved and some remain unsolved in the Internet environment. At the IP level, seamless communication from/to mobile nodes can be achieved by employing Mobile IP[1][2] or VIP[3], i.e., *location transparency* has been solved. At the TCP level, however, communication throughput decreases in some conditions[4], i.e., *performance transparency* is not achieved. Although some middle-ware systems such as the Coda file system[5] take disconnected operation into account, there are only a few applications designed specifically for the mobile computing environment. Domain names are usually used to specify the target computer in the Internet. However, another *naming architecture* should also be considered for the mobile computing environment, where it is very convenient for a user to specify target computer by its location instead of its domain name, e.g., the nearest print server. Security must be taken into account at all levels. Security is generally categorized into authentication, integration, and secrecy. In the current Internet environment, organizations are usually connected to the Internet via firewall machines to protect the intranet from intruders. However, it is very inconvenient for a mobile user if it is impossible to communicate with computers via firewalls. *Secured firewall traversal* must be provided to mobile users.

The NECM (Network Environment for Continuous Mobility) project started in April 1996 to build an actual mobile computing environment. It is a joint project between Keio University, Toshiba Corp., Sun Microsystems, and Stanford University. The NECM project has developed many new technologies such as GLI (Geographical Location Information System)[6], PFS (Personal File System)[7], and LWP (Light Weight Protocol)[8]. We also implemented some standardized protocols such as Dynamic Host Configuration Protocol (DHCP)[9][10] and Dynamic Domain Name System (DynDNS)[11][12][13][14] from scratch. In November 1997, we tested our testbed for a mobile computing environment at Shonan Fujisawa Campus of Keio University.

2   Existing Technologies

Figure 1 depicts existing technologies for a mobile computing environment. At the data link level, wireless communication technologies such as Personal Digital Cellular (PDC)[4] /Personal Digital Cellular Packet (PDC-P) and IEEE802.11 are available. When a mobile node moves to another subnet, it must be reassigned an IP address. DHCP provides mechanisms to assign network parameters such as an IP address. To achieve seamless communication from/to a mobile node, Mobile IP was developed. Dynamic DNS is useful to support node mobility if Mobile IP is not available in the IP level, i.e., the new IP address of a mobile node is immediately reflected to the domain name system. At the middle-ware level, the Coda file system allows disconnected access to a network file system. This section gives overviews of these existing technologies and clarifies the remaining unsolved problems.

2.1   DHCP

DHCP is a client-server type protocol that can be used to dynamically assign network parameters to clients. DHCP supports over 60 parameters, including IP address, netmask, default route, etc. A mobile node can obtain an IP address when it moves to another subnet, and then it can communicate with other nodes. However, the mobile node cannot be identified by an immutable identifier if only DHCP is used.

---

[4] The digital cellular system in Japan

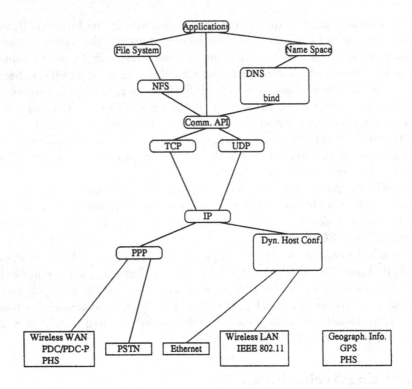

Fig. 1. Block diagram of existing technologies

2.2 Mobile IP

Mobile IP allows seamless communication with mobile nodes. A mobile node can move to subnets served by *FAs (Foreign Agent)*. A mobile node can be identified by its *home address* regardless of its location although its *care-of address* changes when it moves. There are two ways to assign a care-of address: a FA notifies the mobile node of its care-of address or the mobile node obtains its care-of address by using DHCP. The latter case is called *co-located care-of address*. In both cases, the binding between the home address and the care-of address is registered with the *HA (Home Agent)* of the mobile node. The HA announces the routing information for the mobile nodes it manages.

When a node sends an IP packet to a mobile node, this packet first reaches the HA of the mobile node in accordance with the routing information announced by the HA. The HA encapsulates the received IP packet within another IP header and forwards it to the FA that currently serves the mobile node. The FA decapsulates the received packet and forwards the original IP packet to the mobile node. In case of co-located care-of address, the HA directly forwards the encapsulated packet to the mobile node. Thus, every packet sent to a mobile node travels on a redundant route. A packet from the mobile node to its correspondent node travels on the optimal route.

2.3 Dynamic DNS

Dynamic DNS[14] provides a method to dynamically update DNS entries. It is an extension of DNS. The message includes existing entries and update information. When a server receives an update request message, it authenticates the requesting host and updates the entry. Dynamic DNS has a mechanism to keep consistency of the database. If a slave server receives the message, it forwards the message to the master server because only the master server is allowed to update entries.

2.4 Coda File System

The Coda file system, which was developed by CMU as the successor to the Andrew File System, is a file system that supports disconnected operations. It has two operation modes: connected and disconnected. In connected mode, the Coda file system stores files as caches when files are accessed. Also a user can request to store files explicitly. This behavior is almost the same as the Andrew File System. When a host is disconnected, the system provides accessibility to files by using cached data. However, the Coda file system does not take care of characteristics of network connectivity[5] . Heavy traffic is charged to communication links even if a host is connected by PDC. Furthermore, modifications to operating systems are required to install the Coda file system.

2.5 Unsolved Problems

If a mobile node has a single network interface such as Ethernet, DHCP and Mobile IP can provide seamless mobility. Assume that a mobile node uses a wireless LAN interface in a room while it uses a PDC interface outdoors. In this case, *automatic interface switching* must be provided when the mobile node moves across the boundary. In addition, packet routes to mobile nodes are always redundant in Mobile IP. *Route optimization* must be incorporated with mobility support communication protocols such as Mobile IP.

In the mobile computing environment, users want to know the physical location of the target node. Users can know the IP address (or the care-of address if Mobile IP is used) but they cannot know the physical location because there are no mechanisms for mapping IP addresses and geographical location information.

3 New Technologies

To solve the problems described in Sect. 2.5, the NECM project developed some new technologies. Figure 2 depicts the block diagram of the modules to build a continuous mobility environment. In the figure, bold italic fonts indicate new technologies the NECM project developed.

---

[5] LITTLE WORK Project at Michigan University introduced the adopt mode for low bandwidth connection to the Coda File System[15].

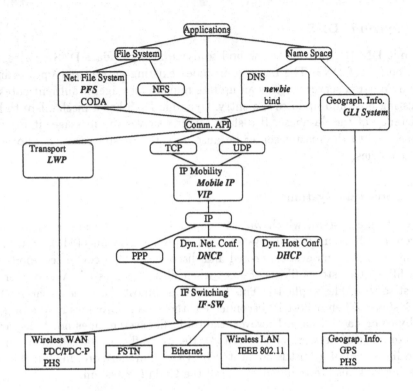

Fig. 2. Block diagram of the NECM system

3.1 Interface Switching

Assume that more than one data link are available at the same time in a mobile computing environment. These data links might have different characteristics. A wireless LAN supports high speed communication in a limited area. PDC and PDC-P provide wide area communication but is expensive. Personal Handyphone System (PHS) can be used in a wide area but cannot communicate with moving nodes.

The technologies to switch currently available data links with user preferences are required in the wireless communication environment. We designed the interface switching technologies to support switching available network interfaces. A user preference description file is stored in a node. According to user preference and availability of the interfaces, the system automatically switches the network interfaces. For example, a car in a garage communicates by a wireless LAN. When the car moves to out of the wireless LAN area, PDC or PDC-P will be automatically started. When the car stops in a crossing, it dumps data with PHS link. After returning to the garage, the interface is switched to the wireless LAN link and PDC or PDC-P link is shutdown. Currently, an implementation on BSD/OS 3.0 is available.

3.2 Virtual IP

Virtual IP (VIP) is another mobile capable Internet Protocol. VIP supports the basic idea of dynamic binding of a a *host identifier* and a *host locator*. VIP capable routers (VIP Routers) have an address mapping table (AMT). AMT is used to bind a host identifier (VIP address) and a host locator (IP address).

The home network of a Mobile Node (MN) has a Home Router (HR) which maintains an AMT entry of the MN. When the MN moves to a foreign network, the MN requests a temporary IP address as a locator by DHCP. The MN announces "the VIP address to IP address" binding to the HR. The HR and intermediate VIP routers between the MN and the HR store the "VIP address/IP address" pair in their AMT as a cache entry. A packet from a Correspondent Node (CN) to the MN is forwarded to the home network of the MN. The HR or a VIP router on the path between the CN and the HR captures this packet and forwards it to the MN location (the destination address in the IP header is rewritten from the VIP address of the MN to the current IP address of the MN). In VIP, the route between a CN and a MN is automatically optimized. When an announce of a VIP address/IP address pair does not reach the HR because of network partitioning, VIP routers provide functions to reroute a packet to the MN. Figure 3 shows the locus of packets to the MN. In this figure, the destination host is a MN. Its HR is called the primary resolver. Currently, VIP is running on BSD/OS 2.1, BSD/OS 3.0, and NEWS-OS 4.2.

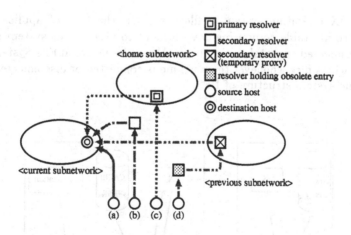

Fig. 3. VIP overview

3.3 Light Weight Protocol

Communication using PDC is unstable in a mobile environment. PDC provides very strong recovery functions. Since PDC recovery looks like congestion of the link, TCP performs retransmission. Thus, performance is degraded further.

In order to utilize the PDC link efficiently, the Light Weight Protocol (LWP) is required instead of TCP. TCP communication with PDC link are divide into two parts. The communication between the Internet node and an access point of PDC link uses TCP while communication between an access point of PDC and the node connected by PDC link is controlled by LWP on the PDC. At the access point, packets are forwarded from TCP to LWP and vise versa. Figure 4 shows the LWP architecture. Currently, implementation on the BSD/OS 2.1 and 3.0 is available.

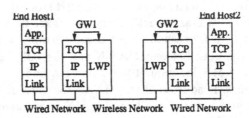

Fig. 4. Light Weight Protocol architecture

3.4 Personal File System

In the UNIX operating system, a file system is the base of applications. To provide a comfortable computing environment to users, a file system that supports disconnected operatable is required. With the Personal File System (PFS), users can access files whenever the machine is connected or disconnected. Figure 5 shows the system structure of PFS.

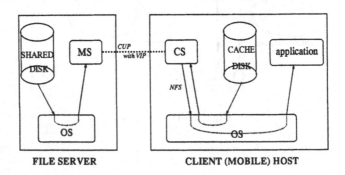

Fig. 5. System structure of PFS

Files are prefetched to the local disk. To consider the status of connection to the Internet (connected, disconnected, and connected with low bandwidth), PFS provides the following four modes.

1. NFS Compatible (Synchronous) Mode
   This mode is used on a high bandwidth connection (such as Ethernet). In this mode, operations to the file system are performed in synchronously. This mode is semantically compatible with NFS operations.
2. Asynchronous Mode
   This mode is used on a mid-bandwidth connection (such as a 9.6Kbps PPP link). In this mode, operations to the local cache data and operations between a client and a file server are performed asynchronously.
3. Fetch Only Mode
   This mode is used on a low bandwidth connection. In this mode, only file fetching is allowed.
4. Disconnected Mode
   This mode is for disconnected operation. Operations to the file system are performed only on local cache data. After reconnecting to the Internet, a house keeping operation will start to keep the consistency of the file system.

Conflicts of updated files are automatically detected by the system. Users solve conflicts manually. Thus, in the current implementation, PFS is suitable for accessing ones home directory and similar files. Currently, PFS is running on the BSD/OS 3.0, FreeBSD 2.2.5, Read Hat Linux, SunOS 4.1, Solaris 2.6, and NEWS-OS 4.2.

3.5 Geographical Location Information

To manage bindings between geographical location information and network location information, we designed the Geographical Location Information (GLI) system. The GLI system collects and manages the geographical location information of each node in the Internet. Mobile nodes continuously announce current geographical location information to a server. By accessing the server, users can extract the current geographical location information of nodes. The current GLI system provides the following two types of queries.

- Where are you?
  Query the current location of the specified node.
- Who is there?
  Query the current members within the specified location.

The current system is designed as a centralized database structure. Thus, it does not scale. We started rebuilding the GLI system with a distributed database structure.

4 Testing and Results

To discuss feasibility of the proposed architecture, we provide two types of test scenarios. The first scenario is the classroom model. This scenario is designed to measure performance of Mobile IP and VIP. Another scenario is the Internet car model. This scenario is designed to confirm the process of the system in a poor communication environment.

4.1 Classroom

In the classroom scenario, Mobile-IP, VIP, PFS and GLI were tested. 34 Portable PCs that supported these software modules were used. These PCs moved between two classrooms. The status logs were saved on the each portable PC and servers of mobile services.

The specifications of the 34 portable PCs are shown in Table 1. BSD machines indicate IBM ThinkPad 560(Pentium 133MHz, 24MB). Linux machines indicate DEC HiNote Ultra II(Pentium 120MHz, 24MB).

Table 1. Portable PCs for the classroom scenario

OS	Mobility Support	GLI	PFS	IF	ping	Num. of PCs
BSD/OS	Toshiba Mobile-IP	Yes	Yes	Wireless	Yes	1
BSD/OS	Toshiba Mobile-IP	No	Yes	Wireless	Yes	9
BSD/OS	VIP	Yes	Yes	Wireless	Yes	10
Linux	Stanford Mobile-IP	No	Yes	10BaseT	No	8
Linux	Sun Mobile-IP	No	Yes	10BaseT	No	6

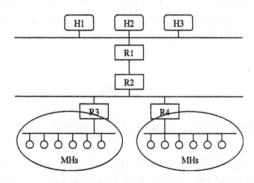

Fig. 6. Classroom testbed

Figure 6 shows the network configuration of the classroom scenario including mobile service servers. H1(Cyrix6x86+PR200, 64MB) performs the following functions: the Home Agent of Mobile-IP, the Home Router of VIP, the Master Server of PFS. H2(Pentium 100MHz, 32MB) is the target machine of the ping from the portable PCs. H3(Pentium ODP 83MHz, 24MB) is a GLI server. The link between R1 and R2 is an ADSL link: from R1 to R2 is 7Mbps and from R2 to R1 is 1Mbps. All other links are Ethernet connections. R3 is a PC running BSD/OS.

In this scenario, at first, all PCs are gathered in the ROOM 2. Then, the PCs were moved to ROOM 1. The Number of the machines that were moved to ROOM1 simultaneously, was 4, 8, 12, 20, and 34. On this situation, we measured the load on each network segment, the load of the each mobile service servers (including Home Agent, Foreign Agents, and Home Router), and mode transition of the PFS client.

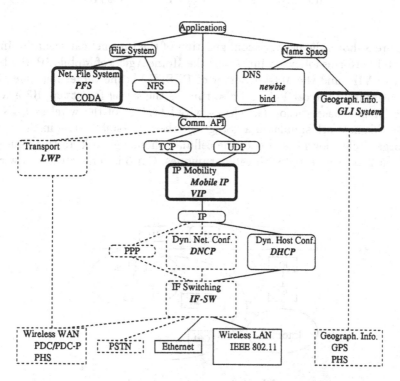

Fig. 7. Test items in classroom environment

The objective of this test is to measure the performance of Mobile IP and co-operability of the various software modules. Figure 7 shows the software used in the NECM system. PFS, GLI system, Mobile IP, VIP, and DHCP were used in this environment.

4.2 Internet Car

In the Internet car scenario, we provide five cars. Each car has a different configuration as shown in the Table 2. The five Internet cars are equipped with a portable PC (Toshiba Portage 300CT, MMX Pentium 133MHz, 64MB), data collection box[6] , GPS, wireless LAN (except car 5), and cellular phone.

Table 2. Internet car configuration

car #	Mobility Support	IF SW	GLI	PFS
car1	Toshiba Mobile IP	Automatic	Yes	Yes
car2	Stanford Mobile IP	Manual	Yes	Yes
car3	Sun Mobile IP	Manual	Yes	Yes
car4	VIP	Manual	Yes	Yes
car5	LWP	NA	Yes	Yes

Figure 8 shows the network configuration of the Internet car scenario. In this figure, H1 performs following functions: the Home Agent of Mobile-IP, the Home Router of VIP, and the Master Server of PFS. H2 is the target machine of the file transfer from the car PCs. H2 also runs as the server for nttcp. H3 is a GLI server. B1 is a base station (wireless - wired bridge) of the wireless LAN. We assume this network simulated a garage for the cars (small circle in the figure). The large circle shows the area of the cellular phone network. In this figure, car 1 and car 2 are connected with cellular phones. Car 3 is connected with wireless LAN.

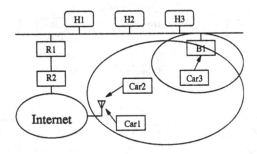

Fig. 8. Internet car testbed

With this network, we accumulated the status logs in the following scenario.

---

[6] This box was developed to obtain raw data of the cars and GPS. Data include latitude, longitude, altitude, pulse count of car speed, switch status of wiper and lights.

1. In the garage, start up the PCs on the car (connected with wireless LAN).
2. Start the programs for GLI and PFS measurement.
3. Start measurement with `nttcp`.
4. Moving to outside of the garage (automatic/hand-operated switching from wireless LAN to PPP with cellular phone).
5. Continue the measurement with `nttcp`.
6. Start file transfer from H1 to PC in the car.
7. Return to the garage (reconnect to the wireless LAN).
8. End of file transfer.
9. Continue the measurement with `nttcp`.

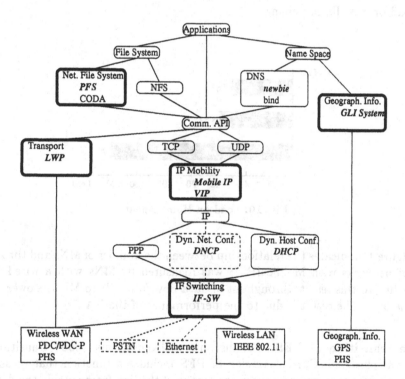

Fig. 9. Test items in Internet car environment

4.3 Results

We analyzed the status log data of tests described in the previous section. In this section, we discuss the result of analysis of status log data.

Performance of Mobile IP. Before discussion on the performance, we have to mention the behavior of Mobile IP in the test environment. In the Internet car test, all implementations of Mobile IP were interoperable. The differences between each implementation were not detected in this test. When the interfaces were switched, Mobile IP software detected it and re-registered the care-of address to its HA automatically. In the classroom testing environment, the software automatically detected Agent Advertisement and switched registered FAs.

Network location transparency is established by Mobile IP and VIP. Tests of classrooms and Internet car show efficient result in load of HA and throughput of network.

On HA, load becomes larger according to the number of MN. Figure 10 shows the load incurred on HA. The values are integration of load averages. The loads were measured, when 8 MNs, 16 MNs and 24 MNs were receiving data from a CH. When MNs sent data, the loads of the HA were also measured. However the load on HA did not change.

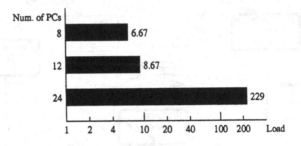

Fig. 10. Load on Home Agent

Figure 11 indicates the relationship between the number of MNs and throughput of networks with Mobile IP. It was measured by MNs with a wired link. According to this result, throughput of data flow from CH to MN is slower than reverse flow. The result is due to the performance of the HA.

State transition of PFS. For disconnected operations, mode transition of PFS was observed. Current version of PFS includes a function that measures link performance in order to check the status of the link from outside the device. In our tests, once PFS moved to an unstable state, PFS did not return to stable state. This means that it is difficult to determine the link status from outside the device.

Automatic configuration. Figure 12 shows the connection status of car 1. This car made a one day round trip from Fujisawa to Tsukuba. The horizontal axis shows the time from start of the round trip. At 0 second, the car is in the garage. In the garage, the car was connected to the Internet by wireless LAN.

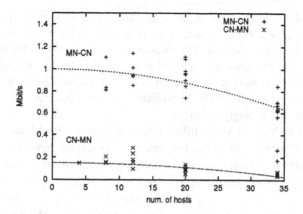

Fig. 11. Mobile IP throughput with wired link

After leaving the garage, the communication link of the car was changed to cellular phone link. In the trip, connection of cellular phone was intercepted by tunnels, but the system automatically reconnects to the Internet. The behavior of the connection is also shown in 5000 seconds units in Fig. 12 . In the figure, disconnection from 8,000 second to 12,000 second is caused by trouble of cellular phone connection. Disconnection from 13,000 second to 26,000 second shows parking at destination. Disconnection from 28,000 second to 33,000 second is caused by trouble of software.

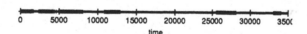

Fig. 12. Connection condition of the car

Geographical Location Information. In the two tests, the geographical location information system was used. MNs in the classroom environment and Internet car environment send GLI update packets to the GLI server every second. The GLI server got the packet and updated the database regardless of the lower layer status such as using an unstable data link status.

5 Consideration

Each implementation of Mobile IP (RFC2002) were interoperable. The implementation of HA could support about 35 MNs. However, the performance of encapsulation decreased as the number of MNs increased. If more than 40 MNs need to be supported, two or more HA are required. Furthermore, when a MN moved, the connectivity of the MN was recovered immediately. However, VIP needed more time to recover. This difference is due to the FA advertisement. When a mobile node runs in co-located care-of address mode, the time needed to recover was the same as VIP. In addition, the co-operation with DHCP and interface status are strongly required.

Interface switching is very difficult to implement. Problems arise because some of the software modules are implemented as kernel modules or as application software. Also, although some state transitions of interfaces can be detected in hardware, the device drivers ignore such state transitions.

The GLI system is currently implemented as a directory service. It works well when there are a small number of users and agents. We are designing the next version of the GLI system. It has a distributed server architecture. Also the application program interface (API) of the GLI system needs to be redesigned. The current API is not familiar with end users.

LWP and PFS can provide performance improvements in an unstable environment. The performance improvements are described in [7] for PFS and [8] for LWP. LWP improves performance by as much as 17 % for an unstable data communication link.

The software structure of this project is designed from network and user side views. Although we were able to run the system as a whole, it was very difficult to implement. Current operating systems have no structure to implement these technologies. To support mobility, the network part of operating systems must be reconstructed.

6 Summary

The NECM project developed a system to provide continuous mobility on the Internet by designing an overall architecture for the purpose, and, by designing and implementing component technologies. The designed architecture provides an explicit use of the geographical location so that a user and applications can map a location in the real world to a logical network location of the mapped object. Also, the system achieves the performance transparency on the mobile node on the Internet by introducing the rapid interface switching mechanism and by LWP, the lightweight protocol system. A seamless computing environment is achieved by introducing a transparent mobile file system called the Personal File System. The basic mobility support functions such as Virtual Internet Protocol, DHCP, Mobile IP and Coda were implemented and tested for evaluation purpose to achieve the integrated system.

In November 1997, integrated tests were executed in Shonan Fujisawa Campus of Keio University to evaluate our approach. Through these implementations and tests, we obtained feasibility of the NECM system. However, we found that our evaluation was insufficient due to lack of measured data. We plan to improve our software and test it again to obtain sufficient data.

Acknowledgments

We would like to thank the members of following groups for co-operation and valuable discussions: WIDE Project and NECM(Network Environment for Continuous Mobility) Project, Sun Microsystems Inc. Technology Development Group, Stanford University Operating Systems and Networking Group, Toshiba Corp., Sony Computer Science Laboratory Inc., NTT Mobile Communications Network Inc., Honda R&D CO., LTD., Isuzu Advanced Engineering Center, LTD., Nippon Telegraph and Telephone Corp. Wireless Lab., NTT Central Personal Communications Network Inc., Soum Corp., and United Motors. Fumio Teraoka and Atsushi Shionozaki provided insightful comments on this paper.

This work was partly funded by MITI(Ministry of International Trade and Industry) through "Advanced Software Enrichment Project" of IPA(Information-technology Promotion Agency, Japan)

References

1. J.D.Solomon: MOBILE IP The Internet Unplugged, Prentice-Hall Inc, (1998)
2. C. Perkins: IP Mobility Support, RFC2002, (1996)
3. F.Teraoka, K.Uehara, H.Sunahara, J.Murai: VIP: A Protocol Providing Host Mobility, Communications of the ACM, Vol.37, No.8 (1994) pp.67–pp.75
4. R.Cáceres,L.Iftode: Improving the Performance of Reliable Transport Protocols in Mobile Computing Environments, IEEE Journal on Selected Areas in Communications, Vol.13, No.5 (1995).
5. J.J.Kister,M.Satyanarayanan: Disconnected Operation in the Coda File System, Proceedings of the 13th Symposium on Operating Systems Principles (1991).
6. Y.Watanabe, A.Shionozaki, F.Teraoka, J.Murai: The Design and Implementation of the Geographical Location Information System, Proceedings of INET'96 (1996)
7. T.Tateoka, K.Uehara, H.Sunahara, F.Teraoka: PFS: A Dynamically Adaptive File System for Networking Environments, Proceedings of the Internet Conference '96 (1996) pp.81-pp.88 (in Japanese)
8. K.Uehara, A.Nishimura, J.Murai: LWPA: Internet architecture for Wide area wireless communication media, Proceedings of Internet Conference 97 (1997) (in Japanese)
9. A.Tominaga,O.Nakamura,F.Teraoka,J.Murai: Problems and Solutions of Dynamic Host Configuration Protocols(DHCP), Proceedings of INET'95 (1995)
10. R.Droms: Dynamic Host Configuration Protocol. RFC2131, (1997).
11. Y.Doi,M.Minami,J.Murai: Implementation of Name Service for New Environment, Proceedings of Distributed System Management Workshop of IPSJ (Information Processing Society of Japan) (1997), pp.85-pp.90 (in Japanese)
12. P.V.Mockapetris, Domain names - concepts and facilities, RFC1034,(1987)
13. P.V.Mockapetris, Domain names - implementation and specification, RFC1035, (1987)
14. P. Vixie, Ed., S. Thomson, Y. Rekhter, J. Bound: Dynamic Updates in the Domain Name System (DNS UPDATE), RFC2136, (1997)
15. L.Huston,P.Honeyman, Disconnected Operation for AFS, Proceedings of USENIX Mobile and Location-Independent Computing Symposium (1993) pp.1–pp.10.

Towards Internationalized Web Creation

KokYong Leong, Hai Liu and Oliver Wu

Internet R&D Unit, Computer Centre
National University of Singapore
10 Kent Ridge Crescent
Singapore 119260

Abstract. Internationalization (i18n) has gained much momentum in recent years. Even the latest HTML 4.0 public draft has taken great strides towards the internationalization of documents, with the goal of making the Web truly 'World Wide'.

This paper starts with describing the various development in HTML standards that has made the Web more global. It then points out the fact that the correct display and rendering of multilingual text is only half the scenario for i18n. Users not only wish to view i18n HTML document, they want to create them! With this in mind, it then goes on to explain why Java has not fully fulfilled its role as an i18n development platform, especially in the area on keyboard input methods. To meet this shortcoming, it explains how the development of a Java Input Method Engine (JIME) fills the gap. The design and implementation of the framework will be described. It concludes with an account of our ongoing development on JIME.

1 Introduction

The integration of Web and I18N are well under way, especially with the World Wide Web Consortium's (W3C) recommendation for HTML 4.0 [1] working draft. Among the i18n features well incorporated from RFC2070 [2] into HTML 4.0 include the use of ISO-10646 (Unicode) as the document character set for HTML, the <lang> tag for specifying the language of content, the <dir> tag for specifying the direction of text, tag for specifying charset in the HTML header, etc. With such enhancements, the Web will be able to broaden its reach.

Although much of the Web used to be dominated by English HTML documents using the ISO-8859-1 character set, HTML documents are increasingly being written in many other native languages and encoding as well. Riding on this trend, major browsers like Netscape Communicator and Microsoft Internet Explorer have included support for viewing i18n HTML documents given that the appropriate fonts are installed. The creation of such documents is also possible, although not without some level of difficulty as will be explained.

1.1 Towards a More Internationalized HTML

The Hypertext Markup Language (HTML) is a markup language used to create hypertext documents that are platform independent. In the beginning, the use of HTML on the World Wide Web was confined to the ISO-8859-1 character set. This only works well for Western European languages. Subsequently, HTML began to be used with other languages using other character sets and encodings frequently at the expense of interoperability.

Prior to HTML 4.0, internationalization features were evidently missing from HTML 2.0 and HTML 3.2. There were no tags to specify the character set of the document (the default charset is ISO 8859-1). Neither were there tags to indicate the text direction which is especially important for right-to-left writings like Arabic and Hebrew.

In the days of HTML 2.0 and 3.2 [3], users encountering multilingual HTML documents while browsing the Web may be subjected to some guessing work to determine the character set which the HTML document is based on. The most intuitive guess would most probably be based on the top-level domain of the website. For example, if the domain is .jp, the HTML documents would most likely be in one of the Japanese encodings - EUC-JP, SJIS or JIS. However, it is also possible that the HTML document could be in one of those double-byte encoding like Chinese GB or Korean KSC or maybe even other character sets. Another approach is to have the HTML document contain an English statement informing the user what character set is used. The user will, upon reading it, switch the browser to the appropriate character set viewing mode.

Along the way, some browsers like Netscape Navigator and Microsoft Internet Explorer began to support the use of a FACE attribute to the FONT [4] tag. With this quick hack, HTML authors can specify a particular font to use to view a certain part of the text within a HTML document. This proved especially useful to 8-bit character set. However, the use of the FONT FACE is considered harmful in many instances since we should not indicate which font set to use to display a document. Rather, we should be specifying the character set a particular HTML document is based on.

With HTML 4.0 public draft, W3C has further enhanced the international capability of the Web. The lastest version of browsers, including Netscape Navigator and IE, can recognize the character set specified in the HTML document header. If the user has provided the appropriate font settings for each language encoding supported, the browser will be able to automatically display the HTML document in the specified language encoding.

2 I18N & Java

Since its inception, Java has been promoted as a cross-platform development language. It is also designed to be a language to support i18n applications right from its initial design. It began with support for Unicode strings in its early version 1.0. However, this primitive implementation really did not do much for i18n.

The current release - version 1.1 [5] - added more support to allow for the development of localizable applets and applications using Java. Enhancements include the display of Unicode characters, a locale mechanism, localized message support, locale-sensitive date and time, time zone and number handling, collation services, character set converters, parameter formatting, and support for finding character/word/sentence boundaries. This is a large step towards i18n in Java. The ability to add fonts to the Java runtime environment made it possible to display Unicode characters. Locales and related services also made it possible to write your application once and port them later to other language contexts through the use of resource bundles. The character set conversion (to and from Unicode) utilities made interchange between current widely used encoding and Unicode effortless.

However, one very important missing feature is the provision for keyboard input methods in Java. Without this, many applications cannot accept non-Roman keyboard input from users. A true localized Java application should not only be able to display localized text, it should be able to accept localized character input from users. Unfortunately, no such functionality has been built into the Java core APIs to date.

3 Java and Keyboard Input Methods

3.1 Why do we need Java Input Methods?

Non-Roman languages require special keyboard mappings to facilitate character input. If you are familiar with Chinese, Japanese or Korean (abbreviated as CJK), you will understand that inputting these characters are not trivial using an English keyboard layout. You need a keyboard manager to trap your keystroke sequence before transforming them into one or more valid characters; some methods require the user to choose from a list of choices. This applies similarly for other languages as well. For example, some Indian languages have phonetic keyboard layouts which are much more complex than direct keyboard mapping. Thai is another instance that needs a keyboard remap to type.

Many a times, a complete GUI application written in Java will need to accept character input from user through widgets like text fields. Currently, such text entry mechanisms are largely based on Roman characters (English keyboards) only. The present core Java APIs framework does not support keyboard input methods for other languages.

Without support for alternative input methods in Java, applications cannot accept non-Roman keyboard input from users.

3.2 JIME

To solve this problem, we focus on developing a Java Input Method Engine (abbreviated as JIME) to allow Java applets and applications to accept non-Roman character input.

273

JIME is being developed on many different fronts. When we started our implementation, due to limited support by browsers for JDK 1.1, we started by writing a Java applet 'jInput' using JDK 1.0. To extend its usefulness, we ported it to a Java plugin for Netscape Composer. Both applet and plugin support various input methods for Chinese, Japanese and Korean.

Along the way, Netscape announced the finalization of JDK 1.1 support for Netscape 4.0 with a patch. As JDK 1.1 support improves, we are re-focusing our development effort toward JDK 1.1 and redeploying our framework to make use of better i18n support from JDK 1.1.

In the sections that follow, we start with introducing our design and implementation of the JDK 1.0 model of our development. Then, we move on to describe our JDK 1.1 model design and implementation issues.

4 Design and Implementation (Based on JDK1.0)

4.1 Design Issues

Input Methods. For languages that require two or more keystrokes to map a character, such as Chinese, we have made use of a very simple lookup array of Strings for our input method mappings from user keystrokes to the corresponding character codes. An example for GB encoding using the PinYin method is shown below .

sourcecode 1. *GB encoding with PinYin method example*
```
static private String[] keys = {
"a",
"ai",
"an",
"ang",
"ao",
........
};
static private String[] mappings = {
"/ub0a2/ub0a1/ubac7/uebe7/ue0c4/uefb9/udfb9",
"/ub0ae/ub4f4/ub0a7/ub0a4/ub0ad/ub0a3/ub0a9/ub0ac/ub0a6/ub0ab
/ub0a5/ub0a8/ub0aa/ub0af/uead3/uf6b0/udedf/ue0c8/ue8a8/ue6c8
/uefcd/ue0c9/uedc1",
"/ub0b2/ub0b8/ub0b4/ub0b5/ub0b6/ub0b3/udacf/uf7f6/ub0b0/ub0b1
/ue2d6/ue8f1/uf0c6/ub0b7/uefa7/udeee/ue1ed/udbfb/ub9e3/ub3a7",
"/ub0ba/ub0b9/ub0bb",
"/ub0c2/ub0c4/ub0c1/ub0be/ub0bd/ucff9/ub0bc/ub0c0/ub0c3/udbea
/ue0bb/uded6/uf7e9/ue6f1/uf7a1/ub0bf/ue1ae/ue2da/ue5db/ue9e1
/uf1fa/ue6c1/uf2fc/uf6cb",
........
};
```

For example, when the user keys in the character 'a', the corresponding to display for the user to select are 0xb0a2, 0xb0a1, 0xbac7, ... etc. If the subsequent key pressed is "n", then the characters selection range will become another set - 0xb0b2, 0xb0b8, 0xb0b4, 0xb0b5, 0xb0b6, ... etc.

Java Bitmap Font Although JDK 1.1 supports the use of host fonts, JDK 1.0 does not. To maintain backward compatibility with older browsers that shipped with a Java 1.0 VM, we designed a bitmap internal font for the applet. It is quite efficient and compact, and bears some similarity to the Hanzi Bitmap Format (HBF). An example of the Chinese GB encoding font is shown below.

sourcecode 2. *Java bitmap font - GB encoding example*
static private final String[] bitmap = {
```
"/u0000/u0000/u0000/u0000/u0000/u0000/u0000/u0000
/u0000/u0000/u0000/u0000/u0000/u0000/u0000/u0000
/u0000/u0000/u0000/u0000/u0000/u0000/u0000/u0000
/u0000/u0000/u0000/u6000/u3000/u1000/u0000/u0000
/u0000/u0000/u0000/u0000/u0000/u0000/u0000/u0000
/u0000/u0000/u0000/u2000/u5000/u2000/u0000/u0000
/u0000/u0000/u0000/u0000/u0000/u0000/u0000/u0300
/u0300/u0000/u0000/u0000/u0000/u0000/u0000/u0000
/u0000/u0000/u0000/u07c0/u0000/u0000/u0000/u0000
/u0000/u0000/u0000/u0000/u0000/u0000/u0000/u0000
....
};
```

We use a 16-by-16 bitmap for each CJK character. So the collection of the first 16 characters in the string above is the hexadecimal bitmap for the first character 0xA1A1 in GB charset. The subsequent 16 characters is for 0xA1A2 and so on.

4.2 Implementation

jInput - a Java applet for non-Roman keyboard input Many search engines around the world are capable of indexing and searching for keywords in languages using double-byte character set, for instance Chinese, Japanese and Korean (CJK). They includes GoYoYo (www.goyoyo.com), Yahoo (search.yahoo.co.jp) and AnySearch (www.anysearch.com).

Usually, the users are expected to find their own ways to enter CJK characters into the text field in the HTML form to search for keywords. This does not pose a problem to those users on a native platform, but users on non-native English platforms will need to source for and install their own third-party applications to input these CJK text. Although many third-party applications for Windows are available (usually running as a keyboard manager), Macintosh and UNIX platforms have limited availability of such applications.

To assist those users on English (and other non-native) platforms, we developed a Java applet allowing the user to input CJK text without having to install any third-party applications.

The advantage of this approach is the user is not expected to install any keyboard manager on his system. The user simply waits for the applet to be downloaded. After the user enters the text into the Java applet, we make use of Netscape LiveConnect technology to retrieve the content from the applet to the HTML form. Netscape LiveConnect [6] allows JavaScript to call methods in Java classes. In this way, the applet works seamlessly with the HTML form as if it is a text field.

The applet currently supports the following language encoding and input methods.

1. Chinese GB2312 with PinYin and CangJie methods.
2. Chinese Big5 with PinYin, CangJie and Simplex methods.
3. Japanese EUC-JP with RomanKana and TCode methods.
4. Korean KSC with Hangul and Hanja methods.

See http://www.irdu.nus.sg/multilingual/jinput/ for a demo of the applet.

This technique will facilitate mobile users who travel to other parts of the world using a different locale operating system platform. In such cases, their native language operating system is not readily available and no native keyboard layouts and display software are at their access.

Composer Plugin - Java Input Method Engine (cpJIME) For cross-platform authoring of i18n HTML pages, we developed a plugin in Java that allows users to input i18n text into Netscape Composer. Since both Netscape and Java runs on platforms from Windows to Macintosh and UNIX, the user can author i18n HTML documents on all the supported platforms using the plugin. This is especially useful for users on English platform but wish to have the i18n capability. If you set your Netscape Messenger to send HTML email message, you can even send email in CJK using the plugin.

We named the plugin - cpJIME which stands for "Composer Plugin [7] - Java Input Method Engine". Installing the plugin is very easy; simply download and copy a ZIP file to the plug-ins directory of where the Communicator application is installed. The plugin is a self-contained unit with its own fonts and keyboard input methods. cpJIME supports various Chinese, Japanese and Korean input methods and encoding. Because Netscape Composer uses Unicode for its internal representation of characters within an HTML document, authoring of CJK documents in Unicode is also possible.

Go to http://www.irdu.nus.sg/multilingual/jinput/cpjime.html to download a beta copy of the plugin.

5 Design and Implementation (based on JDK1.1)

5.1 Design Issues

JDK 1.1 offers better support for writing localized and internationalized Java applications. For example, the ability to add fonts to the Java runtime environment makes possible the display of Unicode characters. Resource bundles, locales and charset converters make localizing your Java applications easier. However, there are still some missing features, which we try to address when designing our JIME framework based on JDK 1.1. JIME API design objectives are -

1. Consistent and convenient font utilities for multiple languages.
   (Java 1.1 cannot let you choose a font of a given encoding, or find out what range of the encoding a font is capable to render.)
2. Various input methods and keyboard input for languages other than US English.
3. Display of multilingual text on AWT widgets such as buttons, menus, etc
4. Complex layout of horizontal and vertical multilingual text.

We break our design into three Java packages for modularity - font, ime and widgets.

jime.font package. It contains typeface implementation to make use of both Java built-in font (system font) and the bitmap font we designed for JDK 1.0 (compiled as Java classes), and provides one consistent interface for user to make use of all kinds of typefaces.

jime.widget package. The widget package, as the name implies, contains necessary components to draw strings, texts, and also layout controllers to layout components in a clean and flexible way. It also provides auxiliary widgets, such as button, pull-down menu, and over-the-spot window, etc.

jime.ime package. This package deals with keyboard mappings and input methods. Generally, the input methods are classified into two classes: direct input and over-the-spot input. Direct input covers keyboards like Thai and most Western European languages. Over-the-spot input covers Chinese, Japanese, Korean keyboard input methods.

5.2 Implementation Issues

Typefaces. The problem with AWT1.1 font is that it does not provide a flexible way use them. Although users can customise the font.properties file to make use of system platform fonts other than default ones, the changes cannot be detected in a Java program, i.e., a user's program cannot request a specific font. With the typeface implementation in jime.font package, Java applications can use

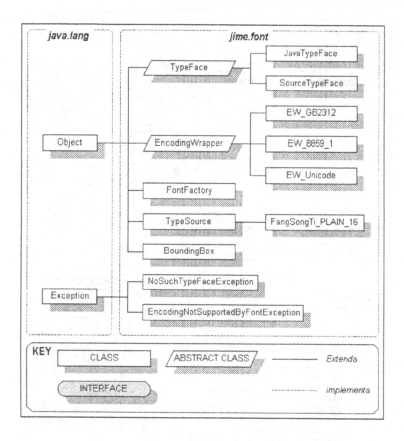

Fig. 1. Overview of jime.font package structure

both system fonts and the bitmap fonts we designed. An unsolved problem is that built-in system fonts cannot be used to render fonts for vertical layout (for ancient Chinese calligraphy for instance). So far, we can only rely on bitmap source font for vertical layout.

FontFactory. FontFactory is designed to provide a convenient way of constructing typefaces. When the user request for typeface, it will search through its database first. It tries to match it with system font first; if no system font can be located for a particular script/language encoding, it will use the bitmap source typeface instead. By grouping typefaces together by font names, encodings, etc., it is very easy to look them up in a hashtable. FontFactory is like a central font repository which gathers the information of all typefaces together so that it can be easily retrieved.

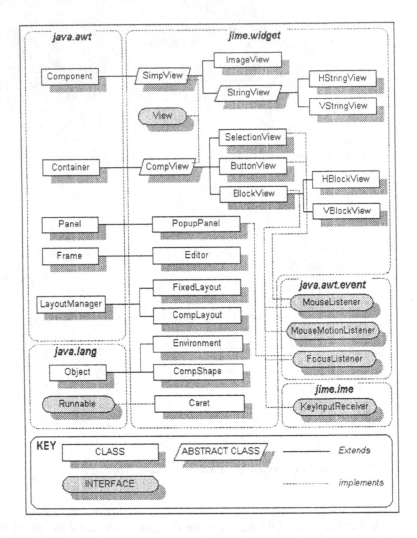

Fig. 2. Overview of jime.widget package structure

View - SimpView and CompView. A view is the basic graphical component in JIME GUI framework. SimpView is like an AWT Component; CompView can contain many SimpView. When laying out a component, SimpView may be asked to split itself into two sub SimpViews, so that it can be laid out one by one. For the purpose of global applicablity, left-right or right-left horizontal layout and even vertical layout are all necessary.

StringView. StringView is the corresponding graphical representation for strings. HStringView is for horizontal representation, and VStringView for vertical. Currently, HStringView has been implemented; vertical font rendering is in the works. A StringView is defined to be a string of one language script, one typeface, one color, of which only color can be changed. The string content can be changed by removing or inserting sub-strings. A StringView can be split into two siblings, and also merged back into one.

BlockView. BlockView is classified as HBlockView for horizontal layout and VBlockView for vertical layout. It maintains a list of SimpViews, aligns them together and lays them out. The SimpViews inside the BlockView are required to split when they come across any interior or exterior boundary.

Input Method. InputMethod basically provides a mapping from keyword to actual input. The mapping can be implicitly committed or waits for the user to choose one from many alternatives. It can include not merely a keyboard mapping in some Western languages, but also sophisticated mappings used in CJK.

KeyInputAdapter & KeyInputReceiver. KeyInputAdapter receives keyboard input from a keyevent listener, classifies keystrokes into input action or input sequence, and redirects them to the KeyInputReceiver. The input sequence is a sequence of Unicode characters of a certain language script. Input actions handles cursor movement, deletion and newline, etc. Input sequence can be preprocessed by some filtering rules before being passed to KeyInputReceiver.

OverTheSpotAdapter OverTheSpotAdapter provides a way to customize users' input sequence, and it is very useful in CJK input because most of the time the user is required to choose one input word from many that all map to the same keyword. It is also useful if some kind of association is needed. OverTheSpotAdapter makes use of OverTheSpotWindow to show possible selections, that is just like a popup window appears just beside the current cursor position. The OverTheSpotWindow will disappear when the user has committed his input sequence.

ImageView, ButtonView and SelectionView. Because AWT widgets are all restricted to simple ASCII text strings, it is very restrictive when it comes to localizing your GUI. So, we wrote some sample lightweight widgets to illustrate the usefulness of the view structure in jime.widget package. They can be used to implement multilingual image buttons, menus and selections.

5.3 Problems & Limitations

While we were carry out testing of our applets (JDK 1.0 model), we noticed some differences in the Netscape Navigator 4.0's implementation of the Java

Virtual Machine on UNIX platforms. Navigator 4 for UNIX does not run the applet well but it works just fine on Windows and Macintosh. Investigation is pending. Sometimes, you really have to "Write Once, Test EveryWhere".

Because of the complex nature of internationalization, it is not easy to get a perfect design. JIME strives to meet its ojective for as many languages as possible and has an extensible structure. However, there will definitely be some limitations along the way.

Current JIME API does provide extensible space for bi-directional horizontal text layout and editing, because they are all left to individual StringView to handle them. In such a way, there need not to be any global changes, but just incorporate another bidi-StringView type into the BlockView. There might be some important things particularly for bidi that are left out, however, and we won't know until a bidi-StringView is on the way.

6 Future Developments

To make the above Java application and applet reusable, we intend to turn them into JavaBeans. With JavaBeans, software developers can easily reuse our Java components and build native keyboard input methods into their Java applications.

Although the above Java solution proves to be feasible, its extensibility has to be further enhanced through adding support for more languages to its portfolio. Development work is underway to add Thai, German, French keyboards to the implementation. We are extending the framework to include other European languages, Tamil, and maybe even right-to-left writings like Arabic and Hebrew.

7 Conclusion

In conclusion, the Web is moving towards a more 'World-Wide' reach and so is Java. With Java, we are close to realizing true internationalization of cross-platform applications. Java Input Methods will make your localized applications more complete.

References

1. Dave Raggett, Arnaud Le Hors, Ian Jacobs
   HTML 4.0 Specification-W3C Working Draft (17 Sep 1997)
   http://www.w3.org/TR/WD-html40/
2. F. Yergeau, G. Nicol, G. Adams, M. Duerst
   RFC2070 - Internationalization of the Hypertext Markup Language
   ftp://ds.internic.net/rfc/rfc2070.txt (Jan 1997)
3. Dave Raggett
   HTML 3.2 Reference Specification, Dave Raggett (14 Jan 1997)
   http://www.w3.org/TR/REC-html32.html

4. FONT FACE considered harmful
   http://www.isoc.org:8080/web_ml/html/fontface.html
5. JDK 1.1 Internationalization Specification (4 Dec 1996)
   http://java.sun.com/products/jdk/1.1/intl/html/intlspecTOC.doc.html
6. Netscape LiveConnect
   http://home.netscape.com/eng/mozilla/3.0/handbook/javascript/livecon.htm
7. Netscape Composer Plug-in Guide
   http://developer.netscape.com/library/documentation/communicator/
   composer/plugin/contents.htm

ISCM
Information System Conceptual Model Oriented to Security Problems and a Tool Implementing It

Pierluca De Maria[1] and Cristiano De Mei[1]

University of Rome "La Sapienza"

Abstract. This paper deals with a new model of an information system. The model is strongly oriented to security problems and in particular it takes in account all the three parameters of availability, integrity and secrecy as stated in [4]. To represent the system, the model defines entities for the system objects, actions for the interactions between them and activities for the system's functionalities.

Based on this model a tool has been created to implement it. Using this tool a system administrator can describe the system, discover security problems, make queries and perform non-intrusive security checks.

This tool and the model which it is based on respond to the need for an advanced security management in an information system both of small and of large dimensions. This work was born to meet the network and security administrators needs collected in a preliminary interviewing phase.

1 Introduction

The increasing development of distributed computing and network applications coupled with the growing number of computer science specialists has led to the arising of security problems in information systems. Plenty of organisations are sensible to these questions and a new need is to guarantee the secrecy, the integrity and the availability of the information stored. Some new professional figures have been created to face these problems and some tools have been developed to assist them (see for example [6]). These tools are mainly aimed to on-line monitor the user activities, but few of them have a strong theoretical base and allow non-intrusive simulations. To start this work we studied university's and non-governative agency's information systems interviewing their system administrators. They expressed some needs: off-line tools to manage and to validate the system security; system models to simulate attacks and faults; tools to establish and support a security policy. This paper's aim is to illustrate a conceptual information system model focused on integrity, availability and secrecy of the system. Upon this model, an off-line tool has been developed which the system administrator can use to simulate all the attacks or accidents without affecting the real information system, therefore with no risks for data.

2 The model

A large number of information system models oriented to security exists in literature [7] [5]. These models can be classified in discretionary or mandatory basing on the object of the rights. In mandatory models all rights are on resources, while in discretionary models they are on activities [3]. It is possible that some operations are permitted, but they aren't legitimate: for example a user can read a file f_1 and write on another file f_2, but he mustn't copy information from f_1 to f_2. In the first kind of model it isn't possible to check this unauthorised information flow; instead, by the second kind of model, it is possible to deny the activity "copy from f_1 to f_2", preventing the flow. On the other hand, tools based on discretionary models are, generally, on-line, so the performance of the system is reduced.

This model shares both mandatory and discretionary models' characteristics, in that it allows to check users' rights on objects and on activities. Furthermore our tool is off-line so it doesn't suffer from the discretionary model's shortcomings.

2.1 Model's structures

This model is based on the concepts of entities, actions and activities[1].

Entity: an entity is a class of components of the system which can perform or undergo actions. A set of objects which share the same characteristics and rights is an entity (eg: a group of users, the project manager, web servers, file servers, firewalls or dbms). More precisely, entities are classified in:
  - Users
  - Hosts
  - Software (applications, operating systems and dbms)
  - Data
  - Networks
  - Rooms

Action: an action is a relationship between two entities. For an action A_{ij}, E_i performs an operation on E_j. An action can be conditioned by predicates. They are conditions which must be satisfied to execute an action.

Authorisation state: the authorisation state $Sa(E_i)$ of an entity E_i is the set of actions it can perform on other entities: $Sa(E_i) = \{A_{ij}^h\}$ where A_{ij}^h is the h-th action E_i can perform on E_j.

Protection state: the protection state $Sp(E_i)$ of an entity E_i is the set of actions which can be performed on E_i by the other entities: $Sp(E_i) = \{A_{ji}^m\}$ where A_{ji}^m is the m-th action E_j can perform on E_i.

Actions may be divided into static actions (SA) and dynamic actions (DA). An action is static if it doesn't modify neither $Sa(E_i)$ nor $Sp(E_i)$; an action is dynamic if it modifies $Sa(E_i)$ or $Sp(E_i)$.

Static actions can be sorted in a hierarchical order as follows:

---

[1] Entity and action are concepts derived from the ACTEN model [1] [3]

1. Use: it means the right to execute an action on a peripheral or to execute a program.
2. Read: it means that an entity can see the information in an other one.
3. Update: is the right to modify an entity.
4. Create/Delete: is the right to create or destroy entities.

Basing on this hierarchy, one entity's E_i active potentiality A_i^+ is the highest action it can perform and its passive potentiality A_i^- is the lowest action it can undergo.

Dynamic actions can be sorted as:

1. Grant/Revoke: an entity E_i can allow or deny another entity E_j the right to execute a static action on one entity E_k.
2. Delegate/Abrogate: an entity E_i can allow (deny) another entity E_j to grant or revoke the right to perform a static action on an entity E_k.

The destination entity E_k of the static action granted (revoked) or delegated (abrogated) is called the parameter of the dynamic action.

Activities are the functionalities of the system and are composed of a set of actions and recursively of other activities.

Activity: an activity is a triple (D_{AC}, P, H) where:

- $D_{AC} \subseteq D \times U^2$
- D is the set of possible actions:
  $D = \{$use, read, update, create/delete, grant/revoke, delegate/ (fabrogate$\}$
- $U \subseteq E$ is the set of the involved entities.
- $P \subset E$ is the set of entities which has the right to perform the activity.
- $H \subset E$ is the set of hosts from which the activity if available.
- E is the set of the system entities.

An example of activity may be the compilation of a source code. This activity involves reading the source file (S), executing the compiler (C), executing the linker (L), writing some temporary files $(F1, \ldots, Fn)$ and finally writing the executable (Ex). If the involved programs are not on the used host, it is necessary to use a network (N) to get them from a remote host (H), probably by NFS (Nfs) or similar, and execute them locally. In this example D_{AC} is as follows:

$$D_{AC} = \{(read, S), (use, C), (use, L), (create, F1), \ldots, (create, Fn),$$
$$(create, Ex), (use, N), (use, Nfs), (delete, F1), \ldots, (delete, Fn)\}$$

---

[2] The couples in D_{AC} are not an ordered sequence, because time-stamps of actions are not relevant in our model.

2.2 Operative structures

This model uses various graphs to represent the different kind of relations between entities and to consider the three security parameters of availability, integrity and secrecy.

Static graph: is a set of nodes and arcs where nodes are entities and arcs are static actions. Eventually an arc may be labelled by a set of predicates.

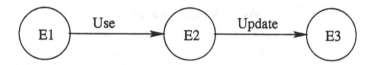

Fig. 1. A static graph.

Dynamic graph: is the graph used to represent the dynamic rights. Its nodes are entities and its arcs are dynamic actions. The static actions granted (revoked) or delegated (abrogated) and the parameter label the arcs. Eventually a predicate may appear in the label.

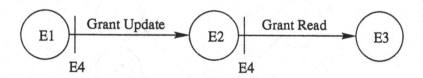

Fig. 2. A dynamic graph

Topological graph: the disposition of hardware and software in the system is represented by the topological graph. The nodes of this graph are entities which may contain some other ones. Two kind of arcs exist: one represents the physical connection between entities and the other represents the relation called inclusion: the entities included in an other one are the entities which lack if the container lacks. In Fig. 3 dashed arcs represent inclusion and bold arcs represent physical connections:

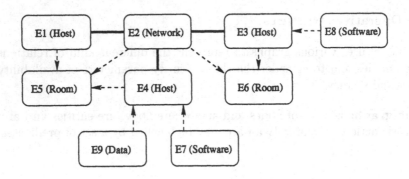

Fig. 3. A topological graph

Functional dependencies graph: a functional dependencies graph
(fdg) exists for each activity in the system. A fdg is an and-or graph, similar
to that in Fig. 4, in which an activity A_1 executed by E_1 needs the group
of entities $\{E_2, E_3, E_6\}$ or $\{E_2, E_3, E_8, E_9\}$. The arcs in *and* are joined
by a dash line and the disjointed groups of arcs indicate *or* possibilities. A
functional dependency exists between the entities contained in E_i and their
container E_i.

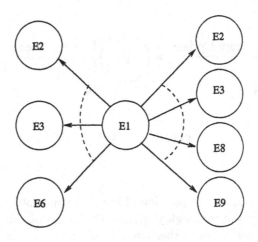

Fig. 4. A functional dependencies graph

2.3 Clearance and sensitivity

One of the purposes of the model is to completely represent the security issues, so all the three parameters of availability, integrity and secrecy are represented in the model. The functional dependency graphs allow to check the availability of entities and the static and dynamic graphs allow to inspect the integrity and secrecy aspects of the system.

Basing on the Bell-LaPadula [2] model we introduce two further concepts: clearance and sensitivity. Clearance is an entity's trustworthiness not to violate the security constraints of the system (i.e. not to violate the privacy of information, not to damage resources, etc.). Sensitivity is the relevance of an entity in the system. Its value is related to the potential damage which could result from unauthorized violation of the system security. These concepts are used to perform some security tests and measurements.

Clearance is related to the probability of the violation of the security and sensitivity is related to the potential damage due to the violation. The probability multiplied by the damage gives the risk, so clearance and sensitivity can measure the risk, too. Security can be considered the inverse of the risk.

The values of clearance and sensitivity available for each entity can be used to compute a value of security for the activities and then for the entire system.

$$\begin{array}{c} System's \\ security \end{array} = 1 - \frac{\left(1 - cl(A_1)\right) * str(A_1) + \cdots + \left(1 - cl(A_n)\right) * str(A_n)}{str(A_1) + \cdots + str(A_n)} \qquad (1)$$

where $cl(A_i)$ is the A_i's clearance and $str(A_i)$ is the A_i's sensitivity.

The two parameters of clearance and sensitivity may be defined for certain objects in the model and then calculated for the other ones, referring to the following rules:

- Inclusion: the clearance of the contained entities is the minimum of its intrinsic clearance and the container's one. The sensitivity of the container is the maximum of the sensitivity of the contained entities.
- Activities: activities have their own sensitivity, but it must not be less than the maximum value of the involved entities' sensitivity. A value of clearance can be calculated for activities. Without losing generality we can suppose that an activity's functional dependencies graph is always similar to the following:

In the case in Fig. 4 the activity's clearance is:

$$cl(A_i) = 1 - \left(\left(1 - min(cl(E_1), cl(E_2), cl(E_3), cl(E_6))\right) * \right.$$
$$\left. * \left(1 - min(cl(E_1), cl(E_2), cl(E_3), cl(E_8), cl(E_9))\right)\right) \qquad (2)$$

where $cl(E_i)$ is E_i's clearance.

In the following table the propagation of clearance and sensitivity is summarised:

	Sensitivity	Clearance
Users	Computation on activities	Assigned
Rooms	Computation on contents	Assigned
Hosts	Computation on contents	Assigned + Computation on container
Software	Evaluated	Assigned + Computation on container
Data	Evaluated	Assigned + Computation on container
Networks	Computation on activities	Assigned + Computation on container
Activities	Assigned + Computation on involved entities[3]	Computation on functional dependencies graph

Table 1. Entity's and activity's clearance and sensitivity.

In the model we adopt the Bell-LaPadula axioms, modifying them. These axioms are the set of properties which must be satisfied for the system to be secure:

1. Basic security property: An entity's clearance must be greater than or equal to its sensitivity.
2. Simple security property: An entity E_i may perform actions on an entity E_j if and only if E_i's clearance if greater than or equal to E_j's sensitivity; an entity E_i may perform an activity if and only if E_i's clearance is not less than the activity's sensitivity.
3. Star property: an entity E_i may have update access to an entity E_j if and only if the E_j's sensitivity is greater than or equal to the E_i's sensitivity; E_i may have read access to E_j if and only if the E_i's sensitivity is greater than or equal to the E_j's sensitivity.
4. Discretionary security property: the only way to access information is to use the activities defined in the model.

2.4 Using the model

Basing on the static graph and the active and passive potentialities of entities, it is possible to compute the indirect rights of entities such as A_{13} (update) in Fig. 5. The algorithm is the following [3]:

1. If $A_{12} \geq A_{23}$ then $A_{13} = A_{23}$
2. else if $A_{23} \geq A_1^+$ then $A_{13} = A_1^+$
3. else $A_{13} = A_{23}$

---

[3] Rooms' and networks' values of sensitivity do not affect this computation.

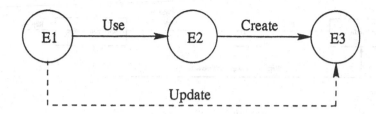

Fig. 5. A static graph

An algorithm similar to the preceding is used to compute the indirect rights in the dynamic graph.

Using the static and dynamic graphs, it is possible to check if an activity is executable, that is if all the users in P own all the rights needed on the involved entities. It is also possible to verify the axioms in Sect. 2.3.

Static and dynamic graphs can also be used to calculate the power of each class of users, so the damages caused by a user who gains another one's rights can be simulated by a simple navigation in these graphs.

The topological graph is used to:

- Propagate clearance and sensitivity according to Table 1.
- Complete the description of an activity defined by the user of the model. This completion is executed by navigating the topological graph from every host in H to the hosts which contain the entities in U.

Basing on the static, the dynamic, the topological graphs and starting from the description of an activity, the various functional dependency graphs may be created.

Functional dependencies graphs are suitable to perform fault propagation: it is easy to notice in Fig. 4, that if E_6 has a fault, the activity can still be executed, but if E_2 has a fault the activity cannot be performed.

3 The tool

The tool is the model implementation and is used to enter the description of the system and to check its security. The tool is based on a client/server architecture: the client side implements an user interface and the server side is fundamentally an inferential engine. The actual architecture is illustrated in Fig. 6:

The user interface is the point of contact between the user and this tool. It provides the user with an environment to draw graphs. Double clicking an icon the user can enter the entity's attributes: type, clearance and sensitivity (when applicable according to Table 1). Output windows display feedbacks from the inferential engine.

The translator is used to produce a rule based description of the system derived from the structures entered by the user.

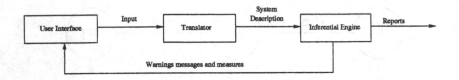

Fig. 6. Tool's architecture

The system description is a set of prolog predicates which constitute a knowledge base used by the inferential engine module.

The inferential engine is a prolog interpreter which elaborates the knowledge base to complete the system description and to produces reports, warnings and measures.

Reports are detailed descriptions of the system composed of:

- a list of entities with all their attributes: both the entered and the calculated ones;
- a description of the topological graph;
- a description of static and dynamic graphs with the direct rights entered by user and the indirect rights computed by the engine;
- a list of activities completed with hosts and actions needed;
- a set of security warnings and measures.

Warnings indicates the violations of security axioms, users' rights which aren't used in any activity, the set of hosts which aren't involved in any activity, users who don't perform any activity.

Security measures are obtained from entities' and activities' clearance and sensitivity. Equation 1 is used to compute a global measure of security on the system.

The interaction with the user proceeds as follows:

1. Preliminary input phase
   (a) the user enters the topological graph dragging & dropping icons;
   (b) the user enters the modelled system's class of users;
   (c) the user enters each entity's attributes (type, sensitivity and clearance when applicable);
   (d) the user enters static and dynamic graphs;
   (e) the user enters the activities;
2. Computing phase
   (a) for each entity E_i the active potentiality A_i^+ and the passive potentiality A_i^- are computed;
   (b) the indirect static and dynamic rights are computed using the algorithm in Sect. 2.4;
   (c) partially defined activities entered by the user are completed;
   (d) sensitivity and clearance are propagated according to Table 1.

3. Interaction phase
   (a) the tool shows some security warnings (if any) and gives some security measures;
   (b) the tool produces a detailed report (a file which describes the entities and the activities with their attributes, the direct and indirect rights, the security warnings and the security measures);
   (c) the user can simulate some new scenarios: masquerading[4], fault propagation, topological changes, alteration of the entities' rights, etc. The knowledge base may the be queried by the system administrator via the pre-built queries offered by the interface or constructing new ones. For each simulation the tool re-computes all the system's values (sensitivity and clearance) and structures re-executing the computing and interaction phases.

4 Conclusions

This model and the tool based on it have been created following the lessons learned by the interviewed system managers. The structures offered by the model are simple and well known and are able to take in account the dynamicity of the systems which use Internet and the web. For example if a web server is moved from behind a firewall to another branch without firewalls then, in the tool, this change is propagated to the description of all the activities in which the server is involved and their functional dependency graphs are automatically updated. Eventual axioms violations are instantaneously evident. Moreover all the risks related to the new configuration can be checked simply querying the tool.

The tool is an off-line program which can be used to test the system's security in non-intrusive mode, so the system administrators can use it without risks for sensitive data and with no need to slow down the normal functioning of the real information system.

References

1. Bussolati U., Fugini N., Martella G.:A conceptual framework for security systems: the action-entity model,IFIP (1983)
2. Bell D.E., La Padula L.J.:Secure computer systems: mathematical foundations and model,ESD-TR-73-278
3. Castano S., Fugini M., Martella G.:Database security,Addison Wesley (1995)
4. Curry D., Longstaff T. et al.:Site Security Handbook. Network Working Group,Request for Comments 1244 (1991)
5. Computer Security - Esorics 96. 4th European Symposium on Research in Computer Security,proceedings (1996)
6. Fugini M.G., Bellinzona R., Martella G.:An Authorisation mechanism for Unix-based Cooperative Environments,Information Systems Vol. 16 No. 5 Pergamon Press (1991)

---

[4] A masquerader is a user who is authenticated as a different one.

7. Landwehr C.E.:Formal models for computer security,ACM Computing Surveys 13 (3) (1981)
8. Siyan K., Hare C.:Internet Firewalls and Network Security,New Riders Publishing (1995)

Design of EDI Security MIB Based on SNMP Protocol

Tae-Kyou Park *

Department of Computer & Information Science
Hanseo University, Seosan, Chungnam, Korea
E-mail : tkpark@gaya.hanseo.ac.kr

Abstract. This paper considers the design and management of security MIB for EDI system. EDI system has to establish security services and mechanisms such as authentication, secure access management, confidentiality, integrity, non-repudiation, message security labeling and security management to protect against security threats. Hence, the EDI system requires appropriate security management to monitor and control the security objects for its security services and mechanisms. In this paper, I identify security management objects for security services defined in the EDI system, and propose the design of a security MIB and describe the use of SNMPv2 network management protocol in its management.

1 Introduction

Computer networks constructed within an open system environment present a very convenient target for attacks and illegal operations. This means that protection of users, resources and assets in every open computer network is becoming increasingly important. Electronic Data Interchange (EDI) is basically the concept of computer-to-computer exchange of messages or information relating to various types of activities in an organization or business. The security in the EDI system has a serious impact on the ways in which organizations and companies conduct their business transactions and manage their documents and messages. The basis for security in the EDI system is the OSI Security Architecture international standard[4]. This document describes a general framework in terms of security services, security mechanisms, security management functions, and some other relevant aspects of security in open systems, and gives some high level recommendations. Key to provision of a security service is its management. An EDI system needs to support the management of these security services as well as how changes in policy and its enforcement can take place. For instance, in the case of data confidentiality and integrity services, it is necessary to manage the keys used in the encryption and decryption process. In the case of message security labeling service, we need to manage the security policy regarding the labeling of documents and messages, and their transactions. Thus, there may be several authorities performing different aspects of these security management

* This research was supported by KOSEF while the author was visiting at Department of Computing, University of Western Sydney, Nepean, Australia.

functions such as access control authorities, authentication authorities, key management authorities and audit management authorities. In practice, several of these functions may be handled by a single authority. One of the difficulties that the network manager has to face, with regard to security management, involves selecting and using the appropriate security management application to be secure against security attacks. In this paper, I identify a number of security-related managed objects which can be contained in Simple Network Management Protocol (SNMP) Management information Base (MIB), and are important for controlling and configuring security measures in the EDI system. In particular, I focus on security management objects and the design of a security MIB (SMIB) using the formal Structure of Management Information (SMI) encoding rules[6]. I propose a common SMIB definition for EDI system components such as user agent (EDI-UA), message store (EDI-MS), and message transfer agent (MTA). This SMIB definition proposed in this paper is based on Simple Network Management Protocol version 2 (SNMPv2) protocol. This paper is organized as follows. Section 2 reviews the security service elements in EDI system and considers as an example the KT-EDI system[5,14]. Section 3 briefly considers the network security management in EDI, and security management using SNMPv2 protocol is described in Sect. 4. In Sect. 5, I identify the security objects, then construct a SMIB for EDI system. Network security protocols with the SMIB are given in Sect. 6. Finally, Sect. 7 concludes the paper.

2   Security Elements in EDI System

ITU-T recommends two kinds of standardization for an EDI system : one is a document standard (EDIFACT)[9], and the other is the communication standard (F.435 / X.435 Recommendations[7]) based on the X.400 Message Handling System (MHS)[8]. That is, the basic activity of the EDI system is the conveyance of electronic messages. The EDI interchanges can be conveyed in many ways, for example, directly over a telephone line or encapsulated in a file transfer. One method of providing a supporting infrastructure for the EDI is to use the MHS. The nature of the MHS should be borne in mind when considering fourteen security elements of security service defined in X.402, and further seven elements appear in X.435. For instance, Korea Telecom-EDI (KT-EDI) system focuses on twenty-seven security elements from X.402 and X.435 documents. Also the functional models, communication protocols, potential threats and transfer message types of the X.435 EDI system have been applied. As shown in Table 1, KT-EDI system has various security services such as origin authentication, EDI Message (EDIM) responsibility authentication, secure access management, data confidentiality, data integrity, non-repudiation of EDIM responsibility, non-repudiation, message security labeling, and security management. The X.400 recommendation belongs to the application layer of the OSI reference model. The originator of the message uses UA to compose a message and to submit it to the message transfer system (MTS). A UA is also involved when the MTS delivers the message to its recipient (the user associated UA). After delivery, the recipient uses the services of its UA to process the received message. Within the MTS, a set of MTAs cooperate in conveying messages to their recipients. Together with MS, the collection of UAs and MTAs comprise the MHS. A principal feature of the MHS is its operation in a store-and-forward manner, which is important for security analysis because of the increased risk to the information while stored temporarily in various network nodes. There are two basic differences

Table 1. Relation between security service elements and MHS components

Security Services	Security Service Elements	*UA/UA	UA/MS	MS/MTA	UA/MTA	MTA/MTA	TA/MTA	MTA/UA	MTA/UA
Origin Authentication (X.402)	Message Origin Authentication	o	o		o				
	Probe Origin Authentication			o	o				
	Report Origin Authentication					o	o	o	
	Proof of Submission							o	
	Proof of Delivery	o							N
EDIM Responsibility Authentication(X.435)	Proof of EDI Notification	o							
	Proof of Retrieval		o						
	Proof of Transfer						o		
Secure Access Management(X.402)	Peer Entity Authentication		o	o	o	o	o	o	o
	Secure Context		o	o	o	o	o	o	o
Data Confidentiality (X.402)	Connection Confidentiality		o	o	o	o	o	o	o
	Content Confidentiality	o							
	Message Flow Confidentiality	o							
Data Integrity(X.402)	Connection Integrity		o	o	o	o	o	o	o
	Content Integrity	o							
	Message Sequence Integrity	o							
Non-Repudiation of EDIM Responsibility (X.435)	Non-Repudiation of EDI Notification	o							
	Non-Repudiation of EDI Retrieval	o							
	Non-Repudiation of EDI Transfer						o		
	Non-Repudiation of EDI Content	o							
Non-Repudiation(X.402)	Non-Repudiation of Origin	o			o				
	Non-Repudiation of Submission							o	
	Non-Repudiation of Delivery	o							o
Message Security Labeling (X.402)	Message Security Labeling	o	o	o	o	o	o	o	o
Security Management (X.402)	Change Credentials		o		o	o	o		
	Register		o		o				
	MS-Register		o						

* UA : EDI_UA, N : Receiver MS to Sender UA

UA : User Agent, MS : Message Store, MTA : Message Transfer Agent between regular network MHS and EDI system. First, EDI information is exchanged in the form of special messages, such as banking transactions, orders, invoices, letters, contracts, and proprietary materials, between companies and business partners. Second, each EDI message is transmitted under some special regime or requirements such as the request for confirmation, the receipt of an "equivalent" message, non-repudiation of content, legal binding, and acceptance of special conditions. The security capabilities in the X.400 system have been achieved using different mechanisms, for example, the inclusion of new elements in the exchanged messages during the association establishment stage or by adding information in the MHS envelope. It should be emphasized that security capabilities included in the MHS system define only how to transfer and use relevant security parameters. Rules about generation and interpretation of these parameters are not in the MHS recommendations. Its aim is to provide security independent of the communication services supplied by other entities of higher or lower levels. Security of the X.400 MHS also requires certain management functions and support. Only the authorized entities may change user credentials or security labels. Most of the techniques (mechanisms) used to implement the described security services are based on cryptography. Security services of the MHS allow the selection of alternative algorithms. The service elements needed to implement security in the X.400 system must be supported by the Directory Authentication environment, defined in the X.509 Directory Service recommendation[12]. The Directory System stores certified copies of the user public keys of the MHS that can be used to provide authentication and facilitate the exchange of user credentials. Thus, mechanisms to secure data confidentiality and integrity are provided. The X.509 recommendation defines a framework for the provision of an entity authentication by the Directory Service to its users. These users include the Directory itself, as well as other applications and services. The Directory can usefully be involved in meeting their needs for authentication and other security services, because it is a natural place from which communicating parties can obtain authentication information about each other. The X.509 recommendation describes two levels of authentication : simple authentication, using a password as a verification of claimed identity, and strong authentication, involving credentials formed using cryptographic techniques. The strong authentication method is based on public-key cryptosystems. For communicating with MHS components and another Directory Service Agent (DSA), Directory Access Protocol (DAP : UA, MS or MTA-DSA) and Directory Service Protocol (DSP : DSA-DSA) are supported. The user certificates are assumed to be formed by "off-line" means, and placed in the Directory by their creator. The generation of user certificates is performed by some off-line Certificate Authority (CA) which is separated from the Directory Service Agencies (DSAs).

3 Design of Security Management Model for EDI System

The design of security management model is aimed to enable the EDI system to provide the various security services defined in Sect. 2. As shown in Fig 1,

KT-EDI system architecture basically consists of MHS components such as UAs (P3 or P7), MSs, MTAs and DSAs for Directory services. The EDI system for communications among MHS components is supported by some protocols such as P1 (MTA-MTA), P2 (UA-UA), P3 (UA or MS-MTA), P7 (UA-MS) and Pedi (defining the heading of EDI). Each system component has a secure EDI subsystem (SES) and a secure management subsystem (SMS). The SES is composed of secure UAs, secure MSs, and secure MTAs according to its functional role as MHS components. Each component transfers the services and related messages to the SES through its SES interface. The SES can access the various information from the SMIB and/or MIB through SNMPv2 interface, hence plays a main role of EDI system. The SMS consists of three management agents such as a key management agent (KMA), a audit management agent (AMA), and a SNMP management agent (SMA). The KMA has two functions, one is a directory service agent (DSA) function to keep and manage public key certificates, and the other is a directory user agent (DUA) function to get and keep secret keys and public keys to be used in security services. The AMA plays the role

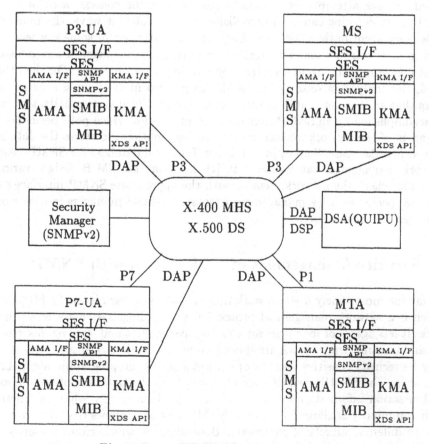

Fig. 1. Secure KT-EDI System Architecture

of storing and retrieving the security relevant events such as a event classifier, audit records, history record, and audit provider. The SMA consists of SMIB, MIB and SNMPv2 protocol, and is the "heart" of the security management of KT-EDI security services and mechanisms, and controls and manages the security related management information base SMIB. Security management has to provide facilities for allowing the network security, manager of the EDI system to control the security-relevant managed objects used in EDI security services and mechanisms such as security service requests, confidential keys, algorithm identifiers and security labels. For these facilities, each EDI-UA, UA-MS and MTA must include its local MIB and SMIB in which it can control its own resources, or grant or restrict access to the entire security manager or selected critical parts of the element security manager. The security manager should have the facilities for archiving and retrieving the appropriate security information and managing and controlling the security objects. In addition, a network management system should provide the network manager with facilities for monitoring and analyzing the security measures. An example of real time monitoring of security measures could be the generation of an alarm when a single user has made numerous unsuccessful login attempts for a network host or the notification of repeated denials of user attempts on a particular service. In the context of SNMP, the real time monitoring can be accomplished in two different ways: the manager polls every agent in the network at frequent time intervals for some key security management information. The agent then notifies the manager of any unusual event concerning the agent's security by sending a trap message. On the other hand, the analysis of security logs is also important in discovering security attacks that are not detectable as they occur. Using a local system MIB, this can be accomplished by an SNMP management application which polls periodically the agent of the network for security related information and stores the data retrieved in a database. This approach using Temporal database for SNMP-based network management can be found in [1]. By using the SMIB design, various tools that check the network security with the appropriate SNMP interface can become specific security management agents or element managers in a network management architecture.

4   Security Management of EDI System with SNMP

By far the most widely used network management standard is the SNMP[3,16], which is a network management protocol for controlling systems across a network. It lets agents or managers set and read parameters and lets systems generate and transmit traps, which are special event notifications. Certain parameters may be security sensitive such as operational status, cryptographic algorithms and keys. The SNMP element manager may keep the database of secrets and authorization information for each community which specify what parameters each community is allowed to access. SNMP version 1 allows read or write access to different subsets of parameters depending on which group a user is in. An SNMP community is a relationship between an SNMP agent and a set of

SNMP managers that defines authentication, access control, and proxy characteristics. The community concept is a local one, defined at the agent. The agent establishes one community for each desired combination of authentication, access control and proxy characteristics. Each community is given a unique community name within this agent, and the managers within that community employ the community name in all "Get" and "Set" operations such as setting passwords. By defining a community, a agent limits access to its MIB to a selected set of managers. By the use of more than one community, the agent can provide different categories of MIB access to different managers. There are two aspects to this access control. First, SNMP MIB view is a set of the objects within an MIB. Different MIB views may be defined for each community. The set of objects in a view need not belong to a single sub-tree of the MIB. Second, SNMP access mode is an element of set READ-ONLY, READ-WRITE. An access mode is defined for each community. However, enhanced security was one of the primary goals behind the design of version 2 of SNMP. SNMPv2 is designed to provide, in essence, three security-related services such as privacy, authentication, and access control. Privacy is the protection of transmitted data from eavesdropping or wiretapping. Privacy requires that contents of any message be distinguished in such a way that only the intended recipient can recover the original message, and uses DES for encrypting the SNMP message. The specification mentions the possibility of algorithms such as using other algorithms, including public key algorithms. A message, file, document, or other collection of data is said to be authentic when it is genuine and came from its alleged source. Message authentication is a procedure that allows communicating parties to verify that received message are authentic. The two important aspects are to verify that the contents of the message have not been altered and that the source is authentic. Each SNMPv2 message can be authenticated and integrity-protected using a shared secret configured into the system being managed and the system doing the management. This is done by creating a cryptographic checksum using a protected MD5 message digest ; the message digest is sent along with the message. I also wish to verify the timeliness of the message, that is, it has not been delayed and replayed, and the sequence relative to other messages flowing between two parties is maintained. In SNMPv2, each message includes a message header, which contains security-related information. The message structures in Fig. 2 show the general format as well as the private and authenticated format . The

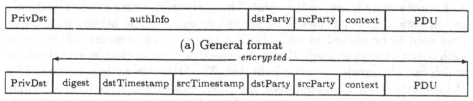

| PrivDst | authInfo | dstParty | srcParty | context | PDU |

(a) General format

encrypted

| PrivDst | digest | dstTimestamp | srcTimestamp | dstParty | srcParty | context | PDU |

(b) Private and authenticated

Fig. 2. SNMPv2 message formats

header consists of five fields. The srcParty identifies the party of the manager or the agent sending the message. The desParty identifies the party of the agent or the manager to whom the message is sent. The context may indicate that this exchange relates to an access to a MIB local to the agent; in this case, the context value serves to identify a subset of the agent's MIB, known as an MIB view. The combination of source party, destination party and context value is used to determine the access control privileges for this exchange. The authInfo field contains information relevant to the authentication protocol. The privDst field repeats the identifier of the destination party. Together with the appropriate parameters, the PDU field contains one of the commands such as "Get", "Get-Next", "GetBulk", "Set", "Trap", "Inform" and "Response". If the message is authenticated and private, then the authInfo field contains information needed for authentication and the entire message, including header and the PDU but excluding the privDst field, is encrypted. The privDst field must remain unencrypted so that the destination SNMPv2 entity can determine the destination party and therefore determine the privacy characteristics of the message. In the context of network management, the purpose of access control is to ensure that only authorized users have access to a particular MIB and that access to and modification of a particular portion of data is limited to authorized individuals and programs. Thus, the access control policy is determined by three parameters. A source party requests a management operation in a destination party and identifies the context of the request. The context may specify an MIB view local to the destination party or may specify a remote proxied entity. For a given pair of source/destination party, there may be multiple access control policies, one for each context. The context is communicated by the source to the destination in the SNMPv2 message header. This approach eliminates the necessity of defining a unique source/destination party pair for access control policy, thus enables a single destination party to perform in a variety of contexts for a given source party. The value of the privileges parameter represents the list of SNMPv2 PDUs that may be sent from the source to the destination. The parameter is encoded by assigning an integer value that is a power of 2 to each PDU. Access control is determined by information in the party MIB. This MIB consists of four tables: party table, context table, access control table, and MIB view table. The best way to describe the function of these tables for access control is to consider their use during message transmission. Consider a message that is sent from a manager to an agent. The message header includes the fields srcParty, dstParty, and context. The party table at the agent contains information about each local and remote party known to the agent. The party information includes authentication parameters that need to be applied to srcParty and privacy parameters that need to be applied to dstParty. The context table contains one entry for each context known to agent. Each entry specifies whether the context is local, in which case the proxied device is indicated. The MIB view table is referenced by the contexts table, The appropriate entry defines a subset of the local MIB that is accessible through this context. Finally, each entry in the access control table has a unique combination of srcParty, dstParty and context, and this indicates which management operations (which PDUs) are allowed for this combination. As a result, SNMPv2 provides the protection against threats such as disclosure, masquerading, message content modification, and message sequence and timing modification. However SNMPv2 does not address threats of denial of service and traffic analysis. Nevertheless, SNMPv2 protocol ensures that the basic security requirements defined in ISO 7498-2 security architecture for an EDI system.

5 Construction of SMIB for EDI System

A network manager can adopt with regard to security management the development of the SMIB that will fulfill our special network security needs. Most of the information needed for security management will be stored in the SMIB. That is, the SMIB is the storage in which the secure network maintains all data pertinent to its security functions such as identities of authorized users, authentication data, user entity capabilities and privileges, security parameters of all network resources, access control privileges and various processing and recovery logs. The individual objects are identified and structured, their mutual dependencies and relations are defined, and their usage for providing all security relevant parameters to various security service elements of the EDI system is described. The SMIB objects in the EDI system must be protected to the highest level of security. The SMIB may be implemented as a distributed information base to the extent that is necessary to enforce a consistent security policy in a logical or physical grouping of end-systems (security domain). In practice, parts of the SMIB may or may not be integrated with the MIB of the open system. There are many realizations of SMIB such as a table of data or a single file or a distributed set of data base segments or rules embedded within the software or hardware of the real system. Rules for inserting, maintaining, deleting and using information in the SMIB constitute security management protocols. Management protocols, especially security management protocols, and the communication channels carrying the management information, are potentially vulnerable. Particular care must therefore be taken to ensure that the management protocols and information are protected. Security management may require the exchange of security-relevant information between various administrations, in order that the SMIB can be established or extended. In some cases, the security-relevant information will be passed through non-OSI communication paths, and the local systems administrators will update the SMIB through methods not standardized by OSI. In other cases, it may be desirable to exchange such information over an OSI communication path, in which case the information will be passed between two security management applications running in an open system. The security management applications will use the communicated information to update the SMIB. Such updating of the SMIB requires prior authorization of appropriate security administrator or access privileges control of other authorized entities. The SMIB purposed in this paper stores security attributes for each association maintained within the EDI system. The attributes include security keys, request flags and identifiers needed by the EDI application and MHS protocol in the

Table 2. SMIB Objects for each EDI component

Object Groups	EDI-SMIB Objects	SYNTAX in SMI
1. Origin Authentication Group	MessageOriginAuthenticationAlgorithmIdentifier	OBJECT IDENTIFIER
	ProbeOriginAuthenticationAlgorithmIdentifier	OBJECT IDENTIFIER
	ProofOfDeliveryAlgorithmIdentifier	OBJECT IDENTIFIER
	ProofOfDeliveryRequest	TruthValue
	ProofOfSubmissionRequest	TruthValue
	ThisRecipientName	DistinguishedName
2. EDIM Group	EDINotificationRequests	TruthValue
	EDINotificationSecurity	TruthValue
	EDIReceptionSecurity	TruthValue
	NonRepudiationOfEDIContentAlgorithmIdentifier	OBJECT IDENTIFIER
	NonRepudiationOfEDINotificationAlgorithmIdentifier	OBJECT IDENTIFIER
3. Data Confidentiality Group	ContentConfidentialityAlgorithmIdentifier	OBJECT IDENTIFIER
	ConnectionConfidentialityAlgorithmIdentifier	OBJECT IDENTIFIER
	ConfidentialityAlgorithmBlockSize	Integer32
	ConfidentialityAlgorithmDecryptKeyLength	Integer32
	ConfidentialityAlgorithmDecryptKey	OCTET STRING
	ConfidentialityAlgorithmEncryptKeyLength	Integer32
	ConfidentialityAlgorithmEncryptKey	OCTET STRING
	ConfidentialityAlgorithmInitVectorIndicate	TruthValue
	ConfidentialityAlgorithmInitVectorLength	Integer32
	ConfidentialityAlgorithmInitVector	OCTET STRING
	ConfidentialityAlgorithmOperateMode	DisplayString
	ConfidentialityAlgorithmSymmetricIndicate	TruthValue
	ConfidentialityAlgorithmSyncIndicate	TruthValue
	ConfidentialityAlgorithmSyncInfoLength	Integer32
4. Data Integrity Group	ContentIntegrityAlgorithmIdentifier	OBJECT IDENTIFIER
	ConnectionIntegrityAlgorithmIdentifier	OBJECT IDENTIFIER
	DigestAlgorithmIdentifier	OBJECT IDENTIFIER
	DigestAlgorithmInitVectorIndicate	TruthValue
	DigestAlgorithmInitVectorLength	Integer32
	DigestAlgorithmInitVector	OCTET STRING
	DigestAlgorithmInputSize	Integer32
	DigestAlgorithmOutputSize	Integer32
	SignatureAlgorithmIdentifier	OBJECT IDENTIFIER
	SignatureAlgorithmCheckKeyLength	Integer32
	SignatureAlgorithmCheckKey	OCTET STRING
	SignatureAlgorithmGenKeyLength	Integer32
	SignatureAlgorithmGenKey	OCTET STRING
	SignatureAlgorithmInitVectorIndicate	TruthValue
	SignatureAlgorithmInitVectorLength	Integer32
	SignatureAlgorithmInitVector	OCTET STRING
	SignatureAlgorithmInputSize	Integer32
	SignatureAlgorithmOutputSize	Integer32
	SignatureAlgorithmSymmetricIndicate	TruthValue
5. Non-Repudiation Group	NonRepudiationOfDeliveryAlgorithmIdentifier	OBJECT IDENTIFIER
	NonRepudiationOfOriginAlgorithmIdentifier	OBJECT IDENTIFIER
	NonRepudiationOfSubmissionAlgorithmIdentifier	OBJECT IDENTIFIER
	ProofOfDeliveryRequest	TruthValue
	ProofOfSubmissionRequest	TruthValue
6. Message Security Labeling Group	MinimumSecurityLabel	DisplayString
	MaximumSecurityLabel	DisplayString
	SecurityPolicyIdentifier	DisplayString
	SecurityCategories	DisplayString
	SecurityClassification	DisplayString
	PrivacyMark	DisplayString
7. Secure Management Group	peerEntitySignatureAlgorithmIdentifier	OBJECT IDENTIFIER
	UserName	Taddress
	UserAddress	OCTET STRING
	InitiatorPassword	OCTET STRING
	subjectPublicKeyAlgorithmIdentifier	OBJECT IDENTIFIER

*All *italic* specified objects have "read-create" in MAX-ACCESS of SMI, and are defined as instances within the object tables. The other objects have "read-write" in MAX-ACCESS of SMI.

implementation of the security mechanisms. The SMIB can be implemented as a table of entries, one of each communicating pair of hosts. It allows the security management applications to control the operation of the EDI system. The steps used in creating a SMIB requires the followings. 1) Gather the security variables want to control the target EDI system. 2) Construct a skeletal SMIB modules. 3) Categorize the security objects class and determine whether there can exist multiple instances of that managed object class. If not, then for each of its attributes, use the OBJECT-TYPE macro to make an equivalent definition. Multiple instances are defined as a conceptual table. 4) Begin compiling SMIB by using a MIB compiler supporting SNMPv2. 5) Refine SMIB observing compiler output for correct data relations. Before constructing SMIB according to the above steps, I first analyzed the data structures of each security services for EDI system, then identified security-related variables as security objects of SMIB. Throughout the analysis, it has been more efficient to construct the common SMIB for each MHS components such as UA, MS, and MTA, because of the similar functions and security objects used among them. However, two object groups in Table 2 namely Message Security Labeling Group and Secure Management Group have multiple instances only for MS and MTA, for MS and MTA may have multiple UAs. In contrast, a UA has only one instance of itself in the case of these groups. KT-EDI system needs SMIBs for three components such as UA, MS, and MTA. Each SMIB has commonly seven object groups, such as Origin Authentication, EDIM Responsibility, Data Confidentiality, Data Integrity, Non-repudiation, Message Security Labeling, and Secure Management group. Table 2 illustrates which security objects belong to which object groups and their object types. Subsequently after the security object types are determined for encoding according to SMI syntax rules for SNMP MIB, I have used the standard MIB compiler (SMIC-compiler[13]) for compiling the SMIB which supports SNMP and SNMPv2.

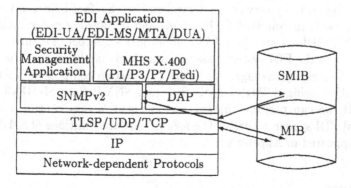

Fig. 3. SMIB and Protocols

6 Network Security Protocols with SMIB

For providing confidentiality and integrity of messages, the adoption of a lower layer security protocol such as NLSP[10] or TLSP[11] may be appropriate. In this EDI security management model, TLSP is adopted for confidentiality and integrity services because it is easier for TLSP to access the SMIB and/or MIB than NLSP. The parameters to be used during the establishment of security associations are also stored as security attributes within SMIB[2]. Some instances of object groups such as data confidentiality and data integrity group can be accessed by the TLSP protocol. Fig. 3 shows which protocols use the SMIB and/or MIB objects. Also EDI applications and security management application can access the SMIB and/or MIB through SNMPv2 application interface. On the other hand, owing to the complexity of the design of the SNMPv2 security and administrative framework, SNMPv3 draft[15] has been published recently as the results of the two approaches SNMPv2u and SNMPv2* towards incorporating security and improvements to SNMPv2. This is the proposal for a complete replacement of the security aspects and administrative framework with a user-based administrative framework. This document also includes a MIB based on SNMPv2-SMI for remotely monitoring / managing the configuration parameters for the Security Model. The principal protection against classical threats can be provided in this document, namely, data integrity, data origin authentication, data confidentiality, access control, message timeliness and limited replay protection. SNMPv3 ensures the basic security requirements defined in ISO 7498-2 security architecture. Therefore, the SMIB proposed in this paper can be used through SNMPv3 also.

7 Conclusion

EDI system needs appropriate security management for controlling the security objects for its security services and mechanisms. So far, I have reviewed the security elements in standard EDI system, and designed security management model for KT-EDI system. Also, I have identified a number of security management objects in the EDI system based on standards, and designed the common SMIB for the security management of the EDI system components such as UA, MS, and MTA using SNMPv2 SMI. By using SNMPv2 or SNMPv3 protocol with SMIB, we can perform the key management, access control, monitoring and control EDI system securely. The formal partial definitions of SMIB in SMI rules are appeared in Appendix.

References

1. T. K. Apostolopoulos, V.C. Daskalou : SNMP-based Network Security Management using a Temporal Database Approach Information Systems Security edited by S.K.Katsikas, and D.Gritzalis, Chapman & Hall, (1996)

2. P. Katsavos, V. Varadharajan : A secure Frame Relay service, Computer Networks and ISDN Systems, 26 (1994)

3. W. Stallings : Network and Internetworking Security, Principles & Practice, IEEE Press, (1995)

4. ISO : Information Processing Systems - Open Systems Interconnection Reference Model - Security Architecture, ISO 7498-2, (1988)

5. ETRI : Development of a Security Service Server for Information Security Services, ETRI Research report, (1995.12)

6. J. Case, K. McCloghrie, M.Rose, S. Waldbusser : Structure of Management Information for Version 2 of SNMPv2 (RFC1902), (1996.1)

7. ITU-T : X.435 Message Handling Systems : Electronic Data Interchange Messaging System, (1992)

8. ITU-T : X.400 Message Handling Systems : Systems and Service Overview, (1992)

9. UN : EDIFACT (Electronic Data Interchange for Administration, Commerce and Transport) Syntax Rules (ISO 9735), UN / ECE, WP.4., (1993.3)

10. ISO / IEC : CD 11577, Network Layer Security Protocol (NLSP), (1991.12)

11. ISO / IEC : DIS 10736, Transport Layer Security Protocol (TLSP), (1991.12)

12. ITU-T : X.509 The Directory- Authentication Framework, (1988)

13. D. Perkins, E. McGinnis : Understanding SNMP MIBs, Prentice Hall Inc, (1997)

14. J. H. Lee : Data Structure of Secure EDI System, The 2nd Symposium proc. of Secure EDI-related technology, ETRI, (1996)

15. U. Blumenthal, B. Wijnen : User-based Security Model (USM) for SNMPv3, IETF Internet-Draft, (1997.11)

16. W. Stallings : SNMP, SNMPv2, and CMIP ; The Practical Guide to Network-Management Standards, Addison-Wesley Pub. Co., (1993)

Appendix : Security MIB Definitions for EDI System

EDI-SMIB DEFINITIONS ::= BEGIN
IMPORTS
OBJECT-TYPE, Integer32, Unsigned32
FROM SNMPv2-SMI
DisplayString, TruthValue
FROM SNMPv2-TC
DistinguishedName
FROM APPLICATION-MIB;
ediSMIB MODULE-IDENTITY

*— The other definitions are omitted intentionally.
—— definition of groups
originAuthGroup   OBJECT IDENTIFIER :: = { ediSMIB 1 }
edimGroup   OBJECT IDENTIFIER :: = { ediSMIB 2 }
dataConfidGroup   OBJECT IDENTIFIER :: = { ediSMIB 3 }
dataIntegrityGroup OBJECT IDENTIFIER :: = { ediSMIB 4 }
nonRepudGroup   OBJECT IDENTIFIER :: = { ediSMIB 5 }
msgSecLabelGroup   OBJECT IDENTIFIER :: = { ediSMIB 6 }
secureMgmtGroup   OBJECT IDENTIFIER :: = { ediSMIB 7 }

*— The definitions of origin authentication group, and EDIM group are omitted
*— intentionally.
—— data confidentiality group
contentConfidentialityAlgorithmIdentifier OBJECT-TYPE
SYNTAX OBJECT IDENTIFIER
MAX-ACCESS read-write
STATUS current
DESCRIPTION
"The algorithm identifier used for Content Confidentiality."
::= {dataConfidGroup 1}

connectionConfidentialityAlgorithmIdentifier OBJECT-TYPE
SYNTAX OBJECT IDENTIFIER
MAX-ACCESS read-write
STATUS current
DESCRIPTION
"The algorithm identifier used for Connection Confidentiality."
::= {dataConfidGroup 2}

confidentialityAlgorithmTable OBJECT-TYPE
SYNTAX SEQUENCE OF ConfidentialityAlgorithmEntry
MAX-ACCESS not-accessible
STATUS current
DESCRIPTION
"The table holding Confidentiality Algorithms."
::= { dataConfidGroup 3}

confidentialityAlgorithmEntry OBJECT-TYPE
SYNTAX ConfidentialityAlgorithmEntry
MAX-ACCESS not-accessible
STATUS current
DESCRIPTION
"The entry containing attributes of Confidentiality Algorithm."
INDEX { algorithmIndex }
::= { confidentialityAlgorithmTable 1}

confidentialityAlgorithmEntry :: =
SEQUENCE {

algorithmIndex   Unsigned32,
confidentialityAlgorithmBlockSize   Integer32,
confidentialityAlgorithmDecryptKeyLength   Integer32,
confidentialityAlgorithmDecryptKey   OCTET STRING,
confidentialityAlgorithmEncryptKeyLength   Integer32,
confidentialityAlgorithmEncryptKey   OCTET STRING,
confidentialityAlgorithmInitVectorIndicate TruthValue,
confidentialityAlgorithmInitVectorLength   Integer32,
confidentialityAlgorithmInitVector   OCTET STRING,
confidentialityAlgorithmOperateMode   DisplayString,
confidentialityAlgorithmSymmetricIndicate TruthValue,
confidentialityAlgorithmSyncIndicate   TruthValue,
confidentialityAlgorithmSyncInfoLength   Integer32 }

algorithmIndex OBJECT-TYPE
SYNTAX Unsigned32
MAX-ACCESS not-accessible
STATUS current
DESCRIPTION
"The algorithm identifier uniquely identifying a particular algorithm."
::= { ConfidentialityAlgorithmEntry 1}

confidentialityAlgorithmBlockSize OBJECT-TYPE
SYNTAX Integer32
MAX-ACCESS read-create
STATUS current
DESCRIPTION
"The block size supported by the algorithm which an identifier uniquely identifies."
::= { ConfidentialityAlgorithmEntry 2}

confidentialityAlgorithmDecryptKeyLength OBJECT-TYPE
SYNTAX Integer32
MAX-ACCESS read-create
STATUS current
DESCRIPTION
"The length of decryption key of the algorithm which an identifier uniquely identifies."
::= { ConfidentialityAlgorithmEntry 3}

confidentialityAlgorithmDecryptKey OBJECT-TYPE
SYNTAX OCTET STRING
MAX-ACCESS read-create
STATUS current
DESCRIPTION
"The decryption key of the algorithm which an identifier uniquely identifies."
::= { ConfidentialityAlgorithmEntry 4}

confidentialityAlgorithmEncryptKeyLength OBJECT-TYPE
SYNTAX Integer32
MAX-ACCESS read-create
STATUS current
DESCRIPTION
"The length of encryption key of the algorithm which an identifier uniquely identifies."
::= { ConfidentialityAlgorithmEntry 5}

confidentialityAlgorithmEncryptKey OBJECT-TYPE
SYNTAX OCTET STRING
MAX-ACCESS read-create
STATUS current
DESCRIPTION
"The encryption key of the algorithm which an identifier uniquely identifies."
::= { ConfidentialityAlgorithmEntry 6}

*− The definitions of the other groups are omitted intentionally.

END

The Block-World Data Model for a Collaborative Virtual Environment

Yoshifumi Masunaga

University of Library and Information Science
1-2 Kasuga, Tsukuba, Ibaraki 305-0821, Japan
masunaga@ulis.ac.jp

Abstract. This paper reports preliminary results for a block-world data model for the realization of three-dimensional virtual work space. In the block-world data model, every real-world object is represented by a "block" which is a three-dimensional interval defined on three orthogonal spatial axes X, Y, and Z. Database users can enter the block-world database space and can see, touch, and move blocks. However, block representation error may occur. In order to minimize the error, a strict interference checking algorithm is developed by introducing null blocks. The block-world database can be realized by integrating a virtual reality system and an object-oriented database system. The virtual reality system is necessary to provide a three-dimensional virtual work space which users can enter to work, while the object-oriented database system is used to provide database function such as query and update processing. A prototype system is developed to evaluate the block-world data model.

1 Introduction

This paper reports the design and implementation of a new generation data model called a "block-world data model" to support a collaborative virtual environment. Needless to say, but traditional database systems such as network and relational data base systems have been used to store and process so-called business data processing data. Well known database systems such as IMS, DB2, and Oracle have been used for this purpose. In recent years, object-oriented database systems have been developed for engineering purposes. They are used to organize and manage multimedia or CAD data.

Although the traditional and object-oriented database systems provide metadata management, query processing, and transaction management capabilities, they cannot support work spaces where users can enter and work together. In order for a user to work in a database space, he/she may want to see, touch, and move objects in the database. For example, suppose that there is a work space where a lot of boxes are piled up to sort according to their shipping destination. In this case, clearly, a worker may want to see the address label of a box to identify the destination and then pick it up to load it on a cargo truck which will take it to its destination.

Unfortunately, any traditional database system cannot support such a function. In a relational database system, a car in the real-world is represented by a tuple in a relation, say Car(id, owner, make, ...). But the tuple is not a car. It is just a tuple representation of the car. The same thing happens in object-oriented database systems. An object is an object and is nothing more, although the behavior of the car can be simulated in object-oriented database systems.

In this paper we propose a new generation data model called a "block-world data model." This is a completely new data model which is different from traditional data models. As with the saying "seeing is believing," users can see, touch, and play with the blocks in the block-world database which is a miniature of the real-world. The block-world database system can be realized by integrating two different types of information systems, a virtual reality system and an object-oriented database system. The virtual reality system is necessary to realize a virtual database work space, while the object-oriented database system is used to provide database function such as object-identity, metadata management, query processing, and transaction management. Some related work has been done in this area. Kuroki et al. [9] have investigated the use of simplicial complexes to represent real-world four-dimensional objects. Although it has been proven in solid geometry that any solid can be expressed by a simplicial complex, it is hard to assign real-world semantic meaning to each simplex, which makes this data model difficult to use. In contrast, in our approach, blocks are used to represent both mathematical and semantic units which are easy to understand. Tokumaru et al. [19] have intended to develop a virtual reality database system for multimedia data handling. Arisawa [3] has been developing a three-dimensional image database system using object-oriented technology. However, their emphasis is on the recognition of three-dimensional objects. There has also been work related to the VRML databases. Tanaka et al. [8] have developed three-dimensional city views in a VRML-object database, Tanizaki et al. [18] have implemented a VRML three-dimensional map generation system, Arikawa et al. [2] have investigated a technique for incorporating live video images into VRML spaces, and recently Uemura et al. [7] have used VRML for human communications. Spatial indexing techniques have been intensively investigated by Nishida et al. [14] and Nakamura et al.[15], and interesting work has been done by Del Bimbo et al. [5] which has implemented an image database system where 2.5-dimensional spatial image retrievals are possible. Much related work has been done in the fields of GIS (Geographic Information Systems) and CAD (Computer Aided Design). We will refer to some of this work in the body of this paper.

The remainder of this paper consists of the following: Section 2 introduces the block-world data model. A strict interference check is introduced. Section 3 shows the system realization technique for the block-world database system. The system integration of a virtual reality system and an object-oriented database system is investigated. A collaborative virtual work space application developed as a prototype system is also mentioned. Section 4 summarizes this paper.

Note that this paper is a revised version of the paper [12] which was presented at the International Symposium on Digital Media Information Base, Nara, Japan, November 26-28, 1997.

2 The Block-World Data Model

Real-world objects are represented by a "block" in the block-world data model. The block is defined using an MBB (Minimum Bounding Block) as shown below. However, the block representation of a real-world object may cause representation error because every real-world object is not always a cuboid. In this section, we will define blocks and investigate the error problem.

2.1 Minimum Bounding Block

[Definition 2.1](MBB)

In the block-world data model, every real-world object is represented as an MBB (Minimum Bounding Block: MBB) which is depicted in **Fig.1**. The MBB is a cuboid whose edges are parallel to either the X, Y, or Z axis, and every one of the six surfaces touches the real-world object.

A real-world object can be represented by a single MBB or a composition of several MBBs. For example, a stereo music player may be represented by a composition of three component blocks, each of which represents a left speaker box, a player, and a right speaker box, respectively. Building a composite block in the block-world database is quite similar to building a structure in the "LEGO" world.

In the field of CAD, CSG (Constructive Solid Geometry) is widely used to design a complex solid object composed of a set of fundamental solid objects named "primitives" such as boxes or cylinders with a set of composition operations like intersection, union, and difference. Unlike CSG, the block-world data model uses only one type of primitive which is a cuboid, and only one type of composition operation to join together the cuboids. In this sense, the representation power of the block-world data model is less powerful than that of CSG. However, we believe that the block-world data model is simple but powerful enough to realize the "seeing is believing" database function.

In the field of GIS, the MBR (Minimum Bounding Rectangle) is used to represent a region of a two-dimensional space [6] . For example, a lake is represented by an MBR. In addition, a one-dimensional object like a road is represented by a concatenation of several component straight roads, each of which can be represented by an MBL (Minimum Bounding Line). Moreover, a temporal object

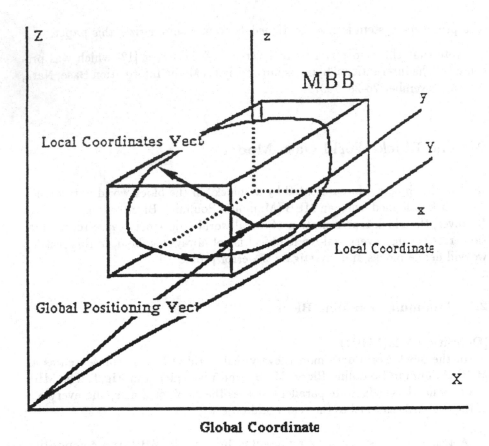

Global Coordinate

Fig. 1. The Minimum Bounding Block (MBB)

such as a video can be represented by a temporal interval [1] . Therefore, the MBB representation is compatible with the MBR, MBI, and temporal interval approach. In other words, it is expected that the block-world data model can provide a uniform representation of both spatial and temporal objects in terms of "intervals." This is depicted in **Fig.2**. In this sense, the block-world data model could be a fundamental data model for a four-dimensional spatio-temporal database system. A basic investigation is given by the author [11] .

2.2 Block, Category and Category Hierarchy

[Definition 2.2](Block)

Suppose that o is a real-world object. Then the block $b(o)$ of o is defined as a triple: $b(o) =(MBB(o), ATTRIB(o), BEHAV(o))$, where $MBB(o)$, $ATTRIB(o)$, and $BEHAV(o)$ are the minimum bounding block, the list of attributes, and the list of behaviors for o, respectively.

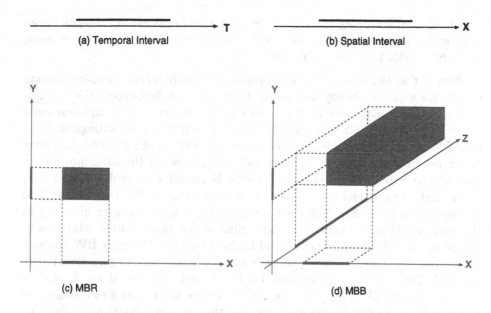

(a) Temporal Interval

(b) Spatial Interval

(c) MBR

(d) MBB

Fig. 2. Compatibility of Interval-Based Representations

For example, if o is an electric home appliance packed in a box, ATTRIB(o) could be a list (ElectricHomeAppliances contents, integer weight, char* shippingAddress, ...), where ElectricHomeAppliances is a category which is the domain of the attribute contents. (The definition of category will be given below.) If o is a car, then BEHAV(o) could be a list (void depart(Destination), ...). Therefore, if a message to depart(Osaka) is sent to block b(o), then block b(o) starts for Osaka as in the object-oriented paradigm. Someone might think that MBB(o) is a kind of ATTRIB(o). This is true, but we clearly distinguish them because "shape" is the first-class citizen in the block-world data model. In other words, the block without attributes and behaviors may exist, but the block without shape may not exist (We call the entities without shape literal.). A block has identity so that it can be recognized even though its shape, Attributes, or behaviors are changed. In order to classify blocks, we introduce the concept of category.

[Definition 2.3](Category)

Let o and o' be real-world objects. Then block b(o) and b(o') of o and o', respectively, belong to the same category if and only if b(o) and b(o') have the same shape, the same attributes, and the same behaviors.

That is, we say that two objects o and o' have the same shape, the same attributes, and the same behavior when MBB(o) is isomorphic to MBB(o'), ATTRIB(o) = ATTRIB(o'), and BEHAV(o) = BEHAV(o') hold, respectively. The relationship between blocks and categories is similar to that between objects and classes in the object-oriented paradigm. Therefore, there exists a category hierarchy among categories. The semantics of this hierarchy are a generalization hierarchy, and, accordingly, shapes, attributes, and behaviors are inherited from a super category to its sub-categories via IS-A hierarchy. Multiple inheritance, override, overload are allowed in this model.

Now, let us examine the built-in category hierarchy of the block-world data model. As we have already mentioned, blocks are the first-class citizen of this model. A block may have blocks as its components as well as alpha-numeric data. Alpha-numeric data are called "literal" in our model to distinguish them from blocks. In other words, blocks have shape, while alpha-numeric data have no shape. However, both of them are called "entities" in the block-world data model. Attributes, relationships, and methods should also be described in the block-world data model so that we can provide category " Characteristic " to accommodate them. **Fig.3** shows a fundamental built-in category hierarchy of the block-world data model. Users can define application-oriented categories as sub-categories of the categories defined in this hierarchy. Category BW_Element is the root category in which two basic categories reside, category BW_Entity and BW_Characteristic. Categories BW_Block and BW_Literal are defined as subcategories of BW_Entity. Composite blocks are located as a subcategory of BW_Block. As we will discuss in the next section, a "strict interference checking algorithm" is introduced to reduce the representation error of composite blocks so that we can define a category BW_Strict_Interference_Composite_Block for this purpose. By introducing category BW_Aggregate_Block, we can define a set of blocks as a block, for example. In designing the built-in category hierarchy, we referred to the built-in class hierarchy of ODMG-93 designed by ODMG (Object Data Management Group) [4] . However, readers can see some essential differences between these hierarchies, in particular where category BW_SpatialInterval is defined to support spatial intervals on the X, Y, and Z axes which are absolutely necessary to define three-dimensional intervals, i.e blocks. Because category BW_Block is the root category of all blocks, the following two essential operations are defined in this category: (a) A set of operations to create, store, and delete blocks, and (b) a set of operations to return the coordinate values of the vertices of a block, the volume of a block, or the movability of a block, etc. according to requests. Users can define arbitrary categories as subcategories of the built-in categories.

2.3 Block Representation Error

Every real-world object is represented by a cuboid whose edges are parallel to either the X, Y, or Z axis in the block-world data model, and every one of the six surfaces touches the real-world object. As a result, representation errors tend to occur due to for the following two reasons: (a) Error due to a cuboid approximation of a non-cuboid object, and (b) error due to the mismatch of the global-space and the local-space axes. **Fig.4** illustrates these two types of errors, using a two-dimensional case for simplicity. As Fig.4 (a) shows, an egg-shaped two-dimensional object is represented by a rectangle, which causes an error that is impossible to correct in the block-world data model. However, it is possible to

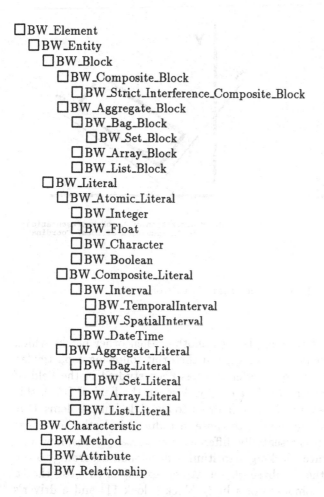

☐ BW_Element
  ☐ BW_Entity
    ☐ BW_Block
      ☐ BW_Composite_Block
        ☐ BW_Strict_Interference_Composite_Block
      ☐ BW_Aggregate_Block
        ☐ BW_Bag_Block
          ☐ BW_Set_Block
        ☐ BW_Array_Block
        ☐ BW_List_Block
    ☐ BW_Literal
      ☐ BW_Atomic_Literal
        ☐ BW_Integer
        ☐ BW_Float
        ☐ BW_Character
        ☐ BW_Boolean
      ☐ BW_Composite_Literal
        ☐ BW_Interval
          ☐ BW_TemporalInterval
          ☐ BW_SpatialInterval
        ☐ BW_DateTime
      ☐ BW_Aggregate_Literal
        ☐ BW_Bag_Literal
          ☐ BW_Set_Literal
        ☐ BW_Array_Literal
        ☐ BW_List_Literal
  ☐ BW_Characteristic
    ☐ BW_Method
    ☐ BW_Attribute
    ☐ BW_Relationship

Fig. 3. A Part of Built-in Category Hierarchy

minimize the representation error if we allow the introduction of a local space axis. For example, the representation error in the egg-shaped representation of Fig.4 (a) can be minimized if a local space axis is introduced, as is shown in Fig.4 (b). But, notice that to handle a new MBR in the local space, it is necessary to handle not only the MBR information but also the mutual spatial relationship between the global and the local space, which requires extra computation cost [13] . The representation error in case (b) can be minimized in this way, but the representation error in case (a) is unavoidable.

2.4 Strict Interference Check

In the block-world data model, we use the word "interference" to indicate the interaction between two blocks in the sense that their MBBs interfere. There-

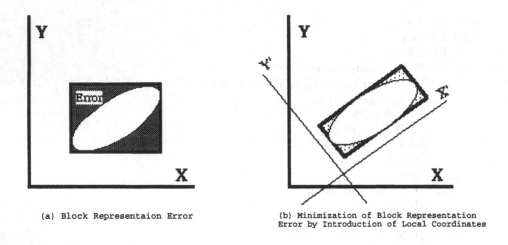

(a) Block Representaion Error

(b) Minimization of Block Representation
Error by Introduction of Local Coordinates

Fig. 4. Block Representation Error

fore, if one block is moved from one place to another, then other blocks which
are located in its orbit should be ejected from the orbit following a particular
dynamics. Of course, this type of interference has been studied in the field of
virtual reality systems in order to reflect reality. Also, in the field of CAD, this
kind of interference has been investigated in order to avoid design problems. Our
interference concept is basically similar to those introduced in both the virtual
reality and CAD systems. It is essentially different from these systems, however,
in that a "strict" interference checking algorithm is developed according to the
composition structure of the database object. As an example, suppose that a
"truck" block (block 1) is composed of a body block (block 11) and a driver's
block (block 12), as shown in **Fig.5** (a). Note that the MBR of the truck is the
outer-most rectangle also shown in this figure because the truck is a composite
block. Then, if we move block 2 south by one unit-length, block 1 and block 2 will
then interfere in the ordinal definition. But, we emphasize that there is no block
at the upper-right corner of block 1, and block 2 should therefore not interfere
with block 1. To reflect such a reality in the block-world data model, we have
introduced the "null block" to represent that there is no block in the real-world.
Moreover, we can create a rule stating that "a null block never interferes with
any other block." Then we can say that block 1 does not interfere with block 2
in the strict sense when the latter moves south by a unit length. This is depicted
in Fig.5 (b). Note that the introduction of null blocks causes an optimization
problem in the following sense. When null blocks are not introduced, we can
say that block 1 does not interfere with block 2 in the strict sense when the
latter moves south by a unit length if the intersection of block 1 and block 2
after moving is disjoint with both block 11 and block 12. In contrast, when null
blocks are introduced, we can say that block 1 does not interfere with block 2
after moving in the strict sense if the intersection of block 1 and block 2 after

moving is included in null block n. That is, the introduction of null blocks saves computation cost for strict interference check, however it requires extra cost for managing null blocks.

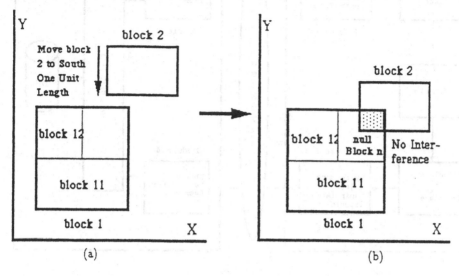

Fig. 5. Strict Interference Check

3 Prototyping of the Block-World Database System

3.1 An Overall System Architecture

The block-world database system can be realized by integrating a virtual reality system and an object-oriented database system via a high-speed network. **Fig.6** depicts an overall system architecture. In the front-end virtual reality system, we define a virtual world and its objects by using a world and shape editor. The editing results are stored in a file in the virtual reality system. The visualizer provides a virtual three-dimensional space for users by accessing the virtual reality file. In order to integrate a virtual reality system and an object-oriented database system, the virtual reality system should be expanded to incorporate two new modules; the first of which can translate the virtual reality objects into object-oriented database objects (module 1 in Fig.6), and the second of which can translate query and update requests from a collaborative user into equivalents which are understood by the object-oriented database system (module 2 in Fig.6), The translated objects and requests are sent to the back-end object-oriented database system via a communication network (a 10 Mega bits Ethernet in our prototype system). Also, the object-oriented database system should be expanded in two ways; we should develop a module which can accept the objects sent by module 1 (module 3 in Fig.6), and another module should be developed

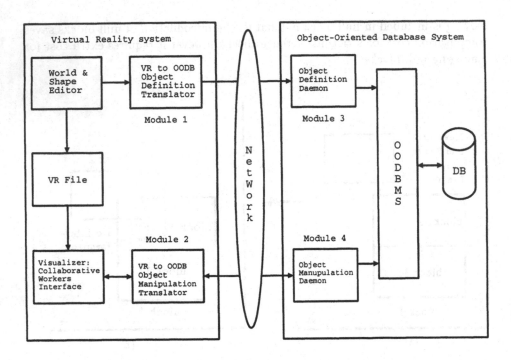

Fig. 6. An Overall System Architecture of the Block-World Database System

which can accept the collaborative worker's query and update requests sent by module 2 (module 4 in Fig.6), Notice that modules 3 and 4 are implemented as "daemons," in that they are running always to capture the input from modules 1 and 2, respectively. Of course another expansion would be necessary for the object-oriented database system to support various types of temporal and spatial relationships between objects, but this is not addressed in this paper.

It is interesting to see that our system integration approach is natural from the well-known database standard system architecture proposed by ANSI/X3/SPARC [20] . This is depicted in **Fig.7**, where a real-world object is represented as a block in the conceptual schema, while a block is implemented as an object in an object-oriented database system, which is defined as an internal schema of the block-world database system. A virtual reality system is used to implement an external schema. In the external schema, a real-world object can be represented as if it exists in the real-world. But the interference check is done according to the algorithm implemented at the conceptual schema level. A user enters the virtual work space either mounting a head-mounted display or interacting with a three-dimensional screen. In the current prototype system, a "data glove" is used to represent a user in the virtual work space so that the user can touch and move the blocks in the block-world database. As has been mentioned several times, this function is essential to support collaborative work, and it has never been realized by any of the traditional database systems.

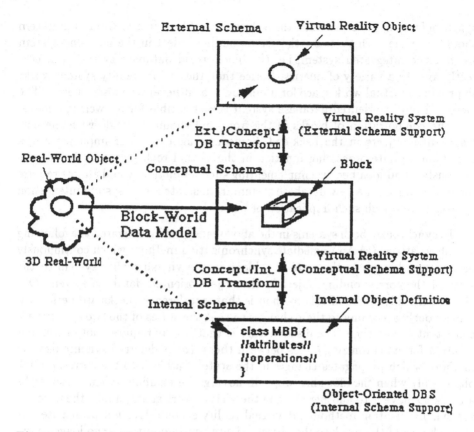

Fig. 7. The Block-World Data Modeling and the ANSI/X3/SPARC Three Schema Structure

To accommodate collaborative work, at least two virtual reality systems are necessary as front-end systems. This situation is not yet implemented in the current prototype system, but the essential technical point is how to maintain data integrity among three different systems, i.e. two virtual reality systems and one object-oriented database system. Basically, two users on the different virtual reality front ends share the same objects stored in the back-end object-oriented database system. A synchronization mechanism for two (conflict) update requests must be implemented to maintain data integrity. This also remains to be studied in the future.

3.2 Synchronizing the Virtual Reality System and the Object-Oriented Database System

The front-end virtual reality system has its state. That is, it has a list of blocks with their values on shape, attributes, and behaviors. The same thing happens for the back-end object-oriented database system. These two states should be synchronized in the sense that the values for a block in the front-end system should coincide with those for the corresponding object in the back-end system so that the integrated system, i.e. the block-world database system, can correctly answer a variety of queries. Notice that the virtual reality system works to provide a virtual work space for users and that it never processes queries. The back-end object-oriented database system is responsible for answering queries. But the configuration of blocks in the front-end should coincide with the corresponding objects in the back-end. Someone might consider implementing a query and update-processing function in the virtual reality system, but this is obviously a bad idea because implementing such a function would almost require the development of a new database system from scratch. Our system integration approach avoids all such duplication of work.

To synchronize both systems in the above sense, we investigated the following two alternatives: (a) An immediate synchronization method, which continuously propagates changes in the state of a block in the virtual reality system to the state of the corresponding object in the object-oriented database system. Obviously, the advantage of this method is that interference checks are performed continuously according to these changes so that the states of the two systems are consistent at any time. The disadvantage is that it may require a lot of communication for synchronizing states between them. (b) A deferred synchronization method, which propagates changes in the state of a block to the corresponding object only when the block has stopped moving. For example, when a user grabs a block to move it to another place in the virtual work space, unlike the immediate synchronization method, the virtual reality system does not propagate any state change of the block to the object-oriented system until it is no longer moving. Therefore, the interference check in the back-end object-oriented database system is deferred. Obviously, the disadvantage of this method is that the states of the two systems are inconsistent during the movement, and the advantage is that it may save communication cost.

Of course, a decision which alternative should be adopted depends on application. However, it is interesting to note that the movement in the virtual reality space by hand (i.e. data glove) may not be made on a straight line even though a user intends to move a block straight towards its destination. This means that the immediate interference check may not be crucial in the virtual reality system, or rather the interference in the virtual world should be calculated in a deferred manner assuming that the block is moved straight towards its destination. By this reason, we implemented the second alternative by adding a rule that the interference check in the virtual world should be calculated in a deferred manner, as with the object-oriented database system.

3.3 Support of the Three-Dimensional Virtual Work Space

In order to verify that the block-world data model is suitable for supporting three-dimensional work space for collaborative workers, we have developed a small application on top of the prototype system. This application is stated as follows: Suppose that there is a set of electric home appliances, each of which is packed in a single box with its shipping destination label. These boxes are laid on a work floor. Workers are responsible for picking up boxes to load on a truck for a certain destination, say Sapporo. Working in collaboration, a worker can ask a partner to tell him the shipping address if he can not see it himself. This collaborative work environment was analyzed using an object-oriented analysis and design method known as OMT proposed by Rumbaugh *et al.* [16] .

Based on the object diagram representing the analysis result [10] , the block-world database schema for this running example was obtained, which was implemented by a commercial object-oriented database system ONTOS. **Fig.8** depicts the class hierarchy of ONTOS used to implement the example. Notice that the class Block is defined to implement category BW_Block. Class StrictInterferenceCheckObject is defined to implement the blocks in category BW_Strict_Interference_Composite_Block. Classes Interval and Label correspond to certain subcategories of category BW_Literal. Class SpatialRelationship corresponds to a subcategory of category BW_Relationship. We used the Virtual Reality Kit as a class library for the realization of a virtual collaborative work space. An SGI's Indigo 2 graphics workstation was used. **Fig.9** depicts a screen image of the virtual collaborative work space implemented for the current prototype system.

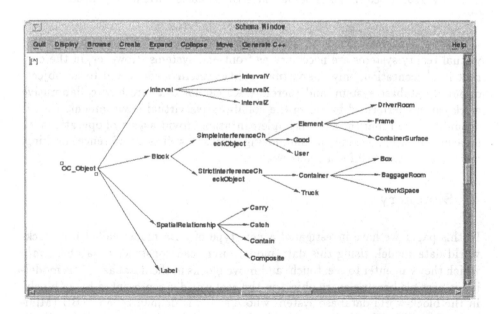

Fig. 8. An Implementation Class Hierarchy of an Object-Oriented Database System

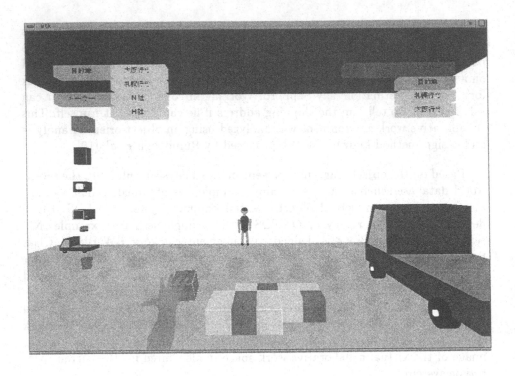

Fig. 9. A Screen Image of the Three-Dimensional Virtual Work Space

As we have mentioned, to accommodate collaborative work, at least two virtual reality systems are necessary as front-end systems. However, in the current implementation, only one virtual reality system is connected to an object-oriented database system, and therefore we cannot evaluate how collaborative work can be performed better in the collaborative virtual environment. But, it should be noted that the current implementation provides a set of operations for creating, deleting, picking up, and moving blocks as well as interference checking, which is working well for a single worker.

4 Summary

In this paper we have investigated a new type of data model called the block-world data model. Using this data model, users can construct a database into which they can enter to see, touch, and move blocks in the database. This modeling is possible because every object in the real world is represented by a "block" in the block-world database system whose shape is defined by an MBB (Minimum Bounding Block), i.e. a cuboid whose edges are parallel to either the X, Y, or Z axis, and every one of the six surfaces touches the real-world object. To minimize the representation error which cannot be avoided in the block-world data model, we have developed a strict interference checking algorithm by introducing "null" blocks which do not interfere with any block. In order to verify our approach, we have implemented a prototype system by integrating a virtual reality system and an object-oriented database system. Particularly, a synchronization mechanism was developed to coordinate the interference checking in both the virtual reality system and the object-oriented database system. A small example of collaborative work is implemented for this prototype, where a worker can pick up a box in which an electric home appliance is packed and carry it to a truck for the shipping destination. We have not yet implemented declarative query capability. Queries in the three-dimensional database system differ greatly from the traditional ones in that they become multimodal as well as spatial position sensitive. Also, query processing needs a combined knowledge of spatial relationships [17] . Implementation of such a query language is left as a focus for a future research, along with the accommodation of more than one virtual reality front-end on top of an object-oriented database system.

Acknowledgements

The author expresses his thanks to Mr. S. Yatsumori and Mr. S. Sato of CRC Corporation who contributed to this work. He is also indebted to a graduate Mr. T. Kameda and undergraduates Mr. H. Kawashima and Mr. Y. Mizuno who worked for this project. He also expresses his sincere thanks to Dr. H. Nakai and all of the person who gave him variable comments and help on this research. This work is partly supported by the Grant-in-Aid on Priority Area of the Ministry of Education, Science, Sports and Culture of Japan; the grant number 08244101.

References

1. Allen, J. F.: Maintaining Knowledge about Temporal Intervals, Communications of ACM, Vol. 26, No. 11, pp.832-843, 1983.
2. Arikawa, M. *et al.*: Incorporating Live Videos into VRML Spaces, Proceedings of Advanced Database Symposium '96, pp. 187-192, December 1996 (In Japanese).
3. Arisawa, H.: Consideration on Real World Data Modeling, Technical Report of IEICE of Japan, DE-96-4, pp.19-24, May 1995 (In Japanese).
4. Cattell, R. (Ed.): The Object Database Standard: ODMG-93, 169p., Morgan Kaufmann Publishers, 1994.
5. Del Bimbo, A., *et al.*: A Three Dimensional Iconic Environment for Image Database Querying, IEEE TOSE, Vol.19, No.10, pp.997-1011, October 1993.
6. Egenhofer, M. J.: Spatial Relations: Models, Inferences, and their Future Applications, Proceedings of Advanced Database Symposium '96, 31p., Tokyo, December 1996.
7. Ishikawa, M., H. Takakura and S. Uemura: Support for Communication in Shared Virtual Space by User Defined Area, Paper of Special Interest Group on Database System of the IPSJ, 97-DBS-113, pp. 299-304, July 1997 (In Japanese).
8. Kamiura, M., H. Oiso, K. Tajima, and K. Tanaka: Spatial Views in VRML-object Databases, Proceedings of International Symposium on Cooperative Database Systems for Advanced Applications (CODAS), pp.282-291, Nara, December 1996.

9. Kuroki, S and A. Makinouchi: Design of the Spatio-Temporal Data Model Universe using Simplicial Complexes, Report of Special Interest Group on Database Systems of the IPSJ, 96-DBS-109, pp. 221-226, July 1996 (In Japanese).
10. Masunaga, Y.: An Investigation on a Three Dimensional Space Data Model for Cooperative Work Support, Report of Special Interest Group on Database Systems of the IPSJ, 96-DBS-109, pp. 227-232, July 1996 (In Japanese).
11. Masunaga, Y.: An Interval-Based Approach to a Spatio-Temporal Data Model for Virtual Collaborative Environments, Proceedings of International Symposium on Cooperative Database Systems for Advanced Applications (CODAS), pp.341-348, Nara, December 1996.
12. Masunaga, Y.: The Block-World Data Model for the Realization of Three-Dimensional Virtual Work Space, Proceedings of International Symposium on Digital Media Information Base (DMIB), pp. 1-10, Nara, November 1997.
13. Nabil, M., J. Shepherd and A. Ngu: 2D Projection Interval Relationships: A Symbolic Representation of Spatial Relationships, Advances in Spatial Databases (M. J. Engenhofer and J. R. Herring (Eds.)), Lecture Notes in Computer Science 951, pp.292-309, Springer, 1995.
14. Naka, A., N. Saiwaki, A. Tsujimoto and S. Nishida: An Adaptive Spacio-Temporal Data Management Structure for Efficient Search, Proceedings of Matsue Workshop on Advanced Databases, pp. 140-144, September 1996 (In Japanese).
15. Nakamura, Y.: Efficient Object Management and Fast Graphics for a Large Scale Virtual City Environment, Proceedings of Knowledge Transfer '96, pp. 533-539, 1996.
16. Rumbaugh, J., M. Blaha, W. Premerlani, F. Eddy and W. Lorensen: Object-Oriented Modeling and Design, 500p., Prentice-Hall International, 1991.
17. Sharma, J. and D. M. Flewelling: Inferences from Combined Knowledge about Topology and Directions, Advances in Spatial Databases (M. J. Engenhofer and J. R. Herring (Eds.)), Lecture Notes in Computer Science 951, pp.279-291, Springer, 1995.
18. Tanizaki, M. and S. Shimada: Study of Spatial Information Service Methods by Active Retrieval Mechanisms, Report of Special Interest Group on Database Systems of the IPSJ, 96-DBS-109, pp. 209-214, July 1996 (In Japanese).
19. Tokumaru, T. and S. Uchinami: Requirement Analysis for Data Model of Virtual Reality Database System, Proceedings of Matsue Workshop on Advanced Databases, pp. 140-144, September 1996 (In Japanese).
20. Tsichritzis, D. and A. Klug: The ANSI/X3/SPARC DBMS Framework Report of the Study Group on Database Management Systems, Information Systems, Vol. 3, pp. 173-191, 1978.

CyPhone – Mobile Multimodal Personal Augmented Reality

Petri Pulli[1], Tino Pyssysalo[2], Kari Kuutti[3], Jouni Similä[3], Jukka-Pekka
Metsävainio[4] and Olli Komulainen[4]

[1] VTT Electronics and University of Oulu
VTT Electronics, P.O. Box 1100, FIN-90571 Oulu, Finland; University of Oulu,
Department of Electrical Engineering and Infotech Research Center, Linnanmaa,
FIN-90570 Oulu, Finland
[2] University of Oulu, Department of Electrical Engineering and Infotech Research
Center, Linnanmaa, FIN-90570 Oulu, Finland
[3] University of Oulu, Department of Information Processing Science and Infotech
Research Center, Linnanmaa, FIN-90570 Oulu, Finland
[4] J-P Metsävainio Design Oy, Kirkkokatu 8A7, 90100 Oulu, Finland

Abstract. Advances in multimedia, virtual reality, and immersive environments have expanded human-computer interaction beyond text and
vision to include touch, gestures, voice and 3D sound. Although there
exist well-developed single modalities for communication, we do not really understand the general problem of designing integrated multimodal
systems.

Recent advances in mobile communication based on picocellular technologies allow the transmission of high bandwidth of data over personal
surrounding networks. The technology offers some more freedom for the
design of mobile multimodal 3D user interfaces but does not solve the
design problem.

In this paper we offer an approach to adding aspects of mobility and
augmented reality to multimodal user interfaces, discuss the technology
and potential future product concept vision, the CyPhone, and depict
the general architecture and integration framework briefly.

1 Introduction

Recent visionary research [1] strongly suggests future information society going
towards virtualisation. Examples of proposed virtual telepresence based services
are: virtual meetings, electronic shopping, games and entertainment, guiding and
tourist services, virtual village, virtual family, personal memory support systems.

Our work is based on the emerging understanding that there is a major
trend towards personal advanced telecommunication services. "Personal" means
that these services are mobile and conveniently available whenever and wherever we want/need to participate in communication activities. We are carrying
out a long-term scientific study for how are we going to bring future increasing
communication bandwidth and computing performance to the personal vicinity
and personal use of individual human beings, meaning everyone of us. We focus on scientific study of user-interaction layer of the future broadband personal

telecommunication products and of services. Through better understanding of user interaction issues of future telecommunication services we believe that, besides scientific contributions, we increase the potential for the telecommunication product and service industry to grow in the future.

Scientifically we are utilising two major approaches to extend the use of computing and communication resources: "ubiquitous computing" and "augmented reality". "Ubiquitous computing" is a term coined by Weiser [2] to mean a situation, where small computational devices are embedded into our everyday environment in a way that allows them to be operated seamlessly and transparently. These devices are suggested to be active and aware of their surroundings so that they can react and emit information when needed. One implementation of ubiquitous computing are active badges, that can trigger automatic doors and give information about the location of a person. Weiser's team and others at Xerox have experimented the idea by using several types of devices, like small pager-sized "Tabs", notebook-sized "Pads" and whiteboard-sized "Boards" [3].

"Augmented reality" [4, 5, 6, 7] is a research approach that attempts to integrate some form of computer media with the real world. When in ubiquitous computing there are many different active devices, in many cases each of them having their own display and interaction devices, the augmented reality approach usually uses much fever devices and aims at a seamless integration between real and digital. The integration may be between paper and electronic documents, like in DigiDesk [4], or even more commonly overlaying digital information (as a non-immersive virtual reality) on real world images [5]. The overlaying of images may take place in several ways, like by using video projection [4, 8], by the means of small, hand-held video screens or palmtop computers [6], or by mixing surrounding reality with non-immersive VR by using head-mounted see-through displays [4].

The core idea of our approach [18, 19] is that by using a very short distance radio communication network it is possible to mix these two approaches. Thus we suggest "ubiquitous computing" in the form where different devices in spaces and places we move around are computationally active and can recognize our presence and identity. But instead of a multitude of different displays and interaction devices we suggest that the interaction with all devices would take place in an "augmented reality", for example by using a head-mounted see-through display and a mobile phone/remote controller.

2   Mobile Virtual Reality Architecture

Several networked virtual reality environments [11, 12, 13, 14] exist today, but none of them supports mobility of users. Most of the networked environments are based on Internet, which could be easily replaced by a mobile multimedia wireless network like SWAN [15] providing mobile connections. However, typical currently available applications and their interfaces, based on immersive virtual reality and heavy desk-top computers, would still restrict the user's ability to move and access services in a natural and convenient way. In the Nara Institute of Science and Technology in Japan [16] an experimental mobile virtual reality system is being developed. This system like ours [17] is based on augmented reality merging both real and virtual environments to provide totally new services and interfaces to mobile observers.

2.1 Picocellular personal surrounding network

The backbone of the mobile virtual reality is a wireless picocellular personal surrounding network (PSN). The PSN network connects user's personal mobile terminals like a head-mounted-display or a pen-shaped input device and provides mobile access to other mobile and fixed networks as depicted in Fig 1.

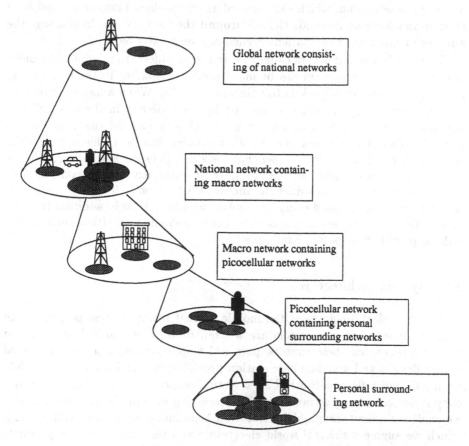

Global network consisting of national networks

National network containing macro networks

Macro network containing picocellular networks

Picocellular network containing personal surrounding networks

Personal surrounding network

Fig. 1. The hierarchy of different mobile networks.

The benefits of using very small cells in mobile virtual reality are obvious. The smaller the cell size, the higher the throughput, because there are fewer users in each cell and higher transmission frequencies can be used. Usually very high frequencies are not used in mobile networks, because of a quick signal attenuation, but if the transmission range is just a few meters, the effect of attenuation is almost negligible. In addition, smaller cell size enables greater frequency reuse. The diameter of a PSN cell in our system is going to be some three meters, which enables the construction of small very low-powered hand held terminals still capable of transmitting high bandwidth multimedia data required by virtual reality applications.

Conventional mobile networks consisting of very small cells have two serious drawbacks: The number of base stations and handovers will be enormous. In our system adjacent PSNs can change information directly without using a fixed base station. This does not only enable wireless communication between user's personal terminals but makes it possible for two users to transmit data to each other directly too. In fact each user's personal surrounding network constitutes a mobile base station, which can forward traffic packets between a fixed base station and some user outside the cell around the base station. In this way the number of expensive base stations needed can be greatly reduced.

The number of handovers cannot be reduced, unless users' ability to move is restricted. But handovers can be made more transparent to the user by e.g. multicasting same data packets to adjacent cells [20]. When a handover occurs, i.e., the user changes a cell, new data packets are already in the new cell and the user does not have to wait the time it takes to forward the data packets from the old cell to the new one. Another problem related to handovers is the availability of services. When a user changes a cell, does the new cell provide the same services as the previous one. In spite of implementing the same services in each network node including the mobile PSNs, it may be more reasonable to get services on demand using e.g. mobile agents [21]. So in addition to data, knowledge about the services required by the user should be multicast in adjacent cells to provide transparent handovers.

2.2 System architecture

In Fig. 2 a block diagram of the mobile virtual reality system is given. The main components of the system are a fixed base station providing access to fixed networks and their services, personal mobile terminals including virtual reality devices and a mobile base station providing connections between mobile terminals and a fixed network. User's virtual reality devices contain input and output devices and an advanced position tracking system. As an output device we shall use a see-through high resolution head-mounted-display (HMD), with which we augment the real world electronics and telecommunication products with virtual properties and interfaces. As an input device we are going to use a 3D pen mouse, which provides very natural way of entering data e.g. editing a text file. In order to provide a reasonable augmented reality we should track both the output and input devices very precisely. Several methods for tracking the position exist. From these an electromagnetic method based on spread-spectrum communication providing an accuracy of a few millimeters [22] seems to be most promising for our purposes.

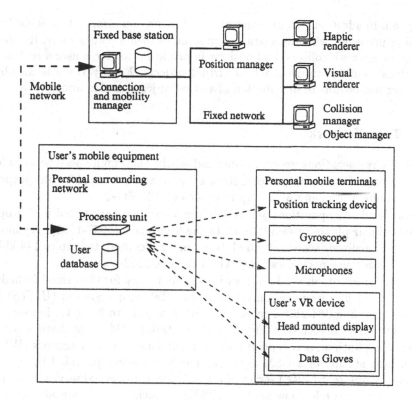

Fig. 2. The components of the mobile VR system.

In order to keep personal mobile terminals as simple as possible, they should not have much storage space or computation capacity. Data routed by mobile PSNs may be buffered, if the destination PSN is temporarily unreachable, but has not left its position from the routing chain. A PSN leaving the chain notifies immediately its downlink PSN, if such exists and uplink PSN or a fixed base station, so that they can re-create an other routing chain, in case there are enough PSNs in the area. Data addressed to a PSN, which has left the routing chain is deleted without buffering, because it will be delivered to the right PSN by multicasting it to a new cell or a new routing chain.

To decrease the amount of computation power needed by a PSN most of the heavy processes should be distributed across the fixed network and executed in different network nodes. For example in one server node a haptic rendering process can be executed, another may contain a visual rendering process and the third node may contain a process generating 3D audio data, as depicted in Fig. 2. One of the most important processes is a position tracking manager, which determines the locations and positions of the users' head-mounted-displays and input devices from the data it periodically receives from users' sensors. One PSN can contain several position sensors, because in addition to user's head and input device it may be desirable to locate his hands and legs or the whole body too. In addition to a fixed network node, position information is used by a collision manager, which is again executed in an own network node. Rendering processes use both collision and position information to give a user a real-world-like visual and haptic feedback of virtual objects. Finally there is an object manager responsible of distribution of virtual objects on demand.

2.3 Trial Network

For in-doors operations we use commercial off-the-shelf high-speed wireless local area network (LAN) with protocol stack adapted and enhanced for our purposes. In-doors operation can operate up to speeds of 2 Mbit/s.

For out-doors operations we are bulding a trial network based on European digital cellular phone system (GSM). In the first phase (1997-1999) very modest speeds of circuit-switched n * 9.6 kbits/s can be accomodated, up to 144 kbit/s. We also study use packed-switched GSM data (GSM2+ services).

The purpose of our dual-strategy is to prepare way for the arrival (scheduled around 1999) of European Universal Mobile Telephone System (UMTS) trial network enabling 384 kbit/s speeds out-doors, and up to 2 Mbit/s indoors. The trial network is depicted in Fig. 3. Mobile stations (MS) can have a wireless access using both an access point (AP) of a wireless local area network (WLAN) and a base station of a GSM network. The services are provided by a virtual reality environment (VRE) server of a WLAN or commercial service provides of a public switched telephone network (PSTN), which a mobile station can access using a mobile services switching centre (MSC).

Cooperation with Japanese 3rd generation digital cellular phone system developers (e.g. DoCoMo) is planned through our industrial support consortium.

3   A Future Product Concept Vision - CyPhone

Our current workis demonstrated by imaginary product concept "CyPhone" in Figs. 4 - 9. Please note that CyberPhone does not exist yet, it is just a vision of the future, and we expect that it can be a consumer product around 2003 - 2008.

CyPhone can serve a s a product platform for many potential value-added services. We have considered services falling in to following categories:

- Telepresence services (tourism, teletaching, nursery)
- Annotation services (guidance, electronic commerce)
- Monitoring & maintenance services (real-estate and property maintenance and alarm systems)
- Home services (child and seniour citized day-care)
- Entertainment services (group games, athletics, training)
- Personal services (pets, tamagotchis, virtual family, virtual friends)

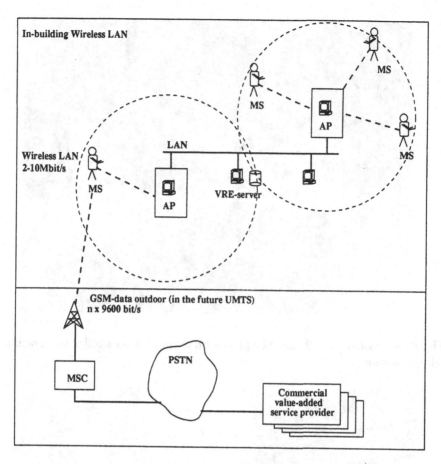

Fig. 3. An architecture of a trial network.

4 Discussion and Conclusions

Virtual reality techniques have received a lot of attention during the last months in the research community. The advantages of contemporary communication and information technologies based on virtual reality techniques offer totally new approaches also to the design of multimodal 3D user interfaces especially through the idea of a common workspace. In this paper, we extend the virtual reality approach to the conceptualization and implementation of a mobile integrated multimodal virtual 3D user interface using picocellular networks as a communication foundation. The potential of the presented approach is examined especially in the case of small, typically hand held electronics and telecommunication products. The problem with these kind of product's standard user interfaces is that they need to contain almost full QWERTY-keyboard and a limited bitmap-display with capability to show WWW-pages.

Currently we are building research environment and experimenting with a multimodal personal augmented reality user interface for CyPhone product con-

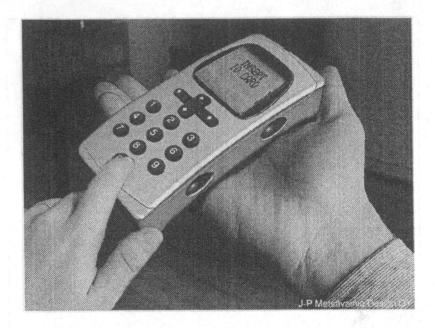

Fig. 4. A visionary CyPhone. The product has appearance similar to an ordinary cellular phone.

Fig. 5. CyPhone with multimedia display screen opened. In this scenario, Cy-Phone is used in tourist guiding service in metropolitan area.

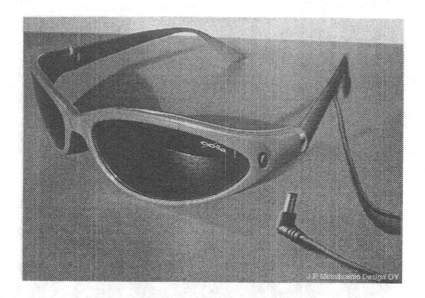

Fig. 6. Augmented reality sunglasses are optional CyPhone accessory. They can be used for more convenient viewing visual information.

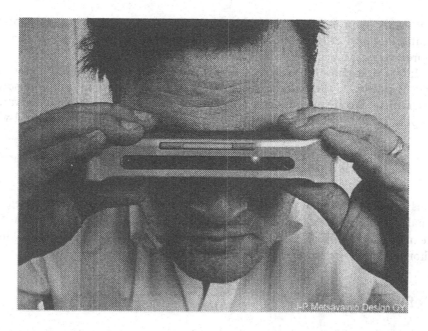

Fig. 7. CyPhone used as a digital stereo camera for "recording" presence in Louvre Art Gallery in Paris.

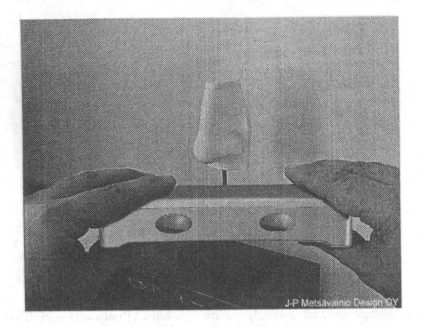

Fig. 8. The user of CyPhone aims at the art object like using a video camera.

cept, which is a small-sized combination of a stereo digital camera, notepad computer and a cellular phone. Beside the current target we believe that our approach has a much wider utilisation reserve.

In the first phase we plan to elaborate telepresence services and annotation type of services in the context of "Mobile City Oulu" future information society programme. We are open for controlled experience exchange and look forward to cooperation with other mobile value-added service trial programmes world-wide.

5   Acknowledgements

This research has been carried out in PIHVI project (Picocellular based personal virtual products and services) co-funded by Technology Development Centre of Finland (TEKES), CCC Software Professionals, Elektrobit, Nokia Mobile Phones, Polar Electro, and Telecom Finland.

References

1. Thalmann, D.: From multimedia to Telepresence. In: Konidaris, S. (coordinator): Communications for Society, Visionary Research. European Commision DG XIII/B. Brussels. February (1997) 173–195
2. Weiser, M.: The Computer for the 21st Century. Scientific American **265** 3 (1991) 94–104

Fig. 9. The observer in Tsukuba, Japan will experience the art object as if being there in Louvre.

3. Buxton, W.: Living in Augmented Reality. Ubiquitous Media and Reactive Environments. Finn, Sellen & Wilber (Eds.) Video Mediated Communication. Hillsdale, N.J.: Erlbaum (to appear)

4. Wellner, P., Mackay, W., Gould, R.: Computer Augmented Environments: Back to the Real World. Introduction to the special issue. Commun. ACM **36** 7 (1993) 24–26

5. Feiner, S., Macintyre, B., Seligmann, D.: Knowledge-based augmented reality. Commun. ACM **36** 7 (1993) 52–62

6. Fitzmaurice, G.W.: Situated Information Spaces and Spatially Aware Palmtop Computers. Commun. ACM **36** 7 (1993) 38–49

7. Cooperstock, J. R., Tanikoshi, K., Beirne, G., Narine, T., Buxton, W.: Evolution of a reactive Environment. Proceedings of CHI'95, New York: ACM Press 170–177

8. Stafford-Fraser, Q.: BrightBoard: A Video-Augmented Environment. Proceedings of CHI'96, New York: ACM Press 134–141

9. MacIntyre, B., Feiner, S.: Future multimedia user interfaces. Multimedia Systems 4 (1996) 250–268

10. Burdea, G.C.: Force and Touch Feedback for Virtual Reality. Wiley, New York. 339 p.

11. Carlsson, C., Hagsand, O.: DIVE-a Multi-User Virtual Reality System. In Proceedings of the IEEE Virtual Reality Annual Symposium (VRAIS'93), September 18–22, 1993, Seattle, Washington, USA 394–400

12. Shaw, C., Green, M., Liand, J., Sun, Y.: Decoupled Simulation in Virtual Reality with The MR Toolkit. ACM Transactions on Information Systems 11 3 (1993) 287–317

13. Snowdon, D., West, A.: The AVIARY VR-system. A Prototype Implementation. In Proceedings of the 6th ECRIM Workshop, June, 1994, Stockholm, Sweden

14. Tarr, R., Jacobs, J.: Distributed Interactive Simulation (DIS). In Proceedings of the 1994 Summer Computer Simulation Conference, July 18–20, La Jolla, California, USA

15. Agrawal, P., Hyden, E., Krzyzanowski, P., Mishra, P., Srivastava, M., Trotter, J.: SWAN: A Mobile Multimedia Wireless Network. IEEE Personal Communications, 3 2 (1996) 18–33

16. http://isw3.aist-nara.ac.jp/IS/Chihara-lab/

17. Pyssysalo, T., Kinnunen, U., and Pulli, P.: Real-Time Distributed Virtual Reality. In Proceedings of the 2nd International Workshop on Mechatronical Computer Systems for Perception and Action, February 10–12, 1997, Pisa, Italy 3–11

18. Pyssysalo, T., Pulli, P., A Picocell-Based Architecture for a Real-Time Mobile Virtual Reality. 9th Euromicro Workshop on Real-Time Systems. Toledo, Spain, 10-13 June, 1997. Pp. 144- 151.

19. Leskelä, J., Partially Decentralised Wireless Routing for Distributed Augmented Reality Applications. Proceedings of the First International Conference on Information, Communications and Signal Processing (ICICS97), p. 210-214, Singapore, 1997.

20. Ghai, R., Singh, S.: An Architecture and Communication Protocol for Picocellular Networks. IEEE Personal Communications 1 3 (1994) 36–46

21. Liu, G., Maguire, G. Jr.: A Virtual Distributed System Architecture for Supporting Global-Distributed Mobile Computing. Technical Report TRITA-IT 95-01, Royal Institute of Technology 1994

22. Bible, S., Zyda, M., Brutzman, D.: Using Spread-Spectrum Ranging Techniques for Position Tracking in a Virtual Environment. In Proceedings of the 1995 Workshop on Networked Realities, October 26–28, 1995, Boston, MA, USA

On Business Intelligence Systems

Won Kim

Cyber Database Solutions, Inc.
2499 S. Capital of Texas Highway, bldg. B, 201
Austin, Texas 78746
tel: 512-329-9034
won.kim@cyberdb.com

Abstract. Business enterprises today face unprecedented competitive pressures, as the pace of advances in computer and information technologies has become maddeningly fast and the standard of living and life styles of consumers have undergone significant changes. Enterprises can gain competitive edges if they can set their business strategies for winning new customers, retaining existing customers, and reducing the cost of doing business better. One promising way is for enterprises to base these strategies on business intelligence that can be analyzed and deduced from the vast amounts of data at their disposal. Today, advances in information technology have made available such technologies as data mining, online analytical processing, and data warehousing. It is now possible to construct business intelligence systems using these technologies. In this paper, we will describe what business intelligence systems are, examine the enabling technologies, and outline several key issues that need to be given serious considerations in successfully building and using business intelligence systems.

1 Introduction

Most medium to large business enterprises today have vast volumes of data at their disposal. These include data about personnel, customers, suppliers, business partners, marketing and sales records and plans, and even data available from other enterprises. In today's competitive market for products and services, those enterprises that can effectively manage these data and obtain business intelligence from the data can realize significant competitive edges, increased revenue/profit, and cost reduction. Business intelligence can help enterprises to set strategic directions and positioning in the market place, to win new customers and retain existing customers, and to reduce the cost of doing business. Enterprises may win new customers and retain existing customers by better understanding the buying behavior and vendor loyalty of customers, and devising more effective and appropriate strategies and tactics for marketing and sales. Enterprises may reduce the cost of doing business by eliminating or re-directing ill-conceived marketing campaigns, by detecting fraud, and by intelligent financial risk analysis in product planning, staff hiring, production capacity planning, etc.

This paper explores feasibility for developing business intelligence systems. A business intelligence system is a software/hardware system that makes it possible for end-users (knowledge workers) to obtain business intelligence by analyzing vast amounts of base data from many different business perspectives, and by discovering significant business information that is not explicitly stored in the base data. Users can use such business intelligence in devising strategies for conducting business in the most profitable way possible.

A successful business intelligence system requires three elements: a sufficient amount of relevant base data, a technology infrastructure that enables the gathering of business intelligence from the base data, and technical expertise in properly organizing the data and integrating the technology infrastructure components. Fortunately, there already exist an adequate technology infrastructure that can be used to derive business intelligence from base data. The technology infrastructure includes three key components. They are the data warehouse (DW) technology for consolidating data from multiple data sources; the multi-dimensional database (MDDB) technology for organizing base data into a number of dimensions (perspectives/views) relevant to particular applications and the online analytical processing (OLAP) technology for querying and analyzing a multi-dimensional database; and the data mining technology for deriving useful conclusions or predictions about relevant business factors from historical data.

In Section 2, we outline an architecture and use of business intelligence systems. In Sections 3, 4, and 5, we examine the status, open technical issues, and product selection criteria for each of the three enabling technologies, data warehousing, OLAP, and data mining, respective. Section 6 summarizes the paper.

2 Constructing and Using a Business Intelligence System

Figure 1 illustrates the software architecture of business intelligence systems. A collection of domain-specific business intelligence applications are built on top of a data mining engine and an OLAP engine, both of which run off a data warehouse or a data mart (a "departmental" data warehouse). The data warehouse / data mart is created by consolidating base data from a wide variety of relevant data sources.

Each business intelligence application is a domain-specific shrink-wrapped software product that shields end-users from the conceptual and product complexities of the underlying technology components. It is very difficult for end-users to properly design and administer a large data warehouse, to analyze a vast amount of business data from many (perhaps hundreds) dimensions directly using an OLAP tool, and to provide many business factors (perhaps hundreds) to a data mining tool and to interpret and fine-tune the knowledge model obtained.

There are two types of users of business intelligence systems: end-user (knowledge worker) and data administrator. The data administrator must design and administer the data warehouse and the metadata, using a DW product. The design and administration tool must provide a rich set of functions via a graphical interface.

The knowledge worker runs a business intelligence application. The knowledge worker's analysis requests are taken by the OLAP engine, which translates them into a series of queries against the data warehouse, and returns the results in business terms that the knowledge worker can easily relate to. The knowledge worker's requests for a knowledge model are taken by the data mining engine, which runs an appropriate knowledge discovery algorithm against the data warehouse. In general, he ends up invoking the OLAP and data mining engines alternatingly, so that he may verify the results of data mining through the use of OLAP tool, thereby iteratively refining the results of data mining. He views and saves the results of his session using a combination of the OLAP and data mining user-interface tools, and desktop productivity applications with which he is already familiar, such as a word processor, a spreadsheet, a personal database, etc.

The knowledge worker needs to understand the metadata for the data warehouse, enough to be able to formulate (graphically) queries, and to be able to interpret the results of data mining in the application's business context. In using these products, he may on occasion need to consult with application domain experts and data administrators.

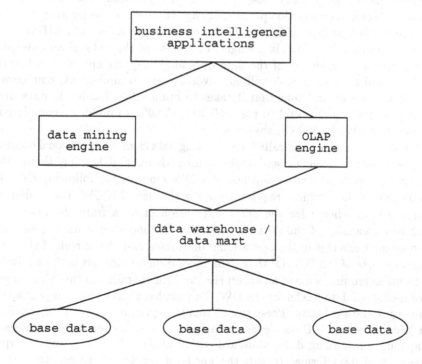

Fig. 1. Architecture of Business Intelligence Systems

The DW component consolidates base data from multiple data sources, including files, relational databases, and hierarchical databases. Consolidation of the base data involves the creation of a global database schema, copying and/or summarization of base data, and cleansing of base data (i.e., fixing incorrect data, filling in missing data, making format changes for some of the data). A DW also provides to the OLAP and data mining components the metadata for all accessible base data. The DW component will include a gateway for each data source, and a gateway controller that controls all gateways. DW vendors typically provide gateways to common data sources, and some of them even offer a gateway controller.

For OLAP analysis, the OLAP engine must be given multi-dimensional views of the consolidated data. Business data may need to be analyzed from many dimensions (e.g., for sales data, the sales region, time, and product line). The number of dimensions may range from only a few to hundreds.

3 Data Warehouse/Data Mart Technology

3.1 Definition and Status

The data warehouse technology is used to design and create an enterprise database for analysis using OLAP and data mining tools. The operational databases of an enterprise are the primary base of a DW. The operational databases are ones that OLTP (online transaction processing) applications access for everyday business. Although a precise distinction between a DW and a data mart (DM) is not available, intuitively, a DW is a single warehouse of the data of an enterprise, while a DM is a warehouse of the data of a single department of an enterprise. A DW is said to require $3-5 million, several years to implement, and grow to terabytes. The cost and time that it takes to build a DW has led to data marts recently. A data mart is said to cost $50,000 -150,000 to build, be completed in 90 days, and have 50-100 Gigabytes.

A DW is constructed basically by extracting data from the operational databases of an enterprise, cleansing and transforming them, and loading them. More specifically, the construction and use of a DW requires the following elements: an analysis of the business requirements for the use of a DW, the design of a metadata (the schema for the DW), extraction of data from the operational databases, cleansing of the data extracts and the operational data, monitoring of subsequent changes in the operational databases and the refresh of the corresponding parts of the DW. Of these, the most difficult element is the analysis of the business requirements of an enterprise, and the mapping of these business requirements to a data model for the DW. The most tedious element is perhaps the cleansing of data extracts. These two elements require a large dose of consulting and training services. Data cleansing includes correcting wrong or inconsistent data, filling in missing data, standardization of data format and data typing, conversion of data format to suit the needs of the OLAP tools, etc. Further, the creation and use of a DW requires not just the purchase of hardware and software (database server, OLAP tools, DW creation tools, system management tools, etc.), but a continuous training of staff in the use of the DW and the software tools, and in the disciplined and correct use of the operational databases and the DW.

The database server technology, which is the core of the data warehouse technology, has become quite mature during the past decade (mainly to satisfy the performance and scalability demands of the OLTP applications). The technology includes integration with TP (transaction processing) monitors (e.g., Tuxedo, Encina, Top End, Forte); three-tier client/server architecture, multiple server process architecture, migration to parallel computers (Symmetric Multiprocessors (SMPs), Cluster SMPs, and even Massively Parallel Processors (MPPs)), parallel and pipelined query processing, parallel and asynchronous disk I/O, etc.

The DW technology is already in increasing use, and its use is expected to increase dramatically in the next several years to $7 billion by 1999. Vendors include all RDB server vendors (Oracle, Informix, Sybase, IBM), NCR, Tandem, Prism Solutions, Informatica, Mentor Communications, Platinum, Evolutionary Technology, etc. RDB vendors IBM and Sybase, and SMP (Symmetric Multiprocessor) vendor Sequent Computer offer "DW Bundles". A DW bundle is a package of (hardware), a database server, tools for extracting, transforming and cleansing data, and OLAP tools. Vendors that offer only data transformation and cleansing products include Trinzic, Apertus Technologies, Information Builders, etc.

3.2 Technical Issues

First, we must recognize that the DMs must be derived from a DW. Some people think that the customers can skip the DW, and go directly to the construction of a DM. If an enterprise only needs one DM, then that DM is in fact the DW of the enterprise. However, if an enterprise constructs more than one DM, one after another, without first having designed a DW, then the enterprise will probably end up with a number of separate DMs that eventually need to be "integrated into a single DW." A DM should really be created within the framework of an enterprise DW.

Second, most of today's DWs and DMs are based on RDBs. They extract data mostly from operational RDBs. They also store the data extracts in some RDBs. In other words, they extract data from RDBs, only to store them in an RDB! The next-generation DWs and DMs will be based on object-relational databases (ORDBs) with multimedia and complex data management capabilities.

Third, a DW often needs to be accessed from a number of different dimensions. This in turn suggests that the data in a DW should be organized in a multidimensional structure to allow for fast access to queries from any of the perspectives. This is what led to the development of the multidimensional database (MDDB) technology. Unfortunately, the current multidimensional database products, although successful in providing efficient retrieval from multidimensional databases, cannot match the maturity of the relational database products in all other standard database services and supported platforms. In theory, a DW should be stored in a multidimensional database for use by OLAP tools. But in practice, most users end up using relational databases (RDBs) and pay the performance penalty of multi-table joins. Most MDDBs are single-user systems and are tuned for multidimensional data access only.

3.3 Importance of Relevant Data and Database Design

One of the primary measures of success for business intelligence systems is the quality of the business intelligence users can extract from the base data. Unless the database contains "sufficient" and "relevant" data, the results of OLAP or data mining sessions are not useful. Simply put, if a DW has "garbage", only "garbage" can be extracted from it. The data administrator must ensure that the DW contains relevant and correct data, that the database be optimally designed for a given application, and for OLAP support, the multi-dimensional model of data be provided, directly or indirectly. Let us examine these issues further.

1. **relevant and correct base data:** It is crucial for the base data to contain a maximum amount of relevant and correct data, but a minimum amount of redundant, irrelevant, or incorrect data, for the application area of the end-users (e.g., demand forecast for Windows/NT, or online sales of Pentium Pro-based PCs). The base data may include customer survey data captured in computer files, technology forecast data stored in relational databases, key stock market data around the world, key economic growth indicator data, subscription and usage data for the internet, subscription data for IT publications, curriculum data in high schools and universities, etc. The data administrator, with help from application domain experts, will need to select relevant data sources and identify relevant parts of the data sources for inclusion in the data warehouse.

2. **optimal database design:** The data that is actually stored in a data warehouse consists of copies of some of the base data, summarization of some of the base data, corrections to some of the base data, consolidations of some of the base data, business rules that led to the creation of the data, etc. Since the data analysis leading up to business intelligence is based on the data warehouse, it is obviously critical that this be prepared properly. The data administrator must see that the metadata satisfy the data analysis needs, and the stored data be sufficient and correct. Further, he must see that the metadata and the stored data both be organized for efficient access (i.e., fast processing of end-user queries); to do this, he must design the metadata to match anticipated access patterns, and also create and manage appropriate access methods (i.e., indexes, sorting) on the stored data. If the base data contains a large amount of relevant textual documents, the data warehouse will need to be connected with a text plug-in (i.e., a link to an information retrieval system).

3. **multi-dimensional data:** The metadata and the stored data need to be organized to support multi-dimensional access (as well as the standard single-dimensional access). Given that the server of choice for managing the data

warehouse will most likely be a relational database, the multi-dimensional database should be designed as views over the stored relational database.

3.4 Key Selection Criteria for Products

The most important criterion for the selection of a data warehouse product is performance and scalability. Scalability is the ability of a product to deliver a satisfactory performance as the amount of data becomes very large (in the terabyte range), and there is a significant number of simultaneous users (tens or hundreds). A product that works well with a few simultaneous users and a small amount of data often becomes unusable as the number of simultaneous users goes past 10 users and the amount of data grows beyond 10 gigabytes. The number of simultaneous users of the business intelligence system is not expected to be large. However, the amount of data is expected to be very large. The large amount of data, and the processing power required for data mining and OLAP queries against such data, may even require a symmetric multiprocessor (SMP) to run the data warehouse server.

4 Decision Support System/Online Analytical Processing Technology

4.1 Definition and Status

The OLAP technology is an extension of the longstanding decision support systems (DSS) and executive information system (EIS) technology. DSS applications are essentially querying and reporting tools that access and analyze data in relational database (RDB) tables (i.e., two-dimensional data). OLAP tools access and analyze multidimensional data. The multidimensional data are created either as views on RDB tables in an RDB, or stored in a multidimensional database. OLAP technology is called ROLAP (relational OLAP) if it uses an RDB; and MOLAP (multidimensional OLAP), if it uses an MDDB. The OLAP technology makes it easy to query a database from various dimensions; for example, report sales results for a company by product line, by territory (East, West; state; city), and by time (year; quarter; month; week). DSS/OLAP tools allow the users to issue sequences of queries in order to verify certain hypotheses; for example, the effects on sales revenue of expanding or reducing the sales force in each region.

OLAP products provide rich sets of analysis functions on the data, including automatic generation of database queries (SQL), and mathematical functions for transforming stored data into business data formats. They also provide rich graphical interfaces for presenting the data. However, perhaps the most important facilities in OLAP products are the multi-dimensional data modeling and manipulation facilities. The number of dimensions may range from a few to hundreds, depending on applications. OLAP tools allow users to analyze data (called metrics, such as revenue, market share, profit margin) from any dimension (e.g., time, region, or product line), and drill-down along each dimension (e.g., in a time dimension, along year, month, week, and day) and pivot (changing from one dimension to another, during analysis).

Vendors include Arbor Software, Andyne Technology, MicroStrategy, Cognos, Business Objects, Pilot Software, SAS Institute, Kenan Systems, Comshare, Information Builders, Platinum Technology, Progress Software, Informix, Oracle, etc.

4.2 Key Selection Criteria for Products

There are a few important criteria for selecting an OLAP product. They include performance and scalability, functionality, ease of use, and vendor viability. The performance of an OLAP product in responding to queries against very large, many-dimensioned data is particularly critical. OLAP products often attempt to strike a balance between the performance advantage of pre-computing all multi-dimensional data and the flexibility of storing only the metric data.

Functionality refers to the richness of functions that a product provides to allow the users to accomplish their objectives. If a product is missing a particular function that a user needs, the user must either find a work-around or implement the function within the user's own application. The functionality that OLAP products provide include automatic generation of SQL queries against the data warehouse, automatic conversion of the result data into a business data format that the end-users can naturally relate to, and sophisticated mathematical analysis functions to apply to retrieved data.

Ease of use refers to the availability of easy-to-use tools and/or intuitive graphical interface for each of the two types of users: the knowledge worker and the data administrator. For the data administrator, the ability to create, modify, and view the metadata is crucial. For the knowledge worker, the abilities to view the metadata, to formulate powerful queries against it, and to view the results of each query are important. Of particular importance is the ease with which the users can manage many-dimensional data. Although OLAP products typically have no limit on the number of dimensions they support, if the number goes beyond 10, it becomes difficult for user to keep all the dimensions straight in their minds. Further, it is highly desirable that OLAP products be integrated with popular personal productivity applications (e.g., word processor, spread sheet, personal database, etc.), so that the end-users may place the retrieved data or the results of analyses in appropriate personal productivity applications for reporting or future reference.

Given the relative youth of the OLAP industry, long-term viability of the vendors is an important consideration. Continued product maintenance and upgrade (performance and functionality) by the vendors are important, since business intelligence systems must be maintained and upgrade over time.

5 Data Mining Technology

5.1 Definition and Status

The data mining/knowledge discovery technology is used to discover useful patterns in business factors from data stored in a data warehouse. There is a clear difference between data mining and DSS/OLAP. A data mining tool searches for patterns and trends; it does not evaluate any precise query that a user may formulate. A DSS/OLAP tool, on the other hand, evaluates a precise query that a user formulates. Data mining technology has been applied in credit card and insurance claims fraud detection, financial risk analysis, segmenting the market and customer base, predicting customer buying habits, new customer profiling, market-basket analysis, etc.

Data mining techniques have a long history. They include neural networks, decision trees, classification and regression trees (CART), radial basis function network, logistic regression and discrimination, etc. Each of the techniques has advantages and disadvantages relative to one another. For example, the neural network technology is not able to explain its discovery. For this reason, data mining products have mostly used symbolic classifiers using machine-learning technology. Some vendors, such as the SAS Institute, offer a number of techniques, so that an appropriate technique may be used for a given application.

Most of the current data mining products are not ready for use in general business settings. In order for a data mining product to generate a result (prediction variable), it may require potentially many business factors (as few as 20 to as many as 2,000), depending on the application's objective. Vertical applications need to be developed to facilitate the use of the data mining technology in general business settings.

There are tens of vendors that sell data mining software products, and customers are beginning to take advantage of the benefits of such products in their business. They include SAS Institute, Information Harvesting, Intelligence Ware, IBM, DataMind, Trajecta, HyperParallel, Thinking Machines, HNC Software, AcknoSoft, ANGOSS Software, Integral Solutions (UK), MIT gmbH (Germany), Osoft (France), Data Distilleries (The Netherlands), Syllogic (Ireland), etc. Some of the vendors, such as Thinking Machines and HNC Software, had originally started out as vendors of proprietary parallel-processing hardware who have decided to apply their hardware technologies to data mining. Some vendors have started to offer shrink-wrapped applications on top of data mining engines. These include S2 Systems, Kenan Systems, and Holistic Systems; all of them offer applications for database marketing aimed at customer retention and discovery of market segmentations.

5.2 Technical Issues

Although the inner workings of data mining products may appear to be magic to some, just like any modern-day software product, there really is no magic in data mining. We must remember that data mining discovers patterns from a "database", not from "thin air". In other words, there must be "sufficient" types and amount of data in a database, before a mere mortal data mining software can discover any useful pattern. To illustrate this point, suppose that the database of sales in a supermarket only contains the names of products sold and the prices of the products. Then how will a data mining software discover the pattern that a customer who buys diapers on Friday evenings are also likely to buy six packs of beer? It will not. The database needs to hold the names of products sold and the prices of the products, for each customer, for each day.

As another example, a greetings card company has learned that between their best selling cards and worst selling cards, the differences in the design, style, and verse of the cards are quite small. They would like to discover these differences, so that they can print more of their best selling cards and less of their worst selling cards. However, as long as their database of greeting cards they sell consists only of the design, style, and verse for each type of card, the data mining software they may run against the database is highly unlikely to discover the differences. Perhaps customers are not attracted to the particular shade of the background color of the card, or to the particular brand of humor in the verse (just as some of David Letterman's jokes go over some people's heads), or to the fact that the card is printed on recycled paper, or whatever.

The customer must capture as much "relevant" data as practicable about their products, their business, their customers, and circumstances that have bearing on their business. However, having "too much" data can often decrease the predictive power of data mining. "Too much" data means "irrelevant" data or multiple representations of the same data. What constitutes "sufficient" and "relevant" data that can yield the best result depends on the applications to a large extent. For example, such factors as the weather (temperature, humidity) and how well college and professional sports teams do may be significant in beer sales, but not in greeting card sales.

We must keep in mind that data mining software often is not terribly useful when used by itself. It must in general be used in conjunction with a Decision Support System (DSS) / Online Analytical Processing (OLAP) software. A DSS/OLAP tool can/should be used in two ways in conjunction with data mining. One way is to analyze the business consequences of the results of data mining. Data-mining software, when used against a reasonable database, will yield some potentially useful patterns. If the customers are to take business benefits from the patterns mined, they will in general need to perform detailed analyses of their business using a DSS/OLAP software of their choice. If these decisions are not made properly, the patterns mined would have served no useful purpose.

Another way in which a DSS/ OLAP software can be used in conjunction with data mining is to verify the user's hypothesis about his business before data mining is done. As remarked earlier, it is difficult to determine what constitutes "sufficient" and "relevant" data for effective data mining. The user may run a DSS/OLAP software to determine the types of data that are relevant to his business. If the user runs his data-mining tool after going through this exercise, he may significantly enhance the quality of the results obtained.

The current data mining products are limited to finding patterns and trends from a database of formatted alphanumeric data, that is, relational database records. In other words, they are pretty much useless against a database of text documents, images, audios, videos, etc. This reflects the current state of database servers. As the database technology transitions to object-relational databases (ORDBs) with multimedia plug ins, data mining products will need to evolve so that they may find patterns and trends in text documents, images, audios, videos, etc. that are stored in a database. Today, technologies for searching precisely-specified patterns (e.g., a combination of the words "football" and "beer" in a document) or fuzzy patterns (e.g., an image of a red fish, a drawing of a face with a scar on the cheek) or even "theme" (related) patterns (e.g., documents that discuss holidays and shopping together) already exist or are starting to emerge for text documents and images from vendors such as Verity, Fulcrum, Excalibur, etc. Some of these technologies are now being "attached" (not integrated) to database servers as multimedia plug ins.

5.3   Key Selection Criteria for Products

There are a few key criteria for selecting a data mining product. These include predictive power, performance and scalability, and ease of use. Ease of use is particularly important with the data mining component, because of the large number of business factors to be input and the complexity of the inductive rules that data mining products generate.

6   Summary

Today, we have rather mature data warehousing technology to consolidating data from a wide variety of base data sources, and organizing it against expected access patterns for different types of application. We also have rather mature OLAP technology for easily analyzing multi-dimensional data stored in a data warehouse. Further, data mining technology has become commercially available to enable discovery of business-significant information from a data warehouse. With the availability of the OLAP and data mining technologies, now it is within our reach to create business intelligence systems that will allow non-specialist knowledge workers to gather significant information relevant to achieving business competitive advantages from raw base data. Further, business intelligence systems should be designed for a collection of domain-specific applications, rather than for a generic application, since the use of data mining technology in particular requires deep domain expertise.

Business intelligence systems can shield users from the technical intricacies and complexities involved in using each of the three technology components. However, the construction of such business intelligence systems require careful design of the data warehouse; an optimal schema design, cleansing of base data, inclusion of application-relevant base data, etc. Further, the component products must be selected that satisfy several key criteria: a data warehouse server must meet performance and scalability, and ease of administration requirements; an OLAP product must meet provide high performance and scalability (with respect to not only the database size but also the number of dimensions in metric data), ease of analysis and presentation, and richness in query and analysis functions; a data mining product must offer high predictive power, as well as high performance and scalability.

Supporting Collaboration through Teleproximity

John C. Tang

Sun Microystems, Inc., JavaSoft Division, 901 San Antonio Road,
Palo Alto, CA 94303 USA

Abstract. Giving distributed collaborators a sense of working near each other involves making it easy to: initiate contact, come in contact at shared events, and set up contact through shared awareness. Three prototypes are discussed that illustrate each of these attributes. *Montage* provides an interface for desktop video conferencing. *Forum* allows people to participate in video-based presentations from their computer desktop. *Piazza* provides shared awareness among distributed group members to help set up good opportunities for making contact. Reflecting on how these prototypes were used raises opportunities for future development.

1 The Need to Support Collaboration

The development of internet technologies has enabled work groups to disperse over large distances while at the same time fueled the demand for higher fidelity connections among distributed group members to support productive collaboration. As companies incorporate sites located around the globe, users of mobile computing devices, and telecommuters working from home, they have come to rely more on network technologies to help them conduct their work. While networks have become a proven mechanism for efficiently distributing electronic raw data around the world, more support is needed to help distributed groups work together productively. Network technologies have the potential to enable distributed groups to enjoy the rich communication opportunities that physical workplaces usually afford. It is this sense of closeness (*proximity*) over distance (*tele-*) that I want to refer to as *teleproximity*.

Research (Kraut et al., 1990a, 1990b, Whittaker et al., 1994) and common experience indicate that being in close proximity enables group members to easily and effortlessly communicate through formal and informal means. Proximally located group members drop by each others' offices to see if they' re available for an impromptu discussion, formally schedule a meeting to talk about a predetermined topic, leave notes and e-mail messages to provide ongoing status, and use many other communication options. They unexpectedly encounter each other at organizational meetings or shared spaces (such as the company cafeteria), sometimes resulting in task-related discussions. They are often aware of each others' comings and goings to know when would be likely and convenient times for establishing contact with each other. The challenge of providing teleproximity is supporting these kinds of facile communication avenues among workers who are scattered over physical distances. Research has begun to explore how technology, especially video, can be applied to address this issue (Bly et al, 1993, Fish et al., 1993, Finn et al., 1997).

I have been involved in a research group that developed several different prototypes to support collaboration among teams distributed over distance. Our work always began by studying actual collaborative activity to identify ways in which they needed more support to conduct their work. These studies guided the design and development of a functional prototype that applied audio, video, shared application, and network technologies to support a more natural collaboration across distance. We deployed these prototypes and qualitatively and quantitatively studied people's everyday use of the technology. Studying the prototype in use not only helped us learn how to refine its design, but also deepened our understanding of collaborative activity.

Our work has identified three key aspects in bringing distributed groups into teleproximity:

- making it easy to initiate contact
- enabling unintended contact at shared events
- facilitating contact through shared awareness

This chapter will describe how three prototypes illustrate each of the aspects above and discuss what we learned from our experiences.

2 Initiating Contact

One of the basic communication mechanisms that physical dispersion disrupts is the ability to easily initiate contact with another colleague. Working in close proximity affords a range of communication options, allowing colleagues to pick the most appropriate method for the occasion. Being in proximity enables them to frequently drop into each other's office when an issue arises for discussion. These impromptu interactions can happen so frequently that they can even take the shape of one ongoing conversation that happens in spurts throughout the day (Whittaker et al., 1994).

Once group members are separated across distance, the communication options become more restricted, typically to the telephone, e-mail, video conferencing, fax, and postal mail. Establishing high-fidelity interactive communication may require more planning and formal procedures (e.g., scheduling video conferencing facilities in advance). The communication mechanisms that distributed workers can conveniently use are typically lower in fidelity (e.g., the phone lacks visual information, e-mail lacks the affect of intonation). Making it easier to initiate contact over distance is one way in which technology can lower the barriers to interaction. Even simple accelerators, such as the "speed dial" buttons on telephones and shorthand aliases for e-mail addresses, are widely popular because they reduce the cognitive effort and time of initiating contact.

Our group's experience with a desktop video conferencing prototype indicated that people liked and used the ability to make audio-video connections on demand among computer desktops (Tang & Isaacs, 1993). However, the fact that our prototype's interface for establishing a desktop video conference was just a little more balky than making a telephone call meant that users were more likely to simply use the phone. They would only go through the extra effort to set up a desktop video conference when they expected visual communication to be important. In fact, sometimes users would call on the telephone to verify that people were available for a desktop video conference before actually initiating the conference. This led us to the design of a prototype called Montage, which was designed to make it easy to initiate desktop video conference connections.

2.1 Montage Design

Montage (Tang & Rua, 1994) provided an easy way to make audio-video connections between computer desktops and integrated other communication applications for coordinating future interactions. Montage used momentary, reciprocal glances among networked, media-equipped workstations to make it easy to peek into someone's office. It was modeled on the process of walking down a hallway to visit a colleague in her office. If you peeked in and saw that it was not a good time to interact (e.g., not in the office, busy on the phone), you might pass by the door without stopping. If you found her in, you might pause at the doorway to indicate what you wanted to talk about before entering in for a discussion. By basing Montage on the hallway model, we hoped to provide a familiar way of increasing the accessibility of colleagues without disrupting their privacy.

To initiate contact in Montage, a user typically selected the name of a person they wished to glance from a menu. Within a few seconds, a sound notified the recipient of the onset of a glance and video windows faded-in on both users' screens (Fig. 1). The fade-in effect provided a graceful sense of approach for the people involved in a glance. Either party could acknowledge the glance by pressing the audio button to open an audio channel. If neither party enabled the audio channel, the glance faded away after 8 seconds.

Once either person pressed the audio button, a two-way audio-video connection was established. The relatively small (128 x 120 pixels) video windows of the glance were intended to support short, lightweight interactions. If participants wanted a more extended interaction, either one could move into a full-featured desktop video conference by pressing the Visit button. A visit offered enlarged video windows (256 x 240 pixels) and access to tools for sharing bitmap graphics and short text messages (Stickup notes). Glances and visits were ended by pressing a button that immediately dismissed the video window.

If the glance showed that the person was not available, the buttons along the bottom of the glance window (see Fig. 1) provided quick access to browse her on-line calender, send her a short text note (Stickup), or send her an e-mail message. The on-line calendar and e-mail functionality were adaptations of existing tools widely used in our company's computer environment. We developed Stickup, which enabled users to type a text note that appeared in a popup window on the recipient's screen (shown in Fig. 2). Stickups also included an embedded "Glance Back" button that quickly started a Montage glance back to the person

352

Fig. 1. Montage glance window, showing the video glance, the audio button, and the buttons for initiating e-mail, calendar browse, and Stickups.

who posted the Stickup, and a Reply button that opened a Stickup to post back. By integrating quick access to these other communication tools, we hoped that Montage would help coordinate opportune times to make future contact.

Since Montage allowed audio-video connections with any other user, it was important to enable users to protect their privacy. Montage addressed this issue in part by building on existing social mechanisms for protecting privacy. Because all Montage glances were reciprocal, users could see if anyone was glancing at them. Just as it is considered rude to stand outside someone's door and stare in, it was equally impolite to do so through Montage, which provided the aural and visual cues to make such eavesdropping obvious. This symmetry enabled users to socially negotiate their privacy. In addition, Montage offered a 'do not disturb' mode that blocked any incoming glances.

2.2 Montage Use

To learn how people would use Montage in their daily work, we deployed the prototype in an existing working group (Tang et al., 1994). We observed a group of ten people who were distributed among three buildings on a campus site using Montage over a couple months. Logs of Montage usage demonstrated how frequently attempts to contact someone were unsuccessful. The Montage

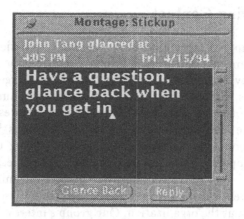

Fig. 2. A Stickup, which pops up on the recipient's screen with embedded Glance Back and Reply buttons to facilitate responding to the message.

logs showed that 75% of the glance attempts were not acknowledged (that is, glances where neither party enabled the audio). This high rate of unacknowledged glances underscored the importance of helping people find opportune times to make future contact. Despite the high likelihood that a glance would not immediately turn into an interaction, people continued to use Montage on a regular basis. We concluded that glancing was sufficiently lightweight and was valuable enough in coordinating future contact that people continued to use it.

The Montage logs showed further evidence of the lightweight nature of interactions in Montage. Of those glances that were acknowledged, the resulting interactions tended to be relatively short, with a median duration of 1 minute 8 seconds. This median compared to 8 minutes 55 seconds in our previous desktop video conferencing prototype, which suggested that Montage glances were used for shorter, more lightweight interactions. Designing the interface to make it easy to initiate glances helped encourage using it for such lightweight interactions.

In the interviews, users were generally enthusiastic about Montage and the visual access provided by the video glances. They felt comfortable using Montage for some interactions that they traditionally reserved for face-to-face visits. They reported that Montage improved communication in the team by making it convenient to contact each other just when an issue arose rather than waiting until they accumulated enough issues to justify making a face-to-face visit.

Both quantitative and qualitative measures indicated that Montage provided a communication medium that was somewhat between face-to-face visits and the phone. Like the phone, it provided quick access to people who were located elsewhere and allowed both participants to remain in their own offices with access to their own resources. Like face-to-face interactions, the video channel in Montage allowed rich interactions and facilitated more frequent, shorter interactions that addressed specific issues just as they arose.

3 Encountering Contact

While Montage supported the kind of one-on-one interaction that is typical of small working teams, we also explored large group interactions that are commonly used to provide a sense of community among a large organization. Presentations, lectures, seminars, and training sessions are common mechanisms for gathering large groups together with some common interest or organizational relationship. These events are important to large groups b ecause they help create common knowledge and shared experiences among the members. They also provide an opportunity to encounter other colleagues, which may result in impromptu work-related interactions. However, as organizations become distributed over different sites, it becomes harder to create these shared experiences for people throughout the organization. Our group's interest in supporting interactions among a distributed large group led to the development of a prototype to enable people from different locations to attend video-based presentations from their computer desktops.

3.1 Forum Design

Forum (Isaacs et al., 1994) was a distributed application that enabled speakers to broadcast talks over a network and enabled audience members to participate in the talks from their workstations. The audience received live audio and video of the speaker as well as the speaker's slides and slide annotations. Audience members could interact with the speaker in three ways:

- speak to the presenter (and audience),
- "vote" anonymously on an issue raised by the speaker, and
- send in written comments.

Speakers gave presentations from a workstation that captured their video and audio to broadcast over the net and provided an interface for controlling Forum. Audience members also sat at their desks and watched the talk through their computer interface. Since they were in a multitasking environment, they could switch their attention between the Forum talk and other applications on their desktop or other activities in their office.

Figure 3 shows the main window of the audience's interface. A window showing a view of the electronic slides would also typically be displayed. The main window showed the video of the speaker, and the controls below it managed the audio parameters. The control panel to the right of the video provided three mechanisms to interact with the speaker: spoken questions, polls, and written comments. An audience member who wanted to speak got in the queue by clicking on the button at the bottom of the window. When the speaker called on her, she pressed and held down the Speak button. As she did so, everyone could hear her speak and see her picture with her name above it. (Fig. 3 shows Ellen Isaacs asking a question.) The poll meter in the upper right showed how many people were voting yes or no on a question posed by the speaker. To vote on

Fig. 3. The interface for Forum allows audience members to watch the video and interact with the speaker.

a poll, an audience member clicked on the "Yes" or "No" option and the bar chart changed accordingly. To submit a written comment, the user clicked on the Comments button, typed a comment into the popup window that appeared, and sent it to the speaker. Audience members saw the speaker's current slide in the slides window, and they could also click on a thumbnail to view a different slide at any time.

Audience members could also find out who else was watching a presentation by clicking on the Audience button, which brought up the Audience window, shown in Fig. 4. In that window, users could click on a name to see that person's icon, their location and phone number. They could send that person a short message by clicking on the "Message" button, which brought up a small window pre-addressed to that recipient. When they sent the message, it popped up on the other person's screen in a small window with a Reply button. These features were aimed at supporting the kind of networking contact among audience members that often occurs before, during, and after a large group meeting.

3.2 Forum Use

The use of Forum was observed using a variety of formal an informal approaches over several months (Isaacs et al., 1994, Isaacs et al., 1995). Most of the studies focused on the asymmetrical nature of video in Forum, where the audience could see the speaker via video, but the speaker only got verbal and written comments

Fig. 4. The Forum audience list shows the other attendees and provides an interface for interacting with them.

and poll responses from the audience. Consequently, audiences were enthusiastic about Forum and in most cases preferred it to local talks, whereas speakers found it less rewarding to give a talk over Forum than in a face-to-face setting.

One of the more subtle insights we learned about large group presentations is that much more is happening than just the transfer of information between the speaker and the audience. The audience is also learning about each other by sharing a common experience and watching how other audience members react. Furthermore, gathering together at the same time in the same place provides opportunities to interact with other people that often prompts serendipitous interactions. Seeing someone at a talk may provide the opportunity to discuss a pending issue. Or the talk may bring together people that share some interests but do not see each other frequently, providing opportunities to catch up with each other. The networking time that happens before and after large meetings often accomplishes work that is unrelated to the purpose of the meeting, but simply a result of encountering other people at the event. Forum explored supporting this type of encountering contact through the audience list and the ability to pass messages among the audience. In some ways, finding someone to talk to in a Forum audience was easier than finding them in a crowded physical meeting room. The list allowed convenient browsing of all the audience members (ordered alphabetically), and passing a message to them could be done at any time, rather than having to wait for a break in the event and negotiating an opportune moment to start a conversation. However, the message passing mechanism in Forum was not on the primary user interface for Forum, and many users may not have been aware of the mechanism or how to use it. In a study of seven Forum talks, an average of 13% of the audiences used the text message feature. Those users sent an average of 2.9 messages per person during the talk (Isaacs et al., 1995). Those who did use the text messages reported that they thought they were an effective means of communicating with other audience members. However, passing text-only messages is a much lower fidelity interaction than face-to-face conversations.

4 Setting Up Contact

Our experience with Montage and Forum helped us recognize the importance of supporting the work of setting up contact. In Montage, we saw that most attempts to make contact with someone were not initially successful, and so we integrated mechanisms to make it easy to coordinate future contacts. In Forum, we noticed that large group shared events provided an opportunity to make contact with others participating in the event. The research literature has begun to draw attention to the importance of interactions that occur opportunistically when people happen to see each other (Kraut et al., 1990b, Isaacs et al., 1997). When groups are co-located, people often "run into each other" in the halls, at the photocopier, in the cafeteria, and other places besides organized meetings. A small but important percentage of the time, they start up conversations that, over time, turn out to be significant to the coordination, productivity, and well-being of a group or community (Kraut et al., 1990b, Kraut & Streeter, 1995, Whittaker et al., 1994).

Workers who are co-located not only have the opportunity to physically encounter each other, but often have an awareness of each others' interests and work rhythms to increase the likelihood of a productive serendipitous interaction. We set out to explore ways of enabling these unintended interactions for groups with members who are distributed among different locations with a prototype called Piazza.

4.1 Piazza Design

Piazza's approach (Isaacs et al., 1996) was to use networked computers to provide opportunities to encounter others through tasks and activities accomplished on-line. As people go about their tasks, it would be useful to know who else is working "nearby" on similar tasks. Every now and then, this awareness of someone else working nearby may result in a serendipitous interaction: to ask a question, find out about the other person's work, or to coordinate activity.

The goal was to integrate Piazza throughout the applications on the desktop, so that people were able to stay aware of others as they went about their usual activity.

They did not have to go to a special place to get this awareness. When they encountered someone else while engaged in a task, the shared task gave them a context that might naturally prompt reasons to start an interaction. The design made it easy for people to enter into interactions once they encountered each other. Adding these elements together, Piazza strove to make interactions between remote colleagues in a distributed environment become as likely and natural as those between co-located ones.

The two main components of Piazza that are most relevant to the issues discussed in this chapter are:

- Encounter, which enabled people to be aware of and easily contact other people who were conceptually "nearby", and
- Gallery, which enabled people to stay aware of and easily contact a pre-selected group of people with whom they worked more closely.

Encounter. Encounter was a desktop component that could be included in any application. It enabled users of that application to be aware of others who were nearby. If, for example, a Web browser incorporated Encounter, a user would be able to see other people who were looking at the same page at the same time. If they then moved on to an Encounter-aware file browser, they would see who else was looking at the same directory at that time. As the user moved from application to application, their Encounter window updated to show who was nearby to their current task. The intention was to give users a background sense of who is "there" as they went about their tasks. In most cases, they might simply note the presence of others but not actively interact with them. However, every once in a while, they might decide to contact someone they encountered as they went about their work.

Figure 5 shows an example of an Encounter window associated with the current application, a document editor. It shows that the current user (the person in the upper right) and two other people were viewing the document at this time. If the user were to move to reading a mail message, then his Encounter window would be associated with that mail message, and he would see what other recipients were reading it at the same time.

The small images in the Encounter window were intended to be unobtrusive, but to give some basic information about the nearby users. In particular, the images indicated at a glance whether the person was actively using their computer during the last 30 seconds. If they were active, their image was facing outward looking "alert" (e.g., the bottom and top right icons in Fig. 5). If they were idle for more than 30 seconds, then their image was looking down and to the side, as if they were attending elsewhere (e.g., the top left icon in Fig. 5). If they were interacting on-line with someone else, their image was turned to the side, speaking and with a "talk bubble" over their heads (see Fig. 6). When someone moved from one state to another, a subtle sound announced the change, and their representation slowly faded from one image to another.

At the bottom of Encounter was a shared text area that could be used for a lightweight group discussion. As people typed, their words appeared in the text area, and anyone else in that Encounter could see it. For example, a user might ask whether anyone has read a file in a directory being viewed, and if so, those people might choose to open an audio-video connection. Or the interaction might remain in the shared text area, much like a chat room interaction.

In Encounter, people were considered to be working "nearby" in the strictest sense when they were looking:

- at the same data
- at the same time

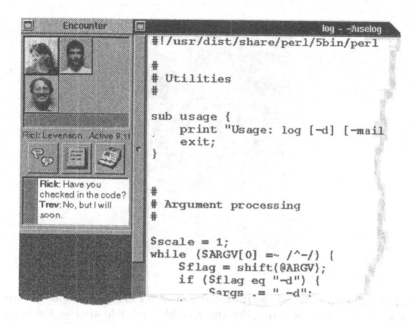

Fig. 5. The Encounter interface shows the user editing a document and seeing two others also accessing it at the same time.

– using the same application.

These three dimensions could be relaxed to gain a broader notion of nearby. Two people might be looking at the same data in different applications (e.g., viewing the same Web page from different browsers), using the same application to manipulate different data (e.g., using the same spell checker on different documents), or looking at the same data at different times (e.g., reading the same e-mail message within a half hour of another). The definition of nearby should be determined separately by each class of application.

Gallery. In addition to the Encounter component, which allowed people to "run into" others, the Gallery component let users remain aware of a pre-defined set of people. Each person populated their Gallery with people they wanted to track, most likely their team members and other close colleagues. The Gallery (shown in Fig. 6) typically remained on the desktop at all times, giving users a low-level awareness of their co-workers' level of activity and the ability to quickly contact those people. The Gallery operated much like Encounter in that it showed who was actively using their computer, who was interacting with others, and who was idle. It also provided the same mechanisms to contact or get information about those people. In addition, Gallery could be used to gain access to Project Rooms, another component of Piazza which defined a place to collect on-line data where

Fig. 6. The Gallery interface shows the activity level of a group of people. The top left and lower middle people are active, the upper middle and right are idle, the lower left is engaged in an on-line interaction, and the lower right is a Project Room.

users could rendezvous to interact with each other and with the data. In Fig. 6, the user included the COCO Project Room in her Gallery so she could quickly go there at any time. The image also indicated whether anyone else was currently in the Project Room, so the user could choose to join simply because she saw that others were generating activity there. Users could also choose to replace their own image with another one, for example, indicating they were out of the office, not to be disturbed, working at home, etc.

The intention of Gallery was to give a member of a distributed group a feeling of awareness similar to what co-located groups share. Over the course of the day, they would have an idea who was working in their offices, who was out for the day, who might have had many meetings, and so on. Kraut, Egido, and Gallagher [1990a] showed that the great majority of interactions that happen at the workplace occur between people located on the same hall. Gallery tried to extend that "hall" to include others who may be doing closely related work but were not physically nearby.

4.2 Piazza Usage

While our group completed a design specification for Piazza and implemented the core features of Encounter and Gallery, we were not able to deploy a fully functional prototype before the group was redirected to work on other things. We would like to see these ideas continue to be investigated in the research community. Our primary goal was to make it possible to have opportunistic and spontaneous interactions with other members of a large distributed community.

Piazza attempted to do so by allowing people to see who else is "nearby" (i.e., working on a similar task at about the same time) and then to naturally transition into an interaction through video, audio, text, or whatever medium was available. By allowing people to see others doing similar tasks, there should be enough context for people to start up lightweight, impromptu interactions.

An interesting issue that would need to be tuned by real use experience is the trade off between making sure that the user saw enough people through Encounter to be interesting and productive, while filtering those encounters so that they were not overwhelming and distracting. Two parameters that affect that trade off is how many people are within Encounter's scope, and how narrowly working "nearby" is defined. If all the Web browsers of the world included Encounter and it was scoped to the world, then users would see far too many strangers every time they looked at a popular Web page. On the other hand, the scope of Encounter must be large enough that users will run into enough people to feel part of a community and lead to occasional interactions. Similarly, if the definition of nearby is too strict, productive encounters with others may be too rare, but if the definition is too lax, the likelihood of a productive encounter decreases. We expect that different applications and different data sources will define their scope and nearby-ness differently, but real use experience is needed to learn how to tune them.

5 Future Directions

Our group's experiences with Montage, Forum, and Piazza have shown the promising potential that network technology has in bringing distributed groups into teleproximity. With the emergence of the World Wide Web and Java™ technologies, we are seeing the development of a platform for supporting collaboration that could span the globe and even cross company boundaries. As we develop this infrastructure, we should ensure that it is easy to: initiate contact with others, come into contact with others who are participating in shared events, and share awareness so that it is easy to set up making contact. I see two opportunities that are ripe for further exploration in this area: providing a standard electronic representation for all the contact information about a person, and applying virtual community technologies to support work activities.

One of the popular features of Montage was integrating together all the relevant mechanisms for contacting people via a computer into a single point of contact. If a glance showed that a person was currently not available for interaction, a user could send e-mail, browse their calendar, or send a pop-up note to the other person without having to separately open those applications. A more powerful notion would be to standardize on a representation of all contact information. We can expect that most contact mechanisms will be mediated by computer control, especially as telephony becomes integrated into the computer platform. Standardizing on a representation would facilitate easy exchange of contact information, similar to how business cards are exchanged today. One vision for this kind of user experience was expressed in the People, Places, and Things architecture by Taligent (Cotter, 1995). An emerging standard for the electronic business card is the vCard (http://www.imc.org/pdi/vcardoverview.html). Adopting a standard electronic respresentation for contact information will make it easy to contact others and allow applications to readily integrate contact accessibility and awareness into their programs.

Virtual community technologies have become increasingly popular in the social entertainment and research realms. On-line chat rooms, where people can interactively engage in text conversations with a group of people with some shared interest, have become one of the more popular services of Internet Service Providers. Research communities have explored this style of interaction even further through Multi-User Domains (MUDs) where users navigate through regions in a virtual world and encounter others via text descriptions and commands. The socially rich interactions that occur in MUDs illustrate how even a text-only system can support unplanned interactions and the creation of complex social organizations (Curtis, 1992). More recent graphical virtual communities (Morningstar & Farmer, 1991) add richer visual representations of places and people, making it that much easier to notice and start interactions with others. The popularity of these virtual communities in social entertainment taken together with the research that highlights the untapped potential of unintended interactions in supporting distributed collaboration suggests an opportunity to apply virtual community technologies to more work-related distributed communities. Work groups that are widely distributed yet rely on the timely sharing of information, such as field sales and service organizations, would be promising candidates to investigate. By designing technology that brings distributed group members into teleproximity, we can create collaboration experiences that are more productive and enjoyable.

6 Acknowledgements

Work reported in this chapter was done in collaboration with several colleagues at Sun: Ellen Isaacs, Trevor Morris, Tom Rodriguez, David Gedye, Monica Rua, Andy Hao, Amy Pearl, Alan Ruberg, Rick Levenson, and George Drapeau (who helped with TeX typsetting). Java is a trademark of Sun Microsystems, Inc. A demonstration version of Forum for the Solaris platform, called Lyceum, is available for download at:
http://www.sun.com/solaris/demo/lyceum/

References

Bly, S.A., Harrison, S.R. and Irwin, S.: Media spaces: Bringing people together in a video, audio, and computing Environment. Communications of the ACM **36** (1993) 28-47

Cotter, S. with Potel, M.: A Human Interface for Organizations. in Inside Taligent Technology, Reading, MA: Addison-Wesley Publishing Company (1995) 75-109

Curtis, P.: Mudding: Social Phenomena in Text-Based Virtual Realities. Proceedings of the Conference on Directions and Implications of Advanced Computing (1992)

Finn, K.E., Sellen, A.J. and Wilbur, S.B.: Video-Mediated Communication. Mahwah, NJ: Lawrence Erlbaum Associates, Publishers (1997)

Fish, R., Kraut, R., Root, R. and Rice, R.: . Video as a technology for informal communication. Communications of the ACM **36** (1993) 48–61

Isaacs, E.A., Morris, T., and Rodriguez, T.K.: A Forum for supporting interactive presentations to distributed audiences. Proceedings of the Conference on Computer-Supported Cooperative Work (CSCW) (1994) 405–416

Isaacs, E.A., Morris, T., Rodriguez, T.K and Tang, J.C.: A comparison of face-to-face and distributed presentations. Proceedings of the Conference on Computer-Human Interaction (1995) 354–361

Isaacs, E.A., Tang, J.C. and Morris, T.: Piazza: A desktop environment supporting impromptu and planned interactions. Proceedings of the Conference on Computer-Supported Cooperative Work (CSCW) (1996) 315–324

Isaacs, E.A., Whittaker, S., Frohlich, D., and O'Conaill, B.: Informal communication re-examined: New functions for video in supporting opportunistic encounters. in K. Finn, A. Sellen, and S. Wilbur (Eds.) Video-Mediated Communication. Mahwah, NJ: Lawrence Erlbaum Associates, Publishers (1997) 459–485

Kraut R.E., Egido C. and Galegher J.: Patterns of contact and communication in scientific research collaboration. in J. Galegher and R. Kraut (Eds.) Intellectual teamwork. Hillsdale, NJ: Lawrence Erlbaum Associates, Publishers (1990) 149–171.

Kraut, R.E., Fish, R.S., Root, R.W. and Chalfonte, B.L.:. Informal communication in organizations: Form, function, and technology. in S. Oskamp and S. Spacapan (Eds.) People's Reactions to Technology. Newbury Park: Sage Publications (1990) 145–199

Kraut, R.E. and Streeter, L.A.: Coordination in Software Development. Communications of the ACM **38** (1995) 69–81

Morningstar, C. and Farmer, F.R.: The Lessons of Lucasfilm's Habitat. in M. Benedikt (Ed.) Cyberspace. Cambridge: MIT Press (1991) 273–301.

Tang, J.C. and Isaacs, E.A.: Why do users like video? Studies of multimedia-supported collaboration. Computer Supported Cooperative Work: An International Journal **1** (1993) 163–196

Tang, J.C. and Rua, M.: Montage: Providing teleproximity for distributed groups. Proceedings of the Conference on Computer-Human Interaction (1994) 37–43.

Tang, J.C., Isaacs, E.A. and Rua, M.: Supporting distributed groups with a Montage of lightweight interactions. Proceedings of the Conference on Computer-Supported Cooperative Work (CSCW) (1994) 23–34

Whittaker, S., Frohlich, D., and Daly-Jones, O.: Informal workplace communication: What is it like and how might we support it? Proceedings of the Conference on Computer Human Interaction (1994) 131–137

A Home Office System Based on a Virtual Shared Room: An Environment Corresponding to Degree of Concentration

Shinkuro Honda, Ken-ichi Okada and Yutaka Matsushita

Department of Instrumentation Engineering, Keio University
3-14-1 Hiyoshi, Kouhoku-ku, Yokohama, 223, Japan

Abstract. In this paper, we describe a system that provides a "work-at-home" environment based on a virtual shared room built on a 3D graphics workstation. We realize "Awareness Space" on the system to avoid a tradeoff between providing facility of informal communication and keeping one's workspace from others' awareness information. Also, this system provides the feeling of the own self presence at virtual office by using "around view" and "sound effect".

Introduction

Recent technological advances made it possible to cooperate or communicate among distributed members by using audio, video and other media. Moreover, these technologies enable us to have a home office environment. In addition to supporting cooperative work and formal communication such as a video conferencing system[1][2], much attention is focused on the research of informal communication[3] and providing awareness information.

Our purpose is providing other members' awareness information at a home office and finding a solution about the tradeoff between providing awareness information and securing personal space.

The advantage of home office is as following: decreasing population of large cities, economizing high cost office space, and giving a chance to the people who are not able to work outside. Nevertheless, the disadvantages of home office includes problems such as burden from less communication and an exclusion from society. To avoid these problems, the home office system should support informal communication. Therefore, we have realized a home office system named Valentine(**V**irtual office environment for transmitting information of networked awareness), which enables the home office workers to go to an office in 3D virtual space and work with his/her colleagues. Valentine provides a virtual shared room as a space for working and communicating. Also, the awareness of other members was provided as a trigger for the communication[4].

The environment which workers can plunge into the work largely affect work efficiency. This is a very important factor to an office environment. For example, it might bother workers, if too much awareness information had been given[5]. In

Valentine, we have defined "Awareness Space" to make possible the coexistence of informal communication and work space where workers can concentrate.

In this paper, we explain the features of our work, which realizes "Awareness Space" to avoid the tradeoff between supporting informal communication and securing personal space, and which provides the feeling of their presence at virtual office by using "Around View" and "Sound Effect".

Scheme of a virtual office environment

In Valentine, we use the 3D virtual space to simulate office, and simulate that the workers go there. Compared with existing conference systems or communication systems, Valentine also considers about worker's personal job when user is not communicating with others. In real office, the workers are able to sense the existence of his/her colleagues while working personally and recognize the occurrences in a realtime manner. But actually, home office worker can not feel such things using existing systems. Valentine provides virtual office on the network, and they can go there, exchange greetings, feel atmosphere, and do their work. Every worker is in his/her own home, and has workstation for personal work and for office system. They connect to server which provides virtual office environment to go to work and come together virtually. Valentine enables the user to receive the other colleagues' awareness information and supports communication while they are in the virtual office.

This paper describes how to realize the environment that is mentioned above, how to keep one's personal space from these awareness information, and explains the way of transmitting awareness in detail. In this paper, we propose two techniques "Around View" and "Sound Effect". Next, we describe "Awareness Space" for the solution of the tradeoff between keeping home worker's personal space and providing awareness. After that, we talk about implementation of Valentine and evaluation of our system. Finally, we conclude this paper.

The way of transmitting awareness in detail

We usually feel other members' awareness such as actions and gaze. For this reason, we are able to feel the atmosphere or tension of the real workplace. This also triggers the occurrence of informal communication. In general, simple audio and video transmission have used to provide other's awareness, but compared to the real world office, these are not enough to transmit other members' awareness in detail.

To realize members' awareness which is similar to the real office, we provide interfaces called "Around View" and "Sound Effect".

Around View

Former methods of viewing 3D virtual workspace could not specify what the next person was doing[10]. But in the real world, one is able to recognize if the person next to him/her sits down or stands up without looking. This is because the field of view of human being extends to more than 180 degrees.

If the interface can view more than 180 degrees, the user has no need of turning his virtual body to communicate with next person. This looks very strange in the point of view of other virtual members, since human usually communicate by looking each other's face. Human can clearly recognize the colors and the shapes only about 60 degrees in front. We cannot clearly see the angles more than that, but are adopted more to the movement of objects.

Therefore we have implemented the interface called "Around View" which is based on the field of view of real human. To be more detail, it has a field of view of 180 degrees. But only the middle 60 degrees is shown clearly, and the rest is shown vague gradually as it moves away from the middle.

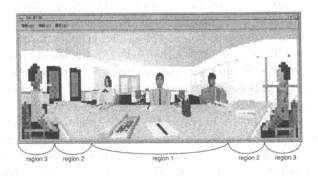

Fig. 1. Office View

Figure 1 shows the office view. The office view is divided into five regions. The center region(Region 1) shows the office view in detail using huge polygons(about 50000). Users can recognize other members' face and other objects in the office clearly. Perspective is set 86 degrees because the larger fields of view introduce serious perspective distortion. Region 2 and 3 are around view that is made of less polygons(about 10000). Perspective of each region is 60 degrees(Figure 2). Around views are mosaicked to express only the movement of members. In this way, Valentine realize the field of view more than 180 degrees. This view realizes seamless office adjusting each region to appropriate width.

By using Around View, the user recognizes the movement and the awareness of the next person, and, of course, the detail of the person in front. So, if the user wants to see the specific person, he/she has to turn his/her virtual body around just like in real world. By this action, other members can notice what the user is looking at.

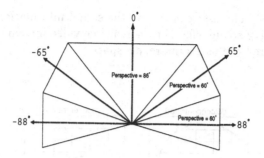

Fig. 2. Realization of the Wide Field of View

Sound Effect

In the real world, we can not only see but also can hear the awareness information. The examples of the awareness information of sound are divided into two types. One type is the sound made by human itself, such as the voice or sneeze. The other is the sound made by human movement, such as footstep, the sound of door opening or closing. If we think of this virtual office system, the former could be heard from audio communication, but the latter could not be heard. So, we provide the sound effect which corresponds to each member's action. The type of sound effect we used are as follows:

- The sound of footsteps.
- The sound chair makes.
- The sound door makes.
- The noise of the office.

By hearing these sounds(excluding office noise), the user can sense other members' action. And the office noise were added to give a reality that the user really works in office.

Awareness space

The Concept of Awareness Space

In good Japanese offices, you should have your own space to work at provided that you can feel the sorroundings. But the tradeoff exists between the facility of communication and keeping one's personal space from other members' awareness information.

To avoid the unlimited flow of other members' awareness information, we have defined the notion of "Awareness Space", and solved the tradeoff problem explained above.

"Awareness Space" is defined as the circled area centering the user in the 3D virtual space. User can sense others' awareness information who is in the circle(see Figure 3). The user can receive the sound information, the movement information from the sound effect, or the realtime video information of the member who had entered the user's awareness space.

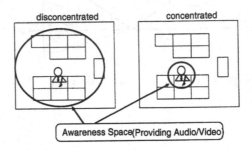

Fig. 3. Awareness Space

In Valentine, the awareness space is provided with 3 levels. The volume of the other members' voice and sound effect and the mosaic of around view are changed in accordance with the level of awareness space. Figure 4 shows three types of mosaicked around view.

NARROW The state of concentration, that is, user does not want to be bothered by others. Only the well selected awareness information, such as the colleagues next to the user or the one who walks behind the user, could be transmitted. Around view is mosaicked much.

NORMAL The state of normal working condition. The awareness information of colleagues in comparably near place could be transmitted.

WIDE The state of trying to feel the atmosphere of the entire office. All of the awareness information could be transmitted. Around view is not mosaicked.

Fig. 4. Three Types of Mosaicked View

In addition, the amount of the awareness information transmitted depends on the distance in 3D virtual space, so as the distance gets farther, the information decreases.

The Parameters for Deciding the Awareness Space

When user is concentrating on his/her project, there is no need of grasping the surrounding information. Giving too much information will lead to the bothering of user's work. In case of working in a project with multiple numbers, even when not working together, some factors such as chatting, knowing other members' mood, or feeling the team's atmosphere are thought to be important. Therefore, we have developed the idea of "Degree of Concentration", about which we talk the details in the later section, to change the awareness space.

In Valentine, the degree of concentration is provided 9 levels, when it is between 1 and 3, his/her awareness space becomes WIDE, when between 4 and 6, becomes NORMAL, between 7 and 9, becomes NARROW(Figure 5). In this way, the awareness space has continuity and doesn't change so frequently. The initial level is 1 because users are disconcentrated when they arrive at office.

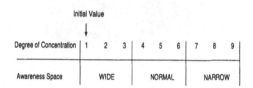

Fig. 5. Degree of Concentration

Elements to Determine the Degreee of Concentration

To detect one's degree of concentration from the usual computer work, we applied two elements itemized below.

  — the frequency of key typing and mouse movement
  — the frequency of chair movement

The reason why these elements are selected is that an interface between computer and human is only keyboard and mouse. So we suppose it is only way to detect one's degree of concentration from the frequency of key typing and mouse movement. In addition, we expect that user do not move chair when he/she concentrate his/her work. Chair movement is easy to detect by simple device, so the frequency of chair movement is chosen. To determine one's degree of concentration from this two elements, we must know which situation of key typing and chair movement indicates concentration.

To derive the relevance between human concentration and these two elements, we have experimented as below.

Experiment

Each of the 25 subjects sat down in laboratory's workstation at a time to work on the menus such as programming, mailing, netscaping, or playing game. While they are working on the menu, we took the measure of the frequency of typing and moving of the chair. At the same time, we observed the brain wave and took the video of the subjects to know whether the subject is concentrating or not. We use IBVA system[11] for measuring brain wave. A subject wears a band with an instrument around his/her head. The information from the instrument is send to Macintosh, analyzed and shown as Figure 6.

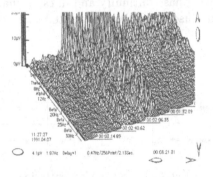

Fig. 6. An Example of Brain Wave on Macintosh

The next two sections explain how to define the period of concentration from the brain wave and video of subjects.

Using Brain Wave As brain wave for a adult, when he/she is awake, and if the eyes are closed or the mental condition is stable, the alpha wave comes out. Coresponding to the mental activity or the opened eyes, the alpha wave is heldback, and the beta wave comes out. In detail, the alpha wave comes out when the eyes are closed and not talking to anyone, and the beta wave comes out when doing a logical, rational thinking like listening deeply into someone's story or solving test questions.

We have defined "the period of concentration" as the situation when the alpha wave is heldback, and the beta wave comes out.

Nevertheless, the beta wave also comes out when in anxiety or in tension. Some subjects had the beta wave at the beginning of the experiment. We consider this is because that the subjects became tense due to the experiment, so we exclude this case from data of experiments.

Using Video We can only determine whether subjects concentrate by using brain wave, but we cannot determine from the brain wave whether the subject is concentrating on his works, or other unrelated materials(e.g. playing games, chatting, etc). We only considered the concentration of users who engaged in their work. For this reason, the video of subjects and the workstation display were taken.

Standardizing the Degree of Concentration

Figure 7 shows the difference of the rate of idle time between concentrating period and disconcentrating period. Most subjects' idle rate of disconcentrating period is greater than that of concentrating period. Figure 8 shows the difference of the frequency of rotating a chair between concentrating period and disconcentrating period. This also shows most subjects' chair movement of disconcentrating period is greater than that of concentrating period. From the result, compared to concentrating period, disconcentrating period has longer idle time and more frequency of moving a chair.

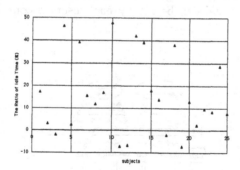

Fig. 7. The Ratio of Idle Time(disconcentrating period–concentrating period)

Based on these results of experiments, we define algorithm to change the degree of concentration(Figure 9 shows).

First, two threshold values (A,B) are defined for idle time and chair movement, and the value is larger than A or lesser than B(when A>B), the degree of concentration is changed. The system measures the percentage of idle time and the frequency of chair movement every minute, and for the idle time when the value is greater than A, the degree of concentration of the user decreases by 1 level. When the value is smaller than B, the degree of concentration increases by 1 level. For the chair movement,the same.

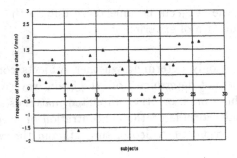

Fig. 8. The Frequency of Rotating A Chair (disconcentrating period–concentrating period)

By calculating the mean value of idle time and frequency of moving a chair, 63% and 1.5 count/min in concentrating period, 47% and 0.8 count/min in disconcentrating period. The default value of A is 63%(keytyping) and 1.5 count/min(chair), B is 47% and 0.8 count/min. For the idle time, if more than 63%, or for the chair, if more than 1.5 count/min, the degree of concentration decreases by 1 level. And for the idle time, if less than 47%, or for the chair, if less than 0.8 count/min, the degree of concentration increases by 1 level. The parameter is variable and can be set by each user to consider the individual difference.

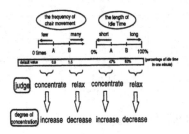

Fig. 9. Algorithm to change the degree of concentration

The Table1 shows the rate of more than 10 seconds of an idle. From this, compared to disconcentrating period, the concentrating period consists mostly of the idle of 10 to 20 seconds. The idle of more than 1 minute were rare. When the idle of more than 1 minute was detected, the system decreases the degree of concentration by 1 level.

Idle time(sec)	Concentrating(%)	Disconcentrating(%)
10-19	64	48
20-29	19	18
30-39	5	10
40-49	5	7
50-59	1	3
60-	6	14

Table 1. The Ratio of Idle Time

The Degree of Concentration Detected by Other Members

The member who is concentrating might not be able to answer others for he/she holds less information of surrounding. Therefore, there is a need of knowing other member's degree of concentration.

In our laboratory, some people put headphone and are listening to music, when he/she don't need others' awareness. Valentine utilizes "Headphone Metaphor" to solve this problem by putting the headphone to the member who has the awareness space level of NARROW. Now, the others are able to recognize that this member is concentrating. To talk with the member with the headphone, others have to walk closer to him/her(Figure 10).

Fig. 10. Headphone Metaphor

Implementation

User Interface

Figure 11 shows the office view of Valentine and the member(the second from right) is sitting and wearing headphone (which indicates his concentration is narrow).

When two of the members look straight at each other, they can communicate in realtime video, by using FDDI. Figure 12 shows video communication with

Fig. 11. Office View

the member who is walking to talk to the user and look straight at each other. The quadrilateral area at the center of the view is video window.

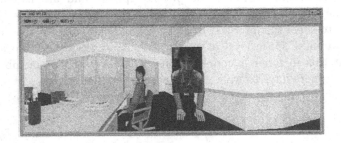

Fig. 12. The Office View With Realtime Video

User can select "GO TO OFFICE" from the dialogbox at the top of the view to enter the office. As we have stated our concept as "A virtual office environment" that the user can go to the office virtually via network, it is important to convince the user that he/she is really going there. When the user goes to a virtual office, there is a simulation of going through the hall and moving across the shared room until he/she sits down. If user wants to go by the other member, he/she can select the other member's name from the dialogbox. Valentine provides him/her the office view animation of going there. The member who is talked to can see the member's movememt(standing up and walking) by CG animation in the virtual office view.

User can change Awareness Space by selecting from the dialogbox if he/she prefer manual change to automatical change.

Providing the Image of Members Each member who participates in a virtual office is provided with images and audio of other members which are defined according to relationships of their positions. In Valentine, user's body is represented in CG and the face picture is attached. Requiring face images of various directions, we use both the continuous video images and the still pictures; Valentine usually uses the still picture taken from 12 directions(Figure 13), and uses the continuous video images when members face each other.

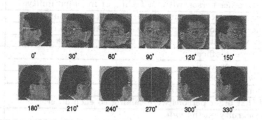

Fig. 13. Still Pictures of User Taken from 12 Directions

Providing Audio According to Distance and Direction To localize the members' voice in real time, the following general and simple methods are used for localization[12].

Direction Attribute The most simple and effective way to give a sound source a direction attribute (i.e., left-right and back-front) is to use stereo speakers or headphones. Stereo-output mixers use differences in amplitude to generate a unidimensional spatial distribution for sound sources. This is so called "panning" of the sound source.

On the other hand, according to the analysis of HRTF(Head Related Transfer Function), we feel that sound from behind is muffled. To give a sound source a back-front attribute, a low-pass filter is employed.

Distance Attribute Valentine uses reverberation to give a sound source a distance attribute. The level and duration of reverberation of the sound source increases in proportion to the distance between the user and the sound source.

View Chair Interface In real world, when people look around, they usually turn their head or body. If the user uses mouse or keyboard to control it, the user might feel different. So we have developed the chair interface named "View Chair" which enables user to turn the virtual chair by turning the real chair.

We added the variable resistance to the shaft of the chair, and by reading the resistance, we calculate the rotating angle. If the user rotates the chair more than 30 degrees to the right, the view of an office rotates to the right, also. This gives a feeling of turning right in virtual office. The same thing happens if the

No.	Question	CaseA	CaseB
1.	I could be well aware of whether there sits a person next to me.	3.85	6.19
2.	I could easily look aroud the office.	5.77	4.41
3.	I could at once nocite the companion who was talking.	3.11	4.41
4.	I could at once nocite other persons who were talking.	5.00	6.11
5.	I could at once feel that other persons were walking in the office.	5.75	5.89
6.	I could at once feel that other persons were walking near to me.	5.00	5.33
7.	I could know well that other persons came to work.	4.77	5.76
8.	I could know well that other persons in front of me came to work.	5.46	6.06
9.	I could talk to other person without feeling of incompatibility.	5.89	6.38
10.	There was no feeling of incongruity on the talking gesture.	5.00	5.12
11.	There was no feeling of incongruity on the picture size.	5.33	6.00
12.	I could know well that person next to me came to work.	3.77	4.94
13.	I felt that I were in office.	5.31	5.63
14.	I wanted to greet or greeted.	5.62	5.00
15.	I felt that I went to office.	5.54	6.06
16.	I felt no incongruity on the 3D office.	5.23	5.12
17.	I knew well that other persons were talking to each other.	4.00	4.94
18.	I felt no incongruity on the video.	5.08	5.00
19.	I knew well who the person next to me was.	4.69	4.94
20.	I knew well what the person next to me did.	3.23	3.82
21.	I knew well where every person sat.	5.46	5.53
22.	The smooth communication was possible.	4.92	5.06
23.	I knew well which direction to which other person faced.	5.31	5.47
24.	I at once knew when other person was sitting down.	5.38	5.53

Table 2. Results of the Questionnaire Data from the Comparative Experiment

user turns left. User can turn the view by clicking left/right button of a mouse if do not want to use View Chair.

This chair is also used for measuring the degree of concentraton.

Figure 14 shows the architecture of View Chair. View Chair is connected to PC9801(NEC) via Multivibrator Unit(MU). MU changes the value of variable resistance to digital signal and send it to PC. PC and workstation is connected by RS232C and communicate information about chair.

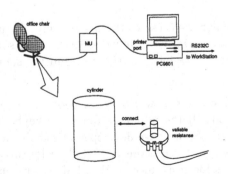

Fig. 14. View Chair

System Overview

Valentine is implemented on SGI Indy, O2 and Sun SparcStation20. The user interfaces are implemented using C, Motif, and OpenGL. Figure 15 shows the system overview.

Valentine uses Ethernet(TCP/IP) for signal connection and FDDI(UDP/IP) for continuous media(i.e., realtime audio/video streams). All workstations are connected by Ethernet. Two sets of Indy and one O2 have video equipment (camera, videoboard) for video communication and connected by FDDI.

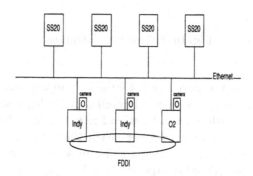

Fig. 15. System Overview

Figure 16 shows the software architecture. The role of servers and a client are described below.

loginServer It administrates each members' login and logout. By connecting to this server, each client is able to get all the informations of other members.

locationServer It notices the rest of the members' position, direction, and degree of concentration which changes dynamically.

audioServer It controls audio and sound effect by receiving the positional information from locationServer.

Client It displays the virtual office implemented by OpenGL, and the precise location of other members by positional information from locationServer. It also transfers video image with other clients through FDDI, if it requires.

concentServer It is run for every clients to calculate the degree of concentration of members every minute, and it informs the result to the client.

Evaluation

Arround View and Sound Effect

We have evaluated Valentine by a comparative experiment. 18 subjects used two types of systems. Table2 shows the results of the questionnaire data from the

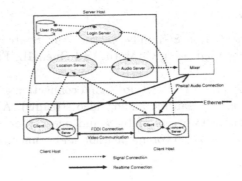

Fig. 16. Software Architecture

comparative experiment. CaseA stands for the system without Around View and Sound Effect and the field of view was limited only 80 degrees. CaseB stands for our complete system with Around View and Sound Effect. For pure evaluation of our techniques, each subject was not heard the roles of Arround View and Sound Effect in advance. The scores are the mean value of respondents. The value has 7 steps from 1(bad) to 7(good).

The questions in the questionnaire have been selected to evaluate the influence of the effects of "Around View" and "Sound Effect" on providing awareness. And some questions are for evaluating the user interface of Valentine.

Our system scores higher than the system of CaseA on most of questions. Especially, providing awareness of the person next to the user is remarkable (question1, 12, 19, 20). This result indicates that Around View and Sound Effect are effective for transmitting awareness information. In addition, many subjects felt the sense of going to office on both CaseA and CaseB(question15). This shows the efficiency of the Sound Effect of footsteps(in CaseB) and office view animation of going through the hall and moving across the shared room until he/she sits down.

However, CaseB has some disavantages(especially in question 2). This is because Arround View and Sound Effect consume high machine resources and it takes longer time to look around the room in CaseB than in CaseA.

Awareness Space

We also evaluate Awareness Space by taking video of user and make a comparison between the degree of concentration and the condition of user. Figure 17 shows the typical result of changing degree of concentration.

This result shows following activities.

Case1 start working(0 min,20 min)
Case2 start chatting with his/her colleague(13 min,49 min)

Case3 start thinking about something(43 min)

In Case1, the subject concentrated on his/her work and the degree of concentration was increasing in both cases(0, 20min). In Case2, the subject turned his/her chair to his/her colleague, not using keyboard and mouse and the degree of concentration began to decrease. In Case3, the subject was thinking with his/her elbows on the desk, not using keyboard and mouse and not moving the chair, and the degree of concentration was decreasing until he/she resumed to work 2 minutes later. This result shows the degree of concentration changed in accordance with state and activity of the subject. However, there is some individual differences: one's concentration changed so frequently and the other's was stable. This is because we used the mean values as thresholds for these experiments. To detect more precise concentration, desirable threshholds should be set by each user after he/she uses Valentine for the time being.

In summing up these results, the degree of concentration detected by Valentine almost(not perfectly) corresponds to the condition of the subject and we can say the efficiency of algorithm we defined in our system.

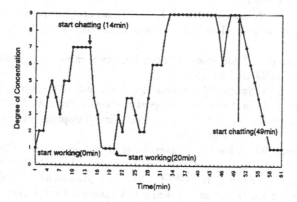

Fig. 17. Degree of Concentration Change

Conclusion

In this paper, we describe Valentine that provides a "work-at-home" environment based on a virtual shared room built on a 3D graphics workstation. Valentine provides the feeling of the ownself presence at virtual office by using "Around View" and "Sound Effect" and the efficiency of these techniques was proved. We also realize "Awareness Space" on the system to avoid the tradeoff between providing facility of informal communication and keeping one's workspace from others' awareness information. To decide the Awareness Space, we have developed the idea of "the Degree of Concentration" which was determined by two parameters: the frequency of key typing and mouse movement and the frequency of chair movement. The degree of concentration detected by Valentine almost corresponds to the condition and activity of user. For the reasons we've mentioned, we can realize the virtual office environment where members can communicate with his/her colleagues naturally and can concentrate on his/her work.

Acknowledgements

This project has been supported by Center Of Excellence (COE).

References

1. T. Inoue, K. Okada, and Y. Matsushita, "Learnign from TV Programs : Application of TV presentation to a videoconferencing system", Proc. ACM UIST'95, 1995.
2. K.Okada, F.Maeda, Y.Ichikawa,and Y.Matsushita, "Multiparty videoconferencing at virtual social distance:MAJIC design", Proc. ACM CSCW'94, Chapel Hill, NC, USA, pp385-393, 1994.
3. Stefik, M., et al, "Beyoud the Chalk board: Computer Support for Collaboration and Problem Solving in Meetings.", Communications of the ACM, Vol.30, No.1, Jan. 1987.
4. P. Dourish, S. Bly, "Portholes: Supporting Awareness in a Distributed work Group", Proc. ACM CHI'92, 1992.
5. S. E. Hudson and I. Smith, "Techniques for Addressing Fundamental Privacy and Disruption Tradeoffs in Awareness Support Systems", Proc. ACM CSCW'96, 1996.
6. J. C. Tang and M. Rua, "Montage: Providing Teleproximity for Distributed Groups", Proc. ACM CHI'94, 1994.
7. M. Sohlenkamp, G. Chwelos, "Integrating Communication, Cooperation, an Awareness: The DIVA Virtual Office Environment", Proc. ACM CSCW'94, 1994.
8. N. Matsuura, G. Fujino, K. Okada, and Y. Matsushita, "VENUS:A Tele-Communicaation Environment to Support Awareness for Informal Interactions", Proc. 12th Scharding Int. Workshop–Design of Computer Supported Cooperative Work and Groupware Systems, 1993.
9. H. Nakanishi, C. Yoshida, T. Nishimura, and T. Ishida, "FreeWalk:Supporting Casual Meetings in a Network", Proc. ACM CSCW'96, 1996.
10. C. Greenhalgh and S. Benford, "MASSIVE: A Collaborative Virtual Environment for Teleconferencing", ACM Transactions on Computer-Human Interaction, Vol.2, No.3 Sep. 1995.
11. http://www.IBVA.com
12. K. Teramoto, N. Oki, K. Okada, and Y. Matsushita, "VCP:Communication System Using Spatial Auditory Interface", Proc. Multimedia Japan'96, pp126-131, 1996.

Electronic Binder System: Promotion of an ISO9001-based Quality System Using the WWW and Experience from Its Application

Atsuo Hazeyama[1] and Miho Hanawa[1]

NEC Corporation, 2-11-5 Shibaura, Minato-ku, Tokyo 108, Japan

Abstract. The authors have been applying an ISO9001-based quality system to a large software project which develops the software product by using electronic media and computer network. To improve sharing documents and quality records, and to facilitate the preparation of internal quality audit and certification activities, the authors developed an electronic binder system that collected necessary documents and quality records by using the WWW (World Wide Web) and applied to their organization. The organization has received the ISO9001 certification using the electronic binder system. To evaluate the usefulness of this system, the authors performed a survey by questionnaire twice: (1) soon after introducing the system (at that time our organization was promoting the deployment of our quality system and was not subject to any internal quality audits and certifications) in our organization, and (2) soon after receiving the ISO9001 certification. The following results were found out from this survey:

– With respect to usefulness of the electronic binder system, in the 1st survey, half of the respondents who had ever accessed the electronic binders evaluated them positively. The other half did not. But in the 2nd survey, more than 90% evaluated the electronic binder system useful.
– The electronic binder system was most effective for ordering the documents and quality records of projects and sub-projects that the respondents themselves were part of in both surveys.
– Planning documents, production specifications and final testing specifications and reports, and configuration management lists are accessed most from the point of view of the accessed number per one document or quality record in both surveys. This means project members regard these documents and quality records as important.

1 Introduction

In recent years, software development companies / organizations have had to overcome global competition in markets. Such companies/organizations are required to provide attractive and high-quality software products on time and within budgetary limits while continuously improving their processes. As a means of continuous process improvements, the implementation of an ISO9001-based quality system[3] has been required in software development companies / organizations.

An ISO9001-based quality system requires the following three points:

- Organizations should create the quality manuals and standards that conform to the requirements of the ISO9001 standard.
- Organizations should implement the procedures specified by the quality manual and standards and should keep records of these procedures (quality records [1]).
- Organizations should confirm the effectiveness of their quality systems.

That is, the spirit of ISO9001 is to define responsibility and authority explicitly and to keep written records of the operations. Document control therefore plays a very important role in ISO9001 (all requirements of ISO9001 relate to document control).

Several papers on experience with ISO9001-based quality systems have been reported. Cramer[1], for example, described the way his company has established an ISO9001-based certified business process model. That paper, however, did not tell how the quality-management team promoted the application of their quality system to the whole organization. Stelzer[2] surveyed dozens of European software firms that had already received ISO9001 certifications and reported whether or not ISO9001 had brought about improvements. However, there are few reports on how organizations tried to promote the application of ISO9001-based quality systems within those organizations.

Our organization has been applying an ISO9001-based quality system where runs several relatively large-scale software projects and received the certification. In our organization, projects develop software products using electronic media and computer network. We have proposed an electronic binder system using the WWW (World Wide Web) for our ISO9001-based quality system and have deployed this system in our organization so that we could share documents and quality records, prepare internal quality audits and certification activities efficiently. In this paper, we explain what electronic binders are, why they are required, and how they are used. We also report the result on two surveys of the use of the electronic binders in our organization.

This paper is organized as follows: Section 2 describes background of the electronic binders, how projects are implemented in our organization, several problems that must be solved before introducing a quality system, the characteristics of our quality system, and several problems that occurred after we introduced our quality system. Section 3 describes what the electronic binder system is and describes its configuration. Section 4 describes the deployment of the system throughout our organization. Section 5 describes the survey, its results, and the lessons we learned from these results. Finally, section 6 gives our conclusions and explain what we intended to do in future work.

---

[1] Quality records are records which are required by the ISO9001 standard to demonstrate conformance to specified requirements and the effective operation of the quality system [3].

2   Background

Our organization develops software products that support software development, and our top management decided to establish an ISO9001-based quality system to improve the quality of our own processes and products. Projects in our organization develop software products by using electronic media and computer network. Various kinds of communication (reporting, notification, discussion, review and inspection, document distribution, etc.) are done using E-mail.

Before our quality system was introduced, each project established some procedures for its own project: procedures such as rules for naming variables and constants in source codes, rules for document control, and guidance for manual writing. A document control rule of a large software project was adopted as the basis of the document control standard in our quality system. But because the document control rule of the project did not explicitly define what documents should be created and managed, the decisions about which documents were to be recorded was left to each of the project / sub-projects. As a result, many important documents were not recorded (they remained in E-mail spools or they were stored only on papers). Some documents were even lost because their authors moved. As a result, problems have occurred that design rationales could not be found out.

In building our ISO9001-based quality system, we established a document control standard as well as a document and quality record list to be created and maintained through our quality system. Here quality records are things which are required to maintain by the ISO9001 standard '4.16 Control of quality records'. On the other hand, documents are things except the quality records of all the things which are required to maintain by the ISO9001 standard.

This list contains around 50 documents and quality records, and for each the following attributes are specified: creator, inspector, approver, distribution, whether it is a quality record, the directory within which it is stored, how long it should be stored, the name of the standard specifying the details about the document and quality record, and whether or not there is a template for the document and quality record (one example is shown in Table 1).

Since we started applying our ISO9001-based quality system, the amount of documents and quality records recorded by projects and sub-projects increased rapidly. Table 2 shows the changes in the number of documents and quality records created and stored during the development of a large project within our organization. This table shows that the introduction of an ISO9001-based quality system (at the time of V4.0 development) resulted in a five-fold increase in the number of recorded documents and quality records over the numbers recorded when the first version was developed[2]. This increase in the number of documents and quality records recorded resulted in increased retrieval cost, too.

---

[2] When V1 was developed, a lot of documents and quality records were created and distributed via E-mail. But because some of them were not recorded in the project / sub-projects directory (i.e., they were archived only in mail spools), they are not counted in this survey.

Table 1. Example attributes and their value of a document controlled under our quality system (in case of development planning document)

Attribute	Attribute value
creator	persons who are appointed by project leader(including project leader him / herself)
inspector	project leader
approver	top management
distribution	the whole project
whether a control document is a quality record or not	none
storage directory	project directory
storage duration	5 years
standard name which specified the details about the document	planning standard
existence of a document template	existence

Considering this background, we proposed an electronic binder using the WWW (World Wide Web) and deployed it in our organization so that we could share information for software development and could prepare the internal quality audits and certifications efficiently.

Table 2. The changes in the number of documents and quality records created and stored of a large software project

product version No.	number of registered documents/quality records	characteristics of the corresponding project
V1	190	first release.
V2	77	minor version-up.
V3	79	porting to another platform and bug fix.
V4	1022	major version-up. Start applying our quality system to our organization. Performed the 1st survey.
V4.1	461	some enhancement and bug fix.
V5	821	major version-up. Received formal examination. Performed the 2nd survey.

3 Configuration of the electronic binder system

The electronic binder uses the WWW (World Wide Web) and HTML (Hyper Text Markup Language) to collect computer-created documents and quality records according to a classification scheme specified in Section 4. Fig. 1 shows a screen image of the electronic binder of a project.

It differs from a paper binder in that a lot of binders can quite easily be constructed from various viewpoints without replicating documents and quality records themselves.

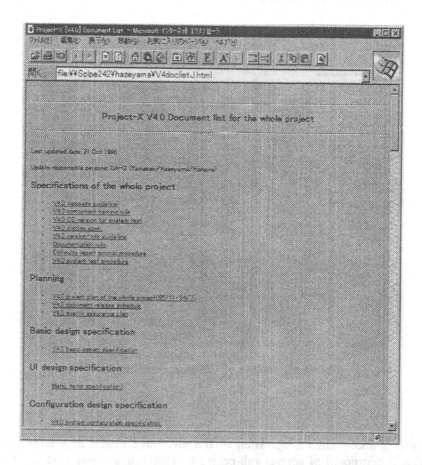

Fig. 1. Example electronic binder

Fig. 2 shows the configuration of the electronic binder system. It is a very simple configuration in that persons register documents and quality records in a center file directory and responsible persons create and maintain an electronic binder by using a template (explained in Section 4). We can view the electronic binders by using a WWW browser such as Netscape Navigator[3] or Internet Explorer[4]. The electronic binders provide various viewpoints because a lot of entries in a lot of electronic binders (HTML files) can link to a single document and quality record regardless of where they are registered. It is particularly useful in a large software project because such a project is composed of several sub-projects which have their own sub-project document directory, and the electronic binder of the whole project can be created by aggregating the binders of its sub-projects. The electronic binder of each product version can also be created very easily. Furthermore the construction cost of the electronic binders is very low because of the use of the WWW.

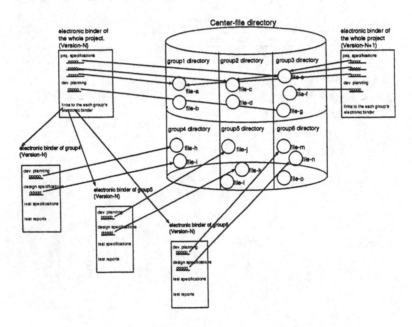

Fig. 2. Configuration of the electronic binder system

Fig. 2 shows the configuration of the electronic binder of a large project which is composed of several sub-projects. This figure shows that the binder of the overall project is composed of documents and quality records which are created for the overall project, and the binders of its sub-projects. This figure also shows the binders for multiple product version of the project (version N and version N+1). Using the electronic binder system, documents which are shared

---

[3] Trademark by Netscape Communications Corporation
[4] Trademark by Microsoft Corporation

among several product version such as file-a, file-c, file-e in this figure can be easily accessed from the binder for each product version.

4 Deployment of the electronic binder system

The electronic binder system has been deployed throughout the whole organization in the following way:

1. Documents and quality records to be managed according to ISO9001 requirements were extracted and defined by an ISO9001 promotion team (The list of these documents and quality records forms a part of our quality system). These documents and quality records were divided into two categories:

   - **Documents and quality records created and maintained by an organization / department.**
     Documents for contracts, internal quality audit plans, training plans, quality records for internal quality audit reports, each personnels' training records, and management review reports, etc. belong in this category.
   - **Documents and quality records created and maintained by projects and/or sub-projects.**
     Development plans, design specifications, test specifications, test reports, various review reports, production specifications, final inspection and testing specifications, final inspection and testing reports, corrective / preventive action reports, and so on belong in this category.

2. Templates of the electronic binder for organization / departments and for projects / sub-projects were prepared by the ISO9001 promotion team.

3. A procedure for the application of the electronic binder system was documented by the ISO9001 promotion team and approved by the top management. This procedure defined who should create and maintain each electronic binder and where each electronic binder should be placed. It also defined the filename conventions of electronic binders. This document was distributed to the whole organization. The organization / departments and projects / sub-projects are required to create and maintain their own electronic binders by using corresponding templates.

5 Survey of the electronic binder usage

We surveyed the usage of the electronic binder system by circulating questionnaires to the whole organization (around one hundred people) twice. The subsequent subsections describe the contents of the survey, the results, and lessons learned from the results.

5.1 Status at the time when the survey was performed

The 1st survey The 1st survey was performed October 1996, soon after having prepared the electronic binder system. When this survey was performed, the status of our quality system was as follows: a large project in our organization had been applying our quality system for the second time (Version 4.1). Around 65 % of our organization have been participating in this project with part-time or full-time. As Table 2 shows, V4.1 development was a minor enhancement and bug fix.

On the other hand, as activities for organization / departments, planning and training record of the quality system, and each personnels' training records had been created and maintained. When the survey was performed, internal quality audits, and management reviews had not been performed yet.

The 2nd survey Our organization received ISO9001 formal examination July 1997 and received the certification September 1997. The 2nd survey was performed September 1997, soon after having received the certification.

5.2 Questionnaire Items

We asked all members of our organization and subsidiary companies for the following information:

(1) their affiliation
(2) whether they had accessed the electronic binders
(3) the frequency with which they had accessed the electronic binders
(4) which electronic binders they had accessed
(5) what documents and quality records in the electronic binders they had accessed
(6) how useful they had found the electronic binders
(7) reasons that the electronic binders are useful
(8) reasons that the electronic binders are not useful

In the 2nd survey, we asked to respond item (3) - (8) per each role a person played.

5.3 Results

We E-mailed the questionnaire to the whole organization. In the 1st survey, sixty-three percent responded and seventy-three percent of those responding had referred to the electronic binders. In the 2nd survey, fifty-six percent responded and eighty-three percent of those responding had referred to the electronic binders. The following results came from the data which people who had accessed to the electronic binder responded.

Accessed pages As Fig. 3 shows, as for accessed pages, in both surveys, the binder of the whole project in a large software project was the one accessed most frequently. The second-most frequently accessed binder was that of the whole organization. Furthermore, in both surveys the binders of system integration group (group-13) and of groups (group-1, 17) that had a lot of technical interfaces

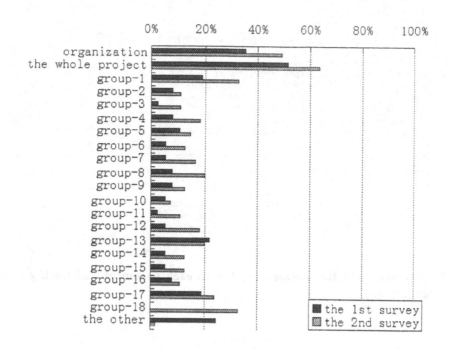

Fig. 3. Result on accessed pages.

with other groups (these groups need to exchange a lot of design information) in a large project have been accessed frequently. The binders of these groups (group-1, 13, 17) have been accessed a lot from members of the other groups.

Accessed documents and quality records Fig. 4 and Fig. 5 shows the accessed number of each document and quality record created for organization and project. As shown in Fig. 4 and Fig. 5, in both organization and project, in almost all documents and quality records, the accessed number in the 2nd survey is more than that in the 1st survey. With respect to organization, in both surveys, the standards and quality manual had been accessed most frequently. On the other hand, with respect to project, in both surveys, development planning documents had been accessed most.

Fig. 6 shows a result on how many kinds of documents and quality records have been accessed by each role in a project using a boxplot diagram [4]. From this result, the number of kinds of documents and quality records accessed by project / sub-projects leaders and members of a project management group of the project was most, the median was 9.5, which was depicted by a bold point within the box. The number of kinds of documents and quality records accessed by developers was second-most, the median was 5. The median of the number of

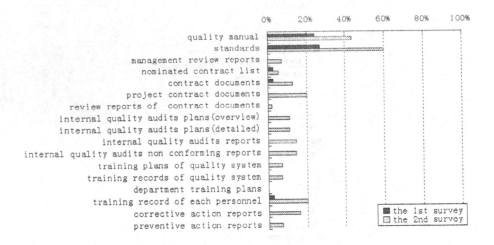

Fig. 4. Result on the accessed number to each document and quality record (organization)

kinds of documents and quality records accessed by testers was 3, testers mainly accessed test specifications, design specifications, and test reports.

Fig. 7 shows the ratio which is the number of each type of documents and quality records to the number of all documents and quality records created in V4.0 and V5.0 development of a project. This figure shows from V4.0 to V5.0, the amounts of test specifications, test reports, review reports increased, on the other hand, design change requests decreased significantly[5].

Based on the data from Fig. 5 and Fig. 7, Fig. 8 derives the accessed number of each document and quality record categorized in Fig. 7 per one document and quality record. The number is normalized (the value for planning documents is the basis, 1.0).

Planning documents, production specifications and final testing specifications and reports, and configuration management lists are accessed most from the point of view of the accessed number per one document or quality record in both surveys in common.

In the 2nd survey, the accessed number of corrective/preventive action report and design review report has grown because of the access by internal quality auditors and examinees (in the 1st survey internal quality audit and formal examination have not been performed yet).

Evaluation on the effectiveness of the electronic binder The results on evaluating the effectiveness of the electronic binder are shown in Fig. 9 and

---

[5] The 1st survey was performed soon after finishing V4.0 development of the project. The 2nd survey was performed soon after finishing V5.0 development of the project.

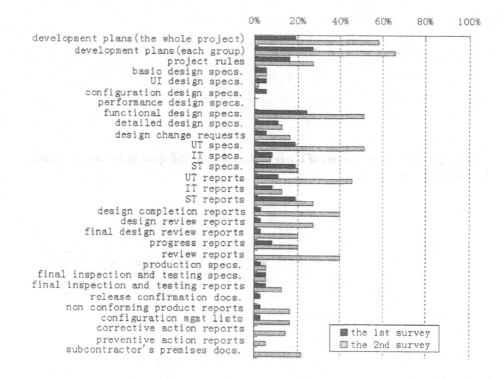

Fig. 5. Result on the accessed number to each document and quality record (project)

summarized as follows: in the 1st survey, half of the respondents who had ever accessed the electronic binders evaluated the electronic binders positively. The other half, however, did not. But in the 2nd survey, more than 90 % people evaluated the electronic binders positively.

Of those who evaluated the electronic binders positively, we asked why they found the electronic binders useful. We did this by asking them to select from the following six choices (multiple choices were permitted). Item (E) was enumerated in the 2nd survey only.

(A) documents and quality records of projects or sub-projects that a respondent belongs to have been ordered by the electronic binders and can be shared/accessed easily.

(B) documents and quality records of other projects or sub-projects have been ordered by the electronic binders and can be shared/accessed easily.

(C) understanding of the ISO9001 standard has been facilitated.

(D) preparing for internal quality audits or ISO9001 formal examinations could be done efficiently.

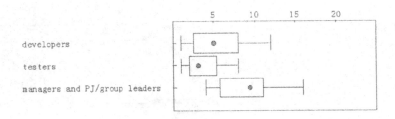

Fig. 6. Result on the number of kinds of documents and quality records accessed by each role (project)

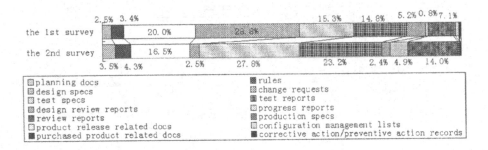

Fig. 7. The ratio of the number of documents and quality records in V4.0 and V5.0 development of a project

(E) internal quality audits and ISO9001 formal examinations could be done smoothly.

(F) the other (the reason can be described free)

The result is shown in Fig. 10. In both surveys, (A) 'documents and quality records of projects or sub-projects that a respondent belongs to have been ordered by the electronic binders and can be shared/accessed easily' was the most answer (around 75 %), (B) 'documents and quality records of other projects or sub-projects have been ordered by the electronic binders and can be shared/accessed easily' was the second most answer (around 65 %). The percentage is also almost same in both surveys. In the 2nd survey (E) 'internal quality audits and ISO9001 formal examinations could be done smoothly' was the third most answer.

We have expected the electronic binders to be useful in helping understand the ISO9001 standard, in helping prepare for internal quality audits, and in helping access to the information of other projects and sub-projects. However, users of the electronic binder system evaluated it useful in helping ordering and

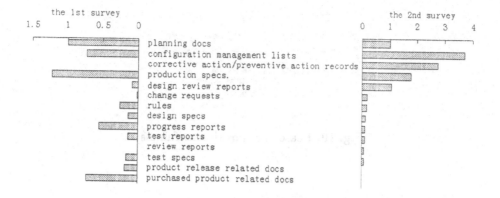

Fig. 8. The accessed number of each document and quality record per one document and quality record

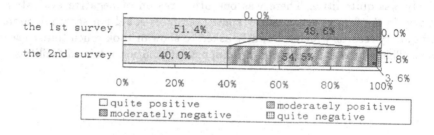

Fig. 9. Result on evaluating usefulness

sharing information of their project or sub-project.

We also asked those who had evaluated the electronic binders negatively why they had evaluated them that way by selecting from the following four choices (multiple choices were permitted).

- the benefit was not worth the effort.
- necessary information has not been found out.
- information has not been latest.
- the other (the reason can be described free)

The result is shown in Fig. 11. In the 1st survey, the most common answer was that the benefit was not worth the effort. The main reason was that almost all documents and quality records registered in the electronic binders had been distributed to the appropriate members by E-mail or that the members had been able to access those documents and quality records by other means (for

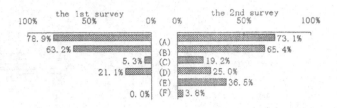

Fig. 10. Reasons of positive usefulness

example, by bookmarking necessary documents and quality records/pages of their own on a WWW browser). Therefore it turned out that the members have not necessarily accessed such documents and quality records via the electronic binders (each person manages his/her necessary documents and quality records for him / herself).

In the second survey, those who evaluated the electronic binder system negatively was quite little. There was one other reason of negative evaluation as follows: in the formal examination, some examinees could not search documents and quality records which examiners asked to show or took much time to search them. This means it is necessary to support information retrieval facilities.

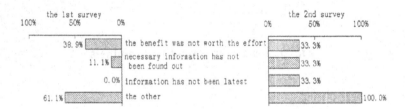

Fig. 11. Reasons of negative usefulness

6 Conclusion

We have proposed an electronic binder system using the WWW (World Wide Web) in order to promote the efficient application and deployment of our quality system. Surveying the status of the electronic binder system usage, we learned the following:

- With respect to usefulness of the electronic binder system, in the 1st survey, half of the respondents who had ever accessed the electronic binders evaluated them positively. The other half did not. But in the 2nd survey which was performed soon after having received the ISO9001 certification, more than 90% evaluated the electronic binder system useful.
- The electronic binder system was most effective for ordering the documents and quality records of projects and sub-projects that the respondents themselves were part of in both surveys .
- Planning documents, production specifications and final testing specifications and reports, and configuration management lists are accessed most from the point of view of the accessed number per one document or quality record in both surveys. This means project members regard these documents and quality records as important.

The purpose of the electronic binder system was originally to prepare for ISO9001 certification efficiently. We have achieved this goal. We are now trying to expand its role toward the information base for software project management. We are now implementing to be able to deal with the following dynamic information of a software project.

- Action item list
- SI (System Integration) status
- open problem report list
- progress graph of bugs
- test status

As some people also required information retrieval facilities, we would like to tackle these enhancements.

Acknowledgement

We would like to thank persons of our organization who cooperated in the survey. We also would like to thank anonymous referees who helped to improve our paper.

References

1. Cramer, J.: The Development of a Certified Business Process Model. Software Process - Improvement and Practice 1 (1995) 27-33
2. Stelzer, D., Mellis, W., Herzwurm, G.: Software Process Improvement via ISO9000? Proc. of the 29th Hawaii International Conference on System and Science **Vol.1: Software Technology and Architecture** (1996) 703-712
3. ISO9001: Quality Systems - Model for quality assurance in design, development, production, installation, and servicing (1994)
4. Yoshizawa, T.: Statistic Processing (1992) 7-14 (In Japanese)

Update Monitoring: The CQ Project

Calton Pu* and Ling Liu

Department of Computer Science & Engineering
Oregon Graduate Institute
P.O.Box 91000 Portland, Oregon 97291-1000 USA
{calton,lingliu}@cse.ogi.edu

Abstract. In rapidly growing open environments such as the Internet, users experience information starvation in the midst of data overload, due to difficulties similar to finding the needle in a haystack. Update monitoring is a promising area of research where we bring the right information to the user at the right time, instead of forcing the user through manual browsing or repeated submission of queries. As an example of update monitoring research, we outline our work in the Continual Queries (CQ) project, including its basic concepts, software architecture, and current implementation status.

1 Introduction and Problem Statement

The World Wide Web (usually referred to as *the Web*) has made an enormous amount of data freely accessible over the Internet. However, finding the right information in the midst of this mountain of data has been likened to finding the proverbial needle in a haystack. This phenomenon has been called "information starvation due to data overload."[2] Commonly used search engines, including web robots (e.g., AltaVista) and indexers (e.g., Yahoo!), have ameliorated the situation somewhat, but the current exponential growth of the Web is quickly aggravating the fundamental problem.

We divide the problem of finding relevant information into two parts. The first part is the search for historical data in the Web. Given its static nature, historical data is best suited for search engines, and generally speaking, data warehousing tools. The second part of the problem is *update monitoring*, which deals with the new information arriving into the Web and the databases. There are many applications in both parts. Let us consider a simple example in decision support systems. On the one hand, historical data is used in long term projections and planning, for example, by Wal-Mart in the selection of inventory. On the other hand, update monitoring is used in (near) real-time decisions, for example, by investment bankers in the buying and selling of stock.

---

* The CQ project is partially funded by DARPA grant MDA972-97-1-0016, and grants from Intel and Boeing.
[2] Gio Wiederhold of Stanford University seems to have been among the first to use this phrase.

While both historical data and update monitoring have interesting applications and research challenges, we focus on update monitoring in this paper. There are three reasons for this bias. First, managing read-only historical data is a more mature area, with many commercial data warehouse systems available. Consequently, many of the most obvious research questions have been answered. Second, update monitoring is a problem that requires solutions that combine writes, which are usually handled by a transaction processing systems, and reads, which are usually handled by database management systems. Third, update monitoring introduces special difficulties when heterogeneous data sources (e.g., from Web pages and relational databases) are being monitored together. As a result, update monitoring presents some interesting new research challenges.

In the Continual Queries (CQ) project at Oregon Graduate Institute we are developing and techniques and a software toolkit for update monitoring and event-driven information delivery on the Internet. The practical result of the CQ project is a "personalized update monitoring" toolkit based on *continual queries* [12]. In contrast to conventional database queries, continual queries are standing queries that are issued once and run "continually" over the source data. As updates to the data sources reach a specific threshold or timed event, the standing query is (conceptually) re-evaluated and new results returned to the user or the application that issued the query. We say that the query is conceptually re-evaluated because of the variety of algorithms and approaches to the standing query re-evaluation.

For each continual query, an update monitoring program (CQ robot for short) creates distributed programs that act together as an intelligent assistant, keep track of information sources that are available (on the Web and elsewhere), how to access them, and the changes that happened. Whenever updates at the data sources result reach a specific update threshold or a timed event, the CQ robot computes and integrates the new results and presents them to the user. Compared with the pure pull (such as DBMSs, various web search engines) and pure push (such as Pointcast, Marimba, Broadcast disks [1]) technology, the CQ project can be seen as a hybrid approach that combines the pull and push models by supporting personalized update monitoring through an integrated client-pull and server-push paradigm.

The rest of the paper is organized as follows. Section 2 introduces the basic concepts of continual queries and the CQ project. Section 3 describes the architecture of CQ software and implementation. Section 4 outlines a client-server design of the CQ architecture. Section 5 describes how continual queries may be executed efficiently. Section 6 describes in some detail the opportunities and problems presented by the push technology. Section 7 summarizes the status of current implementation in the CQ project. Section 8 concludes the paper.

2 Basic CQ Concepts

The goal of the CQ project is to develop techniques and a toolkit for update monitoring with event-driven delivery in an open and dynamic evolving environment such as the Internet and intranets. We pursue this goal along two dimensions: The first dimension is to develop a set of methods and techniques that can incorporate distributed event-driven triggers into the query evaluation and search process to enhance information density and improve system scalability and query responsiveness. The first dimension is summarized in this and the following sections (2 and 3). The second dimension is to build a working system that demonstrates our ideas, concepts, and techniques developed for continual queries using real-world application scenarios. The second dimension is summarized in Sect. 7.

2.1 Concepts and Definitions

A continual query is defined as a triple $(Q_{cq}, Trig_{cq}, Term_{cq})$, consisting of a normal query Q_{cq} (e.g., written in SQL), a trigger condition $Trig_{cq}$, and a termination condition $Term_{cq}$. The initial execution of a continual query is performed as soon as Q_{cq} is issued and the whole result is returned to the user.

The subsequent executions of Q_{cq} happen when the trigger condition $Trig_{cq}$ becomes true. Currently, CQ supports two types of trigger conditions: *time-based event triggering* and *content-based event-triggering*. For time-based event triggering, three modes are supported:

1. immediate, whenever a change to the source data occurs;
2. at a specific time point (e.g., execute Q_{cq} every Monday or every first day of the month); and
3. at regular time intervals (e.g., execute Q_{cq} every two weeks).

For content-based event triggering, we support a variety of content-based conditions. Examples include:

1. a simple condition on the database state (e.g., execute Q_{cq} whenever a deposit of $5,000 is made);
2. an aggregate condition on the database state (e.g., execute Q_{cq} when the total deposits reach $100,000), and
3. a relationship between a previous query result and the current database state (e.g., execute Q_{cq} when a total of $100,000 dollars in deposits have been made since the previous execution of Q_{cq}).

The termination condition $Term_{cq}$ specifies the event that determines the end of a continual query. Both the trigger condition $Trig_{cq}$ and the termination condition $Term_{cq}$ will be evaluated prior to each subsequent execution of Q_{cq}.

2.2 Continual Query Examples

Several examples that illustrate the uses of continual queries. First is *"notify me in the next week each time Microsoft stock price rises by 10%"*. This request is codified by the following three components:

- Query: Result(SC, SP) = SELECT Stock.company, Stock.price
  FROM Stock WHERE Stock.company = 'Microsoft';
- $Trig_{cq}$: Stock.company = 'Microsoft' .and. Stock.price > SP*1.1
- $Term_{cq}$: one week from query creation

Second example is *"tell me the flight number of the plane whenever it has remained in this sector for more than 5 minutes"*.

- Query: Result(FN) = SELECT AirControl.FlightNumber
  FROM AirControl WHERE AirControl.SectorTime > '5min';
- $Trig_{cq}$: AirControl.SectorTime > 5min
- $Term_{cq}$: nil

Third example is *"for the next month, report which manufacturers can supply 1000 units per warehouse whenever the average storage level of canned soup is below 200 units"*.

- Query: Result(MANUF) = SELECT Manufacturer.Name
  FROM Manufacturer WHERE Manufacturer.Supply > '1000'
          .and. Manufacturer.Item = 'Canned Soup'
- $Trig_{cq}$: Inventory.Item = 'Canned Soup'
          .and. Inventory.StockLevel < '200'
- $Term_{cq}$: one month from query execution

Fourth example is *"At 5pm every day, notify me the itemized amount and classification of materials coming into or going out from these ports and their origin or destination"*.

- Query: Result(AMOUNT, CLASS, ORIGIN, DESTINY, PrevLoc) =
  SELECT Materials.Value, Materials.Type, Materials.StartPoint,
          Materials.EndPoint, Materials.Location
  FROM Materials WHERE Materials.Location != PrevLoc;
- $Trig_{cq}$: DayTimer = '17:00'
- $Term_{cq}$: nil

2.3 Continual Semantics

Let us denote the result of running continual query Q_{cq} on database state S_i as $R_{cq}(S_i)$. The result of running a continual query Q_{cq} is a sequence of answers $\{R_{cq}(S_1), R_{cq}(S_2), \ldots, R_{cq}(S_n)\}$ obtained by running query Q_{cq} on the sequence of database states $S_i, 1 \leq i \leq n$, each time triggered by $Trig_{cq}$, i.e., $\forall S_i, Trig_{cq} \wedge \neg Term_{cq}$.

If the termination condition $Term_{cq}$ is nil, Q_{cq} will produce results from $R_{cq}(S_1)$ to $R_{cq}(S_\infty)$. Otherwise, Q_{cq} will produce results from a starting time t_1 to a final time t_n, when $Term_{cq}$ becomes true. In other words, Q_{cq} (the sequence) ends when the termination condition becomes true.

Each time $Trig_{cq}$ is triggered, conceptually Q_{cq} is evaluated against the current state of the database S_i, and the result $R_{cq}(S_i)$ is sent to the user who issued Q_{cq}. In general it is expensive to re-evaluate the whole query over the entire source data for each execution of a continual query, although in some circumstances (e.g., legacy databases and some file systems) it may be unavoidable to reprocess the query from scratch. Therefore, it is important to find optimization steps that can bypass the complete re-evaluation and thus avoid the duplicate computation and unnecessary data transmission. In paper [12] we describe a strategy to generate $R_{cq}(S_i)$ from $R_{cq}(S_{i-1})$ incrementally, thus reducing both processing time and network transmission bandwidth.

3   System Architecture

As mentioned earlier, the ultimate goal of the CQ project is two-fold: On one hand, we intend to develop an adaptive system architecture and a set of techniques for update monitoring in open environments. On the other hand, we provide effective support for enhanced data transparency, data quality, and system scalability and responsiveness. The method and key techniques of the CQ system development include:

– using the notion of continual queries to support customized (or personalized) update monitoring based on users' preference and requirement (user pull followed by server push),
– incorporating broadcast-based server push sources with the pure pull based data sources in the continual queries service provision,
– integrating distributed query processing and dynamic optimization techniques into the continual query evaluation process for achieving effectiveness and responsiveness of the system.

The first generation of the CQ system has a three-tier architecture: client, server, and wrapper/adapter. The client tier is primarily responsible for receiving users' request and expressing such request in the form of CQ query Q_{cq}, CQ trigger $Trig_{cq}$, and CQ termination condition $Term_{cq}$. The client manager is also in charge of user registration and providing CQ users with system utilities such as browsing or editing installed continual queries. The client manager currently has four main components as shown in Fig. 1:

1. The form manager that provides the CQ clients with fill-in forms to register and install their continual queries;
2. The registration manager which allows clients to register the CQ system with valid user id and password, and return the clients a confirmation on their registration;
3. The client and system administration services which provide utilities for browsing or updating installed continual queries, for testing time-based triggers and content-based triggers, and for tracing the performance of update monitoring of source data;
4. The Client manager which coordinates different client requests and invokes different external devices.

For instance, once a continual query request is issued, the client manager will parse the form request and construct the three key components of a continual query $(Q_{cq}, Trig_{cq}, Term_{cq})$, before storing it in the CQ system repository. Although not a direct part of the CQ project, one could imagine value-added update monitoring services based on CQ, where a continual query request can be posted in natural language through either voice or hand-writing or both. Recall the example given earlier: *"notify me whenever Microsoft stock price rises by 10%"*. By hooking up the CQ client with a natural language text recognizer, or hand-writing recognizer, or voice recognizer, we can parse this request and automatically generate the query, the CQ trigger, and the termination condition for this request. The results can be returned to the user either by email, by fax, by phone, or through user-specific bulletin posting.

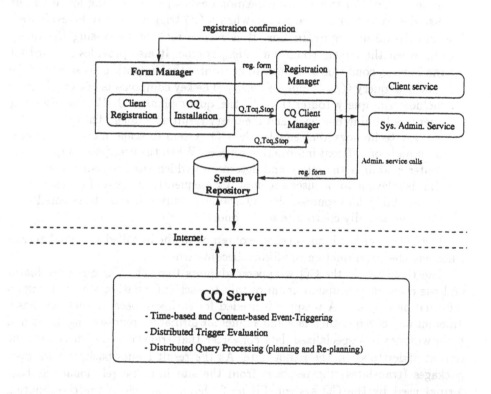

Fig. 1. The CQ Client Tier Architecture

The second tier is the CQ server which is responsible for evaluating continual queries based on the specified update threshold of interest and providing capability for handling distributed event-based triggers. The CQ server manager consists of three key components:

The event-driven update monitor. It coordinates with the CQ wrappers and adapters to track the new updates to the source data. Its main tasks include: (1) the selection of relevant data sources for evaluating CQ triggers, (2) the generation of distributed triggers that can be executed at the selected data sources, and (3) the evaluation of CQ trigger by combining the sub-results of distributed triggers. In short, it decides when to issue an execution of the installed CQ queries.

The CQ-trigger-firing daemon. It is in charge of calling the event-driven update monitor to evaluate the CQ trigger condition for each installed continual query. Two kinds of events are supported in the first generation of the CQ system: (1) a clock daemon checks specified date and time events, and (2) a content-based trigger-firing daemon checks specific update thresholds. In short, the CQ trigger-firing daemon deals with the timing for firing the distributed trigger evaluator, i.e., when a CQ trigger needs to be evaluated.

The continual query evaluator. It is responsible for processing the query Q_{cq} when the trigger condition $Trig_{cq}$ is true. It also provides a guard for the $Term_{cq}$ condition of a query to guarantee the semantic consistency of the continual query $(Q_{cq}, Trig_{cq}, Term_{cq})$. The key components of CQ evaluator include: the query router [11, 10], the query planner [9, 12], the dynamic query replanning manager, and the query result assembler. The query router is a key technology that enables the CQ system to scale in order to handle thousands of different information sources. When the user poses a query, the router examines the query and determines which sites contain information that is relevant to the user's request. Consequently, instead of contacting all the available data sources, the CQ evaluator only contacts the selected sites that can actually contribute to the query.

The CQ server tier is also in charge of removing the installed continual queries whenever their termination conditions become true.

The third tier is the CQ wrappers/adapters tier. The CQ query evaluator and the event-driven update monitor talk to each information sources using an information wrapper. A wrapper is needed for each site because each one has a different way of requesting data and a different format for representing its results. Each wrapper is a specialized data converter that translates the query into the format understood by the remote site. As the result comes back, the wrapper packages (translates) the response from the site into the relational database format used by the CQ system. Figure 2 shows a sketch of the coordination between CQ server and CQ wrappers/adapters, the key components of CQ server and the critical interconnections among them.

4 Client-Server Design

Depending on the need of the application, the CQ client manager, the CQ trigger daemon, the event-driven update monitor, the query router, query planner, and

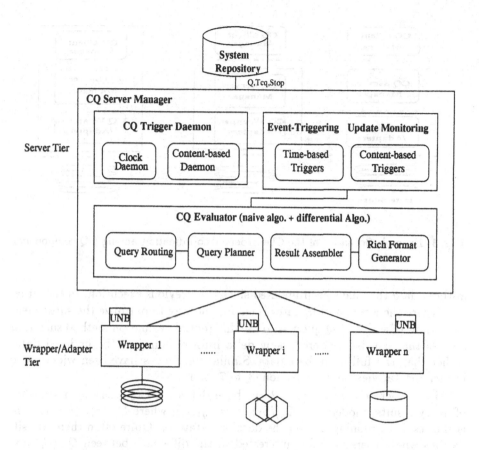

Fig. 2. The CQ Server and Wrappers/Adapters Architecture

query result assembler could be located on a single machine, or distributed among several computers connected through local or wide area networks. CQ uses the most flexible client-server arrangement which is customizable with respect to the particular system requirement of the applications. In this demo, for example, we plan to have the query router running on a powerful server machine, where we also maintain a library of all the current information wrappers including the source capability profiles. Figure 3 shows three different scenarios for multi-layer client/server coordination among CQ components.

5   A Model for Efficient Execution of CQ

Continual queries are standing queries that run continually until the termination condition becomes true. Whenever an relevant update is performed, the CQ system will trigger the execution of the corresponding continual queries. It is obvious that the subsequent executions of a given continual query is only interested

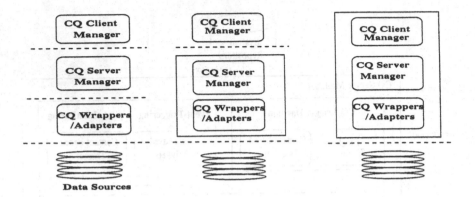

Fig. 3. Example Scenarios of the Client/Server coordination among CQ components

in those data that have been updated since the previous execution. In the situation where the amount of updates is small, one way to optimize the subsequent executions of a given CQ query is to use differential evaluation method such that queries that can be answered using delta information (i.e., the updated data) rather than the full set of base data. Similar techniques have been widely used in incremental view materialization [3, 5, 7, 6, 13].

More concretely, recall Sect. 2, we have defined a CQ query as a sequence of query results, modeled by $Q_{cq}(S_1), ..., Q_{cq}(S_n)$, where $Q_{cq}(S_i), (i = 1, ..., n)$ is the result of running Q_{cq} on the database state S_i. Quite often there are situations where users are more interested in the difference between $Q_{cq}(S_i)$ and $Q_{cq}(S_{i+1})$. This can be accomplished by naively executing the entire query and then filtering out the part of the query result that is the same as the previous result. This simple and straightforward approach can be quite expensive, especially in the Internet environment where query results need to be gathered from multiple source data repositories. An obviously more attractive approach is the differential query evaluation method, which is particularly powerful when $Q_{cq}(S_i)$ is relatively large, and only a small percentage of the result changes from state S_i to state S_{i+1}.

We have proposed a differential re-evaluation algorithm [12]. The key idea behind this algorithm is the following: We produce $Q(S_{i+1})$ by incrementally updating $Q(S_i)$. More concretely, in contrast to a complete re-evaluation, differential re-evaluation means that after the initial execution of a CQ, the re-evaluation of each subsequent execution of this CQ will be performed by using the differential form of the query. This way, we avoid reprocessing the entire query from scratch. When the changes are substantially smaller compared with the latest query execution result, this differential update will be more efficient than reprocessing the entire query.

The differential re-evaluation algorithm (DRA) is invoked by the CQ manager based on the epsilon specification associated with the given CQ. We assume that the information available when the DRA is invoked includes:

- the CQ specification (Q_{cq}, $Trig_{cq}$, $Term_{cq}$);
- the contents of each base relation after the last execution of the CQ;
- the differential relations for each of those operand relations that have been changed since the last execution of the CQ;
- the timestamp of the last execution of the CQ;
- the complete set of the result of the CQ produced by the last execution.

In short, the Differential Re-evaluation Algorithm (DRA) is developed for incrementally computing the new query result from processing updates on top of the previous result. We prove that our differential re-evaluation algorithm to continual queries is *functionally equivalent* to the "recompute the query from scratch" solution, and, in many situations is more efficient. For a formal description of differential (delta) relations and the DRA, refer to [8], where a number of implementation issues is also discussed, including asynchronous evaluation of CQ conditions and strategies for garbage collection of differential relations.

6 Incorporation of Push Data Sources

6.1 Overview of Data Delivery Modes Protocols

Data delivery is defined as the process of delivering information from a set of information sources (servers) to a set of information consumers (clients). There are several possible ways that servers and clients communicate for delivering information to clients, such as clients request and servers respond, servers publish what are available and clients subscribe to only the information of interest, or servers disseminate information by broadcast. Each way can be considered as a protocol between servers and clients, and has pros and cons for delivering data in an open and dynamic information universe.

Client Request and Server Response The *Request/Response* protocol follows the data delivery mechanism that clients send their request to servers to ask the information of their interest, servers respond to the requests of clients by delivering the information requested.

Current database servers and object repositories deliver data only to clients who explicitly request information from them. When a request is received at a server, the server locates or computes the information of interest and returns it to the client. The advantage of the *Request/Response* protocol is the high quality of data delivery since only the information that is explicitly requested by clients is delivered. In a system with a small number of servers and a very large number of clients, the *Request/Response* mechanism may be inadequate, because the server communication and data processing capacity must be divided among all of the clients. As the number of clients continuous to grow, servers may become overwhelmed and may respond with slow delivery or unexpected delay, or even refuse to accept additional connections.

6.2 Servers Publish and Clients Subscribe

The *Publish/Subscribe* protocol delivers information based on the principle that servers publish information online, and clients subscribe to the information of interest. Information delivery is primarily based on the selective subscription of clients to what is available at servers and the subsequent publishing from servers according to what is subscribed.

As the scale and rate of changes for online information continues to grow, the *Publish/Subscribe* mechanism attracts increasing popularity as a promising way of disseminating information over networks. Triggers and change notifications in active database systems bear some resemblance to the *Publish/Subscribe* protocol based on point-to-point communication [2]. The *Publish/Subscribe* mechanisms may not be beneficial when the interest of clients changes irregularly because in such situations clients may be continually interrupted to filter data that is not of interest to them. A typical example is the various online news groups. Another drawback is that publish/subscribe is mostly useful for delivering new or modified data to clients, but it cannot be used to efficiently deliver previously existing data to clients, which the clients later realize they need. Such data are most easily obtained through the request/respond protocol.

6.3 Servers Broadcast

The *Broadcast* mechanism delivers information to clients periodically. Clients who require access to a data item need to wait until the item appears. There are two typical types of broadcasting: *selective broadcast* (or so called *multicast*) and *random broadcast* [4]. Selective broadcast delivers data to a list of known clients and is typically implemented through a router that maintains the list of recipients. Random broadcast, on the other hand, sends information over a medium on which the set of clients who can listen is not known *a priori*. Note that the difference between selective broadcast and *Publish/Subscribe* is that the list of recipients in selective broadcast may change dynamically without explicit subscription from clients.

The *Broadcast* protocol allows multiple clients to receive the data sent by a data source. It is obvious that using broadcast is beneficial when multiple clients are interested in the same items. The tradeoffs of broadcast mechanisms depend upon the number of clients who have the commonality of interest and the volume of information that are of interest to a large number of clients [4, 2].

6.4 Summary of Data Delivery Modes

With the rapid growth of the volume and variety of information available online, combined with the constant increase of information consumers, it is no longer efficient to use a single mode of data delivery. A large-scale modern information system must provide adequate support for different modes of data delivery in order to effectively cope with the various types of communications between clients and servers to improve query responsiveness. Another benefit of providing different modes of data delivery is to allow the system to be optimized for various criteria according to different requirements of data delivery. In this section we identify three potentially popular modes of data delivery and compare them with the types of delivery protocols that can be used. They are client pull-only option, server push-only option, and client pull with server push combined option.

Pull-only Mode In the *Pull-only* mode of data delivery, the transfer of data from servers to clients is initiated by a client pull. When a client request is received at a server, the server responds to it by locating the requested information. The *Request/Respond* style of client and server communication is *pull-based*.

The main characteristic of pull-based delivery is that the arrival of new data items or updates to existing data items are carried out at a server without notification to clients unless clients explicitly poll the server. Also, in pull-based mode, servers must be interrupted continuously to deal with requests from clients. Furthermore, the information that clients can obtain from a server is limited to when and what clients know to ask for. Conventional database systems (including. relational and object-oriented database servers) and most of the web search engines offer primarily pull-based data delivery.

Push-only Mode In *Push-only* mode of data delivery, the transfer of data from servers to clients is initiated by a server push in the absence of specific request from clients. The main difficulty of push-based approach is to decide which data would be of common interest, and when to send them to clients (periodically, irregularly, or conditionally). Thus, the usefulness of server push depends heavily on the accuracy of a server to predict the needs of clients. *Broadcast* style of client and server communication is a typical *push-only* type.

In push-based mode, servers disseminate information to either an unbounded set of clients (random broadcast) who can listen to a medium or a selective set of clients (multicast) who belong to some categories of recipients that may receive the data. It is obvious that the push-based data delivery avoids the disadvantages identified for client-pull approaches such as unnoticed changes. A serious problem with push-only style, however, is the fact that in the absence of a client request the servers may not deliver the data of interest in a timely fashion. A practical solution to this problem is to allow the clients to provide a profile of their interests to the servers. The *Publish/Subscribe* protocol is one of the popular mechanisms for providing such profiles. Using publish/subscribe, clients (information consumers) subscribe to a subset of a given class of information by providing a set of expressions that describe the data of interest. These subscriptions form a profile. When new data items are created or existing ones are updated, the servers (information providers) publish the updated information to the subscribers whose profiles match the items.

Hybrid Mode The hybrid mode of data delivery combines the client-pull and server-push mechanisms. The continual query approach [12] presents one possible way of combining the pull and push modes, namely, the transfer of information from servers to clients is first initiated by a client pull and the subsequent transfer of updated information to clients is initiated by a server push.

The hybrid mode represented by continual queries approach can be seen as a specialization of push-only mode. The main difference between hybrid mode and push-only mode is the initiation of the first data delivery. More concretely, in a hybrid mode, clients receive the information that matches their profiles from servers continuously. In addition to new data items and updates, previously existing data that match the profile of a client who initially pull the server are delivered to the client immediately after the initial pull. However, in push-only mode, although new data and updates are delivered to clients with matching profiles, the delivery of previously existing data to clients that subsequently realize that they need it is much more difficult than through a client pull.

6.5 Pure Push versus Continual Queries

In a pure bush environment such as broadcast services, the server broadcast the update periodically and the clients may tune the channels to listen to those broadcast information that is of particular interest to them. Thus, the data is pushed from source to the broadcast server and then pushed from the server to the client. Figure 4 shows the typical data delivery flow in a pure push environment.

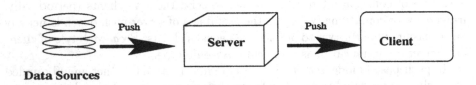

Fig. 4. The data delivery flow in a broadcast-based push service

Continual Queries server is not a pure-push based server since the request is initiated by a client pull. Once the client pulled the CQ server at the time of installing a CQ, the CQ server starts pushing the subsequent updates that satisfy the update threshold specified in the CQ to the client continually until the termination condition is met. The data delivery flow is shown in Fig. 5.

6.6 Incorporation of Broadcast-based Push in the CQ system

In the Continual Queries system architecture, we consider both pull-based data sources such as databases and web search engines and push-based data sources such as Pointcast, Marimba, BackWeb, AirMedia, Intermind. The idea for incorporating push sources into the CQ architecture is to provide a broadcast-based

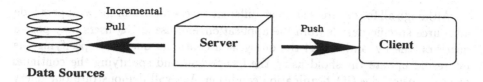

Fig. 5. The data delivery flow in a broadcast-based push service

push client agent on the CQ server for each push source. This push client agent listens to the broadcast lines on behave of a group of CQ clients, grabs the broadcast information of interest, and then responds to the CQ clients' queries by filtering out the irrelevant information. Figure 6 shows a sketch of the data delivery modes in a CQ system that incorporates the push sources in answering queries.

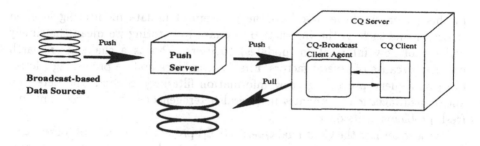

Fig. 6. The data delivery flow in a broadcast-based push service

7 Description of Demo

We demonstrate the latest version of our CQ robot, as described in the previous sections. Specifically we show how to use our CQ robots for monitoring updates in the following four different types of sources containing bibliographic data in the heterogeneous formats:

- A Oracle database which is remotely accessible through SQL, OraPERL, and SQLNet.
- A DB2 database which is remotely accessible through JDBC and SQL.
- A collection of UNIX files which are accessible through a Perl script or a Java Applet.
- A World Wide Web source which is accessible through our semi-structured information adapter and filter utility.

Although all four sources support different access methods, the wrappers hide all source specific details from the application/end-users. CQ users may pose a query on the fly, and install the query as a continual query by specifying the interested update threshold using the CQ trigger and specifying the continual duration using the CQ termination condition. We will demonstrate our query router technology and show how the multi-level progressive pruning improves the overall responsive time of queries as well as trigger evaluation. We also provide a testbed which consists of a user-friendly interface to allow users to experiment the updates at the data sources and watch the CQ system to compute the update threshold and evaluate the trigger, and alert or notify the user by email the new updates that match the query. We will also demonstrate the client and system administration services such as browsing and updating the installed continual queries, canceling some running continual queries upon request, and tracing the CQ trigger evaluation status and the update monitor status.

8 Conclusion

In this paper, we have described the problem of update monitoring in open environments such as the Internet. By update monitoring we mean the timely delivery of new information (updates) to users. This is a challenge research problem because of several factors. First, it combines update processing (detection) and query processing (new information filtering). Second, the detection and synchronization of updates in several heterogeneous data sources presents fresh problems of its own.

We also outline the Continual Queries (CQ) project as an example of research work being done in the update monitoring area. In the CQ project, a continual query is a combination of a normal query and a trigger condition. The query is evaluated when the trigger condition becomes true. The trigger condition may be time-based, e.g., every Monday at 8am, or content-based, i.e., a predicate on the database state such as "Microsoft stock going up by 10%". The query would be in SQL for relational databases, and keyword search for Web pages. A termination condition stops the query execution cycle.

We outline an architecture for the concrete implementation of continual queries in the CQ project. The architecture divides the problem into several components. On the client side, we have the GUIs for the specification of continual queries. These queries are translated into executable sub-queries and triggers by the CQ server. The CQ server consists of a system configuration repository (storing the names and capabilities of data sources), query translator and processing, and distributed trigger execution. The sub-queries are passed to data source wrappers, which translate and execute the local queries. The results are passed back to the CQ server, which assembles them for the user.

We are implementing the continual query capability for DARPA's Advanced Logistics Program. Although a relatively small step towards the lofty goal of generic update monitoring in open environments, the CQ project is making concrete progress. To try out our current demo, please point your Web browser to the following URL: http://www.cse.ogi.edu/DISC/CQ/. We welcome comments, bug reports, and feedback that will bring us closer to the ideal of getting the right information at the right time.

References

1. S. Acharya, R. Alonso, M. Franklin, and S. Zdonik. Broadcast disks: Data management for asymmetric communications environments. In *Proceedings of the ACM SIGMOD International Conference on Management of Data*, San Jose, CA, May 1995.
2. S. Acharya, M. Franklin, and S. Zdonik. Balancing push and pull for data broadcast. In *Proceedings of the ACM SIGMOD International Conference on Management of Data*, Tucson, Arizona, May 1997.
3. J. Blakeley, P. Larson, and F. Tompa. Efficiently updating materialized views. In *Proceedings of the ACM-SIGMOD International Conference on Management of Data*, pages 61-71, Washington, DC, May 1986.
4. M. Franklin and S. Zdonik. Dissemination-based information systems. *IEEE Bulletin of the Technical Committee on Data Engineering*, 19(3):20-30, September 1996.
5. E. N. Hanson. A performance analysis of view materialization strategies. In *Proceedings of the ACM-SIGMOD International Conference on Management of Data*, pages 440-453, San Francisco, CA, May 1987.
6. B. Kahler and O. Risnes. Extending logging for database snapshot refresh. In *Proceedings of the International Conference on Very Large Data Bases*, pages 389-398, Brighton, England, September 1987.
7. B. Lindsay, L. Haas, and C. Mohan. A snapshot differential refresh algorithm. In *Proceedings of the ACM-SIGMOD International Conference on Management of Data*, pages 53-60, Washington, DC, May 1986.
8. L. Liu and C. Pu. The diom approach to large-scale interoperable information systems. Technical report, TR95-16, Department of Computing Science, University of Alberta, Edmonton, Alberta, March 1995.
9. L. Liu and C. Pu. An adaptive object-oriented approach to integration and access of heterogeneous information sources. *DISTRIBUTED AND PARALLEL DATABASES: An International Journal*, 5(2), 1997.
10. L. Liu and C. Pu. Dynamic query processing in diom. *IEEE Bulletin on Data Engineering*, 20(3), September 1997.
11. L. Liu and C. Pu. A metadata approach to improving query responsiveness. In *Proceedings of the Second IEEE Metadata Conference*, Maryland, April 1997.
12. L. Liu, C. Pu, R. Barga, and T. Zhou. Differential evaluation of continual queries. In *IEEE Proceedings of the 16th International Conference on Distributed Computing Systems*, Hong Kong, May 27-30 1996.
13. N. Roussopoulos and H. Kang. Preliminary design of adms+: A workstation-mainframe integrated architecture fopr database management systems. In *Proceedings of the 12th International Conference on Very Large Data Bases*, pages 355-364, Kyoto, Japan, August 1986.

dLIMIT - A Middleware Framework for Loosely-Coupled Database Federations

Henrik Loeser and Theo Härder

University of Kaiserslautern, Dept. of Computer Science,
P.O. Box 3049, D-67653 Kaiserslautern, Germany
email: {loeser|haerder}@informatik.uni-kl.de

Abstract. Today, the Internet offers an everyday increasing number of information sources making search for a certain piece of information a difficult job. By combining existing special-purpose information sources, larger data volumes can be offered to users increasing the chance of finding the needed information. In this paper, we present dLIMIT, a flexible, application-independent framework for building adaptive middleware to easily combine multiple similarly structured databases (DBs). For accessing the related database management systems (DBMSs) residing on heterogeneous platforms different protocols can be used. The dLIMIT-based middleware can be easily configured to requirements of both the application and the DBMSs.

1 Introduction

Today, the Internet offers an every day increasing number of information sources making, on one hand, search for a particular piece of information a difficult job. On the other hand, there may be one among 10^{12} Web pages which provides the needed data. A similar situation exists in large enterprises where departments or divisions, interconnected by a network, have their own special-purpose information systems (ISs). Since data is not explicitly shared, a search request may not be successful in the own IS, although the required information is existing "somewhere". However, due to the lack of an (adequate) integration of these more or less autonomous systems, there is no chance of finding such a piece of information.

To improve the opportunity to find the wanted information, we can use the existent network infrastructure. As mentioned, departments in companies are often interconnected by networks ("Intranets"). Cooperating enterprises use so-called "Extranets", almost every company, nearly every institution, and an uncountable number of private users are on the "data highway" Internet. Thus, to enable data access in autonomous and possibly heterogeneous ISs, we need a framework capable of using different TCP/IP-based database-related communication protocols applied in the Internet. The framework must be adaptable to application-specific demands and the application environments in order to not confine the support to a single field of application. Such environments typically rely on distinct communication protocols for data access, e.g., for the integration of so-called "legacy systems". Furthermore, they have to maintain a high degree of autonomy by using IS encapsulation and other security mechanisms. Homogeneous frameworks would narrow their use only to a small number of platforms. Therefore, bridging heterogeneity should be a prime design goal for the protocols and services of the framework to be built. And, last but not least, the framework must be easy to understand (to enhance user acceptance), easy to configure and to adjust to new application types as well as to new ISs to be integrated. Key properties are run-time performance to serve a large number of users and extensibility to integrate new features.

In this paper, we present dLIMIT [Möc97], a middleware framework for building loosely-coupled DB federations across the Internet (see Fig. 1), to be accessed by application programs (application logic, AL) via graphical user interfaces (GUI). dLIMIT offers a simple but powerful application programming interface (API) to the application developer providing location and communication transparency. dLIMIT facilitates the access of autonomous, heterogeneous information systems. It supports different types of access to underlying DBMSs, and allows the encapsulation of these systems, e.g., for security reasons. dLIMIT, based on Java [GJS96] to achieve platform independence and to support the easy installation and maintenance of applications, is highly configurable. Thus, it is adaptable to the respective kind of application and its environment. dLIMIT can be employed both in Java applets and in applications so that browser-based as well as stand-alone applications can be developed.

In the following, we first motivate different application areas for such a middleware framework and analyze their common characteristics. In Sect. 3, we discuss the requirements for the framework arising from different kinds of users. After that, we outline the architecture of dLIMIT and discuss related performance aspects. In Sect. 5, we describe how dLIMIT supports the development of applications based on loosely-coupled DB federations and how dLIMIT can be adjusted to the particular application requirements. In Sect. 6, we discuss the adaptation of applications resp. of dLIMIT to DBs to be included into the federation, and present dLIMIT's support for the encapsulation of DBMSs. In Sect. 7, we discuss related work. We conclude with a summary and an outlook on future work.

2 Application Areas

Due to the increasing usage of network technology and connections to the Internet or to an Intranet, many DB-based ISs, so far only locally accessible, are made available to a larger group of users. However, every IS must be accessed separately, and every DB must be retrieved in isolation. In the following, we take an exemplary look at some of these ISs to capture their common characteristics. Later on, when discussing dLIMIT, we will keep on referring to these examples.

One of the domains using DBs to administer a more or less huge amount of real objects are libraries and their ISs, library management systems (LMSs). In the past, they provided a telnet access, later in addition a Web-based interface to their data, today often known as OPAC (Online Public Access Catalogue

[LUL97, SM97]). These ISs have a similar structure, i.e., attribute names may differ but a common set of attributes is available, e.g. author, title, isbn, etc. The ISs are used to search for literature in order to find the location of a particular book and to determine its availability. Data access to these ISs is performed in read-only mode, whereas data manipulation is achieved by authorized persons thereby using a separate data access interface. By combining different LMSs the probability of finding the needed book can be increased significantly. When search is being done in such an LMS federation, four steps are performed. A central server is called, the query is distributed by this server to all DBs to be addressed, the answers are collected, merged, and homogenized by the server, and finally the result presented to the user. The origin of each single answer should show the location where to search for the real object, i.e. the book.

Another example having similar characteristics are ISs for biological preparations, e.g., for collections of butterflies. Moreover, in addition to LMSs, not only textual data but also images showing the butterflies may be presented to the user. Other ISs having also non-textual data are, e.g., software libraries resp. repositories allowing the search for software packages (examples are [Gam97, JR97]). These repositories often store hyperlinks to the software and sometimes the software itself, e.g. in case of a private software library. To access such software packages, binary large objects (BLOBs) have to be transferred. A further example of ISs are DBMSs used in hospitals for the management of patient data. If hospitals located in a metropolitan area want to cooperate, e.g., to exchange statistical data or to coordinate preventive steps in health care [CRHT97], data access to ISs of the cooperating hospitals must be provided, e.g. by building a loosely-coupled DB federation across the Internet or a regional public network. Since the data transmitted over the network is very sensitive, extensive security mechanism are needed. These mechanisms concern the authorization of persons using the ISs, the encryption of the transmitted data, and the encapsulation of the DBMSs managing the data to prevent attacks.

As we have seen, there are different application areas having a common set of characteristics:

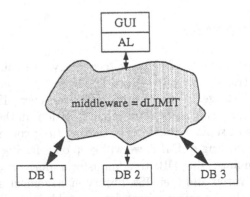

Fig. 1. dLIMIT as middleware

- The ISs to be combined serve the same purpose. Therefore, the information structure, i.e., the set of common attributes is similar, but attributes may be named differently.
- Access to the ISs is performed in read-only mode or without special needs for concurrency control.
- The origin of the answers is important to the user to enable consecutive actions.

An Internet-based DB federation substantially improves data retrieval. However, the application requirements differ in the data types to be transmitted or in their security demands. To avoid the development of tailored solutions for each kind of application, a more general framework handling these application types and their requirements should be developed.

3 Requirement Analysis

When starting to develop such a middleware framework one has to keep in mind the different user group requirements. These groups are the application developers building applications by using the framework for accessing different ISs, the information providers having to adapt the framework-based application to their underlying DBMS, and last but not least the framework developers designing and programming the framework itself. While each group has its own varying demands, there is a set of mutual core requirements.

3.1 Core Requirements

To allow for a broad employment of the middleware framework as well as of applications based on it, the framework should be platform-independent. To facilitate the framework and application development as well as the application installation and maintenance, key features like flexibility and extensibility are required implying an object-oriented, i.e. component-based design. To avoid recompilation of applications and servers when composing, adapting and changing the system, these key properties should be achieved by configuration only.

3.2 The Framework Developer Requirements

Nowadays there exists a broad field of individual platforms whose support often is a cost- and time-intensive job. But to perform its specific task the framework must be available on most of these platforms. Due to the everyday alteration of the Internet and its applied technologies, new communication protocols and methods for data access must be repeatedly integrated to offer their use to application developers and information providers. As we mentioned above, some applications, e.g. the hospital ISs, have special requirements regarding security, etc. Hence, the framework must be extensible even at the level where additional components or new functions are to be integrated. This implies a modular, object-oriented design to enable the replacement of a component by another one.

One of the framework's goal is to support a broad field of applications. As we have seen, data types varying from "classical" SQL-based types (LMS) to large objects (images or software packages) may occur. Therefore, a common, i.e. generic, communication protocol for transmitting the application-specific data structures must be used. In addition, the default communication protocol should obtain high performance behavior for most application types.

3.3 Application Developer Requirements

To provide the application developer with a useful middleware framework, first of all, its use must be easy, and its functionality must seamlessly fit to the application. On one hand, to be easy understandable the framework's application programming interface (API) must have a small set of functions. On the other hand, to be powerful these functions often have a large set of, sometimes esoteric, options making their use difficult. Therefore, the API only should have a small but functional set of options which should be intuitively applicable.

Since each application has its own distinct requirements, e.g., secured communication for the hospital ISs, a set of common communication protocols should be offered to the developer to speed-up the application development. To facilitate development the middleware should be composable and adaptable to the application using a configuration mechanism.

One of the framework's main tasks is to hide the network-related complexities from the application developer, so that he can abstract from communication and related problems. Thus, the framework has to work as a middleware gluing the application (i.e. graphical user interface (GUI), the application logic (AL)) and the various information sources together (see Fig. 1). While access to the potentially large set of DBMSs must be transparent, the information origin must be contained in the answer to enable the user or the application developer for accomplishing consecutive actions.

Additionally, fault tolerance is very important. Thus, communication errors should be handled by the middleware framework and reported to the application to react in an appropriate manner depending on the application semantics.

3.4 Information Provider Requirements

So far, access to information sources was granted to local and "trustworthy" users without the predominant need for rigid isolation. By offering a DB to the Internet community, new security requirements arise. First of all, the information providers want to protect their systems against unauthorized access and data manipulation. To prevent attacks a DBMS can be encapsulated, i.e., data access by an application should be via a server hiding the DBMS from the Internet and managing authorization. To protect sensitive data, e.g. existing in a hospital IS, encrypted data transmission must be provided in an application-specific way.

To enhance acceptance by reducing installation and maintenance costs, adaptation to a given DBMS must be easily done by configuration mechanisms thereby avoiding compilation by information providers. If a JDBC-capable DBMS is to be accessed, the inclusion of proprietary JDBC drivers should be possible by configuration.

An identical DB schema cannot be anticipated for the DBs to be integrated, even when they offer similar data contents. Therefore, a mechanism for mapping a local DB schema to the common schema, i.e., the internal schema of the application, must be provided.

3.5 Summary of Requirements

In the following, we briefly summarize the main requirements for our framework:

– *Easy adaptation/installation*: The framework's components should be easily adaptable to the application and information provider demands by configuration mechanisms.
– *Alterable/selectable components*: The framework should provide a set of components offering common communication protocols. Components should be easily replaceable by other implementations.
– *Security*: Direct access to the integrated DBs as well as unauthorized reading of data should be prevented (in an application-dependent way) by architectural and implementational means.
– *Generic data transfer mechanism*: The framework's default communication protocol should cope with any data to be transferred. High communication performance should be provided for most data types.

Based on these basic requirements we will discuss dLIMIT and its features in the rest of the paper.

4 The Architecture of dLIMIT

In the following, we outline the architecture of dLIMIT and its components (see Fig. 2) and discuss some implementation aspects regarding its performance and key features. While developing the architecture we try to keep in mind the requirements motivated in Sect. 2 and 3. The usage and adaptation of the dLIMIT components will be explained in Sect. 5 and 6.

4.1 dLIMIT - An Overview

One of the application developer requirements is a simple but functional API. This is offered by the *Client Interface* (CI) which provides methods for specifying and executing a task and receiving the answers. As all other dLIMIT components, too, the CI is modeled as a Java interface to support simple and flexible replacement of underlying implementations making dLIMIT highly adaptable. A task passed to the CI by the application is determined by

– its destinations (*locations*), i.e., more or less descriptive names of the servers where the query is to be executed or the task is initially routed to (see below and Sect. 6),

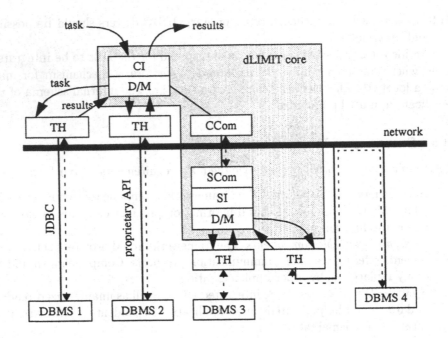

Fig. 2. Architecture of dLIMIT - Overview

- a (short) description, i.e. an identifier, used by the application-specific *Task-Handlers* (THs) to distinguish the task type, e.g., "simple" for a task resulting from a "one-argument-query" and "complex" for a query with multiple search parameters,
- a parameter object. This can be an instance of any Java type resp. class, e.g., an object holding the application- and task-specific parameters.

After starting the task execution at the CI the task is routed by dLIMIT to its final destinations. In each destination, a TH is invoked to evaluate the query. To enable query execution, a TH converts a task with the help of its description and the argument object to a (DB-) system-dependent query that can be executed by the related DBMS. Each result object returned by the DBMS is packed into an *Answer*, i.e., a data structure containing one result object and the location name. The latter one is needed to inform the user about the information source. All Answers of a site are included into a single *AnswerSet* (AS), a data container which is passed back to the CI where it is delivered to the application.

On the task's way down from the CI to the TH responsible for the local query execution, other dLIMIT components may be traversed (see Fig.2). After receiving a task the CI calls the *Distributor/Merger* (D/M) which is the central module that manages the locally available THs. It splits a task according to the locally visible location hierarchies and passes it to a suitable TH (*routing*, see Sect. 6). On the results way up, the D/M merges the received ASs to a single one and passes it to its invoking component (SI or finally CI, see below). In each D/M traversed, the AS may be filtered, for example, to remove duplicate answers.

To find a suitable TH for contacting a location the THs register themselves during start-up at the D/M and specify their protocols. These can be data access protocols like JDBC (Java DataBase Connectivity [HC97]), proprietary APIs (see Fig. 2) or communication protocols like "dLIMIT". The latter one is the protocol used for communication between the *Client Communication* (CCom) and *Server Communication* (SCom) components. This protocol is based on Java *ObjectStreams* which provide automatic marshalling of the transferred objects. Thus, all object types can be transferred making dLIMIT application-independent. To avoid explicit distinction between TH and CCom, the CCom is considered a specialized TH (see configuration example in Sect. 6), i.e., a "real" CCom is an instance of a Java class which implements the TH interface and communicates with an SCom.

While most of the components can be used in a dLIMIT client as well as in a dLIMIT server, the SCom is one of the two modules that is only used in a server. Besides some administrational functions contained in every component it specifies in addition a listen method. After invoking this function with a port number as a parameter, the dLIMIT server is installed listening on the network and waiting for tasks from dLIMIT clients. The network protocol used by the SCom and the CCom depends on the corresponding component implementation.

When a task is received it is passed by the SCom to the *Server Interface* (SI). Analogous to the CI it has a similar interface which only differs in some functions: task construction functions are not needed since complete tasks are delivered. To hide DBMSs to be invoked (see Sect. 6), functions for replacing the task locations have been added, that is, a global name can be replaced by a list of only locally known names resp. DBMSs. Then, the D/M is called by the SI and acts as being directly invoked by a CI, so that other dLIMIT servers or DBMSs can be contacted eventually.

4.2 Communication and Performance Aspects

An important design goal of dLIMIT is run-time performance to serve a large number of users by a dLIMIT server and, at the same time, to offer a fast means for information retrieval to the individual user. In the following, we discuss some design and implementation aspects of dLIMIT regarding run-time performance.

While querying a DB over the Internet, communication is the most time-consuming part. To avoid serial task execution, access to the selected servers has to be performed in parallel, that is, a separate thread for each server to be directly addressed in the task has to be created.

During task execution, communication and system failures are handled by each TH separately, which is achieved in Java by throwing and catching *exceptions*. To inform the application, exception objects are packed as answers including their origin and returned as results. By distinguishing application-dependent answer objects and exception objects the application is able to adequately react

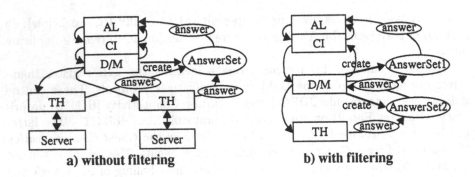

Fig. 3. Result delivery

to failures, e.g., by displaying an error message to the user or by repeating a request to the respective location.

Since typically multiple locations resp. servers are contacted, the reception of all answers may last a while. To shorten the waiting time for the user, we provide an immediate result delivery, i.e., the arriving answers are forwarded to the application as soon as they are received by the CI. This feature has some consequences to the design of the components and data structures involved. As shown in Fig. 3a, the D/M creates an *AnswerSet* (AS) and passes a reference of the AS to all invoked THs as well as to the CI. As a result, the CI returns the reference to the application, i.e., the AS is shared by the THs and the application. As soon as a TH receives an answer, it adds it to the AS. To guarantee consistency of the AS, shared access to it must be *synchronized* which is supported by Java. Furthermore, the application and, as a consequence, the AS must know when the final answer is added. For this reason, it has a counter set by the D/M to the number of created threads resp. invoked THs that is decremented by each TH after task termination. Answers contained in the AS can be accessed by the application in a cursor-like fashion. In order to avoid the application polling the AS for further answers, a *null* object is returned, if the last of all answers has been accessed. If answers are pending and the AS is currently empty (the thread counter has a value greater than zero), the application is blocked, i.e., the application thread is suspended and is resumed on new answers being added to the AS.

If the D/M or CI resp. SI have to fulfill additional jobs like filtering answers, a separate AS must be used (see Fig. 3b). Now, provided the D/M does filtering, it creates two ASs, and passes a reference to AS1 to the THs, a reference to AS2 back to the CI. After that, the D/M can read from AS1 and write the filtered answers to AS2.

Different communication protocols are applicable for the transmission of results from the server to the client. The use of function calls like *next()*, e.g. based on Java RMI (Remote Method Invocation), causes substantial communication overhead. Due to the need to establish a connection every time much processing overhead is provoked. When using ObjectStreams a connection must be established only once, afterwards, data can be transmitted in both directions. This is done by dLIMIT for passing the task to the SCom and the answers back to the CCom.

5 Adaptability to Applications

So far, we have described the architecture of dLIMIT and discussed its components. In the following, we explain how the dLIMIT middleware framework can be used for building applications and how it can be adapted to the application requirements. To use the dLIMIT middleware framework for (developing) a new application only a few things must be adjusted:

- For each dLIMIT component, a suitable implementation has to be selected among the available ones.
- The selected components have to be configured to the application requirements.
- If tailored application requirements must be observed, a new component has to be developed. In the case of the hospital ISs, this may be a CCom and SCom using an encrypted communication protocol like SSL (Secure Socket Layer [FKK96]) to provide a secure data transmission of sensitive data.
- Since application-specific THs are to be used, they must be developed based on a template provided by our framework.

To make TH development as easy as possible, a JDBC TH template for SQL-based queries is made available (see Fig. 4). It consists of four modules and the TH interface implementation (shadowed box):

- *TaskExecutor*: It is the central component invoked by the TH itself. It is responsible for the JDBC-based execution of SQL strings on a DB. The JDBC *ResultSet* is transformed back to an application-dependent answer object. For the SQL string mapping the NameMapperManager and the TaskConverter are invoked.
- *NameMapperManager*: It manages the different location-dependent NameMappers and selects the right one for each specific TH instance resp. thread.
- *NameMapper*: Since not all DBMS supporting JDBC-based access have the same DB schema, a mapping of table and column names must be performed. The mapping is based on Java *Properties*, so that an adaptation to a specific DBMS can be easily achieved (see next section).
- *TaskConverter*: It transforms an application-dependent task into an SQL string. Based on the object type and the attribute values a string containing an SQL command is generated and passed back to the TaskExecutor.

To integrate DBMSs which do not support JDBC-based access, specific THs have to be developed by implementing the TH interface, for example, to enable access to object-oriented DBMSs (OODBMSs). For this purpose, a unique protocol identifier resp. description must be chosen, e.g., "OOSystem1" for a TH querying

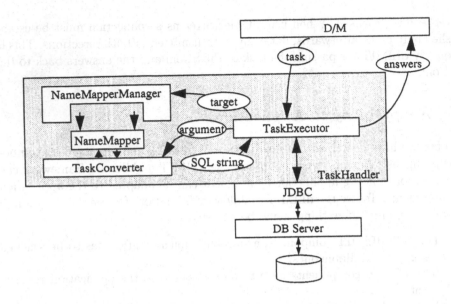

Fig. 4. Template of a JDBC TaskHandler

a particular OODBMS, to identify itself to the D/M. Furthermore, the task execution function has to be implemented. This can be accomplished by, e.g., using the *Java Native Interface* (JNI, [Jav97]) to use non-Java native APIs. Hereby, older systems not supporting Java ("legacy systems") can be integrated and used.

To establish an application-specific network service, the ports used by the SCom implementations can be configured, e.g., a federation of LMSs can agree to use port 4321 for their dLIMIT-based service.

Once, application implementation and selection of adequate dLIMIT components has been completed, a runnable dLIMIT server must be composed. To simplify this job, dLIMIT provides a special *Starter Application* for servers. Based on a configuration file (see Fig. 5) the specified components are loaded and initialized. In our example of a hospital federation, these may be an SSL-based SCom listening on port 911, a standard SI and a standard D/M, a JDBC-based TH, and an SSL-based CCom(-TH). The application developer can attach this configuration file and the Starter Application to the dLIMIT components and deliver this package to the various information providers for low-cost installation.

6 Adaptability to Information Systems

After having finished the application development the client and server programs can be distributed as Java bytecode to all information providers as well as to all

```
SCom=dLimit.server.ServerCommunicationSSL
SI=dLimit.server.ServerInterface
DM=dLimit.DistributerMerger
TH=dLimit.jdbc.TH_SQL_JDBC;dLimit.THdLimitComSSL
port=911
```

Fig. 5. Server configuration - example

users. Since only bytecode has to be shipped, this distribution is straightforward. To enhance the acceptance and to reduce installation costs, the dLIMIT server must be easily adaptable to each participating IS and to its environment. This adjustment includes the

- specification of locations and the communication methods to access them,
- configuration of the IS hierarchies seen by users and ISs,
- adaptation of the local DB schema to the schema used by the application.

Locations and their communication protocols are specified by URLs (Uniform Resource Locators, see Fig. 6). While, in our example for LMSs, the local system named *LMS_local* is accessed with a JDBC-URL using subprotocol DB2 on port 8100 [HC97], *LMS2* located in Munich (SSL-based) as well as KL1 (standard) are dLIMIT servers accessed using the dLIMIT protocol.

```
# Location=URL
LMS_local=jdbc:db2://cs1.informatik.uni-kl.de:8100/lms
LMS2=dLIMIT_SSL://lms.informatik.tu-muenchen.de
KL1=dLIMIT://cs1.informatik.uni-kl.de
```

Fig. 6. Location configuration - example

As mentioned above, dLIMIT supports the building of server hierarchies (to optimize communication). dLIMIT servers, in turn, provide the encapsulation of underlying DBMSs as well as of complete subhierarchies. For this purpose, a configuration file must be provided to the client (see Fig. 7a). It contains the keyword _root used by the *D/M routing submodule* to indicate an entry point. Based on this file a location tree is built, and routing information depending on the (user specified) target location is added to the dLIMIT task. In our example, LMS_local and LMS2 are accessed via the dLIMIT server KL1, i.e., LMS_local and LMS2 are added to the task as sublocations of KL1. To hide access methods for both subnodes, only the URL for KL1 (see Fig.6) needs to be known by the client. Since Java applets can merely open a connection to the machine they are down-loaded from, they have to contact a dLIMIT server or DBMSs residing on this machine. Thus, the configuration given in Fig. 7a is typical for applet-based applications. To route a task the dLIMIT server KL1 has to know the addresses of LMS_local and LMS2 shown in Fig. 6. Since there is no difference between CComs and DB-accessing THs, and, thus, between DBMSs and dLIMIT

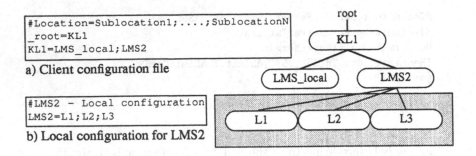

a) Client configuration file

b) Local configuration for LMS2

Fig. 7. Location hierarchy - example

servers, the encapsulation of complete subhierarchies can be easily realized. By performing the filter process in the SI of the dLIMIT server, LMS2 (see Fig. 7) the local LMSs *L1* to *L3* (see shadowed box) can be hidden by LMS2. The only extra thing required is a configuration file specifying the substitutions for LMS2 (see Fig. 7b) and the location URLs (not shown) for these DBMSs.

Another situation occurs when a JDBC-TH based on the template is deployed. In this case, two other configuration files have to be provided. First, to adapt the JDBC-TH to the particular DBMSs, the JDBC-drivers and their protocols must be specified to allow the D/M to select the TH for handling URLs resp. locations using these subprotocols. In the example given in Fig. 8a, the JDBC-TH is responsible for accessing DB2 systems, and DBs of vendor XYZ.

```
protocols=jdbc:db2:;jdbc:xyz:        Author=lms.author
drivers=ibm.netsql.DB2Driver;        Author.lastname=name
        xyz.sql.XYZDriver            Author.URL=WWW_address
                                     . . .
                                     Book=lms.book
                                     Book.ISBN=bnr
                                     . . .
    a) JDBC-TH configuration             b) Name mapping
```

Fig. 8. Configuration examples

To cope with different DB schemas, the dLIMIT NameMapper can be applied. By specifying substitutions for DB table and column names, a DB schema can be transformed into the schema used by the application. This is done by assigning a mapping file to the location name. In the mapping file itself, DB table and column names are assigned to the class resp. attribute names of the application. In the example given in Fig. 8b, the application uses the class *Author* with the attributes *lastname* and *URL*. The DB schema has the table *author* in the schema named *lms* with the attributes *name* and *WWW_address*. Based on this specification the application-dependent names can be mapped to the given DB schema.

As outlined above, only a few configuration files have to be edited to adapt a dLIMIT server to a particular DBMS. Thus, installation and configuration can be achieved easily. Due to dLIMIT's advanced features, a DBMS or complete hierarchies of ISs can be hidden to users as well as to other ISs.

7 Related Work

The focus of many FDBS-based approaches is on the integration of different data models and on schema mapping. An FDBS provides a single homogenized view derived from a fixed number of heterogeneous data sources. Typically, the DB schema is statically defined by using an explicit mapping from all participating source schemas to the target schema representing the global view. In contrast, the dLIMIT approach does not need to know all participating data sources in advance. dLIMIT-based applications refer to a given schema which must be supported by all data sources to be dynamically integrated. For this reason, the individual schemas of the data sources must strongly overlap in their structures (entity types), but may differ in the data models used as well as in specific details (number and naming of attributes). By using dLIMIT's NameMapper, the schemas of the data sources can be mapped to the application schema.

CORBA [OMG96], generally spoken, is a middleware framework, too. Based on stubs and class skeletons generated from the data type specification in IDL (Interface Definition Language) marshalling of data to be transported is automatically obtained. One of CORBA's main advantages is the independence from platforms and programming languages. Using our dLIMIT approach we are restricted to Java. Other programming languages can be used via the JNI [Jav97] while implementing a TH. Since requests are sent directly to a self-written server (library-based ORB) or the stand-alone ORB, dLIMIT-like servers must be developed to provide encapsulation of subhierarchies. When used solely for communication, the type *any*, as one of CORBA's drawbacks, must be used for providing a generic solution. Furthermore, all application-dependent data structures to be transported have to be IDL-defined and, before transmitting them, converted to *any*. Another drawback is that the IIOP (Internet Inter-ORB Protocol) used by most ORBs for communication is not secure. dLIMIT supports the use of secure communication between CCom and SCom as well as in self-written THs.

Today, there exist Web-based interfaces to many LMSs (OPACs, [LUL97, SM97]), a suitable application area of dLIMIT. Similar to dLIMIT they allow for the combined query to more than one LMS thereby directly accessing the specified LMSs. Based on dLIMIT servers and the routing mechanism dLIMIT supports the building of hierarchies for optimizing communication, and for hiding a single LMS or a complete LMS subhierarchy from direct access. By using the CGI (Common Gateway Interface [CGI95]) the OPACs do not need a Java applet on the client-side, i.e. the Web browser, which keeps start-up time short. By developing a CGI program or a servlet, i.e. a server-side applet, which transforms HTTP (HyperText Transfer Protocol) requests to dLIMIT tasks and returns HTML pages containing the answers, a similar environment with all its advantages and drawbacks [Loe97] can be created with dLIMIT. Therefore, dLIMIT may be used for building more powerful OPAC federations.

8   Conclusions and Outlook

In this paper, we have presented dLIMIT, an application-independent middleware framework for building loosely-coupled DB federations across the Internet. Designed for high flexibility and adaptability, dLIMIT offers a simple but powerful API to the application developer providing location and communication transparency. Hereby, access to multiple DBs distributed over the Internet can be integrated into the applications without worrying about their locations and communication protocols. Aiming at DBMS federations with a similar information structure but different DB schemas and applications with read-only data access, dLIMIT provides a set of pre-built but extensible components to compose a communication infrastructure tailored to the application requirements. By the use of configuration files the resulting applications as well as the dLIMIT servers can be easily adapted to the application environments as well as to underlying DBMSs enhancing the acceptance and improving the benefit of using dLIMIT.

As demonstrated by our examples, there is a broad field of applications having common characteristics to be supported. Currently, dLIMIT-based applications in the area of library management systems[1] and biological preparations are tested. Additional applications are being designed. By providing a middleware framework the time-consuming development of application-dependent but less powerful solutions could be avoided. In the future, more sophisticated component implementations will be available to cope with special (secure) communication protocols. To integrate C++-based (dLIMIT) servers directly, a CCom using CORBA-IIOP (Common Object Request Broker Architecture [OMG96], Internet Inter-ORB Protocol) is currently implemented. To support multiple communication protocols within a single dLIMIT server, the Starter Application will be extended. This will allow for, e.g., receiving dLIMIT- as well as dLIMIT_SSL-transported tasks by a single server.

One of the future issues to be achieved is, based on different CCom and SCom implementations, to measure the suitability of communication protocols regarding set-oriented data access for different data types. After that, application-area-specific configuration hints regarding the deployment of CCom/SCom versions can be given to application developers to improve the overall system performance. Another issue to be done is to enhance the D/M component by functionality of the federated DBMS INFINITY [HST97]. By integrating the schema mapping component homogenized views to heterogeneous schemas could be derived thereby supporting combined access to more heterogeneous DBMSs.

---

[1] An applet for JDK1.1-capable browsers using dLIMIT to access library informations is accessable via http://www-agdvs.informatik.uni-kl.de:18070/dLIMIT/

References

[CGI95]   *The CGI Specification*, Version 1.1, University of Illinois, Urbana-Champaign, http://hoohoo.ncsa.uiuc.edu/cgi/interface.html (1995)

[CRHT97]   Castilho, J.M.V., da Rocha, R.P., Härder, T., Thomas, J.: *Global DB Views in a Federation of Autonomous DBS - Supporting ad-hoc Queries in a Distributed Information System for Health Care*, submitted to the Journal of the Brazilian Computer Society (JBCS) (1997)

[FKK96]   Freier, A. O., Karlton, P., Kocher, P. C.: *The SSL Protocol, Version 3.0 - Internet Draft*, Netscape Communications, http://home.netscape.com-/eng/ssl3/ssl-toc.html (1996)

[Gam97]   *Gamelan - The official directory for Java*, http://www.gamelan.com (1997)

[GJS96]   Gosling, J., Joy, B., Steele, G.: *The Java Language Specification*, Addison-Wesley, http://java.sun.com/doc/language_specification.html (1996)

[HC97]   Hamilton, G., Cattell, R.: *JDBC: A Java SQL API*, Version 1.20, SUN Microsystems Computer Company, ftp://ftp.javasoft.com/pub/jdbc/jdbc-spec-0120.ps (January 1997)

[HST97]   Härder, Th., Sauter, G., Thomas, J.: *Design and Architecture of the FDBS Prototype INFINITY*, in: Proc. Int. CAiSe'97 Workshop on Engineering Federated Database Systems (EFDBS'97), Barcelona, Catalonia, Spain, pp. 57-68 (June 1997)

[Jav97]   *JNI - Java Native Interface*, SUN Microsystems Computer Company, http://www.javasoft.com/products/jdk/1.1/docs/guide/jni/index.html (1997)

[JR97]   *The Java Repository*, http://java.wiwi.uni-frankfurt.de/ (1997)

[Loe97]   Loeser, H.: *Linking DBs to the Web - Techniques, Tools and Trends* (in German), in: Proceedings of GI-Fachtagung 'Datenbanken in Büro, Technik und Wissenschaft' (BTW'97), Informatik aktuell, Ulm, pp. 83-99 (March 1997)

[LUL97]   *WWW-gateways to OPAC records*, Collection of hyperlinks, Lund University Library, http://www.ub2.lu.se/opacs/www_gateways_to_opacs.html (1997)

[Möc97]   Möckel, D.: *dLIMIT - A Distributed, Client/Server-based Literature Management System in the Internet, Design and Implementation* (in German), Diploma Thesis, Dept. of Computer Science, University of Kaiserslautern (July 1997)

[OMG96]   *The Common Object Request Broker: Architecture and Specification*, Revision 2.0, Object Management Group, ftp://ftp.omg.org/pub/docs/formal-/97-02-25.pdf (July 1996)

[SM97]   Scott, P., Macdonald, D.: *webCats - Library Catalogues on the World Wide Web*, University of Saskatchewan Libraries, http://library.usask.ca-/hywebcat/ (1997)

Autonomic Buffer Control of Web Proxy Server

Guo Yu, Hiranaka Yukio, Akatsuka Takao

Department of Electrical and Information Engineering,
Faculty of Engineering, Yamagata University,
Jounan 4-3-16, Yonezawa, Yamagata 992, Japan

Abstract. In this paper, we discuss the relation between the communication buffer size and the transfer speed under several web access patterns based on TCP/IP network, and present a scheme of autonomic control for the communication buffer. By this scheme, we could effectively improve the performance of web proxy server or web server, even when any number of accesses happen in a period of short time or large web files are transferred simultaneously. In the scheme, we design a buffer controller to decide the size of buffer for each connection based on socket, and a buffer information table to manager all the transfer buffers on a web server or proxy server.

1 Introduction

Today's Internet and World Wide Web(www) have been recognized as an essential part of human activities, such as education, remote medical treatment and health services, business under EC, etc.. Along with more and more users at different location coming in contact with the Internet to share the resources of the web servers, it is a strong demand to have an effective management of resources.

In the www world, proxy servers are used widely, which play an important role of language translation, caching, distributed processing and firewall function. However, if a number of access requests arrive simultaneously via internet, certain problems will appear. For example, the performance of a proxy server or a web server may decline down and the response time may become long. We all have the following experience. When you want to access a web site to get any useful information at office hours, you will often get messages saying that the host is busy or not accessible.

As we know, for the most communication between browser and web server or proxy server, the client/server process based on connection-oriented socket system calls is usually used. We have to pay attention to both of client and server, especially to the fact that the send/receive queue buffer of a socket is prepared with a fixed-length. The fixed size buffer results in determining the transfer speed of a working socket. In other words, handling capacity of a web server or a proxy server will be affected by the size of its buffer.

In this paper, we propose our solution, namely Autonomic Buffer Control, which is employed in adjusting the buffer size according to the capacity of transferred file to improve the response time and obtain better performance of web proxy server. Additionally, in order to manage the limited buffer resources, we design a Buffer Information Table to manage and coordinate all send/receive buffers on a web proxy server. This paper is organized as following: in Sect. 2, we show a simple description of the principle of network communication and proxy server; the influence of the buffer size upon the server response time is analyzed in Sect. 3; in Sect. 4, we describe our proposed scheme; and give the experimental results and analysis in Sect. 5; the last section is for the conclusions and comments on future work.

2   Network Communication and Proxy Server

Extensively adopted standard model for network communication application is the Client-Server model. In order to communicate with each other, both server process and client process may use API(Application Program Interface), which is the interface providing system calls and some relational functions. Figure 1 is a typical case of using API on one proxy server.

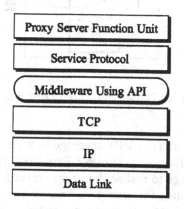

Fig. 1. Using API on Proxy Server

Although API for network programming depends on the operating system, for example, communication API for Unix environment is Berkeley socket or System V TLI(Transport Layer Interface), and Winsock for Microsoft Windows 95 or NT. The principle and procedures for network communication are similar. In this paper, we only discuss the Berkeley socket, because most web proxy servers are based on Unix system environment. We can make sure that the similar results will be acquired under other environments.

The proxy server acts in both a server role and a client role simultaneously. It is a server to receive requests from clients(browser). And also it is a client to relay the requests to the server process on the web server. Therefore, there are two sockets on a proxy server when a connection is established between the browser and web server. Besides, the proxy server doesn't know how much time will be taken to serve one request, and other requests may come during the time. So the web proxy server must be a concurrent server which could handle requests from clients at the same time. The basic architecture of a proxy server is shown in Fig. 2.

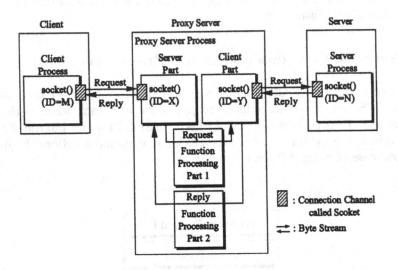

Fig. 2. The Architecture of Proxy Server

A web proxy server accepts URL message unit modified by a special prefix depending on HTTP(Hypertext Transfer Protocol), then strips off the prefix and processes the message to realize the proxy server functions, such as security certifying, etc.. After that, the web proxy server forwards the processed URL message unit to the remote web server requested. Last of all, the web proxy server processes the feedback data from the remote web server to realize the proxy server functions, such as language translating, caching, and relays data to client(browser). The feedback data from the remote web server normally consists of one text file(HTML, Hypertext Markup Language), several graphics files and others described in the same HTML file. According to the HTTP, these files are transferred by different end-to-end connections one by one, first for text file, second for 1st graphics file and then 2nd graphics file, etc.. We take advantage of this characteristic of HTTP in Sect. 4.2.

3 Response Time Analysis

As we described in the introduction, the performance of web proxy server goes down easily when a great number of requests come from different clients in a short period of time, so that users become unbearable. In this session, we discuss the factor which affects the response time of web proxy server.

3.1 Response Time of Web Proxy Server

Users often use the response time to evaluate the performance of a web proxy server. If the web proxy server could not quickly process the requests coming from clients, it becomes the bottleneck. Eventually, the load of the proxy server would become heavy. So it is very important to improve the response time of the web proxy server.

Several factors affecting the response time can be listed, such as network traffic, the size of transferred size, etc.. These factors affect statistically, and can not be decided in a deterministic manner by the designer of the proxy server. Another two factors, namely proxy server processing delay and communication buffer size, also affect the response time of the proxy server. Generally, people concentrate on searching a way to improve the algorithm or program structure, in order to decrease the delay occurring in the period of the proxy server processing. Although the influence of communication buffer upon the server response time is ignored usually.

3.2 Influence of Communication Buffer

According to the client/server process, the receive queue buffer or the send queue buffer is reserved for the socket when one TCP connection is established. The buffer size is usually specified by the default. We do an experiment under the following environment to observe the action of communication buffer size on the response time and the relation between them. In order to avoid the effect coming from unanticipated (indeterminable) factor, such as network delay, we choose an LAN environment separated from backbone network, and directly design a proxy server on a workstation within a web server.

At first, we make the proxy server work only as a relay which receives a URL request from a browser and looks for the resulting URL, then forwards the request to the appropriate web server immediately. The measurement is started when the proxy server relays the result data from the web server to browser. We measured the effect of send queue buffer size to the proxy-browser communication. The result of response time affected along with the change of buffer size, is given in Fig. 3.

In the above test environment, we could consider that the delay of the proxy server is less than the delay of the LAN we used. In other words, the processing delay of all data in send queue buffer on proxy server is less than the network transfer delay of those data. Figure 3 shows that the response time of the proxy server is dependent on the buffer size, when the buffer size is specified to $1,024(2^{10})$ or $2,048(2^{11})$ bytes. Oppositely, if the buffer size is specified bigger than $4,096(2^{12})$ bytes, the response time of the proxy server is not affected by the buffer size. The performance of proxy server is good enough for processing

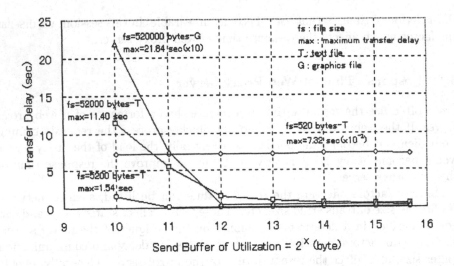

Fig. 3. Response Time on Idealized Proxy Server

the various file types and file sizes, when buffer size is specified to 4,096(2^{12}) bytes.

Secondly, we make the proxy server work with a heavy load in the same test environment, so that the delay of proxy server is larger than the delay of the LAN. In fact, this is a common case in actual web communications. Additionally, we specified the maximum buffer size for one TCP connection to 8,192(2^{13}) bytes. The resultant utilization of the send buffer is shown in Fig. 4. It is necessary to note that the inclined lines, which appear in the period of transfer beginning in Fig. 4, are effects of TCP variable-length window sizing used for reliable transmission and flow control.

Figure 4 means that all the buffer resources, which are reserved in advance with the specified size, are used as much as possible by the socket for TCP connection, if the delay of proxy server is bigger than the delay of the network. It is easy to infer, if a long size buffer is specified in this case, the response time of the proxy server will become shorter and the performance will be improved.

4 Communication Buffer Control

When a client process and a server process are connected over TCP/IP network by socket, system provides send/receive queue buffer for the each socket on both ends of the connection. According to the test result described in the Sect. 3.2, we could increase buffer size to improve the performance of the proxy server.

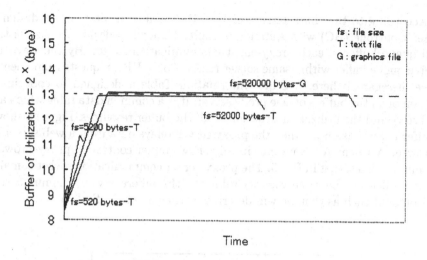

Fig. 4. Buffer of Utilization on Real Proxy Server

4.1 Range of Buffer Control

As we know, the proxy server must be a concurrent server to provide the services to all requests from some clients simultaneously. In order to prevent the total of the buffer memory from overflowing, an upper limit for the buffer size is specified around 52,000 bytes in 4.3BSD. Although the better performance could be achieved by using a larger buffer, fixing the buffer size at 52,000 bytes is not reasonable, for the utilization efficiency of the buffer goes down. For a simple example, if the transferred file size is smaller than 52,000 bytes or less, some parts of the buffer is not used. In addition, according to the test result described in Sect. 3.2, the best buffer size for communicating in the environment with no network delay is around $4,096(2^{12})$ bytes. In fact, today's most web communication applications are designed to use send/receive queue buffer specified with fixed size at $4,096(2^{12})$ bytes.

Consequently, we consider that the response time of the proxy server could be decreased if the size of send/receive queue buffer is dynamically adjusted between 4,096 bytes and 52,000 bytes according to the utilization situation of total buffer and the busyness situation of the proxy server.

4.2 Autonomic Buffer Control

To adjust the buffer size dynamically, we have to solve two problems. One is how to adjust the buffer size to keep the performance better. Another is how to coordinate all the buffers, which are used for sockets from different clients and servers, to prevent buffer overflowing on the proxy server.

According to the characteristic of HTTP described in Sect. 2, we design a Buffer Controller(BC) with Autonomic Buffer Control to decide the size of the send queue buffer of each proxy-client communication socket. By the way, the receive queue buffer within same socket receives only URL requests from clients, so we disregard it here. A Buffer Information Table is designed to coordinate relation of all the buffers on one proxy server. It is a common data table which are used to record the utilization situation of all the buffer resources. Figure 5 shows a buffer control example when the proxy server relays data from a web server to a browser A(Client-A). Note that it only shows buffer control on proxy-browser communication socket in Fig. 5. The proxy-server communication socket can also be controlled by the same way according to the different web communication environment such as that we will describe in the end of the Sect. 5.

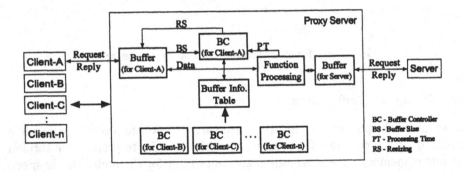

Fig. 5. Autonomic Buffer Control on Web Proxy Server

When the request from browser A(Client-A) is accepted after a connection between the browser and the web proxy server is established, a send buffer for communicating with Client-A is provided with the default of $4,096(2^{12})$ bytes at first. The Function Processing Module modifies the data to act the proxy function, such as language translation, searching engine, etc.. It also feedbacks the Processing Time(PT), which is the handle time for processing the data capacity of the buffer one times. The Buffer Controller(BC for Client-A) only counts the PT, when the specified size of the buffer is used entirely, and calculates the average of PT as the PT_1 for this connection. After above relay processing, the BC increase the size of send queue buffer temporarily to do next relay processing if the next connection is also established for the same client and the same type file is transferred. And then the BC compares PT_{n+1} with PT_n , if $(PT_{n+1} - PT_n) < 0$ then increases the size of send buffer between the minimum 4,096 bytes and the maximum 52,000 bytes according to Buffer Information Table. Otherwise, decreases the size of send queue buffer. The Buffer Information Table is also updated while the send queue buffer is resized. The reply of the web server consists of several connections and the same browser may accesses the same web server several times, so taht above handling loop will be continued until the end of all the connections relayed by the proxy server. Therefore, the utilization of buffer is adjusted autonomically during the period of several connections by one BC. Furthermore, the order of buffer utilization is taken form automatically and works by self-organization by different BCs, when the proxy server serves several connections to clients simultaneously. We call the above buffer control method Autonomic Buffer Control. It affects buffers resizing, and maintains the dynamic changing in stable state to get better response time.

5   Experimental Results and Analysis

In the same test environment described in Sect. 3, we used the Autonomic Buffer Control method to create Buffer Controller(BC) module and Buffer Information Table on the web proxy server. Additionally, specify the upper limit of buffer size to $16,384(2^{14})$ bytes and the lower limit to $4,096(2^{12})$ bytes. In order to compare with the non-Autonomic Buffer Control proxy server, we also transfer same files by using a proxy server with $4,096(2^{12})$ bytes fixed size buffer, which is the common type of the current web communication applications. As a reference, same experiment with fixed size buffer on $16,384(2^{14})$ bytes is also done. Finally, we get results as shown in Fig. 6, in which the transferred sample file is text file; and Fig. 7 in which the sample file is graphics file.

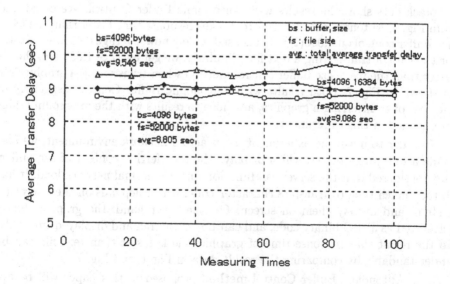

Fig. 6. Average Response Time for Transferring Text File

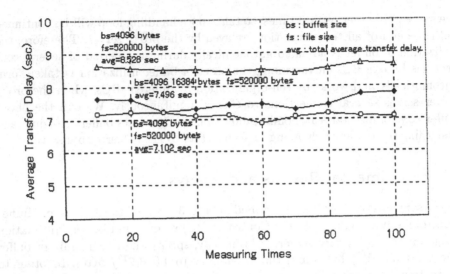

Fig. 7. Average Response Time for Transferring Graphics File

In Fig. 6 and Fig. 7, every marked-node expresses an average response time calculated over 10 successive measurements. The lines marked by white dots are the results measured without Autonomic Buffer Control, and the lines marked by black dots show the results with Autonomic Buffer Control. We could find from Fig. 6, Autonomic Buffer Control makes response time faster than the fixed size buffer control on $4,096(2^{12})$ bytes used widely now, average 0.457 sec in total for the case of transferring a text file. Similarly, we get average 1.032 sec, that is faster than the fixed size buffer control method when transferring a graphics file as shown in Fig. 7. Both results with Autonomic Buffer Control, especially in the case of transferring a graphics, are close to results with the maximum buffer size defined in this experiment.

In order to make the experiment in an actual network environment, we also made a web proxy server, which displays the transferring content of the buffer, and considered that the server can function under a normal network load. It has to take much time to translate character code, which depends on the operating system, and display them on screen. On the other hand, the graphics file is formatted as JPEG binary code, and can be transferred and displayed smoothly. So the result that response time of graphics file is faster than text file can be understandable by comparing the result data in Fig. 6 and Fig. 7.

The Autonomic Buffer Control method proposed in this paper will be applied to the following cases. (1)web FTP proxy servers, which accepts download request from client entity and transfers relational files from different FTP site to them; (2)official homepage servers, which is accessed frequently by a great number of client entities; (3)homepage servers with a large amount of voice, graphics and motion picture files; (4)caching servers, which provides caching service for local client entities; (5)Intranet-Internet gateways, which check transferred data between the Intranet and Internet as security certifying; (6)distributed processing proxy servers, which distribute a large task to several local machines according to the loads of those site, and then gathers the results from them; etc.. In the above cases, the processing delay for the whole data in the buffer of the proxy server is more than the network transfer delay of those data, so we could use the Autonomic Buffer Control method to obtain better response time of the proxy server than the mothod in today's most popular web communication applications. By the way, we also consider that, this method could be applied not only to web proxy servers but also to web servers such as searching engine servers, data base servers and web FTP servers, provided that the response time of web servers are more than network delay.

6 Conclusions and Future Work

Most of the web proxy servers use fixed-length send/receive queue buffer to relay information data between browser(client side) and web server(server side). As clients increase and proxy server's loads grow, it becomes necessary to decrease the response time of proxy servers, and manage the resources effectively on it.

In this paper, we presented a method of Autonomic Buffer Control as a solution. In our scheme, the Buffer Controller was designed to dynamically adjust the size of send/receive queue buffer to increase the swallowing and spitting speed of proxy server, and the Buffer Information Table was designed to keep the order of buffer resource used on the proxy server. Our several experimental results indicate that the Autonomic Buffer Control method could decrease the response time of proxy server effectively. Certainly, this method is significant when the transferred file is quite larger than the buffer capacity.

Although the Autonomic Buffer Control method could make the performance of web proxy servers better than the proxies used widely now, it becomes effective when it is used in a special environment as we described in Sect. 3.2. In the furture work, we are going to improve the Autonomic Buffer Control method to make it work not only with the buffer for proxy-browser communication but also with the buffer for proxy-server communication coordinately, so that the proxy server could fit in with the needs of various communication conditions and environments. And we expect this method to become an additional standard in web communication field which continues its exceedingly rapid growth today.

References

1. Guo, Y., Hiranaka, Y.: Communication Buffer Control on Proxy Server. No. 96-4-9. 4th Workshop of IPSJ(N-E Br.) (1996)
2. Lee, T. B., Fielding, R., Frystyk, H.: Hypertext Transfer Protocol-HTTP/1.0, RFC 1945. MIT/LCS (1996)

3. Fielding, R., et al.: Hypertext Transfer Protocol-HTTP/1.1, Internet Draft. www.w3.org (1996)
4. Claffy, K.: Web Traffic Characterization: An Assessment of the Impact of Caching Documents from NCSA's Web Server. Elec. Proc. 2nd WWW Conf. (1994)
5. Comer, D. E.: Internetworking with TCP/IP, Vol. I: Principles, Protocols and Architecture, 2nd ed. Prentice Hall Inc. (1991)
6. Stevens, W. R.: Unix Network Programming. Prentice Hall Inc. (1990)
7. Nielsen, H. F., et al.: Network Performance Effect of HTTP/1.1, CSS1, PNG. Proc. ACM SIGCOMM'97 (1997)
8. Stevens, W. R.: TCP/IP Illustrated, Vol. 1. Addison Wesley Inc. (1994)
9. Comer, D. E.: Internetworking with TCP/IP, Vol. III: BSD Socket Version. Prentice Hall Inc. (1993)
10. Rieken, B.: Unix Network Applications Programming. John Wiley & Sons Inc. (1992)
11. Hayama, H.: UNIX Network Programming. Ohm Pub.Inc. (1993)
12. Iwai, S., Katai, O.: Problem Solvings and Multi-Layered Autonomous Decentralized Systems. Instr. & Ctrl. Engrs. Vol. 32 (1993)
13. Kitamori, T.: Decentralized Autonomous Systems and Self-Organization. Instr. & Ctrl. Engrs. Vol. 32 (1993)
14. Sasano, H.: Communication Protocol. ASCII Pub. Inc. (1996)
15. Held, G.: LAN Performance Issues and Answers. John Wiley & Sons Ltd. (1994)

Getting Users' Attributes Without Violating Anonymity

Tsutomu Matsumoto

Division of Artificial Environment and Systems &
Division of Electrical and Computer Engineering
Yokohama National University
79-5, Tokiwadai, Hodogaya, Yokohama 240, Japan
tsutomu@mlab.dnj.ynu.ac.jp

Abstract. This paper gives a high level protocol description of a scheme IPADECS (Internet Privacy-oriented Audience Degree Estimation Coupon System) to estimate the distribution of attributes of users who read a web page. The scheme is intended to minimize the violation of users' privacy by adopting some cryptographic techniques. A brief history of development and major properties of IPADECS are also described.

1 Introduction

Subject It is often required to estimate the distribution of attributes, say sex, age group, and so on, of users who read a particular WWW page. There are natural ways to monitor accesses for network resources:

server monitoring that analyzes the access log files of the information provider including identifiers of a set of specified sample users.

proxy monitoring that analyzes the traffic exchanged through a proxy server located between a client and an information providing server.

client monitoring that analyzes the browsers' history files of a set of specified sample users.

However, none of the existing server monitoring schemes such as I/CODE [9], proxy monitoring schemes such as Auditable Metering with Lightweight Security [7], and client monitoring schemes such as PC Meter [10], care the users' privacy sufficiently. Can we get the users' attributes without decreasing the degree of anonymity in the web page access ? This paper records a research activity, stemming from an observation by Kikuchi [1], that tries to answer this question.

Initiation The activity started in 1995. The first result is an idea by Kikuchi et al. [2] to use a nonce "coupon" that certifies the user's attributes. Coupons are produced by the blind signature technique proposed by Chaum [8] to have the unlinkable property. When a user requires to receive a web page from an information providing server, a coupon is also sent to the server. The collected coupons in the server are sent to the analyzing server to calculate the statistics. Hence, the idea of using coupons can be viewed as a kind of server monitoring scheme.

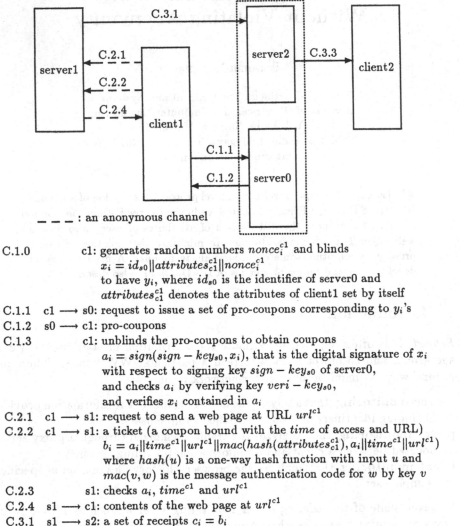

C.1.0   c1: generates random numbers $nonce_i^{c1}$ and blinds
$x_i = id_{s0} \| attributes_{c1}^{c1} \| nonce_i^{c1}$
to have y_i, where id_{s0} is the identifier of server0 and
$attributes_{c1}^{c1}$ denotes the attributes of client1 set by itself

C.1.1   c1 $\longrightarrow$ s0: request to issue a set of pro-coupons corresponding to y_i's

C.1.2   s0 $\longrightarrow$ c1: pro-coupons

C.1.3   c1: unblinds the pro-coupons to obtain coupons
$a_i = sign(sign - key_{s0}, x_i)$, that is the digital signature of x_i
with respect to signing key $sign - key_{s0}$ of server0,
and checks a_i by verifying key $veri - key_{s0}$,
and verifies x_i contained in a_i

C.2.1   c1 $\longrightarrow$ s1: request to send a web page at URL url^{c1}

C.2.2   c1 $\longrightarrow$ s1: a ticket (a coupon bound with the $time$ of access and URL)
$b_i = a_i \| time^{c1} \| url^{c1} \| mac(hash(attributes_{c1}^{c1}), a_i \| time^{c1} \| url^{c1})$
where $hash(u)$ is a one-way hash function with input u and
$mac(v, w)$ is the message authentication code for w by key v

C.2.3   s1: checks a_i, $time^{c1}$ and url^{c1}

C.2.4   s1 $\longrightarrow$ c1: contents of the web page at url^{c1}

C.3.1   s1 $\longrightarrow$ s2: a set of receipts $c_i = b_i$

C.3.2   s2: checks that c_i is valid and that a_i was not received previously

C.3.3   s2 $\longrightarrow$ c2: statistics on $\{attributes \| time \| url\}$

Fig. 1. A sketch of IPADECS Ver. 2

Implementation   Examining a trial implementation by Seo et al. [3], the idea was culminated in the implementation by Okano et al. [4] as IPADECS Ver. 1 (Internet Privacy-oriented Audience Degree Estimation Coupon System, Version 1) and as an operational test for evaluation [4].

Development   Several modifications were made by Matsumoto et al. [6] on IPADECS Ver. 1 to enhance the reliability of estimation, the convenience for installing, and so on. The modified version is called IPADECS Ver. 2, where the coupon is, firstly bound by the URL of the page and the time of access, then sent to the information providing server, to prevent the server illegally reporting the coupon with other URL and time. The idea of binding is borrowed from another privacy oriented scheme proposed by Matsumoto et al. [5] belonging to the client monitoring schemes. The field test of IPADECS Ver. 2 started in November 1997 and will end in the first quarter of 1998 (The author is writing this paper in December 1997).

2 IPADECS

Protocol The core protocol of IPADECS Ver. 2 is described in Fig. 1. Symbol $object_\alpha$ means that the *object* is peculiar to entity α and symbol $object^\beta$ means that the *object* is determined by entity β. Symbol $\gamma\|\delta$ denotes the concatenation of symbols γ and δ.

Entities The entities concerned are client1 (c1, for short), client2 (c2), server0 (s0), server1 (s1), and server2 (s2). Any user with a browser powered by a plug-in for IPADECS is represented by client1. Any information providing server supporting IPADECS is represented by server1. Since coupons are issued with the help of server0 and are finally collected by server2 to calculate statistics, the pair of two servers is called the coupon server. The recipient of the statistics is represented by client2, that may or may not be an information providing server.

Communication Environment All communications between the participating entities are based on HTTP. Channels between client1 and server1 may provide some anonymity for client1. Their realization may vary from a proxy server simply hiding the address of client1 to a full-fledged anonymous communication network.

Mechanism

1. Steps C.1.0 to C.1.3 are for client1 to obtain coupons a_i by the blind signature technique [8]. The signer server0 cannot know the coupons (signatures) acquired by client1. No special mechanism is adopted to confirm $attributes_{c1}^{c1}$.
2. Steps C.2.1 to C.2.4 are for client1 to send a ticket b_i to and receive a web page from server1. A ticket is a coupon bound with the time when the access is made and the URL of the web page. The glue is a message authentication code generated with a key $hash(attribute_{c1}^{c1})$.
3. Steps C.3.1 to C.3.3 are for server2 to analyze the receipts c_i for tickets collected from server1 and to report the statistics to client2.

Difference from IPADECS Ver. 1 The core protocol of IPADECS Ver. 1 is different from that of Ver. 2 in the following two steps:

$$C.2.2' \quad c1 \longrightarrow s1: \text{a ticket } b_i = a_i$$
$$C.3.1' \quad s1 \longrightarrow s2: \text{a receipt } c_i = b_i\|time^{s1}\|url^{s1}$$

Namely, a coupon and the description of how it is used are not firmly combined.

3 Discussion

Anonymity of Access The anonymity of client1 is basically maintained by the property of the channels between client1 and server1. Since a ticket conveys no information about client1 except for $attributes_{c1}^{c1}$, the degree of anonymity of client1 is not severely affected if IPADECS is operated.

Reliability of Statistics In IPADECS Ver. 2, assuming

1. Key $sign - key_{s0}$ is known only to server0
2. Function $hash$ is known only to server2 and client1,

it is very hard for server1 to modify receipt c_i so that the statistics will be deviated. Sending copied receipts is also useless because each receipt is counted only once.

Accuracy of Attributes In IPADECS Ver. 2, the value of attributes for client1 used for making coupons and tickets are just $attributes_{c1}^{c1}$, the self-assessment value. The statistics highly depends on the accuracy of these values.

Incentives for Participants To acquire a lot of participants of IPADECS there will be required some scenario to give incentives to potential participants.

Possible Modifications IPADECS Ver. 2 can be slightly polished by the following modifications:

C.1.2" s0 $\longrightarrow$ c1: pro-coupons and $key_{c1} = hash(attributes_{c1}^{s0})$
C.2.2" c1 $\longrightarrow$ s1: a ticket
$$b_i = a_i \| mac(key_{c1}, a_i \| time^{c1} \| url^{c1})$$
C.3.1" s1 $\longrightarrow$ s2: a set of receipts $c_i = b_i \| time^{s1} \| url^{s1}$

If this modification is applied, condition 2 can be replaced by

3. Function $hash$ is known only to server2 and server0,

that is easier to maintain.

Acknowledgment

The author thanks the program committee of WWCA98, particularly Prof. Shigeki Goto of Waseda University, for the invitation to develop and present this work; Dr. Hiroaki Kikuchi of Tokai University for involving him in this research field; the members of the IPADECS project run by Information-technology Promotion Agency for extensive discussions on IPADECS and related systems; the members of Internet Systems Department of CRC Research Institute for their support; and Kensuke Shimizu and Katsuya Okamoto of his research group in Yokohama National University for their discussions and assistance. The description of IPADECS in this paper is based on the author's personal interpretation and does not necessarily reflect views of the IPADECS project.

References

1. Kikuchi, H.: Some models of audience rating on the Internet. The IEICE 1995 Symposium on Cryptography and Information Security, Inuyama, Japan (Jan. 24–27, 1995) SCIS95-B4.3.
2. Kikuchi, H., Okano, T., Koike, N., Goto, S., Fujioka, A., Nakano, H., Matsumoto, T.: Privacy-oriented audience degree estimation system in the Internet. The IEICE 1996 Symposium on Cryptography and Information Security, Komuro, Japan (Jan. 29–31, 1996) SCIS96-7A.
3. Seo, K., Kikuchi, H., Okano, T., Goto, S., Nakanishi, S.: An implementation of digital coupon privacy oriented browsing system in the Internet. The 1996 Annual Report of the Development and Application of Privacy Technology for the Internet, Information-technology Promotion Agency **8-tech-166** (Mar. 1997) 61–68.
4. Okano, T., Kikuchi, H., Iwai, Y., Koike, N., Goto, S., Nakano, H., Fujioka, A., Matsumoto, T.: A trial and implementation of a privacy-oriented audience degree estimation system in the Internet. The IEICE 1997 Symposium on Cryptography and Information Security, Fukuoka, Japan (Jan. 29 – Feb. 1, 1997) SCIS97-27A.
5. Matsumoto, T., Shimizu, K., Okamoto, K.: Audience counting scheme using additional information to contents and its applications. IEICE Technical Report on Information Security (July 18, 1997) ISEC97-21.
6. Matsumoto, T., Kikuchi, H., Iwai, Y., Koike, N., Goto, S., Nakano, H., Fujioka, A., Shimizu, K., Okamoto, K., Seo, K., Iguchi, M., Tomomura, K., Fujii, S., Inamura, S., Watanabe, T.: Development and application of privacy technology for the Internet — a privacy-oriented audience degree estimation system —. Proceedings of the 16th IPA Symposium, Information-technology Promotion Agency, Tokyo, Japan (Oct. 30–31, 1997) 115–123.
7. Franklin, M. K., Malkhi, D.: Auditable metering with lightweight security. Conference Preproceedings of Financial Cryptography '97, Anguilla, BWI (Feb. 24–28, 1997).
8. Chaum, D.: Blind signature systems. Advances in Cryptology: Proceedings of CRYPTO 83, Plenum Press, p. 153.
9. http://www.ipro.com/
10. http://www.npd.com/

Bayanihan: Web-Based Volunteer Computing Using Java

Luis F. G. Sarmenta

MIT Laboratory for Computer Science
Computer Architecture Group
545 Technology Square
Cambridge, MA 02139
lfgs@cag.lcs.mit.edu
http://www.cag.lcs.mit.edu/bayanihan

Abstract. This paper presents and discusses the idea of Web-based *volunteer computing*, which allows people to cooperate in solving a large parallel problem by using standard Web browsers to volunteer their computers' processing power. Because volunteering requires no prior human contact and very little technical knowledge, it becomes very easy to build very large volunteer computing networks. At its full potential, volunteer computing can make it possible to build world-wide massively parallel computing networks more powerful than any supercomputer. Even on a smaller, more practical scale, volunteer computing can be used within companies or institutions to provide supercomputer-like facilities by harnessing the computing power of existing workstations. Many interesting variations are possible, including *networks of information appliances* (NOIAs), *paid* volunteer systems, and barter trade of compute cycles. In this paper, we discuss these possibilities, and identify several issues that will need to be addressed in order to successfully implement them. We also present an overview of the current work being done in the Bayanihan volunteer computing project.

1 Introduction

The introduction of Java by Sun Microsystems has made it possible to place platform-independent executable programs called *applets* on the Web, so that Internet users can execute them on their own machines without needing anything more than a Java-capable browser. Applets are being used by an increasingly large number of people and organizations to enhance their web pages with such features as animation, interactive demos, user-friendly forms, etc. So far, however, most of these uses have only concentrated on providing local usefulness – that is, additional functionality or ease-of-use for the client user, but few additional benefits for anyone else. The potential for applets to be used for doing cooperative computation has largely been unused

In this paper, we present and discuss one way to exploit this underutilized potential of Java – *volunteer computing*. The idea behind volunteer computing is to allow users from anywhere on the Internet to join in the solving of a parallel problem by simply using a Java-capable browser and visiting a web site. Because it requires no prior human contact and very little technical knowledge on the part of the client user, volunteer computing makes it possible to build very large parallel computing networks very easily. Potentially, such a network can involve thousands, even millions of computers distributed around the world, and make it possible to achieve performance levels far beyond that of any current supercomputer. And, since volunteer computing does not require new hardware to be purchased, it can provide affordable supercomputing capabilities even to financially-constrained organizations such as small universities and universities and companies in developing countries. In fact, since volunteer computing makes it easy for organizations to pool their resources, it opens new possibilities for collaborative research between institutions around the world.

This paper discusses these potential benefits of volunteer computing, as well as the issues and hurdles that must be addressed when implementing volunteer computing systems. It also presents a brief overview of the current work being done in the Bayanihan volunteer computing project. Sections 2 and 3 describe the motivations for implementing volunteer computing, including the disadvantages of current systems and the potential advantages of volunteer computing. Section 4 describes the current state of Project Bayanihan, presenting key research issues, and a framework designed to address them. Finally, Sect. 5 concludes with a brief summary.

2 Motivations

Volunteer computing is actually just a new variation on the old idea of using a network of workstations (NOW) to solve a parallel problem. NOWs first became popular because they allowed people to take advantage of existing (and mostly idle) workstations, enabling them to do parallel processing without having to purchase an expensive supercomputer. Global-scale NOWs, employing computers geographically distributed around the world and communicating through the Internet, have been used with great success to solve large parallel problems as far back as the early 90's [1, 2], and until today [3, 4, 5].

Unfortunately, most of these earlier projects have used *ad hoc* software systems. Typically, a subsystem for providing communication and coordination between machines in the NOW had to be developed mostly from scratch as part of each project. Furthermore, in many cases, the systems were not even fully automatic. Participants had to *manually* request jobs, load them into their computers, execute them, and again manually submit the results. Thus, while these software systems were successfully used to build NOWs containing several thousands of workstations, doing so required a large amount of human effort in terms of setting up, coordinating, and administering the system.

2.1 PVM and MPI

In the past five years, this situation has been notably improved by the development of general-purpose and cross-platform parallel processing systems such as

Parallel Virtual Machine (PVM) [6] and Message Passing Interface (MPI) [7].In such systems, the amount of manual work required is reduced significantly by the runtime system, which takes care of such things as automatically executing the appropriate code on each of the processors involved, keeping track of existing processors, routing and delivering messages, etc. At the same time, programming is made much easier by a general-purpose applications programming interface (API) which hides most of the details of the runtime system, and allows the user to write parallel programs for NOWs using a relatively simple high-level message-passing model. All this allows programmers to concentrate on writing applications instead of worrying about low-level details.

Although systems like PVM and MPI make programming and setting-up NOWs significantly easier than in earlier ad hoc systems, setup requirements still impose practical limits on the size of NOWs that can be used with these systems. To perform a parallel computation using PVM, for example, one must:

1. Install the PVM daemon on all machines to be used in the computation.
2. Compile the application binaries for each target architecture.
3. Distribute these binaries to all the machines (either by explicitly copying them, or by using a shared file system).
4. Provide the owner of the computation with remote shell access (i.e., the ability to execute shell functions and programs remotely) on all machines, to allow remote execution of the PVM daemon and the application binaries.

Clearly, this process not only requires a lot of effort on the part of the system administrator, but also requires a lot of trust between the involved machines, and consequently, a lot of prior human communication between the administrators of different machines. For this reason, the use of PVM and MPI has mostly been restricted to internal use within research institutions, where such close coordination is possible.

2.2 Non-Java-Based Volunteer Computing

On October 19, 1997, distributed.net, a world-wide computing network composed of thousands of volunteer machines, successfully cracked the RSA Systems RC5-56 code challenge [4]. This network achieved an average aggregate computing power equivalent to about 26,000 commodity PCs, and involved as many as 500,000 different computers (as distinguished by their IP addresses) over a span of 250 days [8].

A large part of this success can be attributed to the relative ease with which users are able to join distributed.net. To volunteer, a user only needs to:

1. Go to the distributed.net web site and download a compiled binary for his or her own machine architecture. Versions of the application software have already been coded, compiled, and tested by the distributed.net team for all major architectures.
2. Unarchive and install the software on the volunteer machines.
3. Run the software on the volunteer machines.

At this point, the software takes care of automatically communicating with the `distributed.net` server, requesting work, and sending back results. All the user has to do is leave the software running in the background on these machines. Unlike PVM, `distributed.net` does not require administrators to personally install daemons on the volunteer machines, or contact the volunteer users to acquire remote shell access. Thus, from the volunteers' point-of-view, `distributed.net` is significantly easier to use and understand than PVM.

While this approach to volunteer computing has clearly proven its worth, it still has its limitations. First, volunteers still need some technical knowledge – at least enough to download, install, and run the software. Furthermore, a non-trivial amount of programmer effort is still required to write, compile, and test code for all the possible target architectures. In fact, this step may even be harder with `distributed.net` than with PVM because there might not exist a standardized *cross-platform* library for doing low-level operations, such as communications, and synchronization, that are already provided by PVM,

Perhaps the biggest problem with systems like `distributed.net`, however, is security. Although `distributed.net`, unlike PVM, does not require volunteers to give explicit remote shell access to anyone, it does require them to run programs which implicitly provide the same kind of remote-shell-like access anyway. The code which a volunteer user downloads is executed with user permissions, which means it can access any of its user's files and data, including sensitive data such as credit card numbers and passwords. Clearly, such a serious security risk would (and should) make people wary of volunteering, and thus poses a major obstacle in achieving volunteer computing networks of larger sizes.

2.3 Java-Based Volunteer Computing

Java-based volunteer computing provides an alternative that addresses the problems we have seen so far, improving on both PVM and `distributed.net` in three main areas:

1. **Ease-of-use.** In a Java-based system, volunteering takes only one step: use a Java-capable browser to visit the server web site. There is no technical knowledge required beyond that of using a web browser. The user doesn't even have to be aware of the file system, or understand what downloading an applet really means. Thus, *anyone*, even minimally-computer-literate users of commodity Internet services, can join in such computations.

2. **Platform-independence.** Java-based systems are easy for the programmers and administrators to use as well. Since the Java language and libraries are platform-independent, programmers can "write once, run anywhere" – they can just do their development on any platform, compile the final code into one set of binaries (i.e., Java bytecode), and then post it on the appropriate web sites. Once this is done, any machine that has a Java runtime environment can download these applets and run them. Since free Java browsers and runtime environments have already been implemented on most

major platforms today, practically anybody on the Internet can easily volunteer their computers. In fact, this would include even users of network computers (NCs), whose operating systems may not allow them to download and execute non-Java binary programs such as those used by PVM and `distributed.net`.

3. **Security.** Like `distributed.net`, a Java-based system has the advantage of not requiring accounts or remote-shell access on the volunteer machines. Furthermore, unlike `distributed.net`, the Java applets that volunteers download are executed in a *sandbox* that prevents them from stealing or doing damage to the volunteer's data.

In short, a Java-based volunteer computing system requires minimal setup and distribution effort on the part of the programmers and administrators, minimal technical knowledge and inconvenience on the part of volunteers, and minimal security risk. This characteristic ease with which a volunteer computing system can be set up is what makes it attractive as the next step in bringing supercomputing closer to the reach of the common user.

3 Potentials and Possibilities

3.1 True (or Altruistic) Volunteer Computing

Networks like `distributed.net` can be called *true* volunteer networks – their participants are volunteers in the true sense of the word. Specifically, they are:

1. *autonomous* – they join (and leave) of their own free will.
2. *altruistic* – they generally do not expect to be compensated for volunteering.
3. *anonymous* -- they are unknown to the administrators, and therefore *untrustable*.

The appeal of true volunteer computing is in its potential to pool together the computing power of the millions of computers on the Internet to form a worldwide network more powerful than any single supercomputer by several orders of magnitude. Though the idea of millions of people volunteering their computers may seem far-fetched, the success of projects like `distributed.net`, which managed to involve half a million computers in cracking the RC5-56 challenge, argues strongly to the contrary. The goal of Java-based volunteer computing is to go even further by making volunteering so easy and painless that literally anyone *and* everyone on the Internet can do it.

True volunteer computing has two major problems: One is that of security and correctness of the computation. While the volunteers are reasonably secure against malicious attacks (thanks to Java), the computation itself is not. Since volunteers are anonymous, there is no guarantee that a volunteer is not actually a saboteur who will not do the work assigned to it, but will instead return fabricated results. There may be ways to use cryptography and redundancy to alleviate this problem, but their effectiveness is still unclear (see Sect. 4).

The other problem is motivation – *why* would people want to volunteer their computers to do work for someone else? Some people would say, "Why not?" The typical PC or workstation is idle most of the time anyway, so why not put it to good use? Most people, however, would like to know what these "good uses" are before they volunteer. Thus, the choice of appropriate target problems plays a large part in attracting and motivating volunteers.

One class of target problems that have successfully attracted people are "cool" challenges like Mersenne prime verification [5], the RSA cryptographic challenges [9], and distributed chess [10]. A more interesting and more useful class of target problems, however, is what might be called *worthy causes*. These are realistic and practical problems which can be seen as serving "the common good" – either globally (e.g., protein folding computations for vaccine research), or locally (e.g., simulation studies for a traffic-congested mega-city). A recent and interesting example of a possible worthy cause problem, [1] is the SETI@home project, which aims to use volunteers' home computers to analyze radio telescope data for unusual patterns that may indicate extraterrestrial life [11].

3.2 Forced Volunteer Computing

Interestingly, *forced* volunteer systems are possible as well. These are systems where the participants are *not autonomous* (they do not have a choice about joining the computation), and *not anonymous* (they are known to the computation's administrators) An example of a forced volunteer system would be one where administrators run a background process on all company computers to allow them to be used for parallel computation whenever their users are idle.

Forced volunteer systems cannot match true volunteer systems in potential size and power, but they are more down-to-earth and feasible. For example, forced volunteer networks are not as prone to sabotage as true volunteer networks are. The use of encryption and firewalls can prevent attacks from external sources. Internal saboteurs may still be a problem, but these can be traced and controlled more easily (and punished more severely) than in true volunteer systems. In general forced volunteer systems are more manageable and more secure than true volunteer systems.

Applications. Forced volunteer computing can be used wherever there is a need or opportunity to pool existing (and idle) resources to attain supercomputing power that would otherwise be unaffordable. For example, companies can use computers on their intranet for solving CPU-intensive problems such as market and process simulations, and data-mining [12]. Similarly, research labs and universities can use volunteer computing to turn their existing networks of workstations into virtual supercomputers. In financially-constrained institutions such as universities in developing countries, volunteer networks can also be used to *teach* supercomputing techniques, without requiring actual (expensive) supercomputers.

---

[1] Or maybe just a cool challenge, depending on who one talks to.

By making it very easy for institutions around the world to share their computing resources, volunteer computing opens up exciting new possibilities in world-wide collaborative research efforts. It can enable researchers in *collaboratories* [13, 14] to share not only their data and ideas, but their computing power as well. Research institutions on opposite sides of the globe can also barter-trade for each other's computing power, depending on their need. For example, a university in the United States can allow a lab in Japan to use its CPUs at night (when it is day in Japan) in exchange for being able to use the Japanese lab's CPUs during the day (when it is night in Japan).[2]

Forced volunteer computing is already being done by many institutions using their own ad hoc tools or libraries such as PVM (the PVM home page [15] has some links to PVM-based projects). Java-based forced volunteer computing improves on these by being much easier to use for everyone – users, programmers, and administrators alike. If a company decides to use its machines to do parallel computation, for example, the administrators would not need to spend time manually installing the computational software to be run on all the company machines – they could simply tell their employees to point their browsers to a certain web page on the company intranet, and leave the browser running while they work,[3] or when they go home. In this way, setting-up a parallel computation, a process that would normally take weeks for software installation and user education, can be done literally overnight.

3.3 Paid (or Commercial) Volunteer Computing

So far, we have assumed that volunteers are *altruistic*. That is, the participants work for the benefit of the common good (of the world, or the company), not expecting to be repaid. Non-altruistic, *paid* volunteer systems are also possible.

One way to increase participation in a volunteer computing system is to provide *individual compensation* as an incentive for volunteers. This can take the form of electronic credits proportional to the amount of work that they do (some ideas about this are presented in [16]), or it can be in the form of a *lottery*, such the one used in `distributed.net`, where part of the $10,000 RC5 challenge prize money from RSA Systems was offered to the volunteer team whose computer actually found the key[4]. Such lottery schemes not only require less money from the sponsor, but also encourage participation (i.e., the more one works, the bigger one's chances of winning are), and discourages cheating (i.e., pretending to do the work does not give one any chance of winning).

If we extend the idea of individual compensation to that of group trading of computing resources as commodities, we get a *market system*. Not only can users (or groups of users, such as companies) sell their computing resources, they can also buy the resources from others, or barter trade (like in the example in Sect. 3.2). If reliable mechanisms for electronic currency, accounting, and brokering are developed, market systems promise a practical and productive use

---

[2] I have been unable to find the original reference for this example.

[3] It is possible and easy to write an applet that continues to run in the background, even if the user moves to a different web page.

for volunteer computing technology. The SuperWeb group at UCSB is already actively pursuing this goal [16].

Forced and paid volunteer computing can be combined in *contract-based* systems: clients can be required by contract to volunteer their computers as (part of) their payment for goods or services received. For example, information providers such as search engines, news sites, and shareware sites, might require their users to run a Java applet in the background while they sit idle reading through an article, or downloading a file.[4] Such terms can be represented as a two-sided contract that both sides should find acceptable. While it is actually possible to hide forced volunteer Java applets inside web pages, for example, most users will consider it ethically unacceptable. Sites that require users to volunteer must say so clearly, and allow the user to back-out if they do not agree to the terms. Some of these ideas are discussed in [17, 18].

Some problems in anonymous paid volunteer systems are *cheating* (pretending to do work and getting paid for it), and *spying*. If Company A purchases computing power from Company B, a spy in B may read data from A's computation while he is doing it. For some classes of computations, *encrypted computation* techniques can be used to alleviate this problem[16].

3.4 Networks of Information Appliances (NOIA)

Many experts, both in industry and in the academic community, predict that in the near future, *information appliances* – devices for retrieving information from the Internet which are as easy to use as everyday appliances such as TVs and VCRs – will become commonplace[19, 20]. In the United States today, companies such as WebTV[21] are starting to develop and sell information appliances, and cable companies are starting to include support for cable modems, using the same cable that carries the TV signals[22]. It is not hard to imagine that within the next five or ten years, the information appliance will be as commonplace as the VCR, and high-speed Internet access as commonplace as cable TV.

This brings up an interesting possibility: why not use volunteer computing to harness the power of all these information appliances? Even if an information appliance is not as powerful as a desktop PC, the sheer number of them, potentially in the tens of millions (i.e., the number of people with cable TV), can make up for it.[5] Aside from their great size, these *networks-of-information-appliances*, or NOIAs,[6] have many interesting features.

NOIAs can be *contract-based*. Cable or ISP companies can agree on a contract with their clients that would require clients to leave their information appliance boxes on and connected to the network 24 hours a day, running Java applets in

---

[4] To ensure that the user does not turn Java off, the server can check if it has been periodically receiving data from the applet – if it has not, then the server stops providing service to the user.

[5] Given reasonably appropriate applications.

[6] Interestingly, the word *noia*, Greek for "mind", conjures-up images of a brain-like massively parallel network of tens of millions of small processors around the world.

the background when the user is idle. In exchange, the clients would receive compensation in the form of discounts or premium services. In addition to the option of not participating, clients may also be given a choice of different kinds of computations they can participate in (e.g., charitable or worthy causes, commercial computations, etc.).

NOIAs also have the advantage of being easier to program and administer than other kinds of volunteer networks. Hardware-based cryptographic devices can make NOIAs *secure*, by preventing malicious volunteers from forging messages or modifying the applet code that they are given to execute. Also since users leave their information appliances on all the time, NOIAs are *stable* – the chance of a particular node leaving a NOIA is smaller than that in other kinds of volunteer networks. NOIAs composed purely of information appliances using the same type of processor are also *homogenous*. All these properties lessen the need for adaptive parallelism and fault-tolerance (see Sect. 4.1), and allows greater efficiency and more flexibility in the range of problems that a NOIA can solve.

While actual NOIAs may not be feasible right now, it is useful to keep them in consideration. Techniques developed for the other forms of volunteer computing (especially forced volunteer computing) are likely to be applicable to NOIAs when their time comes.

4 Project Bayanihan

The goal of Project Bayanihan,[7] is to identify and investigate the issues and problems involved in all forms of volunteer computing, and to develop useful technology and theory that can be used to towards turning these concepts to reality. We intend to pursue this goal in manageable steps, starting with the more feasible ideas, and moving on to more complex ones by extension and expansion. Specifically, we intend to start with forced volunteer computing, and move on to true volunteer computing where security and scalability issues become more complex. It is our hope that the results of research in these areas will become applicable to paid volunteer systems and NOIAs when the mechanisms and infrastructure necessary for their implementation (i.e., electronic currency and accounting for paid systems, and hardware infrastructure for NOIAs) become available.

At present, we are developing a flexible software framework that would make it easy to program and set-up forced or true volunteer computing networks for various useful applications. Our goal is to develop a Java-based system that would be for volunteer computing what PVM was for NOW-based computing – an easy-to-understand interface that would allow programmers to write parallel programs for volunteer computing without worrying about low-level details such as network communication, scheduling, etc. In this section, we discuss some issues

---

[7] Pronounced *buy*-uh-*nee*-hun, *bayanihan* is a Filipino word meaning communal unity and cooperation, and is epitomized by the old tradition of neighbors helping a relocating family by physically carrying their house, and moving it to its new location.

we face, and propose possible approaches to them. Then, we give an overview of our current prototype framework, and present preliminary results.

4.1 Research Issues: Problems and Approaches

Adaptive Parallelism. By their nature, volunteer networks are *heterogenous* and *dynamic*. Volunteer nodes can have different kinds of CPUs, and can join and leave a computation at any time. Even nodes with the same type of CPU cannot be assumed to have equal or constant computing capacities, since each can be loaded differently by external tasks (especially in systems which try to exploit users' idle times). For these reasons, models for volunteer computing systems must be *adaptively parallel* [23]. That is, unlike many traditional parallel programming models, they must *not* assume the existence of a fixed number of nodes, or depend on any static timing information about the system.

Various strategies for implementing adaptive parallelism have already been proposed and studied. In *eager scheduling* [24], packets of work to be done are kept in a pool from which worker nodes get any undone work whenever they run out of work to do. In this way, faster workers get more work according to their capability. And, if any work is left undone by a slow node, or a node that "dies", it eventually gets reassigned to another worker. Systems that implement eager schedule include Charlotte [24] and the factoring demo used in Sect. 4.3.

The Linda model [25] provides an associative *tuple-space* that can be used to store both data and tasks to be done. Since this tuple-space is global and optionally blocking, it can be used both for communication and synchronization between parallel tasks. It can also serve as a work pool, which like in eager scheduling, can allow undone tasks to be redone. Linda was originally used in the Piranha [23] system, and more recently implemented in Java by WWWinda [26], Jada [27], and Javelin [28].

In Cilk [29], a task running on a node, A, can spawn a child task, which the node then executes. If another node, B, runs out of work while Node A is still running the child task, it can *steal* the parent task from Node A and continue to execute it. This *work-stealing* algorithm has been shown to be *provably* efficient and fault-tolerant. Cilk has been implemented for NOWs [30], and has been implemented using Java applications (but not applets) in ATLAS [31].

Project Bayanihan aims to develop a framework that does not limit the programmer to using only one form of adaptive parallelism, but instead makes it easy to implement any of these forms and even develop new ones.

Fault-Tolerance. Faults in distributed systems can generally be classified into *stopping faults* and *Byzantine faults* [33]. Stopping faults cover cases of processors crashing or leaving, and are automatically handled by adaptively parallel systems. Byzantine faults cover all other kinds of faults, including unintentional random faults such as data loss or corruption due to faulty network links, or faulty processors, as well as intentional malicious attacks. In general, however, we can think of Byzantine faults simply as faults that result in the generation of incorrect result packets.

Byzantine faults can be handled using *replication* techniques such as *majority voting* or the more sophisticated and reliable algorithms in [33]. (To prevent sabotage by groups, replicated nodes would preferrably belong to different Internet domains.) However, this has the disadvantage of being very inefficient since a replication factor r means a factor r drop in aggregate computational speed.

We can improve efficiency by *spot-checking*. For each work packet that a node receives, there would be some probability p that the server already knows the correct answer, and just wants to check if the node is faulty. Although faulty nodes may be able to slip through for a while, the probability of *not* getting caught approaches zero exponentially in time, so faulty nodes get caught *eventually*.

Once a node gets caught, the server *backtracks* through the results, recomputing any results depending on the offending nodes results, and then *blacklists* the offending node, never allowing it to join the computation again. (More flexible versions of blacklisting can also be used in situations where unintentional and transient occasional errors are expected even from non-faulty nodes, e.g., due to power fluctuations, and we do not want to blacklist a node immediately and forever just because of these temporary failures.)

Another way to achieve fault-tolerance is by simply choosing more fault-tolerant problems. Such problems include those that do not require 100% accuracy in the first place, such as sound or graphics processing where a little static or a few scattered erroneous pixels would be unnoticeable or can be averaged out to be make them unnoticeable. Other problems include those that have easily-verifiable results, such as search problems with *rare* results that can easily be checked by the server without adding significant extra load (e.g., travelling salesman problem), and problems like rendering, where a human user can visually recognize any unacceptable errors and ask the system to recalculate (and blacklist the node responsible for the problematic areas).

Security. Malicious attacks or *sabotage* can take many forms. In general, it involves a malicious node returning erroneous data. This node can either be an internal saboteur who is actually a participating volunteer, or an external *spoofer* – a node that has *not* volunteered, but sends messages forged to look like they came from one of the volunteers.

Spoofing can be prevented with *digital signatures* [34]. These enable the server to verify that a result packet indeed comes from a volunteer. They can also be used in the other direction, to assure a volunteer that an applet really comes from the server, and not from a spoofer. Digital signatures are most useful in protecting non-anonymous volunteer systems, such as forced volunteer networks or NOIAs, from external attack. Unfortunately, however, digital signatures are ineffective against internal saboteurs, and thus useless in true volunteer systems where anyone, even saboteurs, are allowed to volunteer. This is because digital signatures can only authenticate the *source* of a data packet, not its *content*.

One way to authenticate the content of a data packet is to include a *checksum* computation in the code. This way, if the node does not run the code, or runs it incorrectly, the checksum will not match, and the server can be alerted.

In most cases, checksums will catch both unintentional errors, and simple malicious attacks such as returning random packets. We can also use checksums to authenticate sources (and prevent spoofing) by transmitting a *different* checksum key with each work packet. This way, an external spoofer would not know the correct key to use, and cannot forge bogus result packets.

Digital signatures and checksums are only useful against malicious attacks if volunteers are forced to compute them and cannot compute them independently of the work. This is true for NOIAs, where the node hardware and firmware can prevent users from disassembling or modifying the bytecodes they receive from the server. In general, however, it is possible for sophisticated malicious volunteers to disassemble the bytecode they receive, identify the signature and checksum generating code, and use these to forge a result packet containing arbitrary data. One way to guarantee that a node cannot fake a checksum computation is to prevent it from disassembling the code. This is not an easy task, but in some cases, it may be possible to apply *encrypted computation* techniques, such as those that [16] proposes to use against spying.

If cryptographically preventing disassembly is not possible, we can resort to *dynamic obfuscation* techniques to make understanding the disassembled code and isolating the checksum code as difficult as possible. Dynamic obfuscation extends the idea of *static* obfuscation (such as done in Borland's JBuilder [35]) by continously obfuscating code *dynamically* in time. For example, we can randomly vary the checksum formula and its location within the bytecode from work packet to work packet. This would prevent hackers from manually disassembling and modifying the bytecode once and for all. We can also insert *dummy code* at varying locations. These schemes are inspired by *polymorphic computer viruses*, which use them to hide themselves from anti-virus programs [36].

Although very difficult, de-obfuscating polymorphic viruses is not impossible because viruses, being self-reproductive (by definition), contain the obfuscating code. Thus, once one version has been cracked and disassembled, it is possible to reverse engineer this code and develop an "antidote" which can disassemble other instances of the viruses. Dynamic obfuscation in volunteer computing, however, has the advantage of using the server to do the obfuscation. This should make it possible to constantly and arbitrarily replace the code, and make it impossible for hackers to catch up. Provided that the volunteer computing system allows the work code to change from packet to packet, dynamic obfuscation may be easier to implement and more generally applicable than encrypted computation.

Scalability and Congestion. One of the major problems in Java-based volunteer computing is that currently, security restrictions dictate that applets running in users' browsers can only communicate with the Web server from which they were downloaded. This forces Java-based volunteer networks into *star topologies*, which have the disadvantage of having high congestion, no parallelism in communications, and not being scalable.

To solve this problem, we may allow volunteers who are willing to exert extra effort to download Java *applications*, and become *volunteer servers*. Volunteer server applications need to be run outside a browser, but do not have security restrictions. This lets them connect with each other in arbitrary topologies, as well as act as star hubs (centers) for volunteers running applets. Newer browsers such as Netscape and Microsoft Internet Explorer are starting to support *signed applets*, which will also be free of restrictions. These applets can be used as volunteer servers as well.

4.2 System Design

Our current goal in Project Bayanihan is to develop a flexible software framework that will allow us to explore these problems by making it possible to implement various solutions to them. At present we have a basic prototype using HORB [37], a distributed object library that provides remote objects capabilities in Java similar to those of Sun's RMI [38], but not requiring JDK 1.1. In this section, we provide a brief overview of this prototype framework. The details will be discussed in more depth in a separate paper [39].

Architecture. Figure 1 shows a high-level block diagram of a system using the Bayanihan framework.

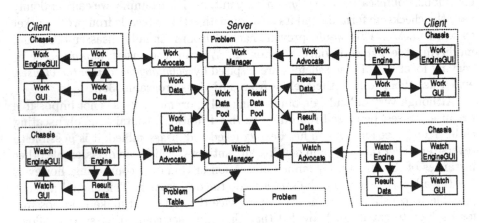

Fig. 1. A Bayanihan system

On the *client* side, an *engine* runs in its own thread, and takes care of receiving and processing *data* objects from its corresponding *manager* on the server. A *work* engine, for example, would take care of getting work data from the work manager, executing the work, and requesting more work when it's done. Data objects are generally polymorphic and know how to process themselves. To execute the work, a work engine passes the work data a pointer to itself, and calls the work data's `process()` method. The work data will compute itself, using the work engine to communicate with the work manager, if desired. Both the engine and the data have associated *GUI* objects which can be used for user interface.

The engine and the GUIs are all contained in a *chassis* object, which can be an applet or application.

On the *server* side, an *advocate* object[8] serves as the engine's representative and forwards the engine's calls to the manager. The manager has access to several *data pools*. These pools may be shared by other managers serving other purposes. In Fig. 1, for example, the work and result pools are shared by the work and watch managers, allowing the watch manager to watch the progress of the computation and inform watch engines of such things as new results and statistics. The whole set of associated managers and data pools compose a *problem*. There may be many independent problems existing in a server at the same time. A *problem table* keeps track of these, and can be used by volunteers to choose the problem they want to participate in.

Flexibility. By using a distributed object system like HORB, the Bayanihan framework hides the details of network communications from programmers, and allows them to program in a fully object-oriented manner without having to worry about communications-level details such as sockets, packet formats, and message protocols. Programmers can write a Bayanihan application by simply filling-in *hot-spots* [40] in the framework. They can use existing library components, or define their own classes, provided that these classes either implement the appropriate interfaces (e.g., the work data interface containing the process() method), or extend library classes that implement these interfaces.

In this way, implementations of the Bayanihan framework can be varied at three main levels:

1. *Applications.* At the highest level, application programmers can write their own data objects and GUIs, and create their own problem objects by putting together appropriate engines, managers, and data pools chosen from a component library. Given a library for eager scheduling, for example, one can write applications for rendering, RC5, and many other applications simply by varying the work data and GUI classes. Within a single application, it is also possible to change the user interface (e.g., to display data in different formats) by changing the GUI objects.

2. *Components.* Programmers can also write their own engines, managers, and data pools to implement additional functionality, or even completely different computation models. Programming at this level allows us to experiment with different forms of adaptive parallelism or different fault-tolerance mechanisms.

3. *Infrastructure.* It is also possible to change other support objects such as the chassis, and the problem table. For example, there may be an application chassis and an applet chassis. Also, different chassis objects may provide different ways to let the user select problems from the problem table. Making changes at this level may allow us to implement different security mechanisms, or address scalability issues.

---

[8] A better name may be *proxy*. However, *proxy* means something else in HORB.

4.3 Preliminary Results

We have used the Bayanihan framework to write a simple application that factors a Java long integer N by dividing the search space $\{1, ..., \sqrt{N}\}$ into fixed-sized work packets which are executed by the work engines. This problem, inspired by [41], although somewhat unrealistic, was chosen because its simplicity and predictability make it easy to measure performance and analyze results.

Figure 2 shows some results for N =12345678901234567 89, with 112 work packets of size 100000000 each. We used five identical 200MHz dual-Pentium machines (one server, and four clients) connected to a 10Base-T Ethernet hub, and running Windows NT 4.0. The server application was run using Sun's JDK 1.1.4, and the worker applets were run using Netscape 4.02. The speeds in the figure represent the average rate (i.e., numbers checked per millisecond) at which work packets were processed, over the course of searching the whole target space. The number of workers represents the number of worker applets run on the client machines. Each client machine was used to run up to two worker applets.[9] The ideal speed is computed as the pure computation speed (measured at the client side) multiplied by the number of workers. With eight workers, we get the figures in Table 1.

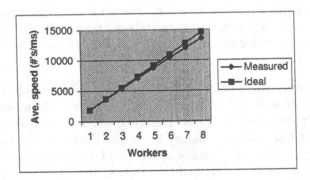

Fig. 2. Timing measurements

To evaluate the performance of Java, relative to C, we wrote a simple C program, compiled it with djgpp [42] (the gcc implementation for MS-DOS). Comparing its performance with the one-worker pure computation performance, we get the results shown in Table 2. These results show that at least for simple tight-loop computations such as our factoring algorithm, the performance of the Java just-in-time-compiler in Netscape is comparable to native C code.

---

[9] Since the worker applet has only one (sequential) computation thread, running only one instance of it does not result in parallelism, even on a dual-Pentium machine. Both processors can be used at full-speed, though, by running two instances of the worker applet in the machine at the same time.

Table 1. Speedup: 8 workers

measurement	num/ms
pure computation (1 worker)	1828
ave. speed (8 workers)	13571
speedup	7.42
efficiency	92.8%

Table 2. Comparing C and Java

version	num/ms
C	1879
Java	1828

While these results are admittedly preliminary and based on a toy problem, we believe that they give us hope that Java-based implementations of volunteer computing will be feasible and practical.

5 Conclusion

In this paper, we have shown how volunteer computing brings potential benefits, but also involves many challenging problems. There is plenty of space in this field for exploration, and indeed many have already started [16, 18, 24, 28, 31, 32, 43]. Project Bayanihan joins these efforts with a different approach: since the perfect approach is not clear, we do not settle on a single one, but instead take advantage of remote object technology to build a flexible framework that we hope would allow us to try *any* approach. Work on Project Bayanihan is ongoing, but preliminary results give us a positive outlook and hope for success.

6 Acknowledgements

Thanks to Dr. Satoshi Hirano of ETL for his valuable support and help in the writing of the HORB version of Bayanihan; to my colleagues and friends who reviewed and edited this paper: Danilo Almeida, Mark Herschberg, Steven Johnson, and Victor Luchangco; to Lydia Sandon and Mark Herschberg for helping out with the demo for SC97; to my thesis supervisor Prof. Steve Ward; and to everyone else who has given me their feedback and support. I have been financially supported in part by the Department of Science and Technology of the Philippines, MIT teaching assistantships, the MIT Japan Program, Ateneo de Manila University, and the Defense Advanced Research Projects Agency.

References

1. Strumpen, V.: Coupling Hundreds of Workstations for Parallel Molecular Sequence Analysis. Software - Practice and Experience. **25(3)** (1995) 291-304
2. Levy, S.: Wisecrackers. Wired, issue 4.03. (Mar. 1996) http://www.hotwired.com/wired/4.03/features/crackers.html
3. Gibbs, W.: CyberView. Scientific American. (May 1997)
4. Beberg, A. L., Lawson, J., McNett, D.: distributed.net. http://www.distributed.net
5. Woltman, G.: Mersenne.org Main Page. http://www.mersenne.org
6. Geist, A., Beguelin, A., Dongarra, J., Jiang, W., Manchek, R., Sunderam, V.: PVM: Parallel Virtual Machine: A User's Guide and Tutorial for Networked Parallelism. MIT Press. (1994) http://www.netlib.org/pvm3/book/pvm-book.html
7. Gropp, W., Lusk, E., Skjellum, A.: Using MPI. MIT Press. (1994) http://www.epm.ornl.gov/ walker/mpi/index.html
8. distributed.net press release. (Oct. 1997) http://www.distributed.net/pressroom/56-announce.html
9. RSA Data Security: RSA Factoring Challenge. http://www.rsa.com/factor/chalenge.htm
10. de Russcher, R.: Possible Projects. http://www.distributed.net/projects.html
11. SETI@home home page. http://www.bigscience.com/setiathome.html
12. Communications of the ACM. (Nov. 1996)
13. Rappa, M.: Solomon's House in the 21st century. Working Paper. (Nov. 1994) http://web.mit.edu/technika/www/solomon.html
14. Wulf, W.: The Collaboratory Opportunity. Science. (Aug. 1993)
15. PVM home page. http://www.epm.ornl.gov/pvm/
16. Alexandrov, A. D., Ibel, M., Schauser K. E., Scheiman, C. J.: SuperWeb: Towards a Global Web-Based Parallel Computing Infrastructure 11th International Parallel Processing Symposium. (April 1997) http://www.cs.ucsb.edu/research/superweb/
17. DigiCrime Computational Services via Java. (June 1996) http://www.digicrime.com/java.html
18. Vanhelsuwe, L.: Create your own supercomputer with Java. JavaWorld. (Jan. 1997) http://www.javaworld.com/jw-01-1997/jw-01-dampp.ibd.html
19. Gates, B.: The Road Ahead. Viking, a division of Penguin Books, USA. (1995)
20. Negroponte, N.: Being Digital. Vintage Books, a division of Random House. (1995)
21. WebTV home page. http://www.webtv.com/ns/index.html
22. Media One home page. http://www.mediaone.com/
23. Gelernter, D., Kaminsky, D.: Supercomputing out of recycled garbage: Preliminary experience with Piranha. Proceedings of the 1992 ACM International Conference of Supercomputing. (July 1992).
24. Baratloo, A., Karaul, M., Kedem, Z., Wyckoff, P.: Charlotte: Metacomputing on the Web. Proc. of the 9th International Conference on Parallel and Distributed Computing Systems. (Sep. 1996) http://cs.nyu.edu/milan/charlotte/
25. Carriero, N., Gelernter, D.: Linda in Context. Comm. of the ACM. (Apr. 1989)
26. Gutfreund, Y. S.: The WWWinda Orchestrator. http://info.gte.com/ftp/circus/Orchestrator
27. Rossi, D.: Jada home page. http://www.cs.unibo.it/ rossi/jada/

28. Cappello, P., Christiansen, B. O., Ionescu, M. F.,, Neary, M. O., Schauser, K. E., Wu, D.: Javelin: Internet-Based Parallel Computing Using Java. ACM Workshop on Java for Science and Engineering Computation. (June 1997) http://www.cs.ucsb.edu/research/superweb/

29. Blumofe, R. D., Joerg C. F., Kuszmaul, B. C., Leiserson, C. E., Randall, K. H., Zhou, Y.: Cilk: An Efficient Multithreaded Runtime System. Proceedings of the 5th ACM SIGPLAN Symposium on Principles of Parallel Programming (PPOPP '95). (July 1995) http://theory.lcs.mit.edu/~cilk/

30. Blumofe, R. D., Lisiecki, P. A.: Adaptive and Reliable Parallel Computing on Networks of Workstations. Proceedings of the USENIX 1997 Annual Technical Symposium. (Jan. 1997)

31. Baldeschwieler, J. E., Blumofe, R. D., Brewer, E. A: ATLAS: An Infrastructure for Global Computing. Proceedings of the Seventh ACM SIGOPS European Workshop: Systems Support for Worldwide Applications. (Sep. 1996)

32. Brecht, T., Sandhu, H., Shan, M., Talbot, J.,: ParaWeb: Towards World-Wide Supercomputing. Proceedings of the Seventh ACM SIGOPS European Workshop: Systems Support for Worldwide Applications. (Sep. 1996)

33. Lynch, N. A.: Distributed Algorithms. Morgan Kauffman Publishers. (1996)

34. Schneier, B.: Applied Cryptography. 2nd ed. John Wiley & Sons. (1996)

35. Borland: JBuilder. (1997) http://www.borland.com/jbuilder/

36. McAfee Associates: Virus Information Library: Polymorphism. http://www.mcafee.com/support/techdocs/vinfo/t0022.asp

37. Hirano, S.: HORB: Extended execution of Java Programs. Proceedings of the First International Conference on World-Wide Computing and its Applications (WWCA97). (March 1997) http://ring.etl.go.jp/openlab/horb/

38. Sun Microsystems: Remote Method Invocation. http://www.javasoft.com/products/jdk/1.1/docs/guide/rmi/

39. Sarmenta, L. F. G., Hirano, S., Ward, S. A.: Towards Bayanihan: Building an Extensible Framework for Volunteer Computing Using Java ACM 1998 Workshop on Java for High-Performance Network Computing. (submitted)

40. Roberts, D., Johnson, R.: Evolving Frameworks: A Pattern Language for Developing Object-Oriented Frameworks. University of Illinois. (1997) http://st-www.cs.uiuc.edu/users/droberts/evolve.html

41. Voelker, G., McNamee, D.: The Java Factoring Project. (Sep. 1995) http://www.cs.washington.edu/homes/dylan/ContestEntry.html

42. Delorie, D.: djgpp. http://www.delorie.com/djgpp

43. Proceedings of the ACM 1997 Workshop on Java for Science and Engineering Computation. (June 1997) http://www.npac.syr.edu/projects/javaforcse/acmprog/prog.html

Architecture of a User Interface Module for Structured Internet Messages

MORIOKA Tomohiko[1]

Japan Advanced Institute of Science and Technology, Hokuriku
1-1 Asahidai, Tatsunokuchi, Nomi, Ishikawa, 923-12, Japan

Abstract. MIME introduces a structured Internet message format. It can represent various data formats and various coded character sets. MIME thus represents an important part of Internet message processing. Conventional message user agents (MUAs) which process Internet messages have different characteristics. The quality of the user interface depends on the user's preference or habits. In this regard, it may be preferable to allow the user to select a good combination of the MUA and a separate MIME module. This paper describes the architecture of a general MIME processing module to provide its features for various conventional MUAs. In the design of such a module, two complementary models are proposed: "representation layer model" which handles complex structured data and the "acting situation model" which processes various kinds of data under various environments.

1 Introduction

MIME (Multipurpose Internet Mail Extensions) is a proposed standard to provide an extension of the traditional Internet message format defined by STD 11[2]. STD 11 messages can represent only US-ASCII[1] plain text. MIME messages, however, can represent various formats specified by a "media-type"[3] for various kinds of information. MIME messages can also represent various coded character sets specified by a "MIME charset"[4] for various languages. Rather than forcing a single unified language coding system or media format, MIME enables the coexistence of different formats. In this way, MIME is an important protocol for Internet message exchange.

There are many existing message user agents (MUAs) built on many user interface models. This is reasonable because the user is free to select the one he is most comfortable with. A number of these MUAs have built in MIME support which the user may or may not be comfortable with. It seems logical to extend the same modular approach used with MUAs to the MIME support. One approach in designing MUAs is to consider the MIME module separately.

MIME offers a "multipart"[4] feature for messages. Structured messages form a hierachical tree in which each node of the tree may be called an "entity"[3]. Each entity has an attribute known as "media-type" for representing its data type. Each message may have multiple entities. Although conventional MUAs such as mail readers, netnews readers, etc, provide message navigational features, they do not typically provide any functionality for navigating structured messages containing multiple entities.

In this study, a preview mechanism based on the notion of a "representation layer model" is proposed to overcome this deficiency. The "representation layer" separates the message contents into "raw message" and "message-preview". "Raw message" is the original information specified by STD 11 and MIME, whereas "message-preview" carries information about the position in the display. The message processing modules described in this paper are based on such a representation system.

A conventional MUA cannot process the entities itself, the MIME module has to be added to process these entities according to their media-type using the appropriate program. There is usually a simple one-to-one mapping between media-type and program. Entity processing is not dependent on media-type alone and a simple mapping may not be adequate. The "acting situation model" is thus proposed as a solution. Instead of a simple mapping between media-type and the appropriate program handler, a generalised MIME processing module is designed.

The proposed system has been implemented on GNU Emacs and its variants, such as "tm"[5] and "SEMI"[6].

2 Display for message contents

Conventional Internet messages are limited to unstructured text that does not require complex message processing. Conventional MUAs thus ignore any internal structure and simply manage messages. The proposed MIME processing module must provide adequate features to process and manage a hierarchy of entities and at the same time it has to offer an interface between a message and its structure. In the present approach, SEMI and tm employ the *"preview"* function for supporting these functions. Entity related information is embedded to allow the user to navigate entities in *preview*. Tm and SEMI manage the mapping between a message and its *preview*. The interface modules between the MIME processing module and an MUA replace the display of a message by its *preview*. *Preview* functions as a message display for MUAs and therefore, MIME processing features are added to the message features of the original MUAs.

The design of the *preview* mechanism is based on the "representation layer model". This model combines layers and allows representation and manipulation of structured data. It organizes a complex system.

2.1 Representation layer model

In the "representation layer model", structured data is represented by several "representation layers". A "representation layer" stores structured data and provides manipulations of this data in a manner determined by its format.

Structured data consists of a number of units. In MIME, an entity is a unit of message content. A "representation unit" is represented by different formats in different kinds of "representation layers". However, they are only different shadows for the same object. The term shadow is used because it may be an incomplete copy of the original. The shadows are attributes of the object and the object is represented by its shadows.

A "representation unit" is a link between "representation layers". "Representation unit" indicates a unit of structured data. A structured data is represented by a unit in a layer. It is called a "shadow". "Representation unit" is a relation between its shadows in "representation layers".

If the user manipulates a shadow in a layer and its operation requires data in another layer, processing is propagated to the other layer by a "representation unit". Each layer has its own manipulating features for shadows and some of them are propagated to other layers.

Thus "representation units" link "representation layers" and organize them into a system. Such systems are called "representation systems".

While it may be possible to represent complex data by one structure, it may be too complicated (Fig. 1). If it is separated into several "representation layers" by format, each representation layers can be simple (Fig. 2). The latter is much simpler to implement and maintain.

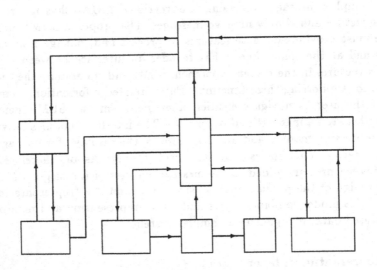

Fig. 1. Example of single structured representation

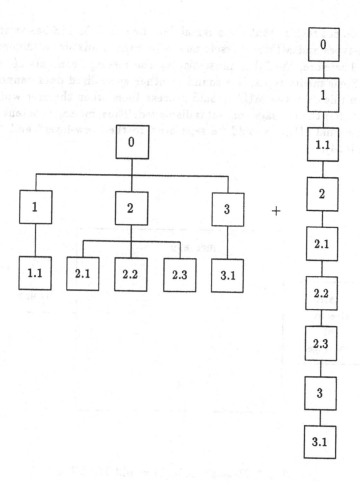

Fig. 2. Example of separated representation layers

2.2 Representation system for Internet message contents

In tm or SEMI, the "representation system" for message content consists of two "representation layers". One is the original content of received message, called the "raw-layer". The other is displayed to the user and is called the "previewed-layer".

Conventional MUAs do not distinguish between the "raw-layer" and the "previewed-layer" (Fig. 3). Because messages as specified by STD 11 do not have structured contents, conventional MUAs can display the original contents. Although they might do some processing of the message [1], the transformations

---

[1] Most conventional MUAs perform header filtering.

involved do not require that the original data be saved. MIME has various kinds of media-types and MIME charsets and it permits a mixture of different kinds of each. Therefore, the MUA must display the message contents after parsing is done. Some media-types, like sound or other specialized data cannot be displayed. In this case, the MUA should process them when the user would like it processed after the message content is displayed. Thus, message content managed by conventional MUAs should be separated to the "raw-layer" and "preview-layer" (Fig. 4).

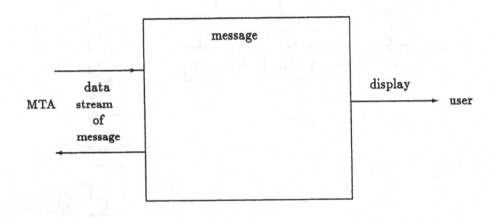

Fig. 3. Message model in non-MIME MUA

The message management of conventional MUAs are classified as two types: "raw-layer" and "preview-layer". The former is the original data. It is usually only used internally. The latter is displayed to user. The interface module between a general MIME module and a conventional MUA must distinguish between them and provide hooks into them.

Construction for both "representation layers" is done by the following steps. First, the "raw-layer" is made from the original message content as parsed by message syntax. After parsing is done, a hierarchy of entities is generated. The "raw-layer" is the representation of the parsing result.

The "preview-layer" is generated from the "raw-layer". Each shadow corresponding entity is flattened and sorted for the display model. The preview generator calls the "preview-filter" for each shadow element. The "Preview-filter" displays and returns the shadow to the "preview-layer". Shadows in the "raw-layer" and "preview-layer" generate the "representation-unit". In tm or SEMI, this is implemented with cell sharing. The shadow in the "preview-layer" has a

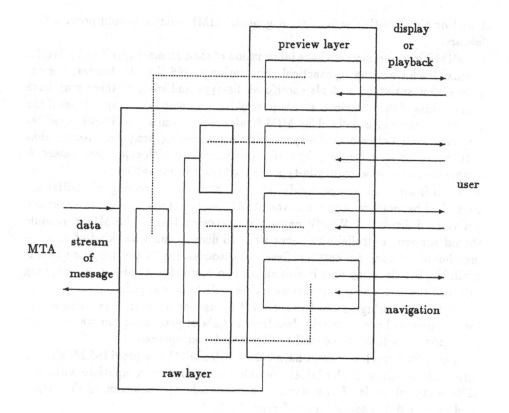

Fig. 4. Message model in MIME processing module

pointer to the "raw-layer". This implementation is able to bypass the high cost of searching in the "preview-layer". A lot of navigations are performed by the user and executed in the "preview-layer", so it is a good method.

Tm and SEMI have multiple "preview-layers" and one "raw-layer". A "preview-layer" may be a hierarchy of "preview-layers". For example, MIME has a "message/rfc822" media-type. Its content can be a MIME message and it's usually used to forward a message. Therefore MIME processing module should allow navigation for message or display as a message. Recursive previewing is available in this case, and several "preview-layers" for one "raw-layer" is good way.

3 Entity Processing

Each entity of MIME message content has a "media-type"[3] to specify the format of its content. It is used for processing by general rule. Of course, conventional MUAs do not use media-types and do not have entity processing features based on the MIME specification. A general MIME module should provide this feature.

MIME message contents have information of their formats specified by MIME syntax. Each entity has syntactical information specified by its header. For example, Content-Type[3] fields specify media-type and some of them may have other values of their attributes. It is possible to automatically play entities if the processing method is defined by MIME rules. For example, mailcap[7] specifies mapping rules between media-types and corresponding programs. Notice that entities are not specified only by media-types but also with other parameters. A simple mapping between media-type and program is not sufficient.

Even if sufficient mapping rules are specified, the processing of entities are controlled by message sender and the MIME module. For example, the user can not control display of WWW pages when viewing them. The MIME module should support controllability about what to display and what kind of processing should be done for entities. System customization of the mapping rule is available, but since the user is also allowed to customize it the system mapping rule and the user's mapping rule should be able to be merged.

MIME processing should be controlled by user operations. It is inconvenient for the user to have to specify low level details of processing, so we use some operation types that correspond to abstracted user operations.

The MIME module should harmonize with the MUA's provided MIME features. The behavior of the MIME module should also be compatible with each MUA's typical mode of operation. In other words, the behavior of the MIME module should be changed for different MUAs.

In the present study, the notion of "acting situation model" is proposed to overcome the above mentioned problems. In the "acting situation model", processing methods for entities are mappings with an "acting situation" instead of simple mappings between media-types and corresponding programs.

3.1 Acting situation model

An "Acting situation" consists of the following elements:

1. information of entity specified by header (ex. Content-Type[3])
2. conditions related to program execution
3. operation type
4. information related to MUA type

An "acting situation" is generated by the operation on entity. In the case of tm and SEMI, an acting situation is represented by an association list:

$$((t_1.v_1)(t_2.v_2)...(t_n.v_n))$$

An acting situation consists of attributes with type t_i and value v_i.

3.2 Information of entity specified by header

It is generated from information of header of each entity. An example of the representation in SEMI is:

```
((media-type . text)(media-subtype . plain)
("charset" . "iso-2022-jp")
(encoding . 7bit)(disposition-type . inline))
```

Media-types (primary type and subtype) are specified by the symbols 'media-type' and 'media-subtype'. Content-Transfer-Encoding is specified by the symbol 'encoding'. Disposition-type is specified by the symbol 'disposition-type'. The parameters of the Content-Type and Content-Disposition fields are specified as strings.

3.3 conditions related to program execution

They are a list of acting situation types. Each acting situation type is a subset of acting situations. It specifies expecting acting situation to run its method. Representation of SEMI is list of association lists.

```
(((media-type . video)(method "xanim" nil "+Ae" -c 'name)
  (mode . play)(encoding binary 8bit 7bit))
 ((media-type . audio)
  (method "tm-au" nil 'file 'type 'encoding 'mode 'name)
  (mode . play)(encoding binary 8bit 7bit))
 ((media-type . image)(method "display" nil 'name)
  (mode play print)(encoding binary 8bit 7bit))
 ((media-type . message)(media-subtype . external-body)
  ("access-type" . "anon-ftp")
  (method . mime-display-message/external-ftp))
 ((media-type . message)(media-subtype . rfc822)
  (method . mime-display-message/rfc822)(mode . play))
 ((media-type . message)(media-subtype . partial)
  (method . mime-combine-message/partials-automatically)
  (major-mode . gnus-original-article-mode)
  (summary-buffer-exp . gnus-summary-buffer))
 ((media-type . message)(media-subtype . partial)
  (method . mime-combine-message/partials))
 ((method "metamail"
          'with-header "-m" "tm" "-x" "-d" "-z" "-e" 'file)
  (mode . play))
 ((method . mime-extract-file)(mode . extract)))
```

Each elements are as same as acting situations, like following:

```
((media-type . message)(media-subtype . partial)
 (method . mime-combine-message/partials-automatically)
 (major-mode . gnus-original-article-mode)
 (summary-buffer-exp . gnus-summary-buffer))
```

3.4 Operation type

tm and SEMI provide three different user operations: 'play', 'file extraction' and 'print'.

3.5 Information related to MUA type

This indicates the kind of running MUA. GNU Emacs and its variants have a variable 'major-mode' to indicate kinds of applications. tm and SEMI use it.

3.6 Composition of acting situation

During an operation on entity, tm or SEMI generates the draft for acting situation with the help of (1) [**information of entity specified by its header**], (3) [**operation type**] and (4) [**information related to MUA type**]. They are unique and therefore they are simply appended. Finally the appropriate condition is retrieved from (2) [**conditions related to program execution**] and it is compared with the draft of acting situation.

Comparing method between two acting situations S_1 and S_2 succeeds when every attributes of S_1 and S_2 are compared successfully. If type of an attribute a_i of S_1 is found in S_2 (a_j), and if values of a_i and a_j are same, then the attributes comparing about type of a_i and a_j succeeds and returns a_i. If type of an attribute a_k of S_1 is not found in S_2, then the attributes comparing about type of a_k succeeds and returns a_k. Similarly, if type of an attribute a_l of S_2 is not found in S_1, then the attributes comparing about type of a_l succeeds and returns a_l. Otherwise attribute comparing fails. If every attributes comparing succeed, comparing between S_1 and S_2 succeeds and return acting situation $S3$ consists of every results of attribute comparing. For example, comparing between $((a.1)(b.2))$ and $((a.1)(c.3))$ succeeds and returns $((a.1)(b.2)(c.3))$, but comparing between $((a.1)(b.2))$ and $((a.3)(c.3))$ fails.

For example, if the draft for action situation is:

```
((media-type . message)(media-subtype . partial)
 ("number" . "2")("total" . "3")
 ("id" . "foo@tsukuyomi.jaist.ac.jp")
 (mode . play)(major-mode . gnus-original-article-mode))
```

and

```
((media-type . message)(media-subtype . partial)
 (method . mime-combine-message/partials-automatically)
 (major-mode . gnus-original-article-mode)
 (summary-buffer-exp . gnus-summary-buffer))
```

is matched with the list of conditions (2), then

```
((media-type . message)(media-subtype . partial)
("number" . "2")("total" . "3")
("id" . "foo@tsukuyomi.jaist.ac.jp")
(mode . play)(major-mode . gnus-original-article-mode)
(method . mime-combine-message/partials-automatically)
(summary-buffer-exp . gnus-summary-buffer))
```

will be generated as the acting situation. Next, the program specified by the 'method' attribute is executed. The remaining attributes are passed to the program.

4 Conclusion

The proposed MIME processing module employs *preview* to provide an adequate mapping mechanism between a message and its hierarchy of entities. It is based on the proposed "representation layer model". This model is available to represent and navigate complicated structured data like MIME message contents.

The functions of the proposed MIME processing module should be consistent with the original MUA functions. The acting situation model allows the user to specify conditions along with various factors. In the proposed method the acting situation is generated dynamically, hence it is flexible. However, the present implementation of the model might generate the wrong acting situation. Therefore, the subject needs further investigation.

References

1. Coded Character Set – 7-Bit American Standard Code for Information Interchange. ANSI X3.4 (1986)
2. Crocker, D.: Standard for the format of ARPA Internet text messages. RFC 822 (1982)
3. Freed, N. and Borenstein, N.: Multipurpose Internet Mail Extensions (MIME) Part One: Format of Internet Message Bodies. RFC 2045 (1996)
4. Freed, N. and Borenstein, N.: Multipurpose Internet Mail Extensions (MIME) Part Two: Media Types. RFC 2046 (1996)
5. ftp://ftp.jaist.ac.jp/pub/GNU/elisp/mime/
6. ftp://ftp.jaist.ac.jp/pub/GNU/elisp/mime/alpha/
7. Borenstein, N.: A User Agent Configuration Mechanism For Multimedia Mail Format Information. RFC 1524 (1993)

Author Index

Springer
and the
environment

At Springer we firmly believe that an international science publisher has a special obligation to the environment, and our corporate policies consistently reflect this conviction.
We also expect our business partners – paper mills, printers, packaging manufacturers, etc. – to commit themselves to using materials and production processes that do not harm the environment. The paper in this book is made from low- or no-chlorine pulp and is acid free, in conformance with international standards for paper permanency.

 Springer

Lecture Notes in Computer Science

For information about Vols. 1–1289

please contact your bookseller or Springer-Verlag